Ulster to America

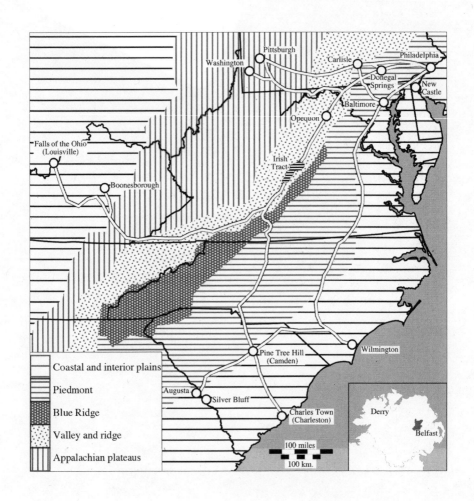

Coastal and interior plains

Piedmont

Blue Ridge

Valley and ridge

Appalachian plateaus

Pittsburgh
Washington
Carlisle
Philadelphia
Donegal
Springs
New
Castle
Baltimore
Opequon
Falls of the Ohio
(Louisville)
Irish
Tract
Boonesborough
Pine Tree Hill
(Camden)
Wilmington
Augusta
Silver Bluff
Charles Town
(Charleston)
Derry
Belfast

100 miles
100 km.

Ulster to America

The Scots-Irish Migration Experience, 1680–1830

Edited by Warren R. Hofstra

The University of Tennessee Press • Knoxville

Frontispiece. Locations of Scots-Irish migration, 1680–1830, and map
of Ulster at same scale.

Copyright © 2012 by The University of Tennessee Press / Knoxville.
All rights reserved. Manufactured in the United States of America.
Cloth: 1st printing, 2012.
Paper: 1st printing, 2016.

Library of Congress Cataloging-in-Publication Data

Ulster to America: the Scots-Irish migration experience, 1680–1830 / edited by
Warren R. Hofstra. — 1st ed.
    p. cm.
Includes bibliographical references and index.

ISBN: 978-1-62190-263-8

1. Scots-Irish—United States—History—18th century.
2. Scots—Ulster (Northern Ireland and Ireland)—History—18th century.
3. United States—Emigration and immigration—History—18th century.
4. Ulster (Northern Ireland and Ireland)—Emigration and immigration—
   History—18th century.
5. Scots-Irish—United States—History.
6. Scots—Ulster (Northern Ireland and Ireland)—History.
7. United States—Emigration and immigration—History.
8. Ulster (Northern Ireland and Ireland)—Emigration and immigration—
   History.
I. Hofstra, Warren R., 1947–

E184.S4U48 2011
973'.0049163—dc23   2011029288

Contents

Figures

Maps

Acknowledgments

A project as large and complex as this one inevitably incurs many debts on its way to completion. It began as an affiliation among most of the authors in consulting with the professional staff of the Ulster American Folk Park in Omagh, Northern Ireland, about the expansion of its outdoor exhibits depicting the North American frontier and the particular locations of signature Scots-Irish settlement. Thus we are in debt particularly to Philip Mowat, head of emigration for the Folk Park and the National Museums of Northern Ireland, for bringing us together and underwriting our initial collaboration. In return, the museum received a concept and design for exhibit development in a physical plan that is also reflected in the intellectual plan of this volume. Insofar as each of the chapters herein reflects themes treated at specific outdoor structures and interpretative sites, the book as a whole serves as a companion volume to the exhibit. Conceived in the service of this exhibit, however, the project has taken on an academic life of its own and stands today on its strengths as a collective study of one of the most important immigrant groups affecting American demographic and cultural identity during the previous three centuries.

Each of us has incurred numerous obligations in the creation of our articles, but we are all indebted collectively to those who read and commented on the manuscript at various stages of its development, namely, Brian Lambkin and Patrick Fitzgerald, director and lecturer/development officer respectively at the Center for Migration Studies at the Ulster American Folk Park, and the anonymous readers recruited by the University of Tennessee Press for manuscript review. For facilitating the various meetings that brought us face-to-face over the ideas that now populate this volume, we are grateful to the staff of the Ulster American Folk Park and to John Herbst, director of the Conner Prairie Museum in Fishers, Indiana. At Shenandoah University, my home institution, work on the volume was eased and speeded by the excellent aid of Sandy Snyder, administrative assistant for the history department, and numerous work-study students in whom the department indulges but most notably Josh Cooper, Dan Radomski, Denise Mitchell, and Charles Buabin. The comprehensive index is owing to the superb work of Robert Grogg, and the generous funding provided by the Woltz-Winchester Foundation of Winchester, Virginia. At the University of Tennessee Press, editor and now director Scot Danforth stood steadfastly by this project through the inevitable delays of complex endeavors. David Miller, author of this volume's lead article, performed the yeoman service of drafting maps for each chapter, and all of the authors in many large and small ways advanced the project with advice, critique, and encouragement at key moments in its development. Without their support, this effort would have foundered long ago. The reward and pleasure of completing it is owing in large measure to their good cheer, high standards of scholarship, and fine spirit of collaboration.

Introduction

From the North of Ireland to North America: The Scots-Irish and the Migration Experience

Warren R. Hofstra

American history, especially early American history, has long been narrated as a migration experience. The movement of English peoples to the portion of mainland North America that became the United States has traditionally dominated the story. The sites of English contact—Jamestown, Plymouth, Philadelphia, Charleston—have become those places where the story—the hardships, the struggle, the courage, the conquests—has been most clearly and forcefully articulated. Americans visit these places today in large numbers to better understand the origins of their nation and the sources of their history.

During the past several decades, however, and due to abundant new work by historians, archaeologists, geographers, and other scholars or writers, the story of the United States as a nation of immigrants has become much larger and more complex, both conceptually and geographically. This development is nowhere more true than for early America, where the settlement areas of varied European nations have gained in significance and influence. British America now includes Caribbean islands as well as the Canadian northeast. Spanish borderlands have been fully integrated into the American story, as have the vast interior territories of French settlement, including Louisiana, Illinois, and the *pays d'en haut*. Dutch outposts have gained in importance, and even Russian settlements along the Pacific Coast have attracted the attention of American historians. Regarding Africa, early American history can no longer be considered apart from the ethnic origins and cultural experiences of millions of African Americans whose story now begins not on the North American coast but in hundreds of communities spread throughout Central and West Africa. And where Native Americans were once regarded, along with the environment, as an object of conquest, they now are considered active agents not only in their own autonomous histories but also in the full panorama of the American past. Places once considered peripheral have come squarely into the focal range of academic research as well as popular attention. No longer can early American history and the movement of peoples into and around the Americas be chronicled without accounts of Barbados, St. Augustine, St. Johns, Halifax, Quebec, Detroit, Santa Fe, New Orleans, the French towns of the Illinois Country, and hundreds of Native American towns from Onondaga to Coweta, Cahokia to Acoma.

There is, however, no single place or collection of sites on American soil that stands out in the story of one of the largest migrant populations in early American history—the Scots-Irish. There is no Jamestown or Plymouth Rock, Williamsburg or Sturbridge Village for these folk from the north of Ireland variously called Scotch-Irish, Ulster Scots, Irish, or sometimes Irish Protestants. Population estimates vary, but upwards of one hundred fifty thousand of them came in numerous waves during the so-called "long eighteenth century" lasting from 1680 to 1830, the extended period during which imperial wars, colonial expansion, political revolutions, and the inevitable mass displacement of European populations engulfed the Atlantic world. A significant portion of this number of Scots-Irish arrived between the 1713 Peace of Utrecht and the American Revolution some sixty years later. Although families and communities were found throughout North America, the large majority helped occupy a broad arc of interior frontier extending from central Pennsylvania to the Georgia upcountry. Theirs was a region defined more by cultural pluralism and intercultural encounters than by the imprint of any single ethnic identity. The Scots-Irish found themselves among large numbers of German-speaking immigrants and other settlers with Anglo-American, Irish, Scottish, Welsh, English, Dutch, or French backgrounds. Native Americans were dispersed throughout the entire region because it was, of course, their homeland. But it is the Scots-Irish and the character of the region they helped shape that compose the subject of essays included in this book.

That there is no single place where the historian or the public can visit and reflect on the Scots-Irish experience in America is not to say that it has

Warren R. Hofstra

been suppressed or its people beaten down as a historical underclass. But some have suggested that the cultural identity of the Scots-Irish was never sufficiently strong to resist the force of Americanization—that the Scots-Irish simply became indistinguishable and were lost in the rising middle class of nineteenth-century America. Others, however, have argued the opposite: due to the enduring power of a compelling Scots-Irish character, American majorities simply became like them. The traits of the Scots-Irish grew into a national identity generalized across the cultural landscape, and they now constitute the core of what it is to be American. Thus the Scots-Irish as a distinct people have vanished in plain sight.

Extravagant as this assertion is, it plays a role in contemporary politics as the captive of conservative movements. The historical Scots-Irish have come to stand today for gun ownership, property rights, anti-tax movements, economic deregulation, Christian evangelicalism, moral conformity, minimal government, and a militaristic foreign policy. In the process, their culture has assumed mythic proportions. Understanding the myth of the Scots-Irish is essential for assessing the essays that compose this book, because collectively they make a case for a Scots-Irish history that contravenes and displaces the Scots-Irish myth. But the myth is no straw man set up only for our authors to beat apart. Their essays have important cultural work to accomplish precisely because the myth plays out so strongly in American popular politics.

The myth of the Scots-Irish has currency because books about it sell. Even academic studies that fuel interest in the myth have a continuing market. Witness the unflagging appeal of David Hackett Fischer's *Albion's Seed: Four British Folkways in America.* A major section entitled "Borderlands to the Backcountry: The Flight from North Britain, 1717–1775" describes the regional character of the American backcountry as an immutable set of folkways transported from the Gaelic marchlands of the British Isles to the frontiers of North America. Something the same can be said about the venerable volume James G. Leyburn published more than forty-five years ago entitled *The Scotch-Irish: A Social History,* now enjoying a renaissance of popular interest remarkable for an academic press book. Leyburn's vivid but static descriptions of Scots-Irish characters, institutions, and settlements hold a continuing fascination for devotees of ethnic heritage in an age in which fixed identities and their ancestral embodiments have become ever more powerfully linked in the American character. Much more recently, geographer Barry Aron Vann has argued along similar lines that the "Bible Belt clearly reflects the culture of a devout people whose ancestors lived in the highlands of Europe's Protestant Celtic fringe."[1]

Popular interests in the Scots-Irish have been fed more directly by the many and imaginative works of Billy Kennedy, a Belfast journalist. In volume after volume, Kennedy has chronicled anecdotes and epigrams about *his* people for the mass market. Even more wondrous is the work of James Webb, professional soldier and popular writer, who launched a combative political career with his book *Born Fighting: How the Scots-Irish Shaped America.* Adopting the title as a moniker for a successful 2006 campaign for a United States Senate seat from Virginia, Webb has emerged as a political iconoclast known for a fundamentalist approach to applying heritage to history as well as current affairs and for switching parties partly out of consistent loyalty to his own Scots-Irish ancestry. Collectively, these authors and their books have not created the myth of the Scots-Irish, but they can be credited with successfully riding the crest of the huge wave of popular interest in it.[2]

Individualism—an "insistent individualism," says Webb—lies at the core of the Scots-Irish culture. More than two hundred years ago, he argues, the mountains of the southern backcountry in America drew an immigrant people from the north of Ireland into cultural strongholds and over the ensuing centuries instilled a "fierce and uncomplaining self-reliance into an already hardened people." Thus for them, "joining a group and putting themselves at the mercy of someone else's collectivist judgment makes about as much sense as letting the government take their guns."[3]

This kind of stiff-necked individualism informed every aspect of life among the mythic Scots-Irish. "The average Scots-Irish frontiersman was a doer," according to Billy Kennedy, "whose values and beliefs were reflected in his everyday behaviour. He was a man who was high-principled and narrow, strong and violent, as tenacious of his own rights as he was blinded often to the rights of others; acquisitive, yet self-sacrificing; but most of all fearless, confident of his own power, determined to have and to hold."[4]

As individualists, the Scots-Irish hated established authority. Fighting anyone attempting to control them has, according to the myth, always defined them. They represent, in Webb's words, a "historically consistent cycle of, among other things, a values-based combativeness, an insistent egalitarianism, and a refusal to be dominated from above." Theirs is a "culture of isolation, hard luck, and infinite stubbornness that has always shunned formal education and mistrusted—even hated—any form of aristocracy."[5]

Included in the authority to which the Scots-Irish stand opposed is the presumptive elite of today's so-called liberal establishment. In only one example: "They are a culture founded on guns, which considers the Second

Amendment sacrosanct, while literary and academic America considers such views not only archaic but also threatening." Class conflict, moreover, is inherent in Scots-Irish anti-authoritarianism because, "in this culture's heart beats the soul of working-class America," according to Webb. "The elites do not have to deal with people from this culture on a daily basis in their classrooms or their neighborhoods or at work. They do not see them in their clubs or go to the same parties. They do not need their goodwill in order to advance professionally. But they ignore them at their peril."[6]

Most perilous to the liberal aristocracy is the mythic construction of the Scots-Irish as a warlike people. Theirs is a culture "conditioned by a thousand years of conflict." From the north of Ireland, they brought this culture to the American frontier in the eighteenth century. There, in Webb's account, "their first task beyond building a cabin was to defend themselves against the bloodcurdling attacks of Indian war parties." Billy Kennedy concurs that they "have always been a patriotic people, with a strong fighting tradition. On the American frontier in the 18th century, one had to possess these sturdy qualities to defend family, home and property and, more than any other race, the Scots-Irish stood out." They fought "Indian-style" even as regular soldiers in the American Revolution. And whereas "German settlers in Pennsylvania . . . were also inclined, like the English Quakers, to retire rather than fight the Indians. Not so the Scots-Irish!" Patriotism and pugilism are confounded in the Scots-Irish myth. According to Webb, the Scots-Irish are "loyal Americans. . . . They show up for our wars. Indeed, we cannot go to war without them."[7]

It is in these ways that the myth of the Scots-Irish has been put to work in the service of numerous conservative causes. In the process, the evangelical right has co-opted the Scots-Irish as well. "They are the very heartbeat of fundamentalist Christianity," according to Webb. "They have produced their share of fire-and-brimstone spiritual leaders, whose conservative views on social issues continually offend liberal opinion-makers." And it is "on these shifting political sands, [that] the hyperindividualistic Scots-Irish . . . will very likely have more influence than at any time since the age of Andrew Jackson."[8]

Clearly the myth confounds past and present, often creating an imaginary past to serve present purposes. And in the light of contemporary political needs, the character of the Scots-Irish has remained fixed and steadfast. "The culture had hardly changed after it crossed the Atlantic Ocean three hundred years ago, and set up its communities in the Appalachian

Mountains," asserts Webb. The Scots-Irish were as individualistic, anti-elitist, egalitarian, working class, warlike, patriotic, and conservative in immigrating to America during the eighteenth century as they are today. The myth then reverses the logic of history. Instead of historical change through long periods of time explaining the present, the present finds justification in an unchanging past. In this essentialist perspective, the character and culture of the Scots-Irish defy history and are derived from a fixed, racialized identity. But what happens to this point of view when the history of the Scots-Irish is examined more closely as responsive to historical forces shaping it and to dramatic changes in these forces over long periods of time? What happens when Scots-Irish lives are examined in the actual places they settled and the communities they created? And what happened to the Scots-Irish when the worlds around them changed and new forces came to bear on ethnic identity? These are the questions raised by the articles in this volume.[9]

As it emerges from these articles, the identity of the Scots-Irish is anything but determined, diffusionist, and immutable. It is, instead, highly responsive to varied cultural and political contexts, themselves changing in time. The identity discussed herein is conditioned and conditional; it is receptive to and reflexive of the main currents of historical change throughout the Atlantic world. Thus, these essays compose an argument against the essentialism of the Scots-Irish myth and the quasi-racial identity it imparts to these people. Theirs has been an identity always negotiated and always being negotiated. As Patrick Griffin, quoted by Richard MacMaster in this volume, comments: "Amid periods of change," the Scots-Irish "defined and redefined their understandings of themselves and the world around them." Constant definition and redefinition lent their experience a complexity that was rich and meaningful but nothing like the singular and linear world described by the myth. In Kentucky, as Griffin recounts, the "Irish story . . . hinged on paradox and contradiction." It was "marked by ambiguity and ambivalence."[10]

Ambiguity and ambivalence were no more evident than in the long transit of culture and tradition plotted by David W. Miller from Scotland to the north of Ireland beginning in the seventeen hundreds and, during the following century, from Ireland to North America. But in Miller's telling, variance and variation, not the diffusion of inert traits, characterized the lives of Scots in Ireland and the Scots-Irish in America. Religion was most telling. Presbyterianism divided between the *great tradition* of the clergy endowed with a Scottish theology dominating both New and Old World churches and the *little tradition* of ordinary congregants and the unchurched with their own interpretation of reformed doctrine and polity. In Ireland the people of the little tradition compelled the clergy to toe more closely than in Scotland to the principles of congregational governance, while in America they often split entirely for the new evangelism of Methodists and Baptists, leaving the old church more reflective of social class than ethnic continuity. Miller's point is that religion, as perhaps the most powerful signifier of Scots-Irish identity, constituted a protean force adjusting constantly to new geographical realities, cultural contexts, and historical meanings.

Understanding individualism is critical. Never absolute, the individualism of the Scots-Irish was alloyed with the ever-present authority of community and the need to live together not only among themselves but also among diverse peoples in various political contexts. In all the sites of settlement examined in this volume, Scots-Irish families engaged in individual searches for good land, but the resulting open-country communities they created did not betray a desire to live unimpeded by neighbors in a frontier of self-sufficient individualism. There is no evidence of their squatting on land in acts of defiance against colonial law or the power of the state. At Donegal Springs in Pennsylvania; at Opequon and the Irish Tract in the Great Valley of Virginia; and in upcountry Carolina, southwestern Pennsylvania, or Kentucky they surveyed land, patented it, purchased it, and nurtured its resources for generations in neighborhoods of like-minded households. Instead of living apart and depending solely on their own resources, they created exchange economies where a quotidian trade in surpluses from farms and workshops fed and sustained large communities. They sought, as Michael Montgomery observes, the "security and self-sufficiency of dispersed rural settlements."

These were ordered communities, but in a seeming paradox, as Richard MacMaster points out for the Donegal Springs settlement, Scots-Irish settlers in the search for order often "valued individual freedom and material gain more than community." In her essay, Marianne Wokeck makes a similar point: Scots-Irish immigrants were opportunity seekers scouting possibilities for self-betterment in the American landscape. This tendency was nowhere more blatantly evident than in the South Carolina upcountry where the Indian trade, as described by Michael Montgomery, provided a "'get-rich' opportunity par excellence to young men . . . who sought enough money to buy land and settle down." The point that all these authors make is that ordered communities emerged from individual pursuits of self-interest. In striving after property and possessions, the Scots-Irish in *Ulster to America* created their own economic and social orders.

The economies the Scots-Irish generated through small-farm, mixed agriculture did not produce much hard wealth, much liquidity, or much capital. But as Warren Hofstra's study of the Opequon settlement reveals, the Scots-Irish living in open-country neighborhoods on the eighteenth-century frontier, even within a few years of settlement, had achieved qualities of life characteristic of wealth and abundant in what can be called social capital. Little cash or other currency lubricated trade in dispersed communities. But the constant recording and balancing of debits and credits in book accounts allowed for the exchange of large volumes of goods and services as the surplus products or labor of one family met the shortfall of another. Reciprocity in time tended to balance accounts, but no one ended up with much cash in the drawer. Distinctions in the size of houses or extent of material possessions were modest. Opequon, nonetheless, presents numerous examples of how social capital brought the comforts, if not the blessings, of wealth. Although a widow, Elizabeth Vance, as Hofstra demonstrates, was related by blood or marriage to practically every Scots-Irish family within a ten-mile radius of her home. She could rely amply on children and kin for care in her old age. By the measure of household goods, William Hoge died very poor, but as a landowner he had enjoyed much prestige in his lifetime and high status among neighbors. By his position on the county court, David Vance worked to secure property throughout his community. Thus, the people of Opequon enjoyed the benefits and privileges of wealth reserved in Europe for the upper classes. They were competent, independent, and beholden only to themselves for land and livelihood.

Out of the collective creation of wealth, Scots-Irish households generated their own social structures. Everyone worked, but the Scots-Irish did not constitute the working classes exclusively. According to Katharine Brown and Ken Keller, a network of families at the Irish Tract in the upper Shenandoah Valley created a republican social order as they sought collective power through mutual control of land, the orderly descent of property, and a wide range of self-created social and cultural institutions. Members of these families constituted the court, governed the church, commanded the militia, and represented the region in state government. They created institutions for the public good such as schools, academies, and colleges. Lodges and fraternal organizations provided mutual assistance and charitable giving. Their library and literary societies, lyceums, and even fire companies promoted civic improvement. In the nineteenth century, this republican social order grew into a middle-class democracy based on landownership, economic competency, and participatory government. All the while, it was never incompatible with the tendency Richard MacMaster identified among the Scots-Irish of valuing individual freedom over community. Freedom in the Irish Tract and elsewhere simply depended upon the wealth or social capital generated by reciprocal economic exchange and the consolidation of this capital in social classes empowered with authority to secure order, property, and stability throughout the community.

Other authors sketch out comparable developments in communities elsewhere. Peter Gilmore and Kerby Miller in their study of southwest Pennsylvania find that the emergence of an autochthonous class structure from the crucible of the market revolution beginning in the late eighteenth century, combined with the contemporaneous formation of national political parties in the era of the New Republic, produced a volatile social chemistry. The emerging Scots-Irish upper class allied with the Federalist program of nationalist economic development and the centralization of power in the federal government. Meanwhile the democratic-republican political philosophy of Thomas Jefferson and James Madison appealed to farmers and small producers. As Gilmore and Miller comment, "Between 1780 and 1810, various groups of Ulster Presbyterians contended with each other to achieve social control, political power, and cultural hegemony over the Ulster American community and to define its relationships with Anglo-America's social and political hierarchies." Wealthier Federalists among an elite of prominent clergy, merchants, and lawyers used the power of status and position actively to suppress political expression among the less privileged. Violence not surprisingly flared up during the Whiskey Rebellion of the mid-1790s but was quickly and decisively suppressed with military force by the Washington administration. One lesson to be drawn from Gilmore and Miller's account of the struggle is that violence was not due to the inbred propensities or cultural inheritance of the Scots-Irish but was instead a response to repressive tensions within a self-created social order destabilized by the explosive admixture of partisan politics. Nor can we conclude that the Scots-Irish in far southwestern Pennsylvania were insulated from the forces of political change embracing the entire nation in their era. Theirs was not a marginal culture nurtured by isolation.

Gilmore and Miller conclude their story with an account of how immigrants from the north of Ireland, inclined to think of themselves as Irish in the eighteenth century, adopted the mantle of Scotch-Irish respectability by the late nineteenth century, partly in resolution of their own internal tensions and partly as an ethnic-group identity adopted in reaction to new waves of poorer, Catholic immigrants from the Ireland of the famine and its aftermath. In his essay on Kentucky, Patrick Griffin recounts a comparable story of how Scots-Irish settlers shed traditional notions of their cultural heritage and adopted new, more nationally integrated identities. On the trans-Appalachian frontier after the American Revolution, the struggle to achieve individual or family independence as American citizens came to rest on universal white male suffrage. Meanwhile, the years of brutal fighting with Native Americans during the Revolution—and particularly in the ensuing struggle over the "dark and bloody" ground of Kentucky during the 1780s and 1790s—led to a loathing for Indian peoples. Indian-hating in turn nurtured the development of "whiteness" or a racialized white identity among the Scots-Irish and practically all European settlers in the new West. Thus, the Scots-Irish became white. "In places like Kentucky, to be white and to be male made one independent," writes Griffin. Here again, however, a new identity for the Scots-Irish emerged in response to powerful forces coursing through the cultural environment of region and nation. Adopting universal white racism belies arguments for Scots-Irish exceptionalism.

Thus, different settlement venues of the Scots-Irish in North America tell different sides of their story. Radical individualism or truculent resistance to authority, however, appear nowhere in this account. And where authority was resisted, violence was not the product of cultural inheritance. Whether in central Pennsylvania, the Shenandoah Valley, upcountry Carolina, southwestern Pennsylvania, or eastern Kentucky, the Scots-Irish in their own open-country communities created indigenous social orders in which authority came to be articulated variously through a republican social consensus, the combination of political faction and class conflict, or the emergence of a new, racialized identity. No doubt each of these developments appeared at all of the sites described in this book. But nowhere did the Scots-Irish live in cultural isolation, nurturing an essentialist and warlike culture based on individualism and an anti-elitist, working-class culture.

The ethnic, cultural, and racial diversity of the world of the Scots-Irish also contradicts arguments about their social and geographical insularity. At none of the settlements under discussion in this volume did the Scots-Irish depend so singularly upon themselves that they could remain apart from an American frontier broadly conceived, as it is today, as an expansive interior zone of cultural diversity, encounter, exchange, and creativity. At Opequon, for instance, practically no Scots-Irish household was without a German, English, or Anglo-Virginia neighbor. Households representing all ethnic groups traded readily with each other in the collective pursuit of economic competency within complex webs of exchange. At George Galphin's settlement and trading post at Silver Bluff, the Indian trade itself created a wide world of cultural encounter among the Scots-Irish and various Native American peoples. It was a "meeting ground where peoples of three worlds—diverse groups of Europeans, Indians, and Africans—came together." The town of Carlisle, Pennsylvania, created similar opportunities for peoples of vastly different backgrounds to engage each other in trade and the mutual exchange of ideas, customs, and perceptions.

Patrick Griffin also argues that cultural diversity made Kentucky a place where "migrants and their children rubbed shoulders with settlers of English descent, men and women from various eastern colonies, German-speakers, African Americans, and even Native Americans." Cultural fusion, accommodation, and synchronism thus made the world of the Scots-Irish on North American settlement frontiers no place for cultural essentialism or the long-term survival of pure ethnic cultures. And just as trade—local in the case of exchange economies and continental for the Indian trade—drew the Scots-Irish into regular and interdependent relations with peoples of varied cultures, so were their lives fully integrated into the much larger cultural geography of the Atlantic world.

Global forces of trade and commerce, European expansion and expansionism, imperial conflict, all in combination with the strategic decisions that were uprooting populations throughout the British Isles, Europe, and Africa, affected not only the lives of the Scots-Irish in America but also the very rationale for their displacement, migration, and relocation on the marchlands of the British Empire. Warren Hofstra makes this point about Opequon where imperial authorities encouraged settlement by the Scots-Irish, German-speakers, and other "foreign" immigrants because as white, Protestant, small farmers they could provide the essential settlement buffers needed to shield Chesapeake plantations not only from external threats posed by French colonists and Native Americans but also from the internal peril of African slave rebellion and maroonage. From this perspective, the planting of the Opequon settlement resembles the much earlier plantations of Ireland by Scottish, English, and other European Protestants undertaken in the security interests of an England caught in a global struggle with Catholicism and the Catholic states of Europe.

Other authors suggest that economic webs of merchant commerce not only explain the dislocation and resettlement of the Scots-Irish but also kept them connected to the Atlantic world wherever they were located in the settlement geography of North America. Marianne Wokeck, for instance, describes New Castle, Delaware, as a primary node in the commercial and personal networks that linked ports in the north of Ireland to centers of trade in North America. This web was also instrumental in directing the flow of immigrants farther inland, where the extension of merchant credit fueled the "development of settlements for both those already established . . . and those striking out anew. At the same time the Scotch-Irish trading community in New Castle extended the lines of communication and business ever more deeply and densely into the countryside, they continued and adjusted their connections to agents and partners across the Atlantic."

At Carlisle, the "farthest bastion of imperial power," Richard MacMaster also finds the commercial connections of the Scots-Irish extending deep into the American interior and even to the far reaches of the Ohio River valley. And in the other direction:

> Carlisle's merchants, like John Montgomery, Robert Callender, and Adam Hoops, traveled to Baltimore and Philadelphia to meet with leaders in the provincial government and in the church as often as they did to order calicoes or arrange the sale of iron or peltry from the frontier. Their city correspondents, as often as not family members, moved in a still wider Atlantic world, returning periodically to Belfast, Londonderry, and London itself and keeping abreast of British and European intellectual and political trends at home.
>
> Thanks in large part to its mercantile community, Carlisle was not an isolated outpost on the frontiers of European settlement and traditional Native American life.

Much the same could be said for towns such as Winchester and Staunton farther along the Great Wagon Road linking Philadelphia to Virginia and beyond. Certainly, as Michael Montgomery makes plain for the Carolina upcountry, new townships and agricultural communities established by imperial authorities in London complemented the activities of men and families engaged in an Indian trade that tied the Mississippi frontier, where native peoples hunted, to the merchant establishments of London and the English outports.

Commodities were not all that flowed throughout the Atlantic world into which the Scots-Irish were so deeply connected. As Richard MacMaster points out, the "intellectual and cultural currents in the Atlantic world [were] mediated through the vibrant life of eighteenth-century Carlisle." And it was through this mediation that the revolutionary ideals of the Society of United Irishmen reached southwestern Pennsylvania from Ireland and helped fuel not only social conflict but also political upheaval at the end of the eighteenth century. If the Scots-Irish brought with them a core set of traits born in the conflict-ridden, anarchic world of North Britain, then it was not isolation in the Appalachian Mountains that preserved them.

That a predilection for fighting was among the inborn traits of the Scots-Irish is an idea for which the articles in this volume provide little evidence. In fact, the only people "born fighting" may be modern politicians election-eering on a hobbyhorse of Scots-Irish heritage. Any discussion of a cult of violence and warfare among the Scots-Irish must be viewed historically in the context of the diversity and interconnectedness of the world in which they lived. That the Scots-Irish would invest so much industry in the creation of social capital, moral and material wealth, and the social structures and political organizations to protect and nurture it belies any tendency toward constantly risking everything in mortal combat. This conclusion is certainly true at Opequon, where isolation from imperial conflict and peace with Native Americans constituted the single-most powerful cultural memory from the first two decades of settlement. Twenty years of political stability allowed for the productive capacity of farms to develop along with the eco-nomic competence productivity engendered.[11] Prosperity permitted govern-ing institutions to mature independently and improve the land with roads, ferries, mills, towns, and public markets. When war did come to Opequon in the 1750s, imperial authorities, not Scots-Irish settlers, provoked it. And the Seven Years' War was a conflict for which the Scots-Irish did not show up. Faced with a global struggle that threatened their own peace, prosper-ity, and security, they evaded militia duty to attend to families and farms. In frustration, George Washington complained, "You may, with almost equal success, attempt to raize the Dead to Life again, as the force of this Country." The reason, as one militia captain explained, was that "his Wife, Family, and Corn was at stake, so were those of his Soldrs therefore it was not possible for him to come."[12]

The image of the Scots-Irish that emerges from the essays in this volume goes a long way toward overthrowing the myth of the Scots-Irish so prevalent in popular literature today. In the place of an essentialist culture forged in the violent peripheries of Europe, brought to America in the cultural baggage of immigrants, and perpetuated at isolated frontier settlements in which a hyperindividualistic, anti-elitist, working-class, egalitarian people given to conservative causes could come to represent the core of American life today, the authors of this book provide a more empirical, less polemic understand-ing of the historic peoples called Scots-Irish. They present a view accounting for the ambiguity of a people who placed self-interest above the interest of the community and, at the same time, established settlements in which the security of property and the uses to which property could be put for achieving economic competence and personal independence relied upon the communal wealth of social capital and the networks of exchange and reciprocity necessary to create it. Theirs is also a view allowing for the complex development of self-generated social orders that, in turns, could be republican in the investment of authority with responsibility for the public welfare, deeply divided by national political conflicts over how best to promote the general good, and paradoxically brought together by the magnetic force of white racism. Although located on the periphery of the Atlantic world, the lifeways of the Scots-Irish depicted herein were regularly stirred by the deep currents of goods and ideas flowing throughout the ocean connecting Europe, Africa, and all of the Americas. Never fixed and static, the world of the Scots-Irish was ever open and responsive to the main tendencies of its times. It was malleable, adaptive, elastic, and protean, in no ways reductive or irreducible, and always as potent in stimulating social change as reflecting it.

What difference did it make to the Scots-Irish if individualism, authority, social order, pluralism, localism, and globalism all at the same time complicated their world? Was it meaningful to have emigrated from the north of Ireland or to be descended from Ulster immigrants; to be Protestant and most likely Presbyterian; to be white, British, and increasingly throughout the long eighteenth century, American? Did, in other words, identity matter?

The answer embedded in the essays of this volume would be a resounding yes. Identity and the power of identity to influence history can be measured in a number of ways. At Donegal, Carlisle, Opequon, and all the settlement sites discussed in this book, Scots-Irish immigrants formed coherent towns or open-country, dispersed communities. None excluded other ethnic groups, and all were in some way affected by Native Americans through trade or contact. But in each of them the Scots-Irish formed webs of social, economic, and political interdependency. At Opequon and probably elsewhere, they married predominantly among their own kind. Everywhere they built Presbyterian churches. They maintained contact with family, friends, and merchants in the north of Ireland. They encouraged their people to come to America and sent something of their produce back home. They created their own highly articulated social structures and nurtured a variety of political, educational, and cultural institutions. Belonging to these institutions or contributing to them were often expressions of being Irish and being Protestant. When their societies became embroiled in the factional and partisan national politics of the New Republic, they looked across the Atlantic to the revolutionary ideology of the United Irishmen to justify protest and rebellion. Later in the nineteenth century, this Irish identity associated with upheaval and disorder was exchanged for the distinction of Scotch-Irish respectability. In all these ways and despite—or possibly because of—its complexity and ambiguity, identity did matter for immigrants from the north of Ireland during the long eighteenth century ending in the 1830s.

Does it matter for us today? This is the challenge presented by popular writers and all those who have politicized Scots-Irish identity for partisan purposes. If the myth of the Scots-Irish can be put to use promoting conservative agendas, what might be the contemporary political implications of the views offered in this volume about Scots-Irish history and identity? Robert Calhoon provides an answer in an Afterword addressed to the idea that political moderation in our own era is not merely the absence of partisanship or party affiliation. Nor is it waffling by those in the middle of the road. Moderation, according to Calhoon, occupies a distinct and autonomous position in American politics. It represents a political stance and philosophy taken not in the absence but in the assertion of ideas. These ideas derive from the experience of diverse peoples living in the same backcountry of America originally settled so famously by the Scots-Irish. Characterized not by the obdurate defense of principle, moderation derives from a highly principled spirit of accommodation and a tolerance born of constant coping with diversity. The tempering of individualism and the untrammeled pursuit of personal gain with an awareness that wealth accumulates as the aggregate of social effort and that authority can perpetuate the benefits of prosperity has, in Calhoon's thinking, compelled the Scots-Irish and their backcountry associates to seek practical solutions to political problems free from confounding ideologies on the right or the left. Calhoon demonstrates that these tendencies can be found rooted in the experiences of backcountry peoples, and most notably the Scots-Irish, as a final witness to the notion that identity matters—as much in the past as in the present.

A final word might be said about the use of identity terms in this volume. Readers should not be confused by the varied appearance of "Scotch-Irish," "Scots-Irish," and "Ulster Scots" in reference to the population of people—the subjects of this book—who made the transit from the north of Ireland to North America from the last years of the seventeenth century to the opening decades of the nineteenth century. Some authors in the volume in certain circumstances might employ these terms with apparent interchangeability, but in context they are never synonymous. No single term stood out in the eighteenth century for these immigrants from the northern counties of Ireland. That they were variously referred to as Irish or Irish

Protestants was consistent with a strong shift to an Irish identity among both liberal and radical Presbyterians. Also during the course of the same century, the term "Scotch-Irish" appeared with greater frequency in the literature of correspondence, travel, and state papers in partial deference to what these immigrants were increasingly calling themselves. Within the next century, however, politically and economically successful Americans of Ulster origin embraced the term "Scotch-Irish" to repudiate the politics and culture of Irish Americans increasingly seen as disreputable and unruly. Thus the term assumed a partisan valence in the religious and ethnic tensions of the day that has persisted and, according to some, intensified in the contentious politics of Northern Ireland since home rule and in the midst of an obstinate anti-Catholicism in American life persisting throughout much of the twentieth century.

It is for this reason that the term "Scots-Irish" has become a contemporary academic and publishing standard in the effort to achieve a politically neutral ethnic identifier for a major segment of the historic American population. As an anachronism more widely employed in the United States than elsewhere, however, the term has ironically become targeted for political correctness in today's culture wars. Thus its very use invites its own dissent and ascriptions of prejudice. Much the same could be said about "Ulster Scots" if it were not for the conscious and partisan affiliation it implies between Ulster unionism and British culture, all the while denying the Irishness of life in Northern Ireland today.

To select any of these three terms as the editorial standard for this volume would, therefore, appear inevitably disingenuous. Imposing interchangeability might be the quickest means of defusing bias but at the expense of authenticity. As the most faithful representation of the differing connotations of these terms and in recognition that the distinctiveness of their usage reflects the ongoing process of identity formation and cultural construction in which this book and its authors are but a part, no universal norm has been adopted; and each author has been encouraged to employ and explain in a note the usage or usages that best suit the context of his or her article. By this means the reader, as well, can better comprehend just how contemporary and how contingent the concerns of this volume truly are.

Notes

1. David Hackett Fischer, *Albion's Seed: Four British Folkways in America* (New York: Oxford University Press, 1989); James G. Leyburn, *The Scotch-Irish: A Social History* (Chapel Hill: University of North Carolina Press, 1962); Barry Aron Vann, *In Search of Ulster-Scots Land: The Birth and Geotheological Imagings of a Transatlantic People, 1603–1703* (Columbia: University of South Carolina Press, 2008).

2. Billy Kennedy, *The Making of America: How the Scots-Irish Shaped a Nation* (Belfast, Northern Ireland: Ambassador International, 2001); Kennedy, *Our Most Priceless Heritage: The Lasting Legacy of the Scots-Irish in America* (Belfast, Northern Ireland: Ambassador International, 2005); James Webb, *Born Fighting: How the Scots-Irish Shaped America* (New York: Broadway Books, 2004). Kennedy's *Making of America* is the latest contribution to a lengthy series of books by him entitled *The Scots-Irish Chronicles,* published between 1995 and 2001 by Ambassador International with individual titles such as *The Scots-Irish in the Hills of Tennessee, The Scots-Irish in the Shenandoah Valley, The Scots-Irish in the Carolinas, The Scots-Irish in Pennsylvania and Kentucky, Faith and Freedom—The Scots-Irish in America,* and *Heroes of the Scots-Irish in America.* See also Rory Fitzpatrick, *God's Frontiersmen: The Scots-Irish Epic* (London: Weidenfeld and Nicholson, 1989).

3. Webb, *Born Fighting,* 9.

4. Kennedy, *Priceless Heritage,* 25.

5. Webb, *Born Fighting,* 20, 12.

6. Ibid., 18–19.

7. Ibid., 12, 10, 19; Kennedy, *Making of America,* 22, 126, 133.

8. Webb, *Born Fighting,* 18, 20.

9. Ibid., 67.

10. Patrick Griffin, *The People with No Name: Ireland's Ulster Scots, America's Scots Irish, and the Creation of a British Atlantic World, 1689–1764* (Princeton, N.J.: Princeton University Press, 2001), 6–7.

11. In the earliest history of the Shenandoah Valley, published in 1833, Samuel Kercheval wrote: "Tradition informs us, and the oral statements of several aged individuals of respectable character confirm the fact that the Indians and white people resided in the same neighborhood for several years after the first settlement commenced, and that the Indians were entirely peaceable and friendly." Due to peaceful relations with Native Americans, the "country rapidly increased in numbers and in the acquisition of property without interruption from the natives, a period of twenty-two years." See Kercheval, *A History of the Valley of Virginia,* 5th ed. (Strasburg, Va.: Shenandoah Publishing House, 1973), 53, 59.

12. Washington to John Augustine Washington, May 28, 1755, in *The Papers of George Washington,* Colonial Series, ed. W. W. Abbot et al. 10 vols. (Charlottesville: University Press of Virginia, 1983–1995), vol. 1:289; Washington to Dinwiddie, October 11, 1755, *The Papers of George Washington,* ed. Abbot et al., vol. 2:104.

Searching for a New World: The Background and Baggage of Scots-Irish Immigrants

David W. Miller

> First and foremost, Ulster Presbyterians moved.
> —Patrick Griffin, *The People with No Name*

What actually moves when someone migrates? If humans were no different from other species, we might be content to concern ourselves solely with the movement of the individual human being and be satisfied with a mere biological explanation of how and why that movement occurs: a description of *homo sapiens'* physical requirements for survival and of the species' bodily resources, such as bipedal locomotion, together perhaps with the latest findings on how the brain gathers and manages the information necessary to reach the desired destination.

At least for historic times, however, we insist on having more than a biological account of humanity's spatial mobility. From a materialist perspective, for example, we want to know what happens to the factors of production—land, labor, and capital. Of course, when individuals migrate, they move their labor from one market to another, and whatever capital they have left after paying for their passage ordinarily migrates with them. If their capital is negative, they barter some of their labor for the cost of the trip; in the case of eighteenth-century Scots-Irish migration, they become indentured servants.[1] Usually a disproportionate share of migrants are of childbearing age, so in addition to productivity, they bring with them reproductive capabilities. If the receiving economy is primarily agricultural, reproduction may well lead to further migration in quest of the one factor of production that never moves: land.

In addition to material resources, migrants bring cultural baggage such as language, identity, religion, assumptions about social relations, and the disposition to produce and use particular artifacts of material culture. When large numbers of people migrate from one society to another, we are especially interested in what happens to this baggage.[2] This essay explores the disposition of cultural baggage in two great migrations: the movement during the seventeenth century of many Lowland Scots to Ulster and the resettlement of many of their descendants on the moving American frontier between 1680 and 1830. In each case we want to understand the relationship of the incoming culture to the preexisting culture as well as to the physical environment of its new location. In addition I offer some reflections on further, post-frontier, mobility—both geographic and social—upon the culture of the descendants of Scots-Irish immigrants.

From Scotland to Ulster

To understand how there came to be a people called the "Scots-Irish," we should begin with the three polities that constituted the British Isles during the Reformation: England, Scotland, and Ireland. The English Reformation was initially *an act of state* by which the Tudor monarch, Henry VIII, had himself (instead of the Pope) made head of the Church in England in 1534, but over the next several generations the character of that church was profoundly affected by *popular religious movements* at home and abroad. In Scotland Protestantism became the state religion in 1559–1560, following a complex political conflict involving not only the Scottish state but also the Catholic state of France and the Protestant English state, and a vigorous popular movement within Scotland (encouraged by some of the Crown's over-mighty subjects) contributed significantly to the outcome. In Ireland the Reformation was an act of state, pure and simple. No significant Protestant popular movement ever emerged among the peoples already present in Ireland at the time of the Reformation.

Scotland and Ireland were each divided into two distinct cultural zones. In Scotland a topographical boundary (see map 1.1) generally demarcated the Highlands, where Gaelic was spoken and the clan system of social relationships flourished, from the Lowlands, where a dialect of English was spoken and the terrain was more suited to tillage farming. Significantly, the term "Irish" was commonly used in Scotland as a label for the Highlanders. In Ireland itself the comparable cultural zones were the result of nearly four centuries of contention and negotiation between Gaelic chieftains and the English successors of twelfth-century Norman invaders who had introduced the feudal system in areas known as the English lordship in recognition of their nominal allegiance to the King of England in deference to his feudal claim to be "lord of Ireland."

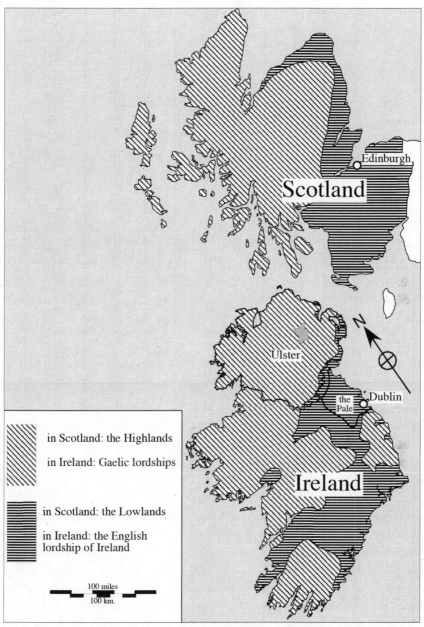

Map 1.1. *Early sixteenth-century Scotland and Ireland. Boundaries of Gaelic and English lordships after Steven G. Ellis,* Tudor Ireland: Crown, Community, and the Confict of Cultures, 1470–1603. *London, 1985.*

In practice, the English Crown had to rely on a few powerful Anglo-Irish aristocrats to maintain a semblance of order beyond a small area around Dublin, "the Pale," outside which the king's writ did not reliably run. Henry's removal of the Irish church from papal jurisdiction and his assumption in 1541 of the title "King of Ireland" were parts of a strategy to "reconquer" the island as a whole. Subsequent Tudor monarchs continued the reconquest of Ireland by several means, including "plantations" of English settlers and subjection of defeated Gaelic chieftains to "surrender and regrant." The latter was a process by which the chieftain relinquished his Gaelic title and the lands associated with it and received an English title and written feudal arrangements restoring the lands to him and clearly defining his obligations to the Crown and his tenants' obligations to him. Meanwhile, Protestantism was making little or no headway in either the Scottish Highlands or the Gaelic lordships in Ireland. The Anglophone character of the Scottish Lowlands no doubt contributed to the popularity of Protestantism there, but in the English lordship of Ireland, the "Old English" aristocratic families mostly remained Catholic. Only a few recent "New English" migrants to Dublin and a few other towns had much enthusiasm for the Protestantism that had been imposed upon the Irish Church.

Among all the Gaelic lordships, those in Ulster under the leadership of Hugh O'Neill put up the most recalcitrant resistance to the Tudor reconquest in a nine-year rebellion that ended in March 1603, the same month that Henry's daughter Elizabeth I died and her cousin James VI, the King of Scots, assumed the throne of England (and of Ireland) as James I. Four years later, dissatisfied with restrictions imposed by their surrender and regrant process, O'Neill (Earl of Tyrone) and Rory O'Donnell (Earl of Tyrconnell), together with a number of their followers, boarded a ship and sailed to continental Europe in what has become known as "the Flight of the Earls." James's government seized the opportunity to treat their departure as evidence of treason, deemed their land (six of the nine Ulster counties) to be forfeited to the Crown, and developed a plan for the most ambitious plantation of the whole reconquest. This time, however, the settlers would include Scots as well as English. Estates, typically between one thousand and two thousand acres, were assigned to members of the gentry called "undertakers," who "undertook" the responsibility to fortify the land and divide it into English-style farms and to recruit British Protestant tenants for them. The Scottish undertakers were chosen exclusively from the Lowlands because a major objective of the Plantation was to encourage by example an alternative to the social order of the Gaelic lordships, which the Scottish Highland clans

4

resembled all too closely. The fact that the Scottish land system was changing in ways that reduced security of tenure no doubt made a more secure tenancy in Ulster attractive.

There had been migration back and forth between the Highlands and Ulster during the middle ages, and the Plantation jump-started a similar pattern of much more numerous migration between the Lowlands and Ulster, including especially the two Ulster counties closest to Scotland—Down and Antrim—which had not been included in the Plantation project. Political and economic crises—for example, the 1641 rebellion of Catholics in Ulster against the Plantation—might reverse the flow for a time, but the direction of flow was generally from Scotland to Ulster. It is estimated that, during the first half of the seventeenth century, between twenty and thirty thousand Scots migrated to Ireland, and that in the second half the flow was between sixty and one hundred thousand, much of that due to harvest failures in Scotland during the 1690s.[3]

Although land never moves, the migrants' culture may affect how the land is allocated and used, what is built upon it, and which of its products the occupiers consume. In the British Isles as a whole, one might envisage agrarian regimes on a continuum from traditional/communal to improved/individualistic. At the traditional/communal end of the spectrum were the clan-based societies of the Scottish Highlands and the Gaelic lordships of Ireland. At the improved/individualist end were those areas in England that had undergone "enclosure"—a process by which common lands shared by a peasant community for grazing livestock and noncontiguous collections of tillage plots held by individual peasants would be consolidated and divided into contiguous farms, each of a sufficient size to sustain a family and, of course, yield a surplus to provide rent to the landlord.

The agrarian regime of the seventeenth-century Scottish Lowlands was somewhere between these two extremes: many farms were held by single lessees, but more communal arrangements known as "runrig" in Scotland and "rundale" in Ireland were still to be found. The typical tenant lived in a gable-ended longhouse with clay or stone walls and a thatched roof. Some, but not all, had chimneys rather than a smoke hole in the center of the roof; many housed livestock as well as the tenant and his family.[4] Between about 1500 and 1750, per capita consumption of meat and dairy products in Scotland declined, while that of food derived from grain rose. With agriculture being less focused on livestock in the Lowlands than in the Highlands, by the time of the Plantation the typical settler would have been used to a diet based primarily on oatmeal.[5]

Migrants from the Lowlands to Ulster encountered a society with a markedly different agrarian regime. In parts of Ulster, the natives maintained a semi-nomadic practice of "booleying" that involved seasonal movement between summer and winter pastures and occupancy of temporary shelters known as "creaghts" in Ulster and "shielings" in the Scottish Highlands.[6] In some parts, however, mixed arable and pasture farming was pursued on the runrig/rundale model. It was often associated with nucleated (rather than dispersed) settlement: the clustering of houses in what was known in Scotland as a "clachan."[7] Typically the initial holdings of Scottish migrants were single tenancies; if settlements were nucleated, it may have been simply the result of security concerns rather than joint tenure. However, population growth and the determination of landlords to exact higher rents seems often to have led to subdivision of land, joint tenancies, and the clustering of additional houses around those that had earlier stood alone.[8]

The settlers' houses themselves were clearly an improvement over creaghts. Whether they bore any specifically Scottish attributes is obscured by the fact that the Plantation explicitly called for "English" houses and that the surveyors, who provided information on how well this requirement was being met, recognized only two categories: "English" and "Irish."[9] Some of the former were timber, box-framed houses, but the already limited Irish woodlands were being so ravaged by the planters themselves to supply fuel and clear land for tillage that timber soon ceased to be viable as a primary building material. By the eighteenth century, most Ulster Scots would have been living in houses whose walls were made of stone or clay, precious timber being reserved for supporting the thatched roof, as it was in Scotland.[10] Meanwhile, the diet in Ireland followed much the same trajectory from animal-based to grain-based foods as it did in Scotland until the late eighteenth century, when the poorest of the native Irish began relying on the potato as virtually their sole source of nourishment.[11] Although the purpose of the Plantation was to create a new landscape conducive to English standards of agriculture and social relations, in material terms the actual outcome of Lowland Scot immigration up to 1750 was perhaps more a convergence between the incoming and the receiving cultures than the replacement of a retrograde agrarian culture with a more modern one.

On their arrival in Ulster, seventeenth-century Scottish immigrants could be identified as such by their dialect and their clothing, but eventually they and their new neighbors would assimilate with each other linguistically and sartorially. However they generally did not assimilate religiously, and the name of their religion—"Presbyterian"—became the most common means

David W. Miller

of identifying these "Ulster Scots" as a group. This does not mean that all Ulster Presbyterians were religiously observant. "From Scotland came many, and from England not a few," wrote one Ulster Presbyterian clergyman around 1670, "yet all of them generally the scum of both nations."[12] Although this assessment may be colored by a Calvinist tendency to discern total depravity in all but the most godly, it does remind us that the primary reason for migration to Ulster was economic, not religious. Nevertheless, the fact that a specifically religious label became essential to the identity of even the unchurched—in the 1860s the number of communicants reported in the denomination's statistical reports was only about a quarter of the number of "Presbyterians" enumerated by the census in Ulster[13]—means that we must unpack the religious component of their cultural baggage.

A useful way to unpack that religious component is to distinguish the high culture of the educated—what the anthropologist Robert Redfield called *the great tradition* of the "reflective few"—from the folk culture of "largely unreflective many" that he called *the little tradition*.[14] In the seventeenth century, Christianity was the great tradition everywhere in the British Isles, though which variety of Christianity would be dominant was being hotly contested. In rural Scotland and Ireland this classic culture coexisted with a folk culture of *sithean* (fairies), gifted healers, charms, and magical wells that, along with other orifices in the landscape, were portals to the otherworld of a pre-Christian Celtic cosmology.[15] Early modern European cultures invite the assumption that such "superstitious" beliefs and practices are the principal component of the little tradition. That view works reasonably well for studies of Roman Catholic communities, whose priests often sought to gain control of the folk culture—by turning magical wells into holy wells, for example—rather than to exterminate it. That very fact helped Protestant clergy to stigmatize folk magic as "popish," but to the extent that a Protestant church or sect owed its origins to a popular movement, its religious professionals were liable to face a different challenge to learned authority.

Migration from lowland Scotland to Ulster contributed to the formation of a new little tradition built around the claim of literate but unreflective laymen to hold their clergyman to account for his fidelity to the Scottish Presbyterian great tradition of the previous century as they understood it.[16] The largest wave of the migration occurred in the 1690s, after the 1688 "Glorious Revolution" settlement secured the status of the Church of Scotland as a Presbyterian body but left the Presbyterian Church of Ireland a dissenting entity in an Anglican confessional state. Much of the migration came from the southwest of Scotland, which had seen the bloodiest conflict during the preceding generation between the government and the Covenanters who had resisted an Episcopal establishment. Memory of the covenanting tradition was sustained in Ulster, as in Scotland, by conducting communion services outdoors reminiscent of the clandestine worship by Covenanters during persecution. Over the next five decades, the newly reconstituted Church of Scotland came to disappoint those who venerated the sacrifices of the Covenanters both because of perceived derogation from Presbyterian doctrinal standards among "moderate" clergy in enlightenment Edinburgh and acquiescence to the reimposition in 1711 of "lay patronage"—that is, the right of the landowner (even if he was an Episcopalian) to appoint a minister in defiance of the wishes of the congregation. One result in Scotland was a schism that began with the withdrawal of several ministers from the General Assembly in the 1730s to form an alternative Presbyterian denomination that came to be known as the Seceders.

Arguably, these developments had a more profound effect in Ulster, where Presbyterian ministers relied for their income almost entirely on their congregations,[17] than in Scotland, where their counterparts automatically received comfortable incomes. There had already been a crisis in the Synod of Ulster in the 1720s initiated by lay suspicions that some ministers were deviating from the Westminster Confession of Faith. From midcentury it was common for a Seceding minister from Scotland to settle in an Ulster locality and attract congregants (and thus income) from an existing Synod of Ulster meetinghouse on the premise that its minister was preaching the "new light"[18] rather than "old light" orthodox theology. The result was a popular tradition of the literate but "largely unreflective many" challenging the well-read—perhaps even wellborn—by grilling ministerial candidates, complaining to presbytery's visitation committee that the minister held unorthodox views, and attending outdoor sermons of itinerant preachers of the covenanting gospel of the previous century.

In a rural district of Ulster Scot settlement, the landlord was typically a member of the established, Episcopalian, Church of Ireland, even if he was of Scottish ancestry. Unlike his counterpart in Scotland, he had neither the power nor the desire to appoint the Presbyterian minister. This meant that authority within the rural community rested mainly with the kirk session, even though that "court" was able to sustain its power to punish only those offenders whose wrongdoings were beneath the notice of the civil courts and the courts of the established church.[19] Map 1.2, which is based on an 1834 religious census, delineates the areas with substantial Dissenting (almost entirely Presbyterian) population from those in which Anglican

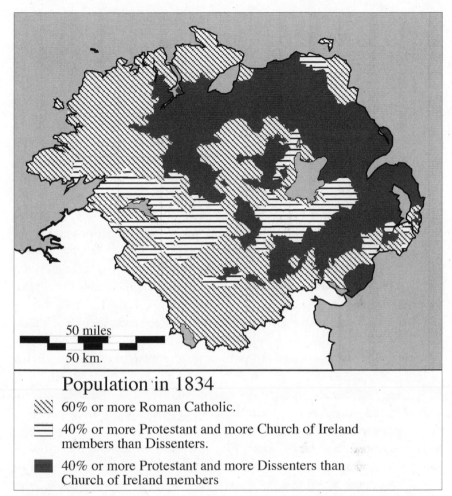

Map 1.2. *Denominational zones in Ulster, 1834. Based on a map that first appeared in Jim Smyth, ed.,* Revolution, Counter-Revolution, and Union: Ireland in the 1790s *(Cambridge, U.K.: Cambridge University Press, 2000).*

landlords had a significant number of subordinates of their own religion. The Presbyterian community as a whole was cast in the role of antagonist to the Anglican confessional state—a reality that present-day Irish people, accustomed to an Ulster politics based on Protestant solidarity against the Catholic ("Nationalist") community, find it difficult to imagine. In the early eighteenth century, the Presbyterians, most of them lacking landed property, posed no serious threat to the Anglicans.

However, a Presbyterian middle class developed in Belfast, and to a lesser extent in Derry, and it was strengthened by the growth of a domestic linen industry in several parts of the Ulster countryside. Its mercantile elite having been denied a share in the governance of a city, every square inch of which was owned by an Anglican landlord, Belfast became a hotbed of opposition to the Anglican confessional state, its corrupt system of parliamentary representation, and its exclusion of both Presbyterians and Catholics from the Irish polity. The outcome was the collapse of that polity, featuring the development of a radical movement known as the Societies of United Irishmen, the adoption of a massive reign of terror by Crown forces in 1797, an unsuccessful popular rebellion in which both Presbyterian and Catholic country folk participated in the following year, and a decision by the British government to dismantle the Irish polity by bribing its Anglican governing class in 1800 into acquiescing in a legislative union of Britain and Ireland. It was under the new polity—the United Kingdom of Great Britain and Ireland (1801–1922)—that the now-familiar political solidarity of Protestants in Ulster developed.

Because a traditional society may place a high value on keeping the local community intact, it is tempting to infer from the relatively early trans-Atlantic migration of Ulster Presbyterians a more modern outlook than that of Irish Catholics who, it might be argued, continued to subdivide their holdings in the old country until the potato famine of the 1840s decimated them and forced the survivors to come to America at last. Actually, the Ulster Scot community of the eighteenth century in many ways had a quite traditional culture. We can make better sense of their behavior by looking not for modern outlooks in general but for what social scientists find in certain Third World communities today: a "culture of migration." In such a culture, "over time migrant communities become culturally 'transnationalized,'" and "migration is increasingly taken for granted."[20] What seems to have happened is that members of the Ulster Scot community, having taken the step of moving from Scotland to Ireland (and perhaps moving back and forth again) had internalized an expectation that having to leave one's traditional community was just part of life.

From Ulster to Frontier America

There had been a trickle of Ulster Presbyterian migration to North America in the seventeenth century, but not until the late 1710s did a fairly steady flow of such emigration begin. During the years 1715–1720 several natural disasters, including drought and an outbreak of smallpox, coincided with the expiration of long-term leases on several estates whose landlords seized the opportunity to raise the rents. The natural calamities were, of course, random events (though no doubt understood in providential terms by many of their victims), but rising rents would become systemic. Low rents and long leases reflected the seventeenth-century effort to entice British farmers to move to a dangerous frontier environment. Both the War of the Three Kingdoms (1638–1652) and the Revolution (1688–1691) had seen substantial violence in Ulster and at least some temporary flight of settlers back to Scotland, but a generation after 1690 life in the province seemed significantly less dangerous. Rents would continue to rise as leases fell in, for the simple reason that it was easier to find willing tenants, even Protestant ones, than it had been in the previous century.

In addition to rising rents, all three of the Irish ethno-religious communities—Catholic, Anglican, and Presbyterian—were experiencing rising population, especially after about 1760. Furthermore, unimproved land suitable for tillage was becoming scarcer. In such an agrarian society, if several male children survive to adulthood the family will face a stark choice: divide the farm into smaller holdings or send all but one son somewhere else. Actually, this reality was somewhat mitigated in Ulster by the growth of the domestic linen industry, for a handloom weaver might make a living from a loom in his cottage on a very small parcel of land suitable only for a garden to supplement the food he would purchase with the cash he received for the sale of his cloth. Fluctuations in the linen market and, ultimately, technological developments including the availability of ginned cotton could, however, eventually force him to leave his traditional neighborhood.

A conservative but demographically sophisticated analysis of very shaky and incomplete data suggests that fifteen thousand Ulster Protestants emigrated to North America during the first half of the eighteenth century and an additional twenty-five thousand between 1751 and 1775. An older detailed study of vessels known to have carried emigrants to America from northern ports offers maximum and minimum passenger estimates that suggest the possibility of three times as many emigrants over the same period. Emigration among Ulster Scots was especially high in 1770 to 1775, a period marked by bad harvests, landlord efforts to ratchet up rents as leases fell in, agrarian violence by Protestant gangs who adopted the name "Hearts of Steel" or "Steelboys," and official efforts to prosecute and punish the offenders. The American Revolution temporarily cut off further emigration. An estimate of

"100,000 or so" Ulster emigrants to America in the three decades beginning in 1783 has the benefit of at least some official efforts to monitor the departures. At the moment, the overall volume of the migration is being contested in the historical literature. Furthermore, the religious composition of the emigrant flow is murky; in addition to Catholic native Irish emigrants, the departures from northern ports included Anglicans and non-Presbyterian Dissenters who probably assimilated much more quickly into the American population of English origin than did either Presbyterians or Catholics. An important current project led by Liam Kennedy and Kerby Miller to assemble and analyze all extant eighteenth-century sources for Irish religious demography promises to shed considerable light on the volume and religious composition of the migration.[21]

During the eighteenth century, passenger ships from northern Irish ports might sail for any major port on the Atlantic seaboard from Prince Edward Island to Savannah, but the initial recipient of the largest share of Ulster emigrants was Philadelphia. Although some found work in the city (or were required to stay there for a time under indentured servitude), most headed for the nearest available farmland. The neighboring colonies of Maryland and Delaware met some of the demand, but the greatest attraction was southeastern Pennsylvania. New arrivals from Ulster competed with English and German immigrants for farms on the exceptionally fertile land between the Delaware River and Blue Mountain, the easternmost ridge of the rugged terrain that blocked development of western Pennsylvania for several decades. As undeveloped land became scarcer in southeastern Pennsylvania, some of the immigrant flow turned southwest near York and began, about 1730, to occupy the Great Valley of Virginia. Settlement of the Carolinas had so far remained in the Tidewater area east of the fall line of the watercourses, but in the 1740s traffic through the Valley began to continue into the North Carolina Piedmont. By 1750, Scots-Irish settlement reached the South Carolina backcountry. Such settlement, quite remote from the Euro-American cities of the Atlantic seaboard, naturally led to conflict with Native Americans, culminating in the French and Indian War of 1754–1763. After the war, British policymakers tried to avoid such trouble in the future by preventing settlement beyond the Appalachians. The American challenge to British sovereignty unleashed the land-hungry along the whole corridor of Scots-Irish settlement beneath the eastern foothills of the Appalachians. In the early 1780s settlers poured into Tennessee and Kentucky from the southern end of the corridor and into western Pennsylvania from the northern end as well as from mid-Atlantic ports, with treks to western Pennsylvania being

David W. Miller

made less arduous by Forbes Road and Braddocks Road, the military paths created by two British generals during the French and Indian War.[22]

The material context of life in America was crucially different from that which the emigrants had left behind. Instead of rising—indeed, often prohibitive—rents, immigrants who were willing to trek to the frontier could be sure of finding inexpensive arable land. Collective land tenure arrangements like rundale and the clustered settlement patterns associated with them had little place in the frontier land market;[23] dispersed and independent farmsteads became the norm. Far from being a scarce commodity, timber was everywhere available and was an obstacle to cultivation. The Scots-Irish adopted the log cabin, although the ground plans of their cabins did bear a close resemblance to those of the stone and clay houses they had left behind.

Perhaps the most notable material change was the return of meat, especially pork, to a prominence in immigrants' diets that their forebears had not enjoyed for two centuries.[24] Of course, grain products continued to be consumed, and the most culturally significant of those products was whiskey. An observer of a predominantly Presbyterian parish in Ulster noted in 1838: "The use of whiskey is too common: not that many drunkards are to be seen, but that it is drunk at all hours upon the slightest pretence."[25] Prior to the temperance movement of the mid-nineteenth century (to the astonishment of many twenty-first-century Presbyterians), whiskey was commonly kept in the kirk session-room, the minister might be handed a glass when he descended from the pulpit, and his congregants were expected to offer him a dram whenever he paid them a visit.[26] The centrality of whiskey in community life definitely crossed the Atlantic. The 1791 federal tax on distilled spirits that triggered the Whiskey Rebellion in Western Pennsylvania three years later should be understood not only as an economic blow to farmers whose raw product was too bulky for overland transport given the state of the roads, but also as a direct assault against Scots-Irish culture. The recent publication of ethnographic "memoirs" of Ulster parishes written by army officers who supervised the Ordnance Survey's monumental mapping of pre-Famine Ireland between 1829 and 1842 has made accessible evidence of the vitality of dancing and accompanying folk music in Ulster Presbyterian communities. Those components of their cultural baggage also made the trans-Atlantic passage and found a home in the Appalachian and trans-Appalachian frontier.[27]

The great tradition of Ulster Scot religion was brought to America initially by the migration of a few Presbyterian ministers, beginning with Rev. Francis Makemie, who founded a Presbyterian congregation in Snow Hill, Maryland, in 1683. More important for the maintenance of that great tradition was the formation in 1727 of a seminary, the so-called "Log College," of which Princeton University was a successor. The founder of the Log College, William Tennent Sr., was born and educated in Scotland. His connection with Ireland was a stint as a clergyman not of the Presbyterian Church, but of the Church of Ireland. He renounced Anglicanism, was admitted by a suspicious Philadelphia Presbytery, and is credited with having taught some of the revivalist preachers of the Great Awakening. The Awakening was the American component of a movement in many parts of the Protestant world during the 1730s and 1740s including Germany, England, Scotland, New England, and Pennsylvania. The movement as a whole emphasized the importance of a palpable conversion experience and is treated by many historians as the beginning of the revivalism that so permeated American religious life in the nineteenth century.

Although there had been some revival-like events in the Sixmilewater district of County Antrim in the 1620s, those events seem to have been forgotten in Ireland over the next two centuries. No evidence of revivals that might have introduced a new little tradition during the 1730s or 1740s in the Presbyterian communities of Ulster has come to light. Indeed, the apparent failure of the famous Cambuslang revival of 1742 to spread to Ulster reflects the fact that, to a much greater extent than their Scottish counterparts, Ulster Presbyterian lay folk had already developed a vigorous and effective little tradition of holding their ministers to account for departures from what they deemed to be sacred and immutable Presbyterian tradition in matters ranging from Christology to the admissibility of pipe organs. It is no wonder that Wesley and his followers made so few inroads among Ulster Scots in the remainder of the eighteenth century. Why bother walking to the crossroads to hear a Methodist denounce your minister as unconverted when your own culture already gave you such latitude to take that minister to task? I call this demotic component of Ulster Presbyterianism's little tradition the "old leaven" to distinguish it from the "new leaven" of revivalism.[28]

That said, it is incontestable that many Scots-Irish on the American frontier—like their Sixmilewater antecedents in a similar frontier situation nearly two centuries earlier—responded positively to revivalism. Furthermore, their festal communions provided a convenient venue for revivals that morphed into the (non-sacramental) "camp meeting" in the early nineteenth century. On the frontier, Scots-Irish immigrants added the revival to the little tradition they had brought with them. Since the revival was an innovation, it might seem to be an odd candidate for inclusion in a little tradition that de-

David W. Miller

plored new ideas and practices. To understand its inclusion, we should remember two circumstances. First, when unreflective folk say that the old ways are best, they are referring to practices that they remember from their own childhood. The pervasive character of revivalism on the American frontier ensured that within a single generation revivals would be so remembered. Second, the mere fact that many clergymen were suspicious of revivals and spent much of the nineteenth century working to gain and maintain control of them placed them in the arena of lay-clerical contention within the little tradition that Scots-Irish immigrants brought with them in their baggage.

Popular accounts of Scots-Irish immigrants often connect their social attitudes and political culture observed in America to their background in Ireland. As Warren Hofstra has indicated in our Introduction, the contributors to this book do not take an "essentialist" view in which attributes of the Scots-Irish are regarded as unchanging. One way to illustrate our perspective is to examine a few examples of attributes of Scots-Irish immigrant culture that contributors to this book have found in the particular frontier communities they have studied by asking how well (or how poorly) they can be explained by the "baggage" metaphor. Richard MacMaster explores conflict between community values and individual material gain, and concludes that the latter was the victor in Donegal Springs. Peter Gilmore and Kerby Miller suggest the opposite when they include a "moral economy" in the world view of Scots-Irish settlers in western Pennsylvania. This apparent discrepancy results from the difference in time of arrival of the two populations: 1720–1750 in Donegal Springs versus 1780–1810 in western Pennsylvania. Some of the immigrants studied by MacMaster may well have had fathers who had learned in the 1690s to drive hard bargains with landlords who were very anxious to recruit Protestant tenants for security reasons. After 1760, population explosion strengthened the upper hand of Irish landlords. The fathers of some immigrants studied by Gilmore and Miller may have acted out community values by participating in the Oakboy and Steelboy protests of the 1760s and 1770s. The individual immigrant often carries perishable cultural goods, but seldom essentialist truisms, in his or her baggage.

Furthermore, the individual immigrant was not the only trans-Atlantic carrier of cultural goods; by the 1770s newspapers on both sides of the Atlantic were copying news from their overseas counterparts. The *Belfast News-Letter* was the first newspaper in Europe to print the Declaration of Independence. Although relatively few immigrants returned to Ireland, literate Irish were receiving news from America regularly. In their account of elite republicanism in the upper Shenandoah Valley, Katherine Brown and Kenneth Keller quote a fascinating 1775 resolution on "a well regulated militia" at the Augusta courthouse. For most American readers, this language evokes the Second Amendment to the Constitution, on the right to bear arms, nearly some seventeen years later, but to the Irish historian it sounds much like the rhetoric that accompanied the Volunteer movement in Ireland only three years later. Trans-Atlantic transmission of political culture could occur in both directions.

A number of the contributors to this book[29] grapple with the meaning and importance of "independence"—freedom from economic dependence upon landlord or employer—that clearly became an objective in the lives of many Scots-Irish immigrants. Was a traditional desire for such independence part of the baggage brought to America from Ulster? Certainly in Ireland aversion to the landlord had been widespread among Ulster Scots. The so-called Ulster custom of tenant right did mean that a farmer who chose to give up his holding and go to America (as opposed to a farmer's son leaving for America) might well collect from the new tenant a tidy sum of money that came to be rationalized as compensation for his improvements to the farm. No doubt such a nest egg could be an incentive to adopt an entrepreneurial attitude once he was in America. However, prior to the 1849 Encumbered Estates Act, outright ownership of a farm in Ireland by anyone other than the hereditary landlord was virtually inconceivable. To the extent that Ulster Presbyterians pursued "independence" within Ulster, they did so by leaving the agrarian economy altogether and seeking their fortune in the mercantile sector or the nascent industrial sector centered increasingly in Belfast. Attaining independence on a farm—or perhaps on a sequence of farms, each improved and sold to enable the seller to buy a larger one—was the product of American possibility, not Irish practice. The emptiness of America (at least as seen by Europeans), and especially its vastness compared to Ulster, was the primary foundation of Scots-Irish independence. Land remains the one factor of production that never moves, and no habit of gaining independence through the exploitation of land was in the baggage of the typical emigrant from Ulster.

From Frontier to Modernity

Each case study in this volume focuses on the period in which the community being studied was on, or not far from, the frontier. Some of the baggage of the immigrants—for example, folk music and dance—flourished in areas where Scots-Irish settlers were thick enough on the ground to constitute a homogenous ethnic community but apparently not among later generations whose geographic and social mobility led them to more diverse social environments. Presbyterianism—the "great tradition"—is the most identifiable surviving baggage of the Scots-Irish immigrations. Ironically, however, Americans who identify themselves as Scots-Irish can be found in almost any of the rich array of American Protestant denominations. Protestant respondents to the General Social Survey between 1978 and 2002 who claimed ancestry in Ireland and/or Scotland were not significantly more likely to be Presbyterians than were those who claimed ancestry in England or Wales.[30] To understand the impact of Scots-Irish Presbyterianism on American society, we must place it in the context of further geographic and social mobility. The culture of migration survived the ocean voyage; farmers' sons and daughters continued to move west until there was no longer a moving frontier of cheap land, by which time there were also increasing opportunities to migrate to the cities of a rapidly industrializing society. For many ethnic groups, however, opportunity in the industrial city started with a job at the lowest rung of the industrial ladder. To use a term that entered the language in the 1960s, the Scots-Irish could pass as "WASPs" (White Anglo-Saxon Protestants), start on a significantly higher rung, and experience social mobility. Of course, not all Scots-Irish continued to experience upward mobility; some no doubt actually moved downward. We should think of the third and later generations of Scots-Irish as arrayed on a social continuum from WASPs to Crackers.

Perhaps the component of the great tradition that most affected the success or failure (depending on one's point of view) of Ulster Presbyterianism in America was insistence on an educated clergy. Presbyterian ministers were determined to admit into their ranks only those who had studied theology at the university level: in Ulster, typically graduates of Scottish universities. (Ulster itself did not have a Presbyterian seminary until 1853.) The flood of new immigrants on the American frontier and (due to revivals) an increasing proportion of recent arrivals desirous of pastoral care created a demand for ministers that rapidly outran the supply of clergy who might meet the Presbyterian educational standard. West of the Appalachians a new denomination, the Cumberland Presbyterians, founded in 1810, met a fraction of this demand by waiving the higher education requirement, but Baptist and Methodist clergy captured most of the market share that the Presbyterians forfeited.

However, if we compare the 1850 census data on religion for western Pennsylvania and western North Carolina—two regions at opposite ends of the settlements addressed in this book—we find drastic differences in the extent of that forfeiture. In western North Carolina there were only 13 Presbyterian churches, representing 5 percent of the 264 Anglophone Protestant churches in the region, while the 422 Presbyterian churches in western Pennsylvania amounted to 44 percent of 954 Anglophone Protestant congregations.[31] The western North Carolina situation was replicated in much of the lower South, where often there was a single Presbyterian church serving the elite of a market town, surrounded by a sea of Baptist and Methodist churches.

A small part of the relative success of Presbyterianism in western Pennsylvania may be attributed to the presence of a rapidly growing city, Pittsburgh, in which there were several middle- and upper-class congregations that actually preferred educated ministers. More significantly, western Pennsylvania differed from other areas of Scots-Irish settlement in rivaling the old country in its rich variety of different flavors of Presbyterianism: the Reformed Presbyterians (strict Covenanters) and various progeny of the eighteenth-century secession in Scotland that eventually merged in 1858 to form the United Presbyterian Church, as well as the mainstream denomination (mostly Old School rather than the revival-friendly New School between 1837 and 1869). One effect of this institutional diversity within orthodox Presbyterianism in the region may have been to help sustain the older Ulster Presbyterian little tradition of contention over who best represented true Presbyterianism. Indeed in Ulster, itself, the old leaven satisfactions of such haggling seem in the early nineteenth century to have trumped the new leaven ecstasies of revival experiences; not until 1859 did a full-fledged American-style revival convulse the province. Although western Pennsylvania certainly had experienced revivals some decades earlier, the old leaven was still alive and well there.

The Scots-Irish great tradition flourished in the Presbyterian denomination as the urbanization and suburbanization of the United States proceeded. Presbyterianism became less and less an ethnic (Scots-Irish and Scottish) denomination and evolved into a denomination whose constituency was defined primarily by social class (middle and upper middle). Presbyterian clergy succeeded in sustaining a religious system attractive to the "reflective few," who, in fact, were becoming much more numerous as higher education became accessible to more and more young middle-class people headed for nonreligious professions.[32] A result was the ability of moderates in the (northern) Presbyterian General Assembly to stave off an effort of the fundamentalists to drive "modernism" out of the denomination in the 1920s. Observers of the culture wars in the past two decades will recognize the Presbyterian Church USA as still an advocate of progressive theological and social views,

David W. Miller

albeit with significant internal conservative resistance. The existence and effectiveness of a centrist party that gives priority to institutional stability over the passionate claims of the contenders in that conflict is an example in the religious realm of the political moderation described in Robert Calhoon's contribution to this volume.[33]

To understand the impact of the Scots-Irish little tradition, we must address the fundamentalist movement that emerged in the late nineteenth and early twentieth centuries. Marsden identifies "the paradox of revivalist fundamentalism"—its amalgamation of the religion of the heart with an insistence on cognitive correctness—as the central problem facing the historian who tries to explain the fundamentalist phenomenon.[34] That paradox becomes easier to resolve if one adds to Marsden's brilliant top-down, "supply-side," analysis of the products on offer from religious professionals a bottom-up understanding of the demand side. Precisely because the Scots-Irish did not all remain Presbyterians, but turned to other denominations wherever there was no Presbyterian church, they spread throughout American Anglophone Protestantism an amalgam of two little traditions: a propensity to resist change in belief and practice (the old leaven) that they had brought with them from Ulster and an enthusiasm for revivals (the new leaven) that they acquired on the American frontier.

Marsden also identified, perhaps inadvertently, the most intriguing excursion of Scots-Irish baggage when he observed that Ulster's is the only culture in the Protestant world in which fundamentalism had become so conspicuous and pervasive as it is in the United States.[35] Actually, both the great tradition of the Scots-Irish—a clergy engaged with the intellectual world of their day—and their little tradition—revivalist fundamentalism—became components of what has been described as "Ulster-American religion." In the late nineteenth century, Princeton replaced Edinburgh as the lodestar of Ulster Presbyterian theology, but not to the exclusion of the higher criticism. During the 1920s Belfast and its vicinity experienced an extended revival that no doubt addressed Protestant anxieties arising from the formation of the Irish Free State and the establishment of the devolved Northern Ireland government. The widely acknowledged leader of this revival was W. P. Nicholson, who had returned to his native Ulster as a missionary from the Bible Institute of Los Angeles. One consequence was the formation of a "Bible Standards League" that precipitated in the Irish Presbyterian Church a fundamentalist-modernist dispute very similar to the one simultaneously occurring in the mainline northern Presbyterian Church USA. Just as in the American case, the outcome was an apparent victory of the great tradition's moderate forces over the fundamentalists.[36] Nevertheless, a convincing argument can be made that the rise of Ian Paisley to prominence in the religio-political culture of Northern Ireland over the succeeding decades owes much to returned baggage containing the uniquely American syncretism of the two little traditions to create Ulster American revivalist fundamentalism.[37] To the extent that the recent political settlement succeeds—ironically, through Paisley's long-awaited compromise—perhaps we will even see some "moderate" recovery of the great tradition.

The cultural baggage that the typical Scots-Irish immigrant brought to America in the five generations or so between 1680 and 1830 was not a precious family heirloom; still less was it loaded with unchanging primordial beliefs and practices. Whatever identity he or she carried—whether ethnic, political, socioeconomic, or religious—was a work in progress. The studies that follow are generally arranged chronologically, and therefore geographically, each focusing on a new locality deeper into the backcountry. The reader will be better served by attending to differences in the experiences and concerns of the actors in each subsequent chapter than by searching for any essentialist characterization of the Scots-Irish in general.

Notes

1. I use "Scots-Irish" and "Ulster Scots" interchangeably. I avoid the term "Scotch-Irish" because of its adoption by some descendants of subjects of this book during the post-Famine era to avoid association with impoverished Catholic Irish immigrants.

2. For an analysis of these issues by an Ulster folklorist, see Alan Gailey, "Migrant Culture," *Folk Life* 28 (1989–1990): 5–18.

3. Thomas Christopher Smout, N. C. Landsman, and Thomas Martin Devine, "Scottish Emigration in the Seventeenth and Eighteenth Centuries," in *Europeans on the Move: Studies on European Migration, 1500–1800,* ed. Nicholas Canny (Oxford: Clarendon Press, 1994), 76–112.

4. Ian Whyte, *Agriculture and Society in Seventeenth-Century Scotland* (Edinburgh: J. Donald, 1979), 137–72.

5. A. Gibson and T. C. Smout, "From Meat to Meal: Changes in Diet in Scotland," in *Food, Diet, and Economic Change Past and Present,* ed. Catherine Geissler and Derek J. Oddy (New York: Leicester University Press, 1993), 10–16.

6. For a discussion of transhumance in Scotland, see James R. Coull, "Crofters' Common Grazings in Scotland," *Agricultural History Review* 16, no. 2 (1968): 142–54.

7. Desmond McCourt, "The Dynamic Quality of Irish Rural Settlement," in *Man and His Habitat: Essays Presented to Emyr Estyn Evans,* ed. R. H. Buchanan, Emrys Jones, and Desmond McCourt (New York: Barnes & Noble, 1971), 126–64; Ian Whyte,

Agriculture and Society in Seventeenth-Century Scotland (Edinburgh: J. Donald, 1979), 145–52.

8. V. B. Proudfoot, "Clachans in Ireland," *Gwerin* 2 (1959): 116–18; Desmond McCourt, "The Decline of Rundale, 1750–1850," in *Plantation to Partition: Essays in Ulster History in Honour of J. L. McCracken,* ed. Peter Roebuck (Belfast: Blackstaff Press, 1981), 119–39.

9. Philip Robinson, "Vernacular Housing in Ulster in the Seventeenth Century," *Ulster Folklife* 25 (1979): 7, 13.

10. F. H. A. Aalen, "Buildings," in *Atlas of the Irish Rural Landscape,* ed. F. H. A. Aalen, Kevin Whelan, and Matthew Stout (Toronto: University of Toronto Press, 1997), 152–55; Roy Tomlinson, "Forests and Woodlands," in *Atlas of the Irish Rural Landscape,* 123.

11. Leslie A. Clarkson and E. Margaret Crawford, *Feast and Famine: Food and Nutrition in Ireland, 1500–1920* (Oxford University Press, 2001), 13–16; L. M. Cullen, "Irish History without the Potato," *Past and Present* 40 (1968): 72–83.

12. Patrick Adair, *A True Narrative of the Rise and Progress of the Presbyterian Church in Ireland (1623–1670),* ed. W. D. Killen (Belfast: C. Aitchison, 1866), 313. The quotation is from a memoir by Rev. Andrew Stewart that Killen includes as an appendix.

13. David W. Miller, "Did Ulster Presbyterians Have a Devotional Revolution?" in *Evangelicals and Catholics in Nineteenth-Century Ireland,* ed. James H. Murphy (Dublin: Four Courts Press, 2005), 53.

14. Robert Redfield, *The Little Community and Peasant Society and Culture* (Chicago: University of Chicago Press, 1962), 40–59.

15. For a summary of folk practices in Scotland, see G. Maxwell-Stuart, *Satan's Conspiracy: Magic and Witchcraft in Sixteenth-Century Scotland* (East Linton, Scotland: Tuckwell Press, 2001), 1–29.

16. Miller, "Did Ulster Presbyterians Have a Devotional Revolution?" 39–45.

17. Since the late seventeenth century, mainstream Irish Presbyterian ministers had received stipends from the government. The ministers valued this *regium donum* because they could interpret it as some sort of recognition of their claims to be the established church, but the stipends were far too small to constitute "livings."

18. The term "new light" began as a label for Arminian scruples over the Westminster Confession. A. W. Godfrey Brown, "A Theological Interpretation of the First Subscription Controversy (1719–1728)," in *Challenge and Conflict: Essays in Irish Presbyterian History and Doctrine* (Antrim, Northern Ireland: W. & G. Baird, 1981), 28–45. Quite logically, the term was adopted in America as a label for those who emphasized the comforts of a conversion experience over the anxieties associated with predestination. In Irish Presbyterianism, however, "new light" ceased to have Arminian connotations and became permanently associated with tendencies toward Unitarianism.

19. Patrick Griffin, *The People with No Name: Ireland's Ulster Scots, America's Scots Irish, and the Creation of a British Atlantic World, 1689–1764* (Princeton, N.J.: Princeton University Press, 2001), 37–64.

20. Douglas Massey, Luin Goldring, and Jorge Durand, "Continuities in Transnational Migration: An Analysis of Nineteen Mexican Communities," *The American Journal of Sociology* 99 (May 1994): 1501.

21. L. M. Cullen, "The Irish Diaspora of the Seventeenth and Eighteenth Centuries," in *Europeans on the Move: Studies on European Migration, 1500–1800,* ed. Nicholas Canny (Oxford: Clarendon Press, 1994), 140; R. J. Dickson, *Ulster Emigration to Colonial America, 1718–1775* (London: Routledge & Kegan Paul, 1966); Maldwyn A. Jones, "Ulster Emigration, 1783–1815," in *Essays in Scotch-Irish History,* ed. E. R. R. Green (London: Routledge & Kegan Paul, 1969), 46–68; Kerby A. Miller, Arnold Schrier, Bruce D. Boling, and David N. Doyle, *Irish Immigrants in the Land of Canaan: Letters and Memoirs from Colonial and Revolutionary America, 1675–1815* (New York: Oxford University Press, 2003), 656–59.

22. James Graham Leyburn, *The Scotch-Irish: A Social History* (Chapel Hill: University of North Carolina Press, 1962), 184–255.

23. Maldwyn A. Jones, "The Scotch-Irish in British America," in *Strangers within the Realm,* ed. Bernard Bailyn and Philip D. Morgan (Chapel Hill: University of North Carolina Press, 1991), 298–99.

24. Leyburn, *The Scotch-Irish,* 24.

25. Angélique Day, Patrick McWilliams, and Lisa English, eds., *Ordnance Survey Memoirs of Ireland* (Belfast: Institute of Irish Studies, 1990–96), vol. 35: 121.

26. W. D. Killen, *Memoir of John Edgar, DD, LLD, Professor of Systematic Theology for the General Assembly of the Presbyterian Church in Ireland* (Belfast: C. Aitchison, 1867), 27.

27. Angélique Day, Patrick McWilliams, and Lisa English, eds., *Ordnance Survey Memoirs of Ireland* 37: 23, 148; Peter Gilmore, "Scotch-Irish Identity and Traditional Ulster Music on the Pennsylvania Frontier," *Journal of Scotch-Irish Studies* 1, no. 2 (2001): 138–48.

28. Miller, "Did Ulster Presbyterians Have a Devotional Revolution?"; David W. Miller, "Religious Commotions in the Scottish Diaspora: A Transatlantic Perspective on 'Evangelicalism' in a Mainline Denomination," in *Ulster Presbyterians in the Atlantic World: Religion, Politics and Identity,* ed. David A. Wilson and Mark G. Spencer (Dublin: Four Courts Press, 2006).

29. Calhoon; Gilmore and Miller; Griffin, Hofstra, Brown and Keller; and Montgomery.

30. David W. Miller, "Ulster Evangelicalism and American Culture Wars," *Radharc: A Journal of Irish and Irish-American Studies* 5–7 (2004–6): 197–215.

31. Includes the following counties: (in North Carolina) Ashe, Buncombe, Burke, Caldwell, Cherokee, Haywood, Henderson, McDowell, Macon, Watauga, and Wilkes; (in Pennsylvania) Allegheny, Armstrong, Beaver, Butler, Clarion, Crawford, Erie, Fayette, Greene, Indiana, Jefferson, Lawrence, Mercer, Venango, Warren, Washington, and Westmoreland. Excluded from the analysis are Roman Catholic, Jewish, Lutheran, Moravian, German Reformed, and Mennonite congregations. For an analysis of the Presbyterian Church's difficulties in part of western North Carolina, see Tyler Blethen and Curtis Wood, ed., "Scotch-Irish Frontier Society in Southwestern North Carolina, 1780–1840," in *Ulster and North America: Transatlantic Perspectives on the Scotch-Irish* (Tuscaloosa: University of Alabama Press, 1997), 217–20.

32. For an interesting analysis of Liberal Protestantism's appeal to the "professional-managerial class" in the early twentieth century, see Eugene McCarraher, *Christian Critics: Religion and the Impasse in Modern American Social Thought* (Ithaca, N.Y.: Cornell University Press, 2000), 7–33.

33. W. J. Weston, "The Presbyterian 'Fidelity and Chastity' Competition as a Loyalist Victory," *Review of Religious Research* 41 (1999). Weston uses the term "loyalist" to mean something like Calhoon's "moderate." In the context of Presbyterian history this analogy can be confusing because the term "Moderate" is used to describe not the reconcilers but one of two contending parties in the eighteenth-century Church of Scotland, its adversary being the "Popular" or (later) "Evangelical" Party.

34. George M. Marsden, *Fundamentalism and American Culture,* 2nd ed. (New York: Oxford University Press, 2006), 43–48.

35. George Marsden, "Fundamentalism as an American Phenomenon: a Comparison with English Evangelicalism," *Church History* 46 (June 1977): 216, n.3.

36. David N. Livingstone and Ronald A. Wells, *Ulster-American Religion: Episodes in the History of a Cultural Connection* (Notre Dame, Ind.: University of Notre Dame Press, 1999).

37. Steve Bruce, *Paisley: Religion and Politics in Northern Ireland* (New York: Oxford University Press, 2007), 12–42.

Searching for Land: The Role of New Castle, Delaware, 1720s–1770s

Marianne S. Wokeck

After almost a century of emigration from Ireland to the West Indies and the Chesapeake Bay colonies, the eighteenth-century migration flow shifted to include New England, South Carolina, and the mid-Atlantic colonies of British North America. Beginning with the first wave in the late 1710s until the American Revolution, the Delaware River ports, New Castle and Philadelphia, attracted the most significant proportion of all Irish voyagers and travelers.[1]

Today Philadelphia, Pennsylvania, comes to mind most often as the entrepôt on the Delaware River that anchored the emigration from Ulster to North America in the eighteenth century. Yet New Castle, Delaware, was an important portal for Irish immigrants in the earlier parts of the long eighteenth century (1680s–1830), handling probably a good quarter to a third of voyagers and travelers from Ulster to the Delaware River (see map 2.1). It acted like a magnet for the Scotch-Irish migration and exerted very strong influence at the beginning of the century but had waned by the time of the American Revolution.[2] Its location and the timing and nature of the migration flow determined New Castle's significance. When sailing vessels laden with passengers and goods reached Cape Henlopen and entered Delaware Bay after long and stressful months at sea, New Castle was the first substantial settlement where ships could take on fresh water and provisions—a most welcome opportunity for everyone on board ship even if the final place of disembarkation, typically Philadelphia, was farther up the Delaware River.

Located on the western shore slightly north of the narrowing head of the bay where the river turns northeastward toward Philadelphia, New Castle was a welcome sight and first port of call for voyagers and travelers alike. Without a protected harbor and tributary connection to its hinterland, however, opportunities for New Castle to grow and develop were limited notwithstanding its prominence and prosperity as a market town, the county seat, and capital of the Lower Counties (New Castle, Kent, and Sussex counties made up the Lower Counties that became the state of Delaware).[3] In the eighteenth century, Philadelphia (to New Castle's north) grew into one of the major cities in North America; Baltimore on the northern end of Chesapeake Bay in neighboring Maryland developed into a sizable competitor of Philadelphia in the later part of the century; and Wilmington, founded less than ten miles up the Delaware before the middle of the century at the tributary confluence of the Christina River and the Brandywine, Red Clay, and White Clay creeks, became a serious and ultimately very successful rival to New Castle in the role of connecting the Pennsylvania and Maryland hinterlands.

Links to the Eastern Shore of the Chesapeake Bay and interests in the tobacco trade allowed New Castle to flourish late in the seventeenth and early eighteenth centuries as a gateway.[4] The commercial functions that shaped the nascent town centered on the export of tobacco and other products and the handling of many kinds of goods in demand by the large number of settlers who peopled and developed William Penn's colony. New Castle persisted in this gateway role until the American Revolution, providing immigrants as well as traders with their wares access to the lower Susquehanna Valley and upper Chesapeake Bay regions and even farther west toward Ohio Country and south toward the Shenandoah Valley. At a time when transportation and communication lines were long, difficult, and expensive, shortening the routes that travelers had to take—whatever their business, destination, or mode of transport—was advantageous and thus put New Castle in an especially attractive position for those with little or no connections or interests in Philadelphia and the northern counties of Pennsylvania and New Jersey.[5]

Over the course of the eighteenth century, New Castle prospered beyond the fort and settlement the Duke of York had established in the seventeenth century to protect his interests in the mid-Atlantic region.[6] It expanded to become a town that included inhabitants of Finnish, Swedish, and Dutch origin and descent as well as those who came later, many from England and Ireland either directly or after they had first settled elsewhere in the colonies. As the center of government of the Lower Counties, it was a town in which lawyers and other professionals as well as traders and merchants resided, most of them with some connections in and to the surrounding counties, including the frontier towns that sprang up in the hinterlands of Maryland and Pennsylvania and the cities developing along the eastern seaboard.

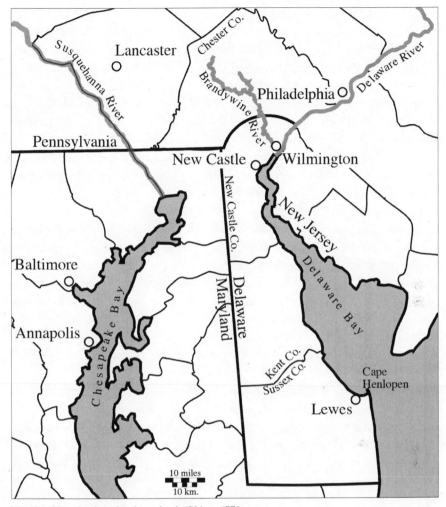

Map 2.1. *New Castle and its hinterland, 1720s to 1770s.*

In recovering and retracing the story of the migration from Ulster to the North American colonies, New Castle's role is difficult to grasp in many of its details. Since the flow of people across the Atlantic was largely unrestricted and few of the immigrants left personal papers, documentary traces are sporadic and sparse in the public and private records that have survived. In addition, because considerable numbers of the voyagers were illiterate and of limited means, those who left marks in official documents, like deeds or tax and probate records, did so only much later—after they had achieved success, often far from where they had disembarked and first settled.[7] Recovering the lives of Ulster emigrants is of keen interest to descendants, genealogists, and historians alike. Most family historians begin their search for kin with the current generation and trace, in effect, those lines that lead to immigrants who succeeded in making their living in the New World, even if those experiences cannot be fully documented. To see the world through the immigrants' eyes requires close and unbroken connections from generation to generation—stories, letters, and diaries.[8] By contrast, historians tend to pursue studies of the migration experience from the north of Ireland to Great Britain's mainland colonies in America with much broader focus and in more general context for which they have to rely on imperfect data gleaned from many different sources.

Since it is typically assumed that the larger the number of immigrants the stronger their ethnic impact on American society and culture, questions about the size of the flow of emigrants from Ulster to the American colonies are considered very important. Yet without complete, systematic, and unambiguous data about the Irish emigration, contemporaries as well as historians have had to estimate the numbers of those who relocated across the Atlantic.[9] Depending on a wide variety of analytical skills and particular interests, estimates of the Irish migration cover a considerable spectrum. Kerby Miller recently divided current migration historians into the proponents whose informed guesses about the size of the migration stream are at the lower end of the scale—minimalists—and those whose "guesstimates" go considerably higher—maximalists.[10] Barring the discovery of new data, there cannot be a definitive end to this lively, even passionate, debate. It is possible, however, to find middle ground and come to some consensus about the most likely range of emigrants from Irish ports even if discussion of the finer points of the differing arguments persists. Much depends on whom historians count over what period of time and also where—from which Irish ports of departure and to which American destinations.[11] Whether the grand total of the Ulster immigration to the American mainland colonies before the Revolution is closer to a lower bound of one hundred thousand than to a higher count of more than two hundred and fifty thousand, for the development of distinctly Scotch-Irish ways of life and communities in America, the number of immigrants alone is less important than the demographically mixed character of the flow of migrants from the north of Ireland across the Atlantic, namely a combination of young single men (and some women) and also family and household groups who survived the relocation and settled successfully.

There is much agreement among maximalists and minimalists about who came, when, and how, and where immigrants settled. There is little doubt that the migration from Ulster was substantial, both in terms of the numbers relative to those who stayed behind and in comparison to other emigration flows such as those from other parts of Ireland, from Scotland, and from German-speaking lands on the continent.[12] Typically in the eighteenth century, the migration stream was made up of significant proportions of boys and young men and, in addition, of families. Ulster emigrants were a mixture of poor and "middling" sorts, the majority of whom were Protestants, usually Presbyterians, rather than Catholics. The flow was small at first, to several select ports of entry along the eastern seaboard. There was a considerable buildup to particular ports over the course of the eighteenth century and an upward trend around which highs and lows in annual numbers fluctuated according to unfavorable conditions at home or special promise overseas. After the end of hostilities in the Seven Years' War in the 1760s, the general volume of the Ulster migration increased markedly, and the proportion of families who relocated as paying passengers rose noticeably until the War for American Independence curtailed trans-Atlantic shipping and trade.

Building on this general agreement about the character of the immigration from Ulster, another important, widely shared insight follows. Excepting circumstances of acute stress or difficulties in the areas of emigration from the north of Ireland, it was the situation in the areas of *im*migration in North America that generated an increase in the number of migrants, including the growing proportion of families among the newcomers to the New World. Overall, economic conditions stabilized in all of Ireland over the course of the eighteenth century. This meant that the need to seek work overseas—in England, on the continent, or in the colonies—gave way to options of pursuing dreams of a decent living for oneself and one's children across the Atlantic.[13] For example, in the first half of the eighteenth century, opportunities beckoned in Pennsylvania, "the best poor man's country" in James Logan's words, and its extensive and expanding hinterland. Later in the century, the Carolinas drew immigrants to settle—through the port of Charleston as well from the north by way of the Great Wagon Road.

The focus on getting the number of immigrants right, however, has tended to divert attention from considering how much the nature of the Ulster migration, in demographic as well as socioeconomic terms, affected the imprints of "Scotch-Irishness"—their ethnic mark—on American society and culture. How immigrants from the north of Ireland could define their identities in America was less tied to their overall numbers than to their situation in particular locales and regions of the colonies and the young United States. Who came early mattered as did what kinds of community those settlers formed and whether those settlements lured kin, neighbors, or coreligionists left behind in Ulster. In addition, and similarly important, how the pioneers raised, trained, and supported their own children and children's children to expand networks farther inland and into new ways of making a living had bearings on distinctively Scotch-Irish characteristics in particular places. Put differently, for immigrants to make an impact locally, it took a critical mass of like and like-minded settlers that included a substantial proportion of families. Moreover, among newcomers, teenage boys and young men with limited life experience in their places of origin and upbringing were less likely to remember, and hence to perpetuate, Old World ways in America. In comparison, more mature men and women brought more and richer memories of life in Ulster that they could bring to bear in recreating and redefining things Scotch-Irish. The expression of Scotch-Irish customs and traditions in the New World—as evident in the use of language, material culture, and shared rituals, foremost among them those rooted in religious beliefs and practices—all point to the importance of families and the strengths of ties that bound them to neighboring communities in the New World as well as those places from which they had emigrated.

In Europe, awareness—and celebration—of local history and culture is well developed. In comparison, local ways in North America often overlap and are mostly synonymous with ethnic customs and traditions. The distinct focus on ethnicity that has developed in the United States is closely tied to the immigrant experience and has become a significant and widely celebrated component of American culture. Historians of ethnicity have recently argued that it is best to explore how newcomers adjusted to their lives across the Atlantic successfully and how they shaped local ways. This perspective differs from more old-fashioned inquiries that delineate increasing deviation of New World manners from Old World standards.[14] Instead of bemoaning the loss of identifiable ethnic traits over the course of two or three generations in North America, the more recent view of ethnicity concentrates on exploring how immigrants and their descendants shaped communities.[15] With the primary focus on how immigrants succeeded in American society has come the realization that being successfully and undeniably American can then give way to *re*defining what Scotch-Irish or Ulster or Irishness means. The view that ethnic labels are fixed and static is giving way to perspectives that recognize the use of ethnic labels not only as a reflection of an acute awareness of

Marianne S. Wokeck

New World circumstances but also as an acknowledgment that developments in the places of European origin factor significantly into the ethnic narratives in America.[16]

Against a background of ethnic pride in the case of immigrants from the north of Ireland, it has been especially difficult to find an appropriately descriptive ethnic term. *People with No Name,* Patrick Griffin's book title, encapsulates the complexity of the Scotch-Irish immigrant and settlement experience in the eighteenth century in light of later developments that have defied the use of a simple, acceptable ethnic label—a problem that reflects the world of past and current political realities more than circumstances over two centuries ago.[17] In a more recent statement, Griffin points not only to the difficulties inherent in defining Scotch-Irishness, especially when considering four centuries of migration from Ireland, but also calls attention to the problem of separating the Scotch-Irish from the Irish in the broader context of people moving from Ireland across the Atlantic.[18]

It is also worth remembering that all such ethnic labels were contextual in that their applications depended in large part on the knowledge and perspectives of outsiders. For colonists ignorant of Ireland, all immigrants and settlers from the island could be labeled indiscriminately Irish or Scotch-Irish, obscuring local and regional differences that remained obvious to the settlers from Ireland themselves but were lost on their non-Irish neighbors.[19] As a consequence, immigrants from the north of Ireland became stereotyped, which meant that all Scotch-Irish could bask in the success of their countrymen but also had to contend with any negative Scotch-Irish images. Moreover, in the complex pluralism of American locales such as New Castle that included other Europeans, Native Americans, and Africans, a variety of ethnic stereotypes flourished and had to be negotiated. At times of prosperity, the various processes of defining ethnic identities presented challenges to the individual and to the group as they charted their ways of becoming American. At times of tension and stress—like war, economic depression, and political instability—ethnic stereotyping was less an option for defining one's place in American society and more a factor that made successful integration difficult.

Descendants as well as immigration historians have typically associated ethnic success and pride with large numbers of immigrants who came to America's shores. In that regard, the Scotch-Irish Americans do not stand out because their numbers are relatively small when compared to others from Ireland who came in the nineteenth century in a much larger stream. What counts more is the substantial proportion of Ulster Americans who made lasting contributions to the fabric of American life and who were successful in making their lives in America because they could found families of their own and pass on their genes, values, and convictions to their children, who, in turn, could perpetuate subsequent successes through their offspring.

In considering measures for determining circumstances under which emigrants from Ulster could successfully become Scotch-Irish Americans and leave notable and lasting imprints on the social and cultural fabric of local communities, it is clear that knowing the overall number of Scotch-Irish immigrants who came during the eighteenth century is important, but that paying attention to the demographic characteristics of the migration flow, especially that of the pioneering generation, is equally, if not more, important. Localities and regions on which Scotch-Irish immigrants left recognizable marks were typically those settlements with a particular set of characteristics among their pioneering cohorts. Places that became widely recognized as Scotch-Irish had their starts with groups in which kin, former neighbors, coreligionists, and countrymen constituted a significant majority and which offered those early colonists and their children continued opportunities to forge and maintain personal and commercial contacts with friends and relatives as well as agents, traders, and merchants in the north of Ireland.

The modeling of three cases illustrates the point. Contemporaries and historians alike noted two distinct strands in the migration from Ulster: single young men and women on the one hand; families on the other. Depending on circumstances, those immigrants, and subsequently also their descendants, had very different chances of finding spouses for themselves or for their children. Some married in; that is, they found other Scotch-Irish immigrants or their descendants to start families and households of their own. Others married out; that is, they took spouses who had no Scotch-Irish experience or background, thereby reducing the degree of Scotch-Irishness of their offspring.[20] Over the course of three generations, the varying opportunities for marrying within Scotch-Irish communities or not figured significantly in the degree of Scotch-Irishness over time. Figure 2.1 summarizes the three hypothetical cases and their variations and is greatly simplified to show the underlying pattern (for Notes on the Modeled Cases of Eighteenth-Century Immigrants from Ulster and the Degree of Their Scotch-Irish Imprint, see the Appendix, below).

The three modeled cases and their variations show that the demographic composition of the immigrant cohort and the choices those pioneers made when they started their families in America had far-reaching effects.

Moreover, the varying impact of those demographic characteristics and different strategies for choosing spouses manifested itself not so much right away but over the course of the following two or three generations. By the fourth generation, or after about a century of settlement in North America, differences in terms of numbers of descendants of Scotch-Irish pioneers and to what degree the immigrants' progenies were Scotch-Irish stand out clearly. Represented on the one side of the spectrum are pioneering cohorts that contained single men and women and a major proportion of families (fig. 2.1: Case I-A and B). They were most successful in keeping the level of Scotch-Irishness high from one generation to the next under circumstances of settlement that enabled adult immigrants as well as the children of immigrants to wed spouses whose backgrounds were also Scotch-Irish (fig. 2.1: Case I-A). The price for such cohesiveness in Scotch-Irishness was the relatively slow pace with which the overall number of those immigrants and their descendants increased over the course of the century. On the opposite side of the scale are pioneering as well as later cohorts made up mostly of single men and women whose partners in marriage came from other than Scotch-Irish backgrounds (fig. 2.1: Case III-B). As a result, the number of descendants of

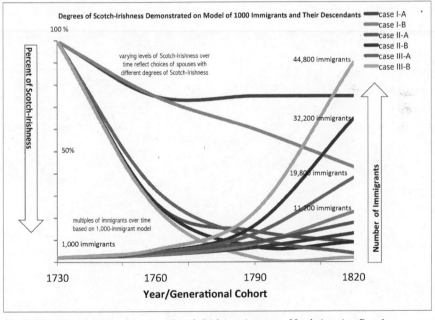

Fig. 2.1. *Imprint of eighteenth-century Scotch-Irish immigrants on North America, Part 1.*

those immigrants rose very rapidly as the generations progressed, but the degree of Scotch-Irishness among the fourth generation had become very small. For real eighteenth-century immigrants who arrived from Ulster on North American shores, the most probable scenarios are likely to lie somewhere between those extremes (fig. 2.1: Case II-A and B).

The implications of this demographic modeling of immigrant behavior are threefold. First, the composition of the migration flow counts in terms of the distribution of men and women and also, more importantly, in terms of single persons and families. Second, the most significant impact of the pioneering cohort manifests itself only in the third and fourth generations of the immigrants' offspring. Third, the decision of single immigrants and, even more significantly, the decision of the immigrants' children whether to marry spouses of the same ethnic parentage as their own or of another background affects not only the number of descendants in the third and fourth generations but also the degree to which those descendants shared directly in the ethnic origin of their immigrant forebears.

In regard to the Scotch-Irish immigrant experience, these insights serve as a reminder that, in the discussion of the numbers of voyagers from the north of Ireland who made it safely and reasonably healthy to the North American

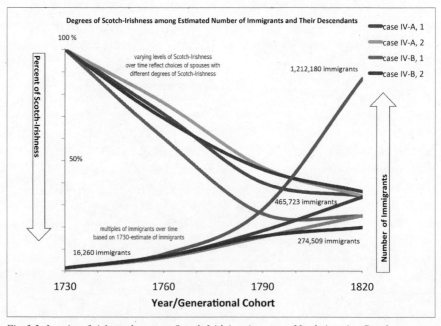

Fig. 2.2. *Imprint of eighteenth-century Scotch-Irish immigrants on North America, Part 2.*

Marianne S. Wokeck

mainland, it is critical to be as discriminating as possible in determining who came when and who landed where. Information about the proportions of young single men and boys and those of families among the immigrants is especially essential for gauging the options those newcomers and their children had in founding families of their own in the New World. Using estimates of migration figures that reflect the actual flow of immigrants from the north of Ireland to the American colonies in the eighteenth century and assuming the same range of choices in marriage partners, as illustrated in fig. 2.2, underscores insights from the hypothetical cases. One is the importance of families in the migration stream in regard to the degree of Scotch-Irishness among the immigrants' descendants; the other is that the delay of the full impact of the pioneering generation on subsequent generations converges with the peak in immigration in the Revolutionary Period. What the data summarized graphically in figures 2.1 and 2.2 cannot show, however, is how the pioneering cohort and their descendants integrated with new cohorts of immigrants who arrived with experiences in Ireland that were increasingly separated by time from those that formed the memories of earlier immigrants.[21]

What is the significance of those insights for the migration from Ulster to New Castle? New Castle in the Delaware Valley offers an especially good example for the case of a century-long migration flow that included single men and women as well as families, some of whom stayed close to where they landed and others who moved on to diverse places in an ever-expanding hinterland. For example, early in the century a group of Donegal Presbyterians settled in New Castle, while entire households removed to settlements in Sussex County.[22] New Castle attracted pioneers from the north of Ireland early, albeit in smaller numbers when compared to those who landed upriver in Philadelphia. The very first immigrants were successful in making a living and building communities in all three of the Lower Counties as well as in the Maryland and Pennsylvania hinterlands. Tobacco planters of Maryland's Eastern Shore played a critical role in extending credit to newcomers from the north of Ireland. Significant commercial connections between Ireland and North America developed because of the tobacco trade, and the success of traders with links to Ulster was essential in creating a positive reputation for the Delaware Valley among kin, neighbors, and coreligionists they had left behind and with whom they kept in touch.[23] The prosperity of the Delaware Valley served to lure others in the pioneers' footsteps, and it enabled plantation owners to invest in additional labor and traders to underwrite the transportation of laborers from Ulster, especially as the trade in tobacco was superseded after 1731 by increasing commercial activities that centered on flaxseed, linen, and emigrants.[24]

In the regular emigration stream from the north of Ireland, the first extraordinary wave of Scotch-Irish immigrants occurred in 1717, which lasted until 1719. It was followed by an even larger influx that numbered in the thousands in the late 1720s.[25] As a consequence, New Castle became a well-established and well-known node in a network of commercial and personal ties that spanned the Atlantic and connected people of similar regional and religious backgrounds over the course of the eighteenth century. The town, moreover, served as a gateway for immigrants from Ulster seeking land and prosperity in the unsettled wilderness of Pennsylvania and beyond.[26] There were, of course, landing sites at other points of intersection of Scotch-Irish and American interests and networks. Philadelphia, farther up the Delaware, first rivaled and then overshadowed New Castle in shipping and attracting immigrants from the continent as well as from the British Isles. Boston, New York, Baltimore, and Charleston, too, were ports on the eastern seaboard of North America with merchant families and communities who had interests in and connections to the north of Ireland and who played mediating roles in channeling immigrants through their respective entrepôts into the hinterlands.[27] Although New Castle could not compete with those major ports, it held its own in influence and attraction as an important base or port of call for shippers and traders with Scotch-Irish ties and as the first stop for a considerable portion of Scotch-Irish immigrants on their way to settlements in the Delaware Valley and beyond. Notices in letters, diaries, and newspapers to that effect, as well as a variety of port records, provide some information about the disembarkation of passengers in New Castle such as Christopher Marshall's entry of July 11, 1774: "*Minerva,* Capt. Lindsey arrived from Newry in New Castle with 450 passengers."[28]

What distinguished New Castle from Philadelphia and New York, and later also Baltimore, was the difference with which it handled immigrants from Ulster. To a large extent, voyagers and travelers who landed in New Castle had some kind of personal connection in Delaware or the hinterlands of Pennsylvania and Maryland. When vessels anchored off New Castle, be it their final destination or, more often, a stopover on the way farther up the river, passengers who disembarked in small boats did so because New Castle was their planned destination.

This point is variously demonstrated by four personal narratives of Irish immigrants to New Castle.[29] Around 1720 Samuel Blair (b. 1712), a future New Side Presbyterian minister, arrived probably in New Castle together

Marianne S. Wokeck

with his parents and siblings. The youth and his family settled not far from where they disembarked in southern Chester County, Pennsylvania, close to the northern border of the Lower Counties, where other Presbyterian Scotch-Irish settlers clustered in close vicinity to neighbors of English and Irish Quaker origins. John Craig (1734–1769/70), a future Old Side Presbyterian minister, left Larne in County Antrim on June 11, 1734, and landed in New Castle on August 17 after a voyage during which he suffered from seasickness and had an accident. When he came ashore, however, he met with the minister of New Castle, Rev. Benjamin Campbell, who treated him kindly and offered useful information and very good advice. A year later, in 1735, yet another future Old Side Presbyterian minister, Francis Alison (1705–1779), sailed from Ulster to New Castle. First, he became tutor in the household of Samuel Dickinson in Talbot County, Maryland; then served vacant pulpits at the forks of Brandywine Creek; in 1737 was ordained and installed as minister of the Presbyterian congregation in New London, Chester County, Pennsylvania; wed Hannah Armitage of New Castle and had six children with her; and founded a classical academy that moved from New London to Newark, Delaware, and evolved into the College and University of Delaware. Even this very limited summary of Alison's life and career demonstrates multiple connections among kin and coreligionists in the region that stretched from the lower Susquehanna River to upper Chesapeake Bay. Such extended and complicated networks were not uncommon, especially among clergy and traders with interests in the backcountry. They provide hints of the rich and far-flung dynamics that shaped the relationships among Scotch-Irish immigrants and their offspring over several generations.

The fourth example, the story of the farmer and weaver James McCullough, underscores the mobility of immigrants. A native of County Londonderry, McCullough and his wife emigrated in 1745 or 1746 and probably landed in New Castle. They settled first in New Castle County, where they made a living with farming and weaving and where their first son was born. In 1750 McCullough moved his wife and two children to Cumberland County, Pennsylvania, where he bought a farm and lived close to several other relations of the same name. Frontier life, which was dangerous because of Indian attacks, also meant the combination of farming and trade, especially in yarns and textiles, that offered opportunities for McCullough to employ poorer immigrants, probably indentured servants, to help with agricultural tasks and weaving. Even though Francis Campble (or Campbell) came to the colonies from County Derry in a more circuitous way via Philadelphia, his role as pioneer merchant in Shippensburg in Cumberland

County can serve as yet another case in which personal and commercial connections among kin, coreligionists, and former neighbors shaped the development of the Ulster American frontier.

In addition to voyagers, New Castle was a destination for travelers and occasional traders. Unlike well-established merchants and their agents, they operated with tiny capital on the margins. Such minor operators brought just a few servants and dealt with small assortments of goods. When they landed in New Castle, they could avoid expenses and competition in Philadelphia and capitalize on their familiarity with local markets in the Lower Counties, upper Chesapeake, and lower Susquehanna. Like Irish scowbankers in the linen and flaxseed trades, who sold linen at cut rates and bid up the price, itinerant Irish and American traders led small bands of servants indented to themselves for sale in port or in the backcountry. The scale of such activities cannot be determined but may well have been significant. If the comment in the *Pennsylvania Chronicle* of February 22, 1768, is correct, such enterprising, albeit small, ventures were deemed profitable: "He [William Graham], an Irish pedlar goes over to *Ireland* every fall with flaxseed &c. and returns in the spring with servants and goods, generally taking shipping and landing at *New Castle,* and is said to be worth money."[30] Nearby farmers and others in need of labor, however, may not have had to rely on such traders because they could go on board to negotiate with indentured servants or redemptioners about contracts for their service without the need for any middleman.

Documentation of the immigration to New Castle is far from complete and much less detailed than the record that historians have been able to establish for Philadelphia.[31] The overall number of emigrants was closely tied to space available to passengers on ships that sailed from Irish ports. These anchored in New Castle for unloading emigrants and a variety of commodities and also for loading agricultural goods such as tobacco, flour, and especially flaxseed.[32] Immigrants who went ashore seem to have done so unhindered and without registration procedures of any kind. Based on the assumption that emigrants from Ulster disembarked in New Castle because they had strong connections to people already settled in town or on land relatively close by, it is likely that a significant proportion of those immigrants relocated as members of a group of kin, countrymen, or coreligionists with affiliations on both sides of the North Atlantic, irrespective of whether they undertook the voyage alone or with others of their family or household. Moreover, many immigrants who chose New Castle as their destination must have been passengers who could afford the trans-Atlantic fare, since there were no procedures in place to handle the sale of large numbers of indentured servants or negotiate contracts for redemptioners.[33] That meant that Scotch-Irish servants brought into New Castle faced limited competition from German or English bound labor. They arrived in small parcels, more often than not as members of a migrating household. Merchants who brokered the transportation and sale of servants in New Castle did so less on a broadly speculative basis—a specialization in transporting emigrants their counterparts in Philadelphia had developed—and more in reaction to well-defined demands in town and the surrounding countryside.[34] As a result, boys and girls as well as single men and women among the Scotch-Irish immigrants to New Castle tended to be either already part of a Scotch-Irish household, or they were likely to serve their terms as bound laborers in an American household that was part of or maintained active ties to the local Scotch-Irish community.

In effect, the relatively smaller, less speculative role of New Castle in the emigrant trade over the course of the eighteenth century acted as a filter in the distribution of immigrants, encouraging the influx of families from certain locales in the north of Ireland and affording poor immigrants from those same places of origin the opportunity to move to America by offering them service in the shops and on the farms of their already-established, better off, America-savvy countrymen. This distribution mechanism through Delaware remained in place but changed somewhat over time as more of the children and grandchildren of the pioneering immigrants moved farther away from New Castle in search of more and affordable land in Maryland, Pennsylvania, and beyond as the interests of the merchants in port and their contacts to agents and partners in the north of Ireland shifted because of different trans-Atlantic trading opportunities and as neighboring Philadelphia and Baltimore were attracting—and channeling—increasingly more of the European immigrants who arrived in ever-larger numbers later in the eighteenth century.

New Castle's role as a magnet for family and household groups from certain places in the north of Ireland, especially early in the eighteenth century, affected the success with which the pioneering immigrants could find places to settle and establish communities that supported their new lives in America and reflected their values and convictions. The lease or acquisition of farms was relatively easier for the pioneers but became increasingly difficult and expensive as the century progressed, pitting the pioneers' children and grandchildren in competition against later immigrants—all vying for land of their own. Overall, the number of settlers who emigrated from the north of Ireland was sufficiently high to allow their coalescing into communities of distinct character—a development that enabled young Scotch-Irish people to look for potential spouses among neighbors of the same origin or ethnic background. The success of planting settlements is evident in the frequency and distribution of place names that signify distinct Scotch-Irish connections in the greater Delaware Valley and well beyond.[35] Yet the building of those Scotch-Irish communities was fraught with difficulties, in large part because the Presbyterians from the north of Ireland disagreed about the proper roles of church and congregation, ministers and laity. Discord created divisions among Ulster American neighbors and more openness toward settlers of different backgrounds even before the upheaval wrought by the American Revolution and the instability during the Early Republic.[36]

In the Ulster American communities of the greater Delaware Valley region and beyond, individual interests competed, even conflicted, as varyingly combined clusters of immigrants from the north of Ireland shaped local ways to suit themselves and, ultimately, to become the accepted and widely embraced norm for all who followed. When settling communities as well as when operating farms, shops, and businesses, early immigrants had certain options. They could continue with or return to ways they knew or cherished before relocating across the Atlantic; they could also abandon or forget former local habits that did not suit the requirements of colonial America or that had little bearing on life in the New World. Typically, the spectrum of immigrants' personal adjustments to new situations in a strange land is very broad, including those newcomers who eagerly embrace new ways, those who find it hard to accept unfamiliar circumstances, and those who are and remain deeply troubled by changes in life as they knew it. In Ireland as well as in eighteenth-century America, the traditionalists in their respective communities tended to hold on to familiar ways. Their more adventurous neighbors more readily embraced new ways, which, if those changes worked, were transformed first into accepted ways and eventually into customary ways. It is for historians to explore why and how such change occurred; it is not for them to disregard or devalue developments that our forebears initiated or adopted because they signaled a departure from certain traditional standards. And yet it is this latter kind of judgment that historians render when they note that, over the course of a generation or two, Scotch-Irish immigrants became indistinguishably American. What has often been interpreted as a loss of ethnic identity over time can, conversely, be taken to mean the measure of success with which Scotch-Irish immigrants and their descendants could bring their ethnic ways to bear on or coincide with customs that defined local communities in North America. Put differently, when Scotch-

Marianne S. Wokeck

Irish ways shaped local rituals and traditions in significant ways, that transformation represents success of the immigrant experience—interesting to explore in all its details and implications and proudly to be celebrated by those on both sides of the Atlantic who share in the same heritage. The following essays, ranging broadly in geographical terms over the course of the eighteenth century, are examples of the variety with which emigrants from Ulster and their descendants built communities and thereby testified to their respective successes in shaping American ways that bear distinctive Scotch-Irish imprints.

In summary, pioneering immigrants were in a position to establish New Castle as an integral part of the commercial and personal networks that connected the Delaware Valley with the north of Ireland. Early in the eighteenth century, the pioneers' mercantile interests included trans-Atlantic connections that developed into long-term partnerships in the emigrant transportation business, which developed as a special form of venture closely tied to the flaxseed trade that flourished after 1731. The way in which Scotch-Irish merchants in New Castle sought profits from this very specialized enterprise differed from the interests that some of their competitors in the trade pursued. For the New Castle merchants, passengers constituted just one part of a diversified cargo, put together not primarily to suit the passengers but to ship goods from Irish to Delaware ports. Scotch-Irish traders and their agents in New Castle facilitated the migration of relatives, former neighbors, and coreligionists to the Delaware Valley because the merchants themselves had interests in the communities that formed in the port's hinterland and could therefore capitalize on personal ties that connected those still resident in Ulster as well as the pioneers' Scotch-Irish American offspring, who set out to pursue opportunities farther inland from the Delaware River's banks. The merchants' investments included the extension of credit as well as the sale of goods—to old-timers as well as newcomers—thus fueling the development of settlements for both those already established in the region and those striking out anew. At the same time the Scotch-Irish trading community in New Castle extended the lines of communication and business ever more deeply and densely into the countryside, they continued and adjusted their connections to agents and partners across the Atlantic, offering passage to voyagers and transporting servants in response to demand in the local labor markets of the Delaware Valley. Throughout the eighteenth century, New Castle played a critical role in this trans-Atlantic network because it attracted and channeled a well-balanced mix of single young men and women and families and households migrating from Ireland to North America. As gateway for a significant and steady flow of Scotch-Irish settlers, New Castle provided and expanded contacts and interaction among early immigrants, their American-born and increasingly American children, their grandchildren, and later immigrants, who brought a different experience of life in the north of Ireland with them. As an important result of New Castle's gateway function, Ulster Americans in the Delaware Valley and well beyond shaped questions about ethnic identity and played prominent roles in the ongoing reevaluation and redefinition of what it meant to be Scotch-Irish—at least in part—in North America.

Appendix

Notes on the Modeled Cases of Eighteenth-Century Immigrants from Ulster and the Degree of Their Scotch-Irish Imprint

Certain assumptions structure the model. Each immigrant cohort is made up of 1,000 Scotch-Irish voyagers, and deaths are reflected as an adjustment to completed family size. Based on estimated averages of family size in pre-industrial Europe, the completed family size was assumed to be 6.8, or, conservatively, 4 surviving children per couple.[37] The four generations—averaged at thirty years each—are grouped in the following way: The first, pioneering generation falls into the years 1716–1745 (noted as the year 1730 in the figures, below). Pioneering immigrants from the north of Ireland came to the Delaware Valley earlier than the second decade of the eighteenth century; but from the founding of Pennsylvania in 1682 until the 1710s, their actual numbers were very small—too small for the model's first generation to coincide with William Penn's early settlement scheme. The second generation of Scotch-Irish colonists extended from 1746 to 1775 (noted as the year 1760 in the figures, above) and includes the children of the pioneering cohort and a new group of immigrants, made up in the same way as the first one. The third generation lasted from 1776 to 1805 (noted as the year 1790 in the figures, above) and includes the descendants of the pioneers, the children of the second cohort, and a fresh group of newcomers, comparable in composition to the ones that had come before. The last cohort of Scotch-Irish immigrants, composed in the same fashion as the earlier ones, arrived in the United States between 1806 and 1835 (noted as the year 1820 in the figures, above), and this fourth generation also included the descendants of the pioneering and second generations and the children of the third set of immigrants.

Assuming that each immigrant cohort of one thousand was composed of seven hundred adults and three hundred children, which were part of the completed families in the next generational cohort, it was the demographic behavior of the adults that determined how prolific that cohort was in numbers from one generation to the next and how "Scotch-Irish" in character. Calculating the numbers is relatively easy; determining "Scotch-Irishness," more difficult. It seems reasonable to assume, however, that when the background of both parents was Scotch-Irish, their children can be counted as Scotch-Irish, too. If the grandchildren continued to "marry in," that is, chose spouses that were Scotch-Irish because of their parentage, they perpetuated Scotch-Irishness in their families, too. Yet the Scotch-Irish factor changed when Scotch-Irish immigrants "married out," or chose spouses from different backgrounds. And it may well be significant whether the men founded families with wives that were "other" or whether "other" men chose Scotch-Irish wives. If women were critical in determining the rituals and customs that governed and shaped family life, their Scotch-Irish imprint on the next generation was likely to be different from that of the men, whose impact may have found expressions of Scotch-Irishness more readily in the workplace or the formal structures of the community.

In the first two cases, the 700 adult immigrants consist of 300 couples (300 men, 300 women) and an additional 100 men (fig. 2.1, Cases I-A and B). In both instances the children and grandchildren of the pioneering couples married in, doubling their numbers with each generation and keeping the Scotch-Irish connection among those descendants strong. The numbers diverged, however, and the ties to the Scotch-Irish immigrant ancestors became more varied when, in the one instance, the extra men, and also their descendants, married in while, in the other instance, the single men, and subsequently their offspring, married out. The former marriage strategy kept the overall numbers of Scotch-Irish descendants across the generations small (Case I-A: 6,400); the latter almost doubled them (Case I-B: 11,200), albeit at the expense of the degree of Scotch-Irishness in the fourth generation. In the first instances, it remained at 75 percent after three generations in American (fig. 2.1: Case 1-A); in the second instance the strength of the Scotch-Irish connection had by then fallen to less than half (fig. 2.1: Case I-B).

The second case differs from the first in that the number of couples among the immigrant cohort is reduced to half. Of the 700 adults, 150 men and women were assumed to be couples whose children and grandchildren chose spouses of Scotch-Irish parentage when it was their turn to start families in America. For the remaining 250 men and 150 women, it was first calculated that they married out and that, in turn, their children and grandchildren sought spouses who were part Scotch-Irish (Case II-A). As a result, the overall number of Americans in the fourth-generation cohort who were part Scotch-Irish was considerably higher (fig. 2.1: Case II-A) than when only 100 single men in the immigrant cohort married out (Case I-A), but the relative strength of their Scotch-Irish bond was much weaker (fig. 2.1: Case II-A). If the descendants of the 400 men and women in the pioneering cohort who chose spouses from outside of the Scotch-Irish fold repeated that pattern when they started their own families, their numbers in the fourth-generation cohort increased dramatically and at the expense of the overall degree of Scotch-Irishness (fig. 2.1: Case II-B).

The third case models two variations of situation that assumes that all 700 adults (400 men, 300 women) were single (fig. 2.1: Case III-A and B). In the first scenario, 200 of the men and 150 of the women married out, as did their children and grandchildren. The remaining 200 men and 150 women married in, and so did their children and grandchildren when it was their time to choose spouses. Clearly one of the effects of the choice in spouses that the immigrant cohort had was an impressive number of offspring with some Scotch-Irish connection in the fourth generation (fig. 2.1: Case III-A). This effect was augmented further in the second scenario of this case, when not only all of the adults in the immigrant cohort married out but also their children and grandchildren (fig. 2.1: Case III-B). In demographic terms, the strategy to marry out paid off especially well for a multitude of fourth-generation American offspring when the majority of immigrants were single adults. Over the course of less than a century, however, the Scotch-Irish part in fourth-generation descendants had become very small (fig. 2.1: Case III-B).

The model of the fourth case uses actual immigrant statistics, which are grouped in the same generational cohorts as in the standardized hypothetical models, above, but incorporates the immigrants who came later into the generations of the pioneers' children and grandchildren.[38] Following the assumptions laid out in Case I, all couples in the pioneering generation chose spouses of Scotch-Irish parentage (fig. 2.2: Cases IV-A and B). If, in the subsequent generations, the immigrants' offspring started families with spouses that were fully, half, or part Scotch-Irish, the numbers of those descendants in the different generational cohorts are shown in figure 2.2 (Case IV-A, 2). If, in another scenario, half of the children in the subsequent generations married in and half of them married out, this particular change in the way in which American-born offspring of Scotch-Irish parents chose their own

Marianne S. Wokeck

spouses had significant impact on their children and grandchildren. In the third and fourth generations, the number of descendants with some Scotch-Irish ties increased dramatically, while the degree of intensity of their Scotch-Irishness diverged noticeably from that of their grandparents, who were in some part Scotch-Irish, and that of their great-grandparents, who were Scotch-Irish (fig .2.2: Case IV-B, 1 and 2).

Notes

1. Bernard Bailyn uses "voyagers" in his study of 1770s migrants from Great Britain to the American mainland colonies as an aptly descriptive term that captures the migrants' common experience of the voyage across the Atlantic. Trevor Parkhill called attention to the fact that, especially toward the end of the eighteenth century, there were significant, albeit difficult to count, numbers of "travelers" who took trans-Atlantic passage not with the intent of becoming permanent settlers in the New World but to return to reside in Ireland or elsewhere. Bernard Bailyn, *Voyagers to the West: A Passage in the Peopling of America on the Eve of the Revolution* (New York: Knopf, 1986); Trevor Parkhill, "Philadelphia Here I Come: A Study of Letters of Ulster Immigrants in Pennsylvania, 1750–1875," in *Ulster and North America: Transatlantic Perspectives on the Scotch-Irish,* ed. Tyler Blethen and Curtis Wood (Tuscaloosa: University of Alabama Press, 1997), 118–33.

2. North American colonists used, inconsistently, a variety of descriptions for immigrants who had boarded ships in Irish ports, not always distinguishing whether vessels embarking on the trans-Atlantic voyage originated in Ulster or any of the other provinces. Since the label "Scotch-Irish" has become a common self-identifier among the descendants of the voyagers and settlers who emigrated from the north of Ireland and also as a convenient and much-used term in the literature about that particular immigrant experience, "Scotch-Irish" is the preferred use in this chapter.

3. In addition to New Castle, Gabriel Thomas described Chester, Germantown, and Lewes in 1698 as "great market towns" in the Delaware Valley. Albert Cook Myers, *Narratives of Early Pennsylvania, West New Jersey and Delaware, 1630–1707* (New York: Barnes & Noble, 1946), 318; in the same collection of early narratives, see also William Penn's comment in "Further Account of the Province of Pennsylvania" (1685), 262.

4. Thomas M. Truxes, *Irish-American Trade, 1660–1783* (Cambridge: Cambridge University Press, 1988), chapter 1, provides the best background even though the focus is more generally on Philadelphia and New York.

5. The literature of the history of colonial Delaware is divided in its focus between the period of the seventeenth century, when Swedish, Dutch, and English interests competed in the region, and the time beginning with William Penn's "holy experiment" in the early 1680s. When Penn obtained his charter for Pennsylvania, its southern boundaries were in conflict with Maryland's northern border, which resulted in a long-fought dispute that was not settled until well into the eighteenth century. The three Lower Counties abutted the

disputed area, explaining in part New Castle's success in taking on the gateway role that linked hinterland areas of Pennsylvania as well as Maryland. Evan Haefeli, "The Pennsyl vania Difference: Religious Diversity on the Delaware before 1683," *(Project Muse) Early American Studies.* Spring 2003, 28–60, http://muse.jhu.edu/journals/early_american_studies _an_interdisciplinary_journal/v001/1.1haefeli.pdf), 60; C. A. (Clinton Alfred) Weslager, *The English on the Delaware, 1610–1682* (New Brunswick: Rutgers University Press, 1967), 223; John A. Munroe, *Colonial Delaware: A History* (Millwood, N.Y.: KTO Press, 1978), 160; John A. Munroe, *History of Delaware* (Newark: University of Delaware Press, 2001), 55.

6. For a commemoration of that founding by the governor in 1724, see *Early American Imprints,* Series I: Evans Readex Digital Collection, 1st ser., no. 2542 (filmed).

7. The scarcity of personal records makes the few that have survived the more valuable and has forced historians to mine other kinds of sources for useful information about those immigrants and settlers who left few writings of their own. Kerby Miller underscores the point about the paucity of personal records; John Bedell demonstrates in an example of combining archaeology evidence with information gleaned from estate inventories how to understand better the material lives of farmers in Delaware who left few other records. Kerby A. Miller, Arnold Schrier, Bruce D. Boling, and David N. Doyle, *Irish Immigrants in the Land of Canaan: Letters and Memoirs from Colonial and Revolutionary America, 1675–1815* (New York: Oxford University Press, 2003 [electronic Resource 2004]), 156; John Bedell, "Archaeology and Probate Inventories in the Study of Eighteenth Century Life," *Journal of Interdisciplinary History* 31, no. 2 (2000): 223–45.

8. For example, the country singer Emmylou Harris captured this connection with an example from a more recent immigration in her album *Songbird* that features her rendition of Guy Clark's "Immigrant Eyes."

9. The literature about Irish immigration to North America is extensive, and estimates vary widely. Miller et. al., *Irish Immigrants,* appendix 2 (Irish Immigration and Demography, 1659–1831), esp. 656–58, provides a good starting point from which discussions in the literature about the size of the migration flow from Ireland can follow.

10. Miller et al., *Irish Immigrants,* 656–58; see also Kerby Miller, "Re-Imagining Irish Revisionism," in *Re-Imagining Ireland,* ed. Andrew Higgins Wyndham (Charlottesville: University of Virginia Press, 2006), 223–43, 231.

11. Many of the specialized studies about migration from Ireland focus on certain particulars, like the following select examples: Maurice J. Bric, "Patterns of Irish Emigration to America, 1783–1800," in *New Directions in Irish-American History,* ed. Kevin Kenny (Madison: University of Wisconsin Press, 2003), 17–35; Louis Michael Cullen, "The Irish Diaspora of the Seventeenth and Eighteenth Centuries," in *Europeans on the Move: Studies on European Migration, 1500–1800,* ed. Nicholas Canny (Oxford: Clarendon Press, 1994), 113–49; R. J. Dickson, *Ulster Emigration to Colonial America, 1718–1775* (London: Routledge & Kegan Paul, 1966, 2nd ed. 1980); David N. Doyle, *Ireland, Irishmen, and Revolutionary America, 1760–1820* (Cork: Mercier, 1981); Audrey Lockhart, *Some Aspects of Emigration from Ireland to the North American Colonies between 1660 and 1775* (New York: Arno, 1976); Audrey Lockhart, "The Quakers and Emigration from Ireland to the North

American Colonies," *Quaker History* 77 (Fall 1988): 67–92; Marianne S. Wokeck, *Trade in Strangers: The Beginnings of Mass Migration to North America* (University Park: Pennsylvania State University Press, 1999).

12. See, for example, T. C. Smout, N. C. Landsman, and T. M. Devine, "Scottish Emigration in the Seventeenth and Eighteenth Centuries," in Canny, *Europeans on the Move,* 76–112; Wokeck, *Trade in Strangers.*

13. Cullen has presented this argument most persuasively and called attention to the fundamental shift in the nature of the migration when emigrants, especially families, moved overseas in response to opportunities there. Cullen, "The Irish Diaspora of the Seventeenth and Eighteenth Centuries."

14. Kathleen Neils Conzen has presented this perspective, using German immigrants to America as examples: "German-Catholic Communalism and the American Civil War: Exploring the Dilemmas of Transatlantic Political Integration," in *Bridging the Atlantic: Europe and the United States in Modern Times,* ed. Elisabeth Glaser-Schmidt and Hermann Wellenreuther (Cambridge: Cambridge University Press, 2002), 119–44; "Phantom Landscapes of Colonization: Germans in the Making of a Pluralist America," in *The German-American Encounter: Conflict and Cooperation between Two Cultures, 1800–2000,* ed. Frank Trommler and Elliott Shore (New York: Berghahn Books, 2001), 7–21.

15. Richard MacMaster points to this in the different views of order in Donegal Springs, see below, where longer-established immigrants and more recent arrivals battled with each other because they insisted on differing understandings of the rules to guide Presbyterian congregations that should apply to their situation in colonial America. The difference between New and Old Side Presbyterian ministers can also be seen in terms of different upbringing—in America and Europe, respectively. Miller et al., *Irish Immigrants,* 385.

16. Miller has called attention to the political nature of the "meaning" of the Irish migration, and Griffin has articulated best the difficulties that arise when appropriate and acceptable ethnic labels are lacking. Miller, "Re-Imagining Irish Revisionism," 231; Patrick Griffin, "The Two-Migrations Myth, the Scotch Irish, and the Irish American Experience," in Wyndham, *Re-Imagining Ireland,* 244–50, 245–46.

17. Patrick Griffin, *The People with No Name: Ireland's Ulster Scots, America's Scots Irish, and the Creation of a British Atlantic World, 1689–1764* (Princeton: Princeton University Press, 2001).

18. "Most people still see the Scotch-Irish as a distinct group, not really Irish, and view their movement as smaller in scale and not as significant, say, as the huge and influential movement of Catholics that dwarfed the earlier migration." Griffin, "The Two-Migrations Myth," 245–46.

19. Similarly, the labels "Palatines" or "Pennsylvania Dutch" for German-speakers from the continent were used broadly and irrespective of the places from where those newcomers had emigrated.

20. It is important to point out that this demographic measure of Scotch-Irishness is not a reflection of the ways in which individuals or communities defined themselves as Scotch-Irish.

21. Tension between immigrants belonging to different generations of newcomers is a common feature shared by many ethnic groups in North America.

22. Graeme Kirkham, "Ulster Emigration to North America, 1680–1720," in Blethen and Wood, *Ulster and North America,* 77–117, 79, 95 (246, n.110).

23. Kirkham, "Ulster Emigration to North America," 78, 84; Truxes, *Irish-American Trade,* 21, 25.

24. Truxes, *Irish-American Trade,* 21–40.

25. Before the American Revolution, other significant peaks occurred in the 1740s and 1750s and especially in the 1760s and 1770s, when the migration flow was very heavy. Wokeck, *Trade in Strangers,* 117–18 (figure 3, table 4 [note that the labels of the two right-most columns contain a misprint: the last column includes the numbers from vessels that stopped over in New Castle]); Wokeck, "Irish and German Migration to Eighteenth-Century North America," in *Coerced and Free Migration: Global Perspectives,* ed. David Eltis (Stanford: Stanford University Press, 2002), 152–75, 154 (Figure 1).

26. Kirkham, "Ulster Emigration to North America," 81.

27. Truxes, *Irish-American Trade,* and also Thomas M. Doerflinger, *A Vigorous Spirit of Enterprise: Merchants and Economic Development in Revolutionary Philadelphia* (Chapel Hill: University of North Carolina Press for the Institute of Early American History and Culture, 1986), both provide valuable details about the connections among merchants in major Irish and American ports, especially Philadelphia, but they pay only passing attention to smaller ports such as New Castle.

28. William Duane, ed., *Extracts from the Diary of Christopher Marshall: Kept in Philadelphia and Lancaster, During the American Revolution, 1774–1781* (Albany: Joel Munsell, 1877), 7. Although Marshall records other ships stopping in New Castle in 1774, more consistently useful are the customhouse notices published in the newspapers, especially the *Pennsylvania Gazette.*

29. The following examples are found in Miller et al, *Irish Immigrants,* 21, 39, 46, 47, 55. This collection of letters and memoirs is an extraordinarily useful resource—in hard copy as well as in the electronic, searchable version.

30. Truxes, *Irish-American Trade,* 135, n.50. Richard MacMaster has been studying the workings and networks of backcountry traders in the Pennsylvania and Maryland hinterlands, and his book, *Flaxseed and Emigrants: Scotch-Irish Merchants in Eighteenth-Century America* (Belfast: Ulster Historical Foundation, 2009) is a very welcome addition to the literature of Irish American commerce.

31. Historians have mined ship registers, merchants' accounts, customs records, and newspaper notices in order to reconstruct the ships' traffic to Philadelphia and goods transported on those vessels. The customhouse notices published in the *Pennsylvania Gazette* are the best sources over several years and suggest that New Castle was for some of the vessels their only port of call in the Delaware River, while others made it a stopover on their way to Philadelphia.

32. Truxes, *Irish-America Trade,* chapter 10.

33. Indentured servants contracted their labor for the trans-Atlantic passage in the port of embarkation, typically with the master of the vessel that transported them or the agent of the merchant(s) who organized or invested in the voyage. After landing in America, those indentured were usually sold to farmers, craftsmen, and others in need of labor. Redemptioners negotiated contracts upon arrival in the American colonies, using their labor to redeem the debt of the fare they owed to the master or owner of the vessel. Among eighteenth-century emigrants from Ireland, the proportion of indentured servants was considerable, with well-established markets for such laborers in and through Philadelphia and, later, Baltimore.

34. James A. Munroe, *History of Delaware* (Cranbury, N.J.: Associated Universities Press, 2006), 55.

35. James T. Lemon, *The Best Poor Man's Country: A Geographical Study of Early Southeastern Pennsylvania* (Baltimore: Johns Hopkins Press, 1972), delineates the expansion of European settlement radiating out from the banks of the Delaware River.

36. The following essays by Griffin and MacMaster focus on the uncertainties and instability of that period in Scotch-Irish communities on the Pennsylvania and Ohio frontiers.

37. P. M. G. Harris guided me to the appropriate demographic literature and helped me to understand—and apply—how historic demographers calculate mortality and fertility and figure completed family size.

38. For the immigrant statistics, I relied on data that I presented in *Trade in Strangers,* chapter 5, and "Irish and German Migration" for the period before the American Revolution. For the following decades in the new republic of the United States, I relied on Hans-Jürgen Grabbe, *Vor der Grossen Flut: Die Europaeische Migration in die Vereinigten Staaten von Amerika, 1783–1820,* vol. 10, USA Studien (Stuttgart: Franz Steiner Verlag, 2001). These statistics clearly belong to the "minimalist" camp and are reasonably consistent over time. Even if considerable numbers were added to make up for serious underreporting and cautious estimating, they affect the levels, not the shapes of the lines.

Searching for Order: Donegal Springs, Pennsylvania, 1720s–1730s

Richard K. MacMaster

In October 1727 Sidney Gamble Smith, wife of Samuel Smith, made the long journey from the Donegal settlement on the banks of the Susquehanna River to Philadelphia "on purpose" to explain to James Logan, agent for the Penn family, a disagreement about land on the Pennsylvania frontier.[1] It was no easy trip (see map 3.1). A minister sent in 1723 to the Presbyterian congregation at Donegal Springs as supply preacher lost his way in the thickets and swamps and had to turn back "for want of a guide."[2] A young wife and mother would hardly go so far without an expectation of success.

Logan found himself in the middle of a dispute between James Patterson, a prominent Indian trader, who wished "John Carr to Settle on a vacancy not far from his [Patterson's] father in Law Thomas Howard," and Samuel Smith and his wife, who believed Carr encroached on their land along Conewago Creek. Apparently the issue was over a spring of water on Smith's land. Patterson and Carr were raising "a new Quarrel about Meribah that thou and I had our ears sufficiently fill'd with before." Logan was in a difficult situation. On the one hand, he tried to oblige "those who depend on me in Trade," but not at the cost of injustice to others. He resolved it by having John Wright and Andrew Galbraith, "whom I take to be as impartial a man as any in their settlem[en]t" act as arbitrators.[3]

This argument over the metes and bounds of land along a creek at the edge of Donegal Township in Lancaster County is interesting precisely because it was a boundary dispute. Carr did not obtain a warrant for his 468 acres until ten years later, in 1737, and Smith held his 305 acres for a dozen years before he registered a survey in 1739, but Logan's letter made clear there *were* boundaries and even fences in 1727. The arbitrators were "to view the place and sett bounds," which neither Carr nor Patterson "may pass to molest Smith any further," and this was to be done "without any regard to [their] new fences or their late attempts of any kind."[4] The Donegal settlers may have lived on the farthest limits of Pennsylvania, but they were as concerned for security of tenure and the laws of trespass as any landowner or tenant in Ulster. In other words, the quest for order was one of their goals from the beginning of their settlement.

Their desire for order is in sharp contrast with the romantic notion of frontiersmen as footloose and prone to move on if they saw the smoke of another settler's chimney, bridling at any restraint, and reluctant to accept any effort to bring them into a community or extend its authority over them. This popular image of the Scotch-Irish as "kings of the wild frontier" from Donegal Springs westward has a long history, but it was left for George W. Franz in his study of Paxton—and incidentally, neighboring Donegal— townships to document what he termed "A Community of Strangers" as the result of high mobility and out-migration.[5] Franz concluded that "the entire backcountry around Paxton" was "a society that had no roots and rapid turn-

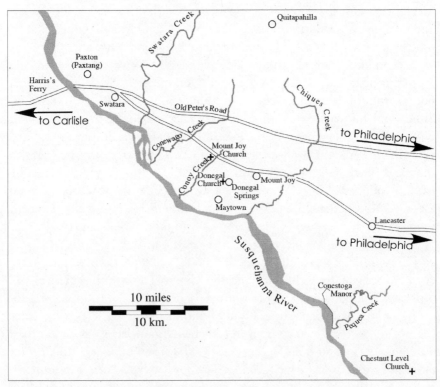

Map 3.1. *Settlement on the Susquehanna, 1720s and 1730s.*

Richard K. MacMaster

over in population was commonplace." He relied primarily on tax assessments from 1750 (the earliest extant) through 1782 to make his case.[6] Even if the Scotch-Irish settlements in the lower Susquehanna Valley had as high a mobility rate as Franz claimed, did this correlate with rootlessness and disorder? In his study of German settlers, Aaron Fogleman put local migration in context, finding that all Germans, including the Amish, moved at least once from their initial location in Pennsylvania before settling down, and at least "a minority made a second move sometime later."[7]

Patrick Griffin is also convinced that in the early years of settlement, "isolation and disorder on the frontier" presented "the greatest challenge to Ulster's migrants." This interpretation undergirds his main argument. "With drunkenness, poverty, and lawlessness threatening the stability of settlements, some settlers reinvented Old World traditions to bring order to chaos and meaning to isolation." In this, they were only partially successful, since "the mobility and contention that stemmed from the formative years of settlement were the defining features of a group inhabiting a rapidly changing frontier."[8] Griffin would seem to be posing his question in familiar terms of tradition and environment, but his interpretation is more nuanced. "Amid periods of change," Ulster settlers on the Pennsylvania frontier "defined and redefined their own understandings of themselves and the world around them."[9]

One institution was present from the beginning—the Presbyterian Church. The earliest settlers had dispatched Andrew Galbraith to meet with New Castle Presbytery in August 1721 and present a petition "in the names of the people of Chiken's Longus desiring a supply of preaching ye Gospel unto them," and Presbytery arranged for ministers to visit them. Five years later, the congregation called the Reverend James Anderson as their pastor.[10] The new minister was a Scot, educated at Glasgow and ordained by the Presbytery of Irvine in 1708 for mission work in Virginia.[11] He had never been in Ulster, and his experience was of the Church of Scotland. Anderson articulated the concept of a permanent, settled community. The Donegal settlers, in his view, had established "a Settlem't of so many families" who shared their "religious Principles as might be requisite to form a Religious Society and to Support a Minister." He wanted them discouraged from selling their improvements and moving away.[12]

The eighteenth-century concept of "improvement" is important for any understanding of a search for order. The wilderness would be improved by bringing it into cultivation and society by making it "more demonstrably British," more like the established societies in the Old World.[13] How was that to be done? The Donegal Springs story is less a search for order to be imposed on a disorderly frontier community than a contest between at least two different visions of what an orderly community should be. Each is an economic outlook, the productive relations that reshaped the environment, but they are not limited to economic issues. Proponents of one envisioned a more traditional society, not precisely the pre-commercial outlook described by historian James Henretta but certainly one, innocent of market forces, in which "acquisitive hopes yielded to geographic realities."[14] It involved an orderly distribution of land by the Penn family and their agents and established communities that could support a minister and other institutions. The other view is that put forward emphatically by historical geographer James T. Lemon, who believed settlers placed "individual freedom and material gain over public interest," planning "for themselves much more than they did for their communities."[15] In each case, they sought order and improvement but with a different vision of the goal to be achieved. Those differing visions arose in large part from their understanding of the land itself.

Land as a Commodity

Emigration from Ulster to Pennsylvania began in 1717, but it became more significant two years later. A Philadelphia merchant wrote in 1719, "This summer we have had 12 or 13 sayle of ships from the North of Ireland with a swarm of people."[16] The first settlers at Donegal Springs were part of that swarm. On their arrival from Ulster in 1719, the first settlers in Donegal Township found only a few breaks in the woods, where fur traders had cleared a patch of ground, built a rough cabin, and turned their horses and cattle into the forests to graze.[17] Although Swiss and German Mennonite settlers had taken up land some miles south and east of Donegal, only one rough track, Old Peter's Road, led from a fur trader's home base on French Creek in Chester County to his trading post on the Susquehanna.[18]

When emigrants from Ulster came ashore at New Castle or Philadelphia, they had not far to go on their way to their new homes in Pennsylvania before they found themselves traveling in thick forests. A squirrel leaping from branch to branch could have gone from Philadelphia to the Donegal settlement along the Susquehanna without need to set foot on the ground. Long after Scotch-Irish settlers began clearing their land, the region retained most of its forest cover. Land grants were large, averaging three hundred acres, and it took time to down trees and grub out stumps. In his last will written in 1728, one settler directed his sons to turn their inheritance into farmland, "Thirty acres of Land to be cleared in three years."[19] Of twenty-one tracts in

Donegal Township mortgaged between 1736 and 1741, the owners described sixteen as unimproved and only five as improved by buildings or any amount of cleared land. The proportion of timbered to cleared land changed in time, with only three of eleven tracts mortgaged between 1742 and 1747 described as unimproved.[20]

Heading west from Philadelphia, or more likely New Castle, newly arrived Ulster folk looked for available land where they could find it, settling in adjacent parts of Maryland, Delaware, and southeastern Pennsylvania. Land was not there for the taking, of course. Each jurisdiction prescribed an orderly process for obtaining a land grant. Some found the land they wanted, settled on it, and only then began the process of acquiring a legal title.[21] Others went first to the colonial land office and sought direction. The normal procedure for obtaining a clear title in Pennsylvania was first to obtain a warrant for a certain number of acres at a specific location. The warrant authorized a county surveyor to make an exact survey of the metes and bounds of the tract, so that a patent could be issued by the land office confirming the grant. At each stage there were fees to pay, and the patent required retroactive payment of quitrents, essentially a land tax due to the proprietor (the Penn family). It was easy for landowners to put off the inconvenience and expense of going through all the steps, since warranted land sold as readily as patented land.[22]

James Logan, confidential agent for the Penn family and "permanent under-secretary for all affairs" in Pennsylvania, controlled both the fur trade and the land office.[23] Logan and some of his Indian traders held large grants along the Susquehanna, and it was there to what became Donegal Township that Logan directed one group of Ulster emigrants in 1719–1720.[24] He later recalled that Pennsylvanians "were under some apprehensions from ye northern Indians" of the Five Nations, or Iroquois, who claimed "the Lands on Sasquehannah" as their own and "About that time considerable Numbers of good Sober People came in from Ireland, who wanted to be Settled." Logan, himself a native of Ulster, told Thomas Penn that he thought "it might be prudent to plant a Settlement of fresh men as those who formerly had so bravely defended Derry and Enniskillen as a frontier in case of any Disturbance." The settlement of Donegal Township began accordingly, "some few by Warrants at the certain price of 10 pounds per hundred [acres]," but more without any official sanction.[25] They had made as good a bargain as could be had. The death of William Penn in 1718 suspended land grants in the usual form. With or without a warrant for a survey, they selected land for themselves and marked it off in substantial quantities.

The first settlers in Donegal Township found James Logan and his agents busy surveying land for the Penn family, himself, and his business associates in the fur trade. As Francis Jennings observed, "The fur-trade interest, which was pre-eminently James Logan, was not a political and social factor protecting Indians from the encroachments of settling farmers; rather, in Pennsylvania, the trade was a means of accelerating settlement."[26] Logan and his friends held title to thousands of acres near the mouth of Chiques Creek, and he encouraged the newcomers to take up and improve nearby tracts.[27] As they took up lands in Donegal Township, adjacent property would automatically increase in value. With that in mind, the heirs of William Penn held back substantial blocks of land as proprietary manors, and their agent Logan followed their lead with strategically placed holdings of his own.[28] It was a lesson the Scotch-Irish of Donegal Township were not slow to learn. Land was a commodity to be acquired as cheaply as possible and sold for as much as the market would bear.

This was not a new concept for the Donegal settlers. They would have had experience in Ulster bargaining with landlords for the best terms.[29] But they wanted no landlords here, even on generous terms. They sought to own their land outright as a freehold to be disposed of at will. In a petition to Thomas Penn, they declared: "We have been before we came here so much oppressed and harassed by under-landlords in our own country from which we, with great losses, dangers and difficulties came, with this chief and principle view of going, in this foreign world, freed from such oppression."[30]

They were alarmed when in 1723 Governor Keith promised the Conoys and Shawnees that "no English Settlements shall hereafter be made too near your Towns" and that they might remain in peace where they were. Logan immediately had "a very pressing application from some Inhabitants on this side the River . . . who have not yet obtained titles to their settlements" and were afraid the governor might "turn them out of their possessions and Improvements."[31]

They were equally anxious not to be limited in their choice of additional land by other settlers. In October 1727 Logan received a petition from "ye Inhabitants of Donegal, requesting yt ye Dutch may not be allowed to settle between them and Sohatoroe."[32] Their motivation became clear when in November "Rowland Chambers presented a Petition to Sec't'y Logan subscribed by 40 or 50 Persons, requesting the grant of about 10,000 Acres of Land at Sawhatara, near Paxtang, for Settlements for themselves and familys."[33] Logan reported "one of ye Irish applied to me, in the name of 400, as he said," who wanted directions where to settle. The petitioners felt that they

Richard K. MacMaster

deserved so substantial a grant. "They say the Proprietor invited People to come & settle his Countrey, they are come for that end, & must live."[34]

With the greatly increased emigration from Ulster in 1728 and 1729, a flood of new settlers took up lands above the Donegal settlement in Paxton and Derry and began to encroach on Conestoga Manor, a tract set aside for the Penn family to develop later on. Others settled on unclaimed land in and around Donegal. Their haphazard methods of finding land that suited them irritated James Logan, who complained often enough "of the Scotch-Irish (so called here)" who felt entitled to take up unpatented land and "sit frequently down on any idle land without asking questions," or paying quit-rents.[35] Logan complained to Hannah Penn about "unruly Palatines" and "disorderly persons" from Ireland who had settled on either side, but he exempted his own settlement of Donegal from such criticism.[36] He had in fact recognized their right to lands of their choice, for Logan had promised the Donegal settlers that "we should have the first refusal of purchasing the Lands we have made improvements on."[37]

It would be a mistake to think that this tendency to claim unclaimed land indicated a disorderly community or a haphazard attitude to property rights. Land and the security of tenure was a major issue for the Scotch-Irish of Donegal Township. What we see are different definitions of what each meant. From the viewpoint of the Penn family and their agents in the land office, Pennsylvania was a very large personal estate to be managed like the Abercorn or Brownlow lands in Ulster, but on a larger scale. The family's income depended on the regular collection of quitrents, so the steps to land-ownership should be followed in order and quitrents paid thereafter. Settlers should be put on the land by the landlord's agent, and it was appropriate to set aside parts of the estate for future use as the proprietor and his agent determined. Thus Logan "sent the obviously penurious applicants into the region disputed with Maryland, where clear titles could not be guaranteed anyway; the other sort of immigrants—people with money—were sent to selected settlements with active surveyors and magistrates."[38] Opposed to this view was the understanding of the Scotch-Irish settlers that the man who scouted good land could make an improvement and sell it to the highest bidder and move on. They had come to Penn's woods to settle it and make it more valuable to the proprietor, and they needed land to live, so they should not be hindered in finding the most valuable land and staking a claim to it.

Provided they had control of the available land, the Scotch-Irish of Donegal Township had no objection to German land-seekers. Their pastor complained that many of them "with a regard to their own private Interest only are for disposing of their Improvement to the best Bidders who are generally the Dutch."[39] No fairer statement of land as commodity could be found.

Their attitude to land contrasted sharply with the vision of stable Presbyterian farming communities, like New England towns, advocated by the clergy. Since coming to Donegal, Rev. James Anderson had helped "Some new settlers At Swatara" to build two meetinghouses and form themselves into the united congregations of Paxton and Derry.[40] But the availability of land in the backcountry militated against such closed communities. The new Presbytery of Donegal complained in 1732 about "a considerable number of families" living "between ye Cong[regatio]ns of Dunnagal and Swatara, who tho they do not join themselves to any Congn. are ready (as they have occasion) to Seek Sealing ordinances for themselves and children."[41] The ministers did not want Presbyterians settling beyond the bounds of organized congregations.

A generation later the problem was more widespread. Edmund and William Burke ascribed the settlement of the southern backcountry to Irish migrants, "who not succeeding so well in Pensylvania, as the more frugal and industrious Germans, sell their lands in that province, and take up new ground in the remote counties in Virginia, Maryland, and North Carolina. These are chiefly presbyterians from the Northern part of Ireland, who in America are generally called Scotch Irish."[42] Longer-settled parts of Pennsylvania gradually became more German as the Scotch-Irish moved to the backcountry. The Presbyterian Synod of Pennsylvania declared in 1759 that the "Inhabitants are inconstant and unsettled, and are always shifting their Habitations, either from a Love of variety, or from the fair Prospect of more commodious Settlements on the Frontiers of this, or the Neighbouring Provinces. . . . When our People remove they are generally Succeeded by Strangers from Europe, who incline at their first arrival to purchase or hire cultivated Lands; [so that] one of our most promising Settlements of Presbyterians, may in a few Years, be entirely possessed by German Menonists, or Moravians, or any other Society of Christians."[43]

Once their right to both land and improvements was established, Donegal settlers began selling both and either moving a short distance within the community or across the Susquehanna to newly available lands in Cumberland County and beyond. Robert Buchanan and his family went to the Marsh Creek settlement, the later Gettysburg in Adams County. Samuel Smith sold his land, gristmills, and sawmill on Conewago Creek in 1750 to Thomas Harris after moving to Cumberland County. Smith was the first to transfer his operations to Cumberland County and its newly founded town of Carlisle. William Buchanan, Robert Buchanan's son, was another.[44] With "near fifty Houses built, and building," in 1751, Carlisle promised to be a considerable place, "a great thorough fare to the back Countries, and the Depositary of the Indian Trade."[45] In other cases, some family members remained in Donegal, while others took off for newer settlements or for commercial centers like Baltimore and Philadelphia. William Spear, merchant, and his brother Joseph Spear, "Indian trader," moved to Carlisle, while a third brother, Robert, farmed in Donegal Township.[46] John Fulton also left Donegal Township for Carlisle, leaving his brother James on the land acquired by their father, Samuel Fulton. James Fulton became a chapman or shopkeeper as well as a farmer, retailing goods sent by his kinsman, James Fullton, a merchant in Philadelphia. This was a gradual out-migration, spread over many decades, and it left the Scotch-Irish community in Donegal Township intact until well after the American Revolution.

Disorder in Donegal?

The Donegal settlers escaped the tyranny of landlords, as they understood it, until 1733, when Thomas Penn, established as heir to his father's Pennsylvania Proprietary, moved to the colony from England. Scotch-Irish pioneers in Donegal Township marked out their lands as early as 1719, but few, if any, had bothered to initiate the process of taking a secure title or pay any quitrents before 1733. From his arrival, Penn attempted every year to collect back quitrents in Lancaster County, and every year through 1740 the sheriff reported that no one would pay, since they thought such taxes unfair.[47]

Donegal Township seemed to be seething with disorder in the spring of 1733. The settlers informed a surveying party sent out by Penn's land office that no surveys would be permitted until they had definite assurance they could have deeds for their land at an agreed price of no more than five pounds for every hundred acres. The surveyors met with Samuel Smith on Conoy Creek, who explained that "the inhabitants met and was come to a general resolution not to admit of any survey to be made, neither in Donegall, Swatara, Pextan [Paxton], Quitapahilla nor any lands there or thereabouts." They withdrew altogether when "the people flocked in on all sides of the road to a very great number, nearly forty or sixty in about one hour, many of them having clubs with them in a very unbecoming manner and by their words and actions, appeared fully determined to offer an abuse if we had proceeded to a survey." Did this mob action imply a breakdown of order? Before the mob assembled, the surveyors appealed to Andrew Galbraith to accompany them, since "his presence as a magistrate might greatly awe the disquietude of the people, but he absolutely refused to go along." It is worth underscoring that opposition to the surveying party was not a spontaneous mob action but the policy adopted at a meeting of the inhabitants, and that Justice Galbraith, like Sheriff Buchanan, refused to cooperate with the provincial authorities against his own community and their just cause. This incident seems to suggest a community united in upholding its own version of decency and order against what they perceived as unjust and rapacious demands by a landlord.[48] When James Logan heard what had happened in Donegal, he persuaded William Allen to write a letter to the Reverend James Anderson, although Allen was certain the minister "had now very little interest or influence over the people."[49] An able and gifted man, as evidenced by his own writings, Anderson offered to negotiate with Logan and Penn in his people's behalf—and he did—but they did not rely only on his letters, sending their own delegations and petitions to Logan at Stenton and to Philadelphia. Anderson gave more of his time to Presbytery affairs and to missionary journeys in the next few years, notably a visit to Virginia where he organized congregations and worked with the authorities in Williamsburg to obtain full religious liberty for Presbyterians.[50]

A few days after the incident with the surveyors, the Donegal settlers drew up a petition to Proprietor Thomas Penn, asking that the purchase price and quitrents for lands in Donegal be less than what Penn charged settlers elsewhere because they were "so far back from markets" and "the poverty and erosion of much of our lands" put them at a disadvantage. They made two basic arguments: land in Donegal and the other townships on the Susquehanna was less valuable, and they had agreed to specific terms with James Logan.[51] Six months later, deputies from Donegal brought another petition. This one, Logan reported, made the case that "some of their Tracts are so exceeding mean" that "they are scarce worth holding." They also insisted that Logan had directed them to these lands and given them verbal promises as to the purchase price and quitrents. Logan agreed some of their land was of poor quality and used that fact to rebut Penn's suggestion that he had offered his own countrymen more favorable terms. "If I had, I should have acted a more friendly part by them, than to place them on a Tract so full of Barrens."[52]

Penn left the problem in Logan's hands but then overruled his solution. He questioned "granting those people their Lands at a Rate much more moderate than other persons generally pay," especially since they had been living on the land "for 12 or 15 years" and had "paid no Consideration for that favour neither do they think they ought."[53] In the end he capitulated.

Richard K. MacMaster

They could have their lands at the agreed price, but they would have to pay both purchase price and quitrents at once.[54] They did not hurry to take his offer. James Smith, who died in 1739, instructed his executors to "pay the Proprietor for the tract surveyed for me in Dunigall" and "procure a patent for my son William Smith."[55] Others delayed patenting their land even longer. Throughout this struggle, the Scotch-Irish of Donegal Township insisted on their ownership of whatever improvements they had made on the land, reflecting Ulster tenant rights. As historian Mary Schweitzer noted, this was more important than landownership in capital formation.[56]

A Rural Economy

Donegal Township settlers practiced mixed farming, selling their surplus produce, hence their concern about distance from markets. James Patton, for instance, grew rye, wheat, barley, oats, hay, hemp, flax, and buckwheat in 1746. His appraisers found three cows, three heifers, a steer, a calf, three horses, and sheep when they made an inventory of his estate. They listed a plow and coulter, dung fork, pitchfork, scythes, axes, other tools, and "a cloath for cleaning grain." Patton had "a slad and carr" like those used in Ulster to haul loads.[57] Some settlers had substantial numbers of livestock early on. Absent fences and cleared pastures, they found sustenance in the forests and natural meadows. In his 1730 will, Robert Middleton left "a chestnut horse now in the woods" to his son and ordered an unspecified number of horses and cows divided equally among his children.[58] Thomas Mitchell, whose 1734 will included a request to be "desently entered in the Meeting house Yard at Donnegal," left his plantation, two working horses with the plough, farming implements, and a "mare called Beess" to his wife, together with three cows of her choice, two heifers, a black bullock, all the sheep, and household goods. He distributed another horse, four mares, four heifers, two other cows, four bullocks, "the brown mare's foal," and "all the sheep called her own" among the children.[59]

The houses built by the first generation were understandably small. In his 1728 will, John Allison instructed his sons to build a house on the land he destined for one of them. He wanted "a well Dug and walled and a Dwelling house built with the Floor layd and Chimney built, And likewise a Barn."[60] In a similar case in 1760, Samuel Fulton specified that it be "a Square Log House 28 Feet by 20 & a Store & a half high with a Stone Chimney."[61] Log houses predominated, actually log-framed houses with the gaps between the logs filled with a rough plaster, rather than cabins built with tight-fitting notched logs. Samuel Fulton's original dwelling house, built over a spring, and his later "House I now dwell in, with all ye Office houses, belonging thereunto" were constructed of stone. The Presbyterian meetinghouse; taverns like the Sign of the Bear, erected by Thomas Harris in 1745; and, as the settlement prospered, many farmhouses were built with stone.

Inventories suggest sparse workaday furnishings. James Patton's appraisers listed an iron pot, three pots, three pair of pot hooks, a crock, a churn, a cider tub, two pair of wool cards, a hackle for breaking flax, a reel, a spinning wheel, a wool wheel, a weaver's reed, a weaver's loom, a smoothing iron, a cake of tallow, and quantities of yarn, coarse yarn, coarse cloth, and linen. The household goods are few—an old chest, a bed, feather bolster, two sheets, a rug and blanket, and six pewter spoons. Benjamin Sterrett's inventory, taken in 1739, included a loom, tow cards and hackles, and 105 yards of linen. This prosperous Donegal Township farmer had an indentured servant, and several neighbors owed him money, but his appraisers listed no furniture of any kind, only pewter and wooden dishes. Fine furniture was not unknown in Donegal Township. When David McClure and William Allison inventoried James Smith's property in 1739, they began with an oval table, five walnut chairs, a walnut chest, and "a walnut bedstead with a poplar board at the head of it and bolster and Clo[the]s belonging to it."[62]

Some Donegal settlers were influential beyond their own community. Business ties with Logan in the Indian trade certainly helped, but social standing was also a factor. Robert Buchanan, James Mitchell, George Stewart, and John Galbraith were the most substantial taxpayers among the Scotch-Irish of Donegal Township in 1722 and in turn held most of the county offices and represented their neighbors in the Pennsylvania Assembly. James Mitchell was a justice of the peace when the township was formed the same year, an emissary from Pennsylvania to different Native American tribes, although he spoke none of their languages, and in 1729 the first representative from newly formed Lancaster County in the Pennsylvania Assembly. John Galbraith was the first sheriff, to be succeeded by Robert Buchanan and Samuel Smith. George Stewart, Andrew Galbraith, and Samuel Smith followed Mitchell in the assembly. Such men obviously looked for order wherever they lived and made it happen.

Enterprising Ulstermen

From the beginning of the Donegal Springs settlement, the search for markets was crucial. John Galbraith's well-known petition to the Chester County authorities in 1726 for permission to brew and sell beer claimed that "by reason of the great distance from a market, with no public houses here," the

Richard K. MacMaster

great quantity of barley grown and malted in Donegal Township would go to waste. He added that the lack of roads in the backcountry meant that "Trade and Commerce among ourselves" was "mostly by way of Barter."[63] Galbraith had a gristmill on Donegal Run by 1722, when another settler asked for a grant of land "two miles from Galbraith's Mill to the Northward."[64] Galbraith was not a man to be contented with a subsistence farm in the wilderness. Other enterprising Ulster emigrants like Robert Allison, James Roddy, and Samuel Smith on Conewago Creek and Alexander Hutchinson on Conoy Creek built mills on Donegal Township's creeks and runs. John Allison had a fulling mill on Conewago Creek, where he thickened and scoured cloth. Early on, some millers were entrepreneurs with a complex of services. Mills were important enough even in a barter economy among isolated farmers but were essential once grain production was linked to a growing export market. By midcentury, they were found about two miles apart on every major stream. Some were merchant mills buying grain for sale as flour as well as custom grinding.[65]

The Donegal economy did not take long to move from subsistence to specialization. The loss of Lancaster County tax records between 1722 and 1751 has made it difficult to chart the pace of change, but there are many clues in extant records. The Sterretts, for instance, were distillers and did well. By the time John Sterrett died in 1748, he left his heirs two slaves, the time of a servant man, copper stills, and three hundred gallons of distilled liquor in addition to a plantation in Donegal Township, livestock, farming utensils, and household furniture.[66] John Sterrett's brother-in-law and neighbor, Joseph Work, another early settler, developed a tannery on his farm that in his son's time employed a half-dozen indentured servants.

It was the fur trade, however, that brought some of Donegal's early settlers into the commercial mainstream. Like other settlers in Donegal Township, Samuel Smith found the Indian trade at his doorstep. A decade or two before the coming of the Scotch-Irish, Native American tribes—Piscataways or Conoys, Shawnee, and Delaware—drawn by English trade goods, migrated to the banks of the Susquehanna and settled there in their own villages. Traders followed and established their posts along the river.[67] Smith set up his own trading post on Conewago Creek as early as 1725.[68]

The traders on the western fringe of settlement have been described as a crude, violent, and raffish lot, "renegade Frenchmen like Peter Bezaillon, tough, hard-bitten Scotch-Irishmen like James Patterson, backsliden Quakers like John and Edmund Cartlidge." But they were carrying on a trade of great value to the Pennsylvania economy.[69] The Indian trade was always about distributing British-manufactured products to native peoples. They paid for these purchases with furs or deerskins, but this was only a small part of a trader's profits. He made most of his money in the markup on the trade goods he sold, especially rum. A few of the newcomers from Ulster joined them, selling rum and store goods to Indians and settlers alike, men like Samuel Smith[70] and James and Thomas Harris. Thomas Harris arrived in 1729 from Raphoe, County Donegal, and settled on Conoy Creek some miles upstream from the Conoy village by 1730. Lazarus Lowrey and his sons also came from Ireland in 1729, and the following year he was licensed as an Indian trader.

The rapid growth of the Donegal settlement alarmed the native people. They were concerned "to behold all their Lands invaded by swarms of strangers that they have an aversion to, for the Irish are generally rough to them."[71] As more settlers came into the lower Susquehanna Valley, Shawnees and Delawares retreated to the upper reaches of the Susquehanna and over the mountains to Ohio.[72] But trade itself was beginning to change at this time. Instead of dealing primarily with Native Americans living on Pennsylvania's doorstep, traders began to open new routes far up the Susquehanna and Juniata in Pennsylvania and down the Monocacy and Shenandoah into western Virginia. Soon they would be trading west of the Alleghenies to the Ohio Country. For this expansion, they needed more capital and more credit from their suppliers. The Lowreys, for example, joined forces with Joseph Simon, who linked them to the principal Jewish merchants in Philadelphia. With this backing, they extended their operations far enough to challenge the French traders in the Miami Valley.

Others saw their role as assembling goods for traders to take by packhorse over the Susquehanna River. Local farmers could also find necessities at this frontier store. The Indian trader in this way became over time a backcountry merchant. Thomas Harris, for example, located his store and tavern where the main road from Lancaster to Harris's Ferry crossed Conoy Creek. Harris built a substantial stone tavern, the Sign of the Bear, a short distance from his original cabin in 1745 and continued as storekeeper, with interests in the Indian trade until 1751 when he sold everything to Lazarus Lowrey, well known in the Indian trade.[73] The inventory of John Murray, storekeeper, of Paxton Township, taken in 1745, is an indication of the variety he offered in his frontier store, some of his stock clearly trade goods, other items more likely of interest to settlers. Appraisers listed many pairs of "Mocksons," black and white wampum, match coats, guns, and several hundred pounds of tobacco as well as cloth, "a Remnant Lining," ribbons, stockings, paper, looking glasses, and Murray's own household furniture and tools. [74]

Another sort of businessman emerged on the frontier: the chapman, or peddler. The goods sold by a Scotch-Irish chapman were designed to appeal to the pioneer farmer and, more especially, his wife. Samuel Shaw, who died in 1743, instructed his executors to sell "the merchant goods" as well as his horse and saddle, so a list was made of them, including from five to eighteen yards of cloth identified as "Checker," "Killimanco," Muslin, "Kellico," linen, and blue linen. His inventory also included three handkerchiefs ("three hangchirchefs of other sort"), eight clasp knives, another "one dussin of Clasp Knives," six razors, three knives and forks, five inkhorns, plus "nine brace Inkhorns," five pair of worsted stockings, eight worsted caps, laces and tapes, combs, four silk laces, gartering, ribbon, five pair of buckles, and "some Little small goods." The total value was less than £20, but Shaw held bonds, notes, and book debts amounting to £160. [75]

Backcountry chapmen and storekeepers depended on Philadelphia merchants for their stock in trade. A few evidently returned to Ulster periodically to get a fresh assortment of linens and other manufactures and to recruit servants to return with them. In the summer of 1735, James Coulter sailed from Belfast on the *John and Margaret* bound for New Castle and Philadelphia. Coulter, who was originally from Banbridge, County Down, was on his way home to Pennsylvania, where his wife and two young children awaited him on his plantation on Pequea Creek in Lancaster County. He never reached America, dying at sea. Captain Archibald McSparran of the *John and Margaret* landed Coulter's goods at New Castle, where his executors came to inventory them and bring them up to Lancaster County. They recorded "the true value of the goods of James Coulter who departed this Life at Sea about the—of august 1735" as "six Servant men at 18 pounds a peas," "two Servants Maids 29 pounds," and "one Servant Maid 12 pounds." They also appraised "Six Score parts of Linin Cloth" and "other Smal goods." (A second inventory the following April listed the usual household goods and farm implements as well as six bonds to secure debts due to him.) James Coulter's home in the lower Susquehanna Valley was on the Pennsylvania frontier. Was Coulter a backcountry shopkeeper or chapman or simply bringing his money to America in a readily saleable form? Whatever the case, he was typical of both Ulster merchants and emigrants, who dealt on a larger or smaller scale in linen and servants. [76] Such folk left few records, although they persisted in all colonial markets. Only the chance of an unpaid bill preserved a notice of

"William Graham, or Grimes, an Irish pedlar," who "goes over to Ireland every fall, with flaxseed &c., and returns in the spring with servants and goods, generally taking shipping and landing at New Castle, and is said to be worth money."[77]

By 1740 Philadelphia merchants were intent on developing backcountry networks of storekeepers and traders whom they supplied with dry goods, hardware, wine, and liquor, and who in turn supplied them with the flax-seed, flour, iron, and barrel staves they shipped to their correspondents in the British Isles. Samuel Carsan from Strabane and Hugh Davey from Londonderry were partners in a Philadelphia firm before 1738, buying primarily flaxseed and flour for merchants in Strabane and Derry.[78] Justice Samuel Smith of Donegal Township was one of their customers in 1739 and for six frustrating years failed to pay for goods sent him from Strabane.[79] Apart from this reference and one to problems over payment for servants in Chester County, Davey and Carsan's letters gave no clue to their backcountry connections.

The ledgers and letter book of James Fullton, another Philadelphia merchant from Ulster, on the other hand, provided a detailed record of his customers, many of whom sold him flaxseed and flour.[80] But Fullton's extant records begin only in 1763. His flaxseed suppliers then were backcountry storekeepers as far from Philadelphia as York and Gettysburg. Fullton had many dealings with a kinsman of the same name in Donegal Township, who regularly ordered hogsheads of rice, rum, sugar, tea, and other store goods. This James Fulton lived in a stone house on Donegal Springs Road that was moved to the Ulster American Folk Park in 1998. His Philadelphia cousin also supplied rum, rice, sugar, tea, two dozen sickles, and other goods to Margaret Craig, who evidently had a store on Conoy Creek in Donegal Township.[81]

Records of storekeepers in Donegal Township are rare before the 1760s. William McCord's ledger and daybook is the record of a Lancaster merchant from 1762 to 1767 with extensive backcountry business. McCord recorded the store goods advanced him by Philadelphia merchants, including James Fullton. His cashbook and invoice book both include detailed records of iron sent by wagon to Philadelphia merchants and of purchases of rye and hemp subsequently shipped to other Philadelphia merchants. Among his accounts are those with Widow Haines, a shopkeeper in Maytown, a newly founded town within a mile of Donegal meetinghouse, whom he supplied with dry goods and liquors. James Knox and James Dysart, partners in a store at an unknown location, relied on McCord for goods advanced on credit.

He evidently also supplied goods for John Grattan, a shopkeeper in Augusta County, Virginia, shipping iron and other goods by wagon to Winchester, Virginia, where Grattan presumably brought his own wagons.[82]

The vibrant provincial economy of the 1760s cannot be projected back into the 1740s, to be sure, but the market orientation of the backcountry and the dependence of backcountry consumers on British manufactures began even earlier. There is a continuity of personnel, too. Justice Samuel Smith and Thomas Harris were still active in new enterprises; and Buchanans, McClures, Smiths, and Sterretts of the next generation moved into the ranks of merchants in the 1760s.[83]

"Some Uneasiness in Donegal"

The Presbyterian Church was a powerful force for order from the first settlement in Donegal Township. Filling a variety of both religious and secular needs, the church in Donegal, as elsewhere, played a part in assimilating emigrants from the British Isles to a common Scotch-Irish Presbyterian identity. [84] But this rock of stability threatened to split asunder from divisions caused by the revival known as the Great Awakening.

The Reverend James Anderson, the first pastor of the Donegal Presbyterian Church, died in July 1740. His last public action was to attend a meeting of Donegal Presbytery at his own congregation's meetinghouse, where consideration was given to "ye unhappy divisions of ye Church in this part of the world."[85] The presenting issue dated back to 1735 when an overture was submitted to Presbytery regarding strangers preaching in vacant pulpits. This was a question of order. The Presbyterian Church provided supply preachers for vacant congregations by appointment of Presbytery and traditionally held parish boundaries sacrosanct. A minister could not intrude into another parish without permission from Presbytery or the settled pastor of the congregation. To some younger ministers this seemed unduly limiting. They wanted to preach the Gospel whenever and wherever there was an opening. Between 1737 and 1739, a series of controversies over this supposed right divided Pennsylvania Presbyterians. The Synod of 1738 attempted to solve the problem by forbidding the pulpit to visiting ministers if *any* minister in that Presbytery thought "his Preaching in that Congregation will have a tendency to procure Divisions and Disorders." The same Synodal meeting at Philadelphia authorized a new Presbytery of New Brunswick composed of the Reverend Gilbert Tennent and four other New Light ministers who advocated preaching in any vacant congregation. They chose to ignore the Synod's ruling against them, arguing Synod and Presbytery were only advisory. By so opposing the Synod's authority, the New Brunswick group radically reduced the powers of the Presbyterian judicatory system.

Two staunch New Lights supplied the vacant pulpit of Nottingham in Chester County and sparked a revival there. In March 1740 they invited Tennent to help them and encourage the congregation to call a New Light pastor. On this visit, Tennent gave a sermon on "The Danger of an Unconverted Ministry," assailing those ministers who lulled their hearers into false security by never preaching, as the New Lights did, on the terrors of damnation, which would awaken backsliders to their Christian duty. It was an infringement of Christian liberty to bind men and women to such ministers. "Let those who live under the Ministry of dead Men repair to the Living, where they may be edified." Tennent thus dissolved the bond of the church covenant between lay members and their minister. When the Synod met again in 1740, Tennent and the New Brunswick Presbytery went a step further, repudiating all efforts to regulate itinerant preachers, since "Rules that are serviceable in ordinary Cases, when the Church is stocked with a faithful Ministry, are notoriously prejudicial when the Church is oppressed with a carnal Ministry."[86]

For the New Lights, the definition of a carnal minister embraced all the members of Donegal Presbytery, since they opposed "ye work of God in their Seaming to condemn ye crying out of people at Sermons" as well as opposing "these ministers that Seem instrumental in carrying on these things."[87] Attitudes towards the revival, commonly known in America as the Great Awakening, underlay the Presbyterian quarrel, but theological issues were never in dispute. The subscription issue in the American church meant a pledge to follow the church structure laid out in the Westminster Directory and not an affirmation of orthodox teaching. When Presbytery met at the Donegal meetinghouse in May 1741, the minister and elders of the Chestnut Level congregation submitted an overture requiring lay members to subscribe to the Westminster standards and "promise to submit to the Government of the presbyterian Churches as laid down in the Westminster Directory" and never to "countenance or encourage" itinerant preachers "intruding irregularly into our Congregations."[88] The meeting of the Synod of Philadelphia on June 1, 1741, was the final act in the drama. A harsher version of the Chestnut Level overture led to the Presbytery of New Brunswick and its supporters being read out of the Presbyterian Synod.[89]

Donegal Presbyterians echoed the divisions in the denomination. Presbytery sent two young students, both "lately from Ireland," as supply preachers at Donegal. The congregation called one of them, James Lyon, as Donegal's second pastor in May 1741, but Presbytery soon learned there was "some uneasiness in Donegal" about the new minister.[90] It surfaced when Presbytery met at Donegal in October 1741 and received two separate supplications from the Donegal church, both asking that Lyon be removed. One came from those in the congregation "who had been drawn aside by the New Brunswick ministers, wherein they profess that they still adhere to the congregation & Presbytery of Donegal & by their commissioner James Harris promising to be subject to this Pby & farther declaring that tho they could not join in calling Mr. Lyon yet they would cordially join in calling another with their brethren."[91]

The Donegal congregation did unite in calling another minister, the Reverend Hamilton Bell, in 1742; but within a few months there was more unease in Donegal. Presbytery met with the Donegal elders in April 1743 to investigate rumors about him and decided there was no basis for them. John Allison, one of the elders, returned to report that Samuel Smith and Nathaniel Litle, both New Lights, were criticizing the action taken by Presbytery. Presbytery invited them to come in and agreed to hear their witnesses, who presented damaging but inconclusive testimony.[92] Nearly a year later, James Mitchell, John Allison, John Jamison, and Andrew Boggs, elders of Donegal Presbyterian Church, brought more damning evidence, and Bell was deposed from the ministry.[93]

Lay Presbyterians insisted they had the right to use the church judicatories to make sure their minister toed the line. They became skilled at that. "Protests of the laity against unsound ministers set in motion administrative corrections and trials."[94] Shaming unworthy ministers was usually the province of New Lights; but in both cases at Donegal, all parties in the congregation agreed that the minister had to leave. Both parties clearly favored a decisive lay voice in church matters.

This event nevertheless precipitated the withdrawal of the New Light minority from the Donegal congregation. They called the Reverend John Roan as their pastor in the Mount Joy Presbyterian Church. The 1745 membership roll of the congregation can be reconstructed from his account book.[95] The split evidently divided many Donegal families as the twenty-eight heads of households in the Mount Joy congregation included members of the Allison, Campbell, Clingan, Harris, Howard, Litle, Lowery, McFarlane, Mays, Mitchell, Ramsey, Sterrett, Stevenson, Wilson, and Woods families, all prominent in Donegal.

James Harris and Gordon Howard, spokesmen for the New Lights in the Donegal congregation, were men who had both made money in the Indian trade and were substantial landowners. Harris's brother Thomas Harris, another New Light, had a store, a tavern, a gristmill, and sawmill as well as farms and served as captain of the company of associators raised in Donegal Township in 1745. Thomas Harris was a partner in the Philadelphia Company in the development of settlement at Pictou in Nova Scotia. Matthew Harris, Thomas's son, was also a member of the Mount Joy congregation. He managed the mills on Conewago before moving with his family to Nova Scotia. Gordon Howard, who "wrought for a considerable time for James Logan" before the Donegal settlement began and was rewarded with large land grants, died prior to formation of the new congregation; his widow, Rachel McFarlan Howard, and several of her relatives were members.

Sheriff Samuel Smith and Assemblyman Samuel Smith were both subscribers to the Reverend John Roan's salary. Sheriff Samuel Smith moved across the Susquehanna to Cumberland County before he sold his mills and acreage on Conewago Creek to Thomas Harris and was named one of the original justices of the county court. In the 1742 election, Sheriff Samuel Smith and Robert Buchanan represented the Penn family interests, and their successful opponents bruited about that they had been bribed with land to sell out the liberties of the people. The other Samuel Smith, who gave the land for the Mount Joy meetinghouse, had served in the Pennsylvania Assembly and as county treasurer and county commissioner.[96] David Wilson, the first elder of the Mount Joy congregation, was Lancaster County treasurer.

James Sterrett, county sheriff in 1745–1747 and treasurer in 1748, also subscribed for the minister's salary. He was the eldest son of John Sterrett, farmer and distiller, who was county treasurer in 1742–1747 and died in 1748. James Sterrett left Donegal Township for Baltimore, Maryland, in 1761 and formed a partnership with William Smith, his wife's cousin, as distillers and general merchants.

These few examples are enough to suggest that the division between Old Lights and New Lights was not between the haves and the have-nots or the young and restless on one side, the establishment on the other. Rather we find a mix of both sorts in both Donegal Township congregations. The New Lights included men of an entrepreneurial bent, interested in making the most of their opportunities in a market-oriented world, but the Old Lights had their share of such men, too, enough to allow us to conclude that by 1745 the search for order in Donegal embraced an order that valued individual freedom and material gain more than community.

But community certainly survived the frontier experience of the first generation. Division in the church was more meaningful to the clerical members of Donegal Presbytery than to laymen, and there is no indication that families divided between Mount Joy and Donegal congregations were themselves divided. As in every early American community, a network of interrelated families upheld a common vision of order.

Notes

1. Sidney Smith was the daughter of John Gamble, a merchant in Strabane, County Tyrone, and the wife of Samuel Smith, who had leased one-quarter of the nearby townland of Ballymagorry in 1720. His father, Hugh Smith, an agent for the Abercorn estate, held half of the same townland. (Will of John Gamble, T408/4787; Thomas Nevill, "The True Map & Survey of BallymcGorry and Mill Town Lands," D623/D/1/2, Public Record Office of Northern Ireland, Belfast.) Her husband sailed for America a year or two later to recoup his fortunes. He may have intended to set up as a merchant or linen draper in Dublin. As a grandson told the story in 1823, Samuel Smith "preferred the society of his jovial friends of the four Bottle Club in Dublin to the necessary attention to his own affairs, those he entrusted to a partner who collected their funds and ran off, which compelled my handsome Grandfather to come off to America in 1721 where his education and manners introduced him to the Proprietors of Pennsylvania and he became a man of consequence and High Sheriff of Lancaster County" (Samuel Smith to My Dear Daughter, May 5, 1823, Smith Family Papers, 1729/178, Alderman Library, University of Virginia, Charlottesville). This Samuel Smith as a young man lived with his grandfather in Baltimore, so he would have heard this story from him.) Smith returned to Tyrone for the wife and son he left behind.

2. "The Records of the Presbytery of New Castle upon Delaware," *Journal of the Presbyterian Historical Society* 15 (June 1932): 88.

3. James Logan to John Wright, October 23, 1727, Logan Letterbooks, III:16, Historical Society of Pennsylvania, Philadelphia (hereafter cited as HSP). "Meribah" is an allusion to Exodus 17:7. Logan's intervention did not end their quarrel, as both "Samuel" and "James" came to town soon afterward to make their case in person and to reject Galbraith as a mediator. James Logan to John Wright and Samuel Blunston, October 30, 1727, Logan Letterbooks, HSP, III:17.

4. Carr obtained title to his land in 1739 and Smith in 1742. Patent Books A-10–412 and A-12–156. Pennsylvania State Archives, Harrisburg. Logan to Wright, October 23, 1727.

5. George W. Franz, *Paxton: A Study of Community Structure and Mobility in the Colonial Pennsylvania Backcountry* (New York: Garland, 1989), 121ff. I have used the term "Scotch-Irish" in preference to "Scots-Irish" or "Ulster Scots." It is a purely American term, in common usage since the mid-eighteenth century. Edmund Burke, for instance, wrote of backcountry settlers: "These are chiefly Presbyterians from the Northern part of Ireland, who in America are generally called Scotch-Irish," in *An Account of the European Settlements in America* (London: R. and J. Dodsley, 1760), vol. 2:216. In ordinary American

speech, "Scotch-Irish" lacks the implied ethnic or geographic specificity of "Scots-Irish" and "Ulster Scots." Ned Landsman observed that nice distinctions among emigrants from Scotland, Ireland, the north of Ireland, or elsewhere in the British Isles were rarely made by contemporaries. Scots, Englishmen, Irishmen, and Welshmen who found themselves in predominantly "Scotch-Irish" Presbyterian settlements in the Pennsylvania or Virginia backcountry readily assimilated to the majority and became "Scotch-Irish." Landsman concluded that "Ethnic identifications in the eighteenth century, among British immigrants at least, were not fixed in quite the way that is sometimes supposed," reflecting "both a circumstantial and a volitional quality to ethnic identifications in the eighteenth-century British and Anglo-American worlds." Ned C. Landsman, "Ethnicity and National Origin among British Settlers in the Philadelphia Region," *Proceedings of the American Philosophical Society* 133 (1989): 170–77. An individual with few or no Scottish ancestors might be considered "Scotch-Irish," while Ulster-born and Presbyterian-bred William Henry, gunsmith and leader of the German-speaking Moravian Brethren in Lancaster, Pennsylvania, and others who emigrated from Ulster as Quakers would be identified with those quasi-ethnic groups.

6. There are significant gaps in the extant series, but the problematic nature of the Lancaster County tax lists surviving from the 1750s is a more serious problem. Analyzing Donegal township assessments for that decade—one of which inexplicably assigns only thirty acres to most landholders—Franz concluded that the average holding was 60.8 acres and that only one person owned more than 100 acres, a statement belied even by other individual lists in extant Donegal assessments 1750–1759 (Franz, *Paxton,* 157, 193; Donegal Tax Assessments, Lancaster County Historical Society, Lancaster, Pa.).

7. Aaron S. Fogleman, *Hopeful Journeys: German Immigration, Settlement, and Political Culture in Colonial America, 1717–1775* (Philadelphia: University of Pennsylvania Press, 1996), 93–97.

8. Patrick Griffin, "The People with No Name: Ulster's Migrants and Identity Formation in Eighteenth-Century Pennsylvania," *William and Mary Quarterly,* 3rd ser., vol. 58 (July 2001): 587–614.

9. Patrick Griffin, *The People with No Name: Ireland's Ulster Scots, America's Scots Irish, and the Creation of a British Atlantic World, 1689–1764* (Princeton, N.J.: Princeton University Press, 2001), 6–7.

10. "Records of the Presbytery of New Castle upon Delaware," *Journal of Presbyterian History* 14 (December 1931): 379–80; 15 (September 1932): 160–62. Chiken's Longus is Chiquesalunga or Chiques Creek.

11. Howard McKnight Wilson, *The Lexington Presbytery Heritage* (Verona, Va.: McClure Publishers, 1971), 10.

12. James Logan to James Anderson and Andrew Galbraith, March 2, 1730, Logan Letterbooks, HSP, III:170.

13. Jack P. Greene and J. R. Pole, *Colonial British America: Essays in the New History of the Early Modern Era* (Baltimore: Johns Hopkins University Press, 1984), 15.

14. James A. Henretta, "Families and Farms: *Mentalite* in Pre-Industrial America," *William and Mary Quarterly,* 3rd ser., vol. 35 (October 1978): 14. But see Allan Kulikoff, *From British Peasants to Colonial American Farmers* (Chapel Hill: University of North Carolina Press, 2000), 203ff.

15. James T. Lemon, *The Best Poor Man's Country: A Geographical Study of Early Southeastern Pennsylvania* (Baltimore: Johns Hopkins University Press, 1971), xiv–xv.

16. Wayland F. Dunaway, *The Scotch-Irish of Colonial Pennsylvania* (Chapel Hill: University of North Carolina Press, 1944), 34.

17. Alexander Mitchell, Deposition, 1770, W. H. Egle, ed., *Notes and Queries,* 3rd ser., vol. 1:236–38.

18. Martin H. Brackbill, "Peter Bezaillon's Road," *Journal of the Lancaster County Historical Society* 43 (January 1939): 4–10.

19. Will of John Allison, 1728, Chester County Wills, Chester County Courthouse, West Chester, Pa., A-291.

20. Analysis based on property listed in James M. Duffin, comp., *Guide to the Mortgages of the General Land Office of the Province of Pennsylvania, 1724–1756* (Philadelphia: Genealogical Society of Pennsylvania, 1994).

21. Lemon, *Best Poor Man's Country,* 54–57.

22. Thomas Sergeant, *View of the Land Laws of Pennsylvania* (Philadelphia: J. Kay and Brother, 1838), 36–41; Mary M. Schweitzer, *Custom and Contract: Household, Government, and the Economy in Colonial Pennsylvania,* (New York: Columbia University Press, 1987), 97–100.

23. Francis Jennings, "Miquon's Passing: Indian Policy in Pennsylvania, 1683–1730," PhD diss., University of Wisconsin, 1967, 104.

24. James Logan to Thomas Penn, February 28, 1733/4, *Pennsylvania Archives,* 2nd ser., vol. 7:158–59.

25. James Logan to James Steel, November 18, 1729, Logan Papers, X:46; also in Penn Manuscripts, Official Correspondence, HSP, II:101.

26. Francis Jennings, "The Indian Trade of the Susquehanna Valley," *Proceedings of the American Philosophical Society* 110 (December 1966): 420–22.

27. Jennings, "Miquon's Passing," 230. Chiques Creek was also called Chiquesalunga Creek.

28. Lemon, *Best Poor Man's Country,* 55.

29. William H. Crawford, *The Management of a Major Ulster Estate in the Late Eighteenth Century* (Dublin: Irish Academic Press, 2001), 13–14.

30. Donegal Township Petition to Thomas Penn, June 12, 1733, Penn Physick Papers, HSP, VI:29.

31. Logan to Henry Goldney, May 7, 1723, *Pennsylvania Archives,* 2nd ser., vol. 7:77.

32. Swatara Creek emptied into the Susquehanna at present Middletown, Pennsylvania. James Logan to John Wright and Samuel Blunston, October 30, 1727, Logan Letterbooks, HSP, III:17.

33. Land Book H, *Pennsylvania Archives,* 2nd ser., vol. 19:755.

34. James Logan to John Penn, November 25, 1727, *Pennsylvania Archives,* 2nd ser., vol. 7:96–97.

35. James Logan to Rev. James Anderson, December 23, 1730, Logan Letterbooks, IV: 273, HSP, 92–94. Martin H. Brackbill, "The Manor of Conestoga in the Colonial Period," *Journal of the Lancaster County Historical Society* 42 (March 1938): 22–26.

36. Logan to Hannah Penn, February 9, 1724, Penn MSS., Official Correspondence, HSP, I:313.

37. Rev. James Anderson to William Allen, June 26, 1733, Penn-Physick Papers, HSP, VI:29.

38. Jennings, "Miquon's Passing," 292.

39. James Logan to Rev. James Anderson and Andrew Galbraith, March 2, 1730, Logan Letterbooks, HSP, III:170.

40. Richard Kerwin MacMaster, *Donegal Presbyterians: A Scots-Irish Congregation in Pennsylvania* (Morgantown, Pa.: Donegal Society, 1995), 16.

41. Donegal Presbytery Records, I:6. Presbyterian Historical Society, Philadelphia. By not joining a congregation, they escaped the financial obligation of supporting the minister, an obligation enforceable on all members.

42. [Edmund and William Burke], *An Account of the European Settlements in America* (London: R. and J. Dodsley, 1760), vol. 2:216.

43. Minutes of the Corporation for the Relief of Poor and Distressed Presbyterian Ministers, 1759, in Maurice W. Armstrong, Lefferts A. Loetscher, and Charles A. Anderson, eds., *The Presbyterian Enterprise: Sources of American Presbyterian History* (Philadelphia: Presbyterian Historical Society, 1956), 71.

44. When he moved to Baltimore in 1760, William Buchanan sold a building that is still standing at 137 East High Street in Carlisle to James Pollock of Carlisle, tavern keeper, for £1200.

45. Judith Anne Ridner, "A Handsomely Improved Place: Economic, Social, and Gender Role Development in a Backcountry Town, Carlisle, Pennsylvania, 1750–1815," PhD diss., College of William and Mary, 1994, 26–27.

46. Merri Lou Scribner Schauman, *A History and Genealogy of Carlisle, Cumberland County, Pennsylvania, 1751–1835* (Dover, Pa.: the author, 1987), 107–9.

47. Schweitzer, *Custom and Contract,* 95. The sheriffs in this period were Robert Buchanan and Samuel Smith of Donegal.

48. Report of William Webb, June 4, 1733, "Donegal: Surveying Land on Susquehanna Once Hazardous Venture," *Internal Affairs Monthly Bulletin* 22 (November 1954): 3–5.

49. James Logan to Thomas Penn, June 14, 1733, *Pennsylvania Archives,* 2nd ser., vol. 7:143–44.

50. Howard McKnight Wilson, *Lexington Presbytery Heritage* (Verona, Va.: McClure Publishers, 1971), 18–20.

51. Petition of Inhabitants of Donegal to Thomas Penn, June 12, 1733, enclosed in Rev. James Anderson to William Allen, June 26, 1733, Penn-Physick Papers, HSP, VI:29.

52. James Logan to Thomas Penn, February 28, 1733/34, *Pennsylvania Archives,* 2nd ser., vol. 7:158–59.

53. Thomas Penn to Joshua Minshall, December 22, 1733, Thomas Penn to James Logan, January 23, 1733/34, *Pennsylvania Archives,* 2nd ser., vol. 7:161–62, 164–65.

54. Thomas Penn to James Logan, January 24, 1733/34, Thomas Penn to John Wright, January 24, 1733/34, *Pennsylvania Archives,* 2nd ser., vol. 7:162–64.

55. Lancaster County Wills, A-1–34. Lancaster County Court House, Lancaster, Pa. (hereafter cited as LCCH).

56. Schweitzer, *Custom and Contract,* 219.

57. Lancaster County Inventories, 1746, Lancaster County Historical Society. For a contemporary description of these cars, see Richard K. MacMaster, ed., "Reminiscences of the Rev. Samuel Houston," *Augusta Historical Bulletin* 23 (Spring 1987): 28.

58. Lancaster County Wills, LCCH, A-1–4.

59. Lancaster County Wills, LCCH, A-1–17.

60. Chester County Wills, A-291.

61. Lancaster County Wills, LCCH, B-1–322.

62. Lancaster County Inventories, 1739, 1746, Lancaster County Historical Society.

63. Until the creation of Lancaster County in 1729, Donegal Township was part of Chester County. Franklin Ellis and Samuel Evans, *History of Lancaster County, Pennsylvania* (Philadelphia: Everts and Peck, 1883), 778.

64. *Pennsylvania Archives,* 2nd ser., vol. 19:727.

65. Lemon, *Best Poor Man's Country,* 200–207; Kulikoff, *From British Peasants to Colonial American Farmers,* 208–9.

66. Lancaster County Will Book LCCH, A-1–146.

67. Jennings, "Miquon's Passing," 83–95.

68. Charles A. Hanna, *The Wilderness Trail* (New York: G. P. Putnam's Sons, 1911), 175–76.

69. Frederick B. Tolles, *James Logan and the Culture of Provincial America* (Boston: Little, Brown, 1957), 89–90.

70. There were two or three Samuel Smiths in Donegal Township at this time. The Indian trader "Justice Samuel Smith" owned land on Conewago Creek and served as sheriff, later moving to Cumberland County, Pennsylvania, where he was also on the county court, and then to Baltimore, Maryland. Samuel Smith of Conoy may or may not have been the same person. A different Samuel Smith, with land near Donegal Springs, represented Lancaster County in the Pennsylvania Assembly. Joseph S. Foster, "Samuel Smith," in *Lawmaking and Legislators in Pennsylvania: A Biographical Dictionary* (Philadelphia: University of Pennsylvania Press, 1997), vol. 2:930–31.

71. James Logan to John Penn, August 13, 1729, Penn Manuscripts, Official Correspondence, HSP, II:83.

72. James H. Merrell, *Into the American Woods: Negotiators on the Pennsylvania Frontier* (New York: W. W. Norton, 1999), 166.

73. Robert Stewart, *Colonel George Stewart and His Wife Margaret Harris: Their Ancestors and Descendants* (Lahore, India: the author, 1907), 84–87.

74. John Murray, Inventory, August 5, 1745, Lancaster County Historical Society. His will is in Lancaster County Will Book, LCCH, A:1–105.

75. Samuel Shaw, Inventory, May 23, 1743. Lancaster County Historical Society. His will is in Lancaster Will Book, LCCH, A:1–79.

76. Lancaster County Wills, LCCH, A:1–23; Inventory, October 28, 1735, Inventory, April 1736, and Accounts, March 24, 1740, Lancaster County Historical Society, Lancaster, Pa.

77. *Pennsylvania Chronicle,* February 28, 1768.

78. Samuel Carsan to Arthur Vance, February 15, 1746/7. Davey and Carsan Letterbook, Library of Congress, Washington, D.C.

79. Samuel Carsan to Alexander Auchinleck, November 25, 1745, Davey and Carsan Letterbook.

80. Richard K. MacMaster, "James Fullton: A Philadelphia Merchant and His Customers," *Familia* 17 (2001): 23–34.

81. James Fullton, Day Book, 1763–1764, York County Historical Society, York, Pa.

82. William McCord Papers, MG-2, Pennsylvania State Archives, Harrisburg.

83. Richard K. MacMaster, "Scotch-Irish Merchants and the Rise of Baltimore, 1755–1775," *Journal of Scotch-Irish Studies* 1 (Summer 2001): 19–32.

84. Landsman, "Ethnicity and National Origin among British Settlers," 170–77; Hubertis Cummings, *Scots Breed and Susquehanna* (Pittsburgh: University of Pittsburgh Press, 1964), 53.

85. Donegal Presbytery Minutes, I:278–79, Presbyterian Historical Society, Philadelphia.

86. Milton J. Coalter, *Gilbert Tennent, Son of Thunder* (New York: Greenwood Press, 1986), 68–71.

87. Donegal Presbytery Minutes, I:309.

88. Donegal Presbytery Minutes, I:317–30.

89. Coalter, *Gilbert Tennent,* 81–85; Leonard J. Trinterud, *The Forming of an American Tradition: A Re-Evaluation of Colonial Presbyterianism* (Philadelphia: Westminster Press, 1949), 135–36.

90. Donegal Presbytery Minutes, I:311–14, 331–35, 346.

91. Donegal Presbytery Minutes, I:351–55.

92. Donegal Presbytery Minutes, I:376–83.

93. Donegal Presbytery Minutes, I:396–409.

94. Marilyn J. Westerkamp, *Triumph of the Laity: Scots-Irish Piety and the Great Awakening, 1625–1760* (Oxford, U.K.: Oxford University Press, 1988), 151–57.

95. Rev. John Roan, Account Book, 1745–1761, Dauphin County Historical Society, Harrisburg, Pa. Photocopy in Lancaster County Historical Society, Lancaster, Pa.

96. Foster, "Samuel Smith," II:930–31.

Searching for Community: Carlisle, Pennsylvania, 1750s–1780s

Richard K. MacMaster

In 1769 an anonymous writer in the *Pennsylvania Chronicle* sketched a picture of a potential Scotch-Irish, linen-making region in the Pennsylvania backcountry. He had seen an advertisement for a proposed new town to be laid out on the Juniata River and took this as his starting point: "The proposed erection of a town on Juniata seemed to me to point out the proper place for the erection of a linen manufacture; the distance from maritime navigation must ever keep provisions low. These countries abound in great tracts of fresh land, proper for the produce of hemp and flax, and Cumberland County is seated in great measure by natives of Ireland, who, many of them, understand that employment, and would, no doubt, engage therein with alacrity, if properly encouraged."

The writer expanded on the advantages of his scheme for more than a page, but they need not detain us, other than his insistence that the back inhabitants could not readily send their produce to market. "And inasmuch as the provisions raised in those inland parts are too remote from marine navigation, to bear the expence of exportation, or encourage the industry of the farmers, the erection of trading and popular towns is become absolutely necessary."[1]

Pennsylvania west of the Susquehanna was the domain of the Scotch-Irish. They crossed the river in the 1730s, and by 1745 settlers had formed ten Presbyterian congregations within the bounds of what was soon to be Cumberland County. Settlement spread beyond the Susquehanna and followed the river and its tributaries, like the Juniata, deep into the Pennsylvania backcountry by 1769. But settlers had difficulty in transporting goods. Farm surplus went to market in Philadelphia by wagon over roads that were little more than rutted trails. Even iron was hauled in wagons. "The traveler who headed west from Philadelphia would find the road rutted and muddy, thanks to heavy use by hundreds of Conestoga wagons loaded with produce."[2] Wagons and teams crossed the broad Susquehanna with some difficulty by ferryboat.[3] This would change in time. While backcountry merchants continued to ship farm produce and pelts to market in Philadelphia, a network of improved roads drew much of their trade to Baltimore and encouraged the growth of towns west of the Susquehanna. The river itself became a highway into the interior. By 1775, according to one Middletown boomer, merchants there traded up the Susquehanna, and produce was brought down the river to Middletown "with many thousand bushels of wheat, rye, and Indian corn annually unloaded here" (see map 4.1).[4]

James T. Lemon wrote of a "town-making fever" that led to the founding of more than twenty-nine new towns in the Pennsylvania backcountry between 1756 and 1765, more than in all of Pennsylvania in the previous seventy-five years.[5] This fever reached its peak in the 1760s, with the end of the French and Indian War and a positive economic outlook based on wartime profits on backcountry produce. It also reflected the commercial development of the county towns in the backcountry, notably Lancaster, York, and Carlisle, as secondary centers for the distribution of manufactured goods and the shipment of wheat, flour, flaxseed, beef, and pork to Philadelphia and a market overseas. Lemon suggested that some of the new towns, such as McAllisterstown (Hanover) in York County and Chambersburg and Shippensburg in Cumberland County, developed in the 1760s as satellites of the county towns, being important transport centers at major crossroads. He also recognized a different network for which the established county towns and the new towns were nodal points, the commercial network linking city merchants and backcountry shopkeepers.[6]

Given the difficulties in transportation, which were beyond the ability of an individual farmer, towns became "absolutely necessary" as collection points for the shipment of produce and the distribution of imported goods as well as a market for nearby farmers. Philadelphia (and later Baltimore) merchants were essential middlemen in getting the flour, flaxseed, and iron of the backcountry to consumers in the Atlantic world and in bringing an increasing variety of European and East India goods to backcountry farmers. They depended in turn on backcountry shopkeepers to supply the exports they needed and to alert them to the goods demanded by their customers.

Commercial networks were also information highways, with backcountry towns as nodal points in a complex web of credit, goods, and ideas that linked them through Baltimore and Philadelphia with Belfast, Dublin, and London. Called into being to serve the needs of government and trade, these

Richard K. MacMaster

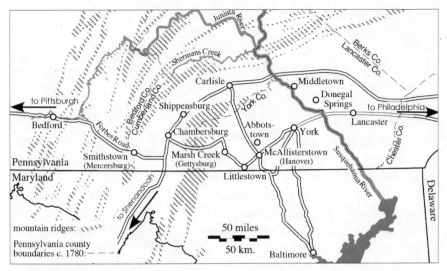

Map 4.1. *Carlisle region, 1750s to 1780s.*

inland towns became centers for spreading news and developing social and political culture. They supported schools and institutions of higher learning. They thus reflected the goals of an "improved" society and fostered genuine community. Lancaster, York, and Carlisle, the three most important inland towns, shared similar roles, but this essay will focus on Carlisle, county town of Scotch-Irish Cumberland County.

The merchants and traders of Carlisle were links in a commercial network that brought the shopkeepers of crossroads villages and the backcountry farmers and millers who supplied them with flour, grain, flaxseed, and other produce into contact with the wider world of Baltimore and Philadelphia. It was a two-way street, with city merchants providing markets for the rural producer and tailoring the assortments of dry goods they forwarded to local tastes. Their contacts went beyond mere exchange of goods and advance of capital. Carlisle's merchants, like John Montgomery, Robert Callender, and Adam Hoops, traveled to Baltimore and Philadelphia to meet with leaders in the provincial government and in the church as often as they did to order calicoes or arrange the sale of iron or peltry from the frontier. Their city correspondents, as often as not family members, moved in a still wider Atlantic world, returning periodically to Belfast, Londonderry, and London itself and keeping abreast of British and European intellectual and political trends at home.

Thanks in large part to its mercantile community, Carlisle was not an isolated outpost on the frontiers of European settlement and traditional Native American life. The Scotch-Irish of Cumberland County and beyond were aware of intellectual and cultural currents in the Atlantic world, mediated through the vibrant life of eighteenth-century Carlisle.

"A Handsomely Improved Place"

Settlement had spread beyond the Susquehanna to such an extent that two new counties were created in 1749 and 1750. York County included an area along the southern boundary of the colony. Cumberland County formed a wide arc around York, from the Susquehanna to the Maryland line. The new counties demanded a place where local government could be conducted with the erection of a courthouse, jail, and other public buildings. The proprietor of Pennsylvania, Thomas Penn, authorized two new "Proprietary towns," as they were called, to meet this need. Penn took a personal interest in planning Carlisle, the county town for Cumberland County. With "near fifty Houses built, and building," in 1751, Carlisle promised to be a considerable place, "a great thorough fare to the back Countries, and the Depositary of the Indian Trade."[7] Never simply an administrative center, Carlisle was intended from the first as a channel for the trade of central Pennsylvania.[8]

In 1750 Thomas Cookson, Thomas Penn's agent, purchased four farms as the site for the new town of Carlisle and laid it out in 312 lots, measuring 60 by 240 feet, on a symmetrical gridiron pattern of parallel streets and alleys punctuated by a central square or diamond. John Armstrong, a native of County Fermanagh, did the actual surveying in 1750–1751 and settled with his family in Carlisle to continue doing business as county surveyor. Lot owners were expected to build a substantial dwelling house at least twenty by twenty feet of stone, brick, or frame, with a stone or brick chimney, within one year. "Persons that settle in the Town are to have Patents for their Lands as soon as they begin to build and they may have two years time given them from the time of taking up to pay the Rent."[9]

Established athwart the main road leading from Harris's Ferry on the Susquehanna into the backcountry, Carlisle was fourteen miles from the ferry and fifty miles by road from Lancaster. The new town was thirty-two miles from the slightly older York.[10] Only a generation after the first Scotch-Irish settlers made their way through the wilderness to Donegal Springs, Carlisle had its beginning in a more complex world than they had known. The Pennsylvania town was as much as its Cumbrian namesake a part of the

Richard K. MacMaster

British Atlantic community and of a dynamic and changing trans-Atlantic commercial enterprise. At the same time a frontier outpost, Carlisle was the collection point for Indian traders as well as a distribution point for back-country grain, flour, flaxseed, and British manufactured goods. Within a few short years of its founding, Carlisle became a frontier outpost of a different kind, the farthest bastion of imperial power, a refugee camp for settlers fleeing more exposed frontier settlements, and the base for the British army's operations in western Pennsylvania. These war years proved a blessing for Carlisle's merchants and shopkeepers, as army contracts provided capital to expand their own operations and join the ranks of Baltimore and Philadelphia merchants in overseas trade.

Just as in Irish historian L. M. Cullen's words, "novel traffics—flaxseed and emigration—gave a new dynamism" to Belfast and Londonderry in the eighteenth century, so the same trade directed settlers to the Pennsylvania backcountry and increased demand for its produce. Philadelphia and Baltimore merchants and their backcountry networks were dynamic agents for change in this process, facilitating the movement of passengers, redemptioners, and servants and providing the necessary commercial, financial, and transportation support for the orderly exchange of backcountry produce for manufactured goods. These business networks helped bring the eighteenth-century consumer revolution to the backcountry and also contributed to its peopling.[11]

The importance of such business networks on both sides of the Atlantic has been recognized in recent years by scholars who rejected "the implicit assumption that the process of getting goods from the producer to the wholesaler was relatively transparent and trivial."[12] And the process of moving goods from wholesaler to backcountry consumer merited scholarly investigation, too. Thomas Doerflinger indicated the importance of backcountry networks to Philadelphia dry goods merchants.[13] John Smail, writing about the English woolen textile industry, began his study with a Yorkshire manufacturer's agent in Philadelphia in 1767 who found he could not compete with London suppliers because Philadelphia dry goods merchants, with an eye on what retail storekeepers would buy, "could rely on getting [from London] the correct assortment of cloth—type, colour, quality, and finish—which guaranteed a quick sale."[14] In other words, British manufacturers had to meet the wants of increasingly demanding backcountry consumers. The eighteenth-century consumer revolution, by then in high gear, has been the subject of several recent studies.[15] In his 1986 monograph, Doerflinger adumbrated its impact on the Pennsylvania backcountry and more fully explored the Philadelphia dry goods trade and its relevance to "the region's rural economy as a whole" in an important essay published in 1988.[16]

Dependence on transportation by wagon over difficult roads added another element. Philadelphia was a great distance from the backcountry, even in the days when the frontier ran along the Susquehanna. Merchants as well as backcountry farmers sought a more accessible collection point for country produce, following roads that led south into Maryland. This was especially true of the region west of the Susquehanna, where no fewer than eight major roads led south to Baltimore by 1770.[17] Baltimore, founded a year before Carlisle, was situated at the mouth of the Patapsco River on the west shore of Chesapeake Bay.[18] Baltimore began its upward trajectory as a major commercial center only in the 1760s, after the coming of the Scotch-Irish merchants who made it, in one scholar's phrase, "a Scotch-Irish boom town."[19] In 1771, a Philadelphian could write that "Baltimore town in Maryland has within a few years past carried off from this city almost the whole trade of Frederick, York, Bedford, and Cumberland Counties, its situation on the West side of the river Susquehannah and its vicinity to these counties will always be a prevailing inducement with the inhabitants of those parts to resort to Baltimore for trade, rather than to be at the expense of crossing the river Susquehannah and afterwards to drag their wagons along a road rendered almost impassable by the multitude of carriages which use it, and the insufficiency of our road Acts to keep it in repair."[20]

Another Philadelphian observed that "immense quantities" of wheat and flour "are now carried to Baltimore in Maryland" and "that, not only all the Inhabitants to the westward of Susquehanna, but also a large tract of the country adjacent, on the east side of said river, transport their commodities to that growing town."[21]

Baltimore claimed a lion's share of the trade in grain, flour, and flaxseed within the Cumberland Valley. In 1771 a number of persons living near Carlisle petitioned for "a Road from Captain Robert Callenders and Chambers Mills at the mouth of Letort Spring to fall into the Baltimore Road," because they had "no direct Road from said Mills to the Baltimore Markett."[22] They were obviously interested in sending flour to Baltimore. Carlisle merchants with ties to Baltimore significantly dealt with their former fellow townsmen, William Buchanan, John Smith, and William Neill, who was Captain Robert Callender's son-in-law.[23]

Carlisle, like York and the smaller west shore towns that rose in the 1760s—Chambersburg, Shippensburg, Hanover, and Bedford—was within

Baltimore's commercial hinterland, but Philadelphia merchants were no less active there. Newspaper essayists like "Philo-Pennsylvaniensis" might talk of Baltimore as "a dangerous rival of Philadelphia in her foreign trade," but it was less a rivalry than a symbiotic relationship. Philadelphia merchants like Sam Carsan and Samuel Purviance established branches of their firms, and others found correspondents in the new town, supplying one another's needs.[24]

"A great thorough fare to the back Countries"

Samuel Smith, former Sheriff of Lancaster County, was appointed Justice of the Court of Common Pleas for the new County of Cumberland on March 10, 1750. He was one of the early settlers in Donegal Township and had served as a Lancaster County justice continuously since 1741. The court met for its first session on July 24, 1750, "before Samuel Smith, Esquire and his Bretheren Keepers of the Peace of our said Lord the King."[25] The town of Carlisle did not yet exist, and the first Cumberland County court met at Shippensburg, a more centrally located settlement whose sparse inhabitants believed their "town" should be made the county seat.[26] Smith's large family relocated to Carlisle as soon as the town was laid out. He evidently lived in Carlisle with his son and his family until he moved to Baltimore in 1779.[27]

Smith transferred his Indian trade interests to Cumberland County, working with George Croghan, whose trading post was at Aughwick in present Huntington County. In a letter to Governor Hamilton in 1754, Conrad Weiser, Pennsylvania's Indian agent, complained, "It is a surprising thing that no means can be found to prevent the inhabitants in Cumberland County from selling strong liquor to the Indians. I am creditably informed that some of the magistrates of that county sell the most. Mr. Smith was at Aughwick, I suppose to gather some money for the liquor he sent. He is an old hypocrite."[28]

Many Carlisle merchants were also actively engaged in trade with the western Indians for deerskins and furs. Carlisle became the central point between Philadelphia and the remote tribal villages of the upper Susquehanna and the Ohio Country for the accumulation of trade goods and the return shipments of pelts. Carlisle merchants were essentially middlemen, working with dry goods importers in Philadelphia and equipping the packhorse men who carried the goods beyond the frontier. For most of them, Indian trade was one among several business interests. They were usually shopkeepers, selling dry goods and buying local produce for shipment to their correspondents in Philadelphia. In this they paralleled the Lancaster Indian traders, like Joseph Simon who worked with the Lowerys trading to the Ohio and with Nathan Levy and David Franks of Philadelphia.[29] As Judith Ridner concluded for men engaged in the fur trade "Carlisle was the real and symbolic mid-point . . . of an expansive economic universe that stretched from the furthest reaches of the Ohio Valley to the export markets of western Europe."[30]

One surviving eighteenth-century building in Carlisle has associations with the Indian trade. Joseph Simon owned Lot 101 in Carlisle in 1760. Nine years later Joseph Simon and Rosa, his wife, sold the property to Captain William Trent, another Indian trader. William Trent and his wife, Sarah, promptly mortgaged Lot 101 to Joseph Morris of Philadelphia, probably to finance the purchase price. The property was then improved by a two-story stone house, an attached one-story stone kitchen, and a log stable. This house is still standing at 7 North East Street in Carlisle. The Trents later sold the house to Alexander Blaine, who was also an Indian trader.[31]

The nature of the Indian trade made it a template for backcountry commercial networks. This business could only be conducted with the backing of established firms who could supply the required trade goods and trusted agents at each stage to bring them closer to the Native American consumer. As Nicholas Wainwright explained, trade goods were normally shipped on credit to frontier trader-merchants. They divided the goods into small cargoes and allowed independent traders to take an assortment of trade goods on credit (or else entrusted them to their own employees or indentured servants to carry into the wilderness). The goods thus passed from hand to hand on credit at ever-increasing prices.[32] It was a trade fraught with dangers, where a miscalculation could easily lead to ruin, so both the Philadelphia merchant and his frontier associate spread their risks. Partnerships shifted, and one Indian trader might work with many merchants in his time.

The complexity of these networks can be seen from a single example. Robert Callender, "perhaps Carlisle's best-known Indian trader," and his partner, Michael Taaffe, were obligated in 1752–1753 to the Philadelphia merchant Jeremiah Warder in the considerable sums of £1,352 and £321.[33] Just as frontier merchants provided loans to trustworthy customers, the major Philadelphia merchants trading to the frontier and beyond often acted as a syndicate advancing money secured by land to Indian traders. Edward Shippen, Thomas Lawrence, David Franks, and Joseph Simon joined with Warder in numerous mortgages to Indian traders in the 1750s.[34] Warder was interested in the fur trade because he was a hatter; an advertisement in 1771 mentioned beaver, raccoon, and castor hats "made by Jeremiah Warder."[35] But he was much more. A Quaker artisan of humble origin, Warder entered the beaver hat trade in Bucks County; by 1745 he was making hats on a large enough scale to buy seventy-three "hat bloks" from his father-in-law, John Head. He soon expanded into shirt-making as well as the fur trade and eventually became one of Philadelphia's most prominent dry goods merchants and importers.[36] He supplied stores as far away as Staunton in Virginia's Shenandoah Valley.[37]

Robert Callender of Carlisle, in partnership with Michael Taaffe and George Croghan, traded to the Ohio Country in the early 1750s. Callender, a prominent landowner, miller, and merchant, was one of the founders of Carlisle. As a trader, he had important connections in Philadelphia and commanded the respect of provincial authorities. Callender was one of the "suffering traders" who lost goods sent to the Miami tribe at Pickawillany in Ohio when the French attacked and destroyed the town as a warning to British traders and their Native American allies in 1752.[38] He and his associates were eventually compensated with large grants of western lands. Joseph Spear and Thomas Smallman of Carlisle were among the other suffering Indian traders.[39]

William Buchanan was involved in several trading ventures cut short by Pontiac's War in 1763. Buchanan and his partner, Barnabas Hughes,[40] joined Thomas Smallman, a Carlisle Indian trader, in sending goods to the Ohio and Illinois countries. George Croghan was a silent partner, backing his cousin Smallman financially. When the Indian trade reopened at Fort Pitt, they were among the first to ship trade goods to Smallman's store there. Croghan took an active role in the business. According to Smallman's clerk, James Harris, "Any thing we do here is promoted by the influence of Mr. Croghan, without which it would not be worth while to keep a store open at this place."[41] The partners lost heavily in ventures beyond Fort Pitt in 1763. Their severest loss was a shipment of goods valued at £3,000 sent "under the care of Hugh Crawford to Waweachteny [on the Wabash] and Miamy [upper Miami in Indiana]." Other losses were incurred on trade goods sent to the Lower Shawnee Town (near the juncture of Scioto Creek and the Ohio River) with Thomas Smallman, to Muskingum (in Ohio) under the care of John Bard, and to Illinois under Smallman's charge as well as "two Houses Destroyed at Fort Pitt by the Indian War in June 1763" and "two Cows Drove from Fort Pitt in June or July 1763."[42]

Joseph Spear, trader of Carlisle, also suffered losses by the Indians in 1763, giving a power of attorney, in association with his partners John Baynton, Samuel Wharton, and Robert Callender, to William Trent to negotiate for compensation.[43] The fur trade was the anchor for Philadelphia interests in

Carlisle, since much of the western trade passed that way. Among the Carlisle merchants in this trade in the 1760s, Ridner documented the activities of Sligo-born Francis West, brother of Philadelphia merchant William West, and Ephraim and Alexander Blaine, who were agents of the Philadelphia firm of Baynton, Wharton, and Morgan in their unsuccessful efforts to garner the trade of the Illinois Country. Stephen Duncan, a Carlisle shopkeeper interested in the fur trade, dealt initially with Baynton, Wharton, and Morgan, and later with William West.[44] Because of the fur trade, Carlisle still looked eastward over Harris's Ferry to commercial links with Philadelphia. Between 1763 and 1775, twelve Cumberland County residents, including five Carlisle shopkeepers, mortgaged property to Philadelphia merchants to secure debts; and only three, all local merchants, mortgaged property to Baltimore merchants.[45] Robert Callender, Indian trader of Carlisle, for instance, borrowed money from the trustees of the College of Philadelphia in 1762, mortgaging acreage on the Conodoguinet to secure payment.[46]

"This town has become the frontier"

Rivalry over fur trade brought the imperial ambitions of France and Great Britain for control of the Ohio Valley to a crisis in the early 1750s, beginning with expulsion of British traders from western Ohio in 1753. The British government sent General Sir Edward Braddock with two regiments of regulars to America in 1755 to dislodge the French from western Pennsylvania. The general planned to advance on the Forks of the Ohio by way of the Potomac and asked for two roads to be constructed to facilitate his army's march and the movement of materiel and supplies. George Croghan, John Armstrong, William Buchanan, James Burd, and Adam Hoops were appointed commissioners to oversee construction of two roads, one to Wills Creek, where Braddock planned to locate his base camp, and the other to the Forks of the Ohio. The commissioners started from Carlisle at the end of March 1755 and followed an old traders' path from Shippensburg across the mountains and along Raystown Creek. Deserted by their Indian guides and threatened by scouting parties of French and Indians, they stopped short of the Youghiogheny River and retired to the safety of Fort Cumberland at Wills Creek.[47] Armstrong and Buchanan advertised in April and May for "two Hundred Labourers . . . to work on Clearing the new Road . . . thro' Cumberland County towards the Ohio."[48]

By the time he was ready to march toward Fort Duquesne, Braddock had 2,500 men at his command, regulars and colonial troops. Pennsylvania supplied wagons and wagoners to haul the supplies this army needed as it inched its way through the wilderness. On July 9, 1755, Braddock's column blundered into a French and Indian ambush, and after two hours of slaughter, the remnants of his army withdrew from the field.[49]

William Buchanan wrote from Carlisle on July 21, 1755, to William Franklin, the future royal governor of New Jersey, with news of Braddock's defeat: "It is now reduced to a certainty that our Army are defeated, the General & Sir John are dangerously wounded, about the number of one thousand men lost with the train of Artillery & baggage. The remain[in]g part of the Army have destroy'd all their baggage except two Six pounders which was in Dunbar's Regiment and Provisions necessary for their retreat to Wills' Creek where I expect they are by this time."[50]

Governor Morris was at Carlisle when news came of Braddock's defeat. In the immediate aftermath of the disaster, Morris "at the request of the People laid the Ground for a Wooden Fort in the Town of Carlisle and . . . formed four Companies of Militia to whom I distributed some Powder and Lead." Pennsylvania, alone among the American colonies, had no militia, since the Quakers in the assembly were unwilling to impose a burden on others that they could not conscientiously carry themselves. Companies of volunteer associators formed to meet the emergency and elected their own officers. William Buchanan commanded the company raised in Carlisle.[51]

The frontier waited through the summer and early autumn for the Indians to strike. On Saturday afternoon, November 1, 1755, a hundred Delaware and Shawnee fell upon the Big Cove settlement (present McConnellsburg) and destroyed it. When news reached Carlisle the next day, John Armstrong, John Smith, and William Buchanan decided to send Captain Hans Hamilton and a company of York County volunteers to Shippensburg.[52] For the time being, Carlisle and Shippensburg served as refuges for settlers fleeing more exposed frontier settlements.

The Pennsylvania Assembly overcame its scruples and voted to construct forts and take the voluntary militia into provincial pay. In February 1756 the province counted 919 men under arms, of whom five companies, totaling 350 men, were stationed in Cumberland County. In May, Colonel John Armstrong was given the command of all forces west of the Susquehanna, and William Buchanan and Adam Hoops shared responsibility for provisioning all the military posts west of the river. Armstrong was unhappy with "an Extravagant sum thrown into the hands of two private persons for a Service of not more than two months in ye whole year." Buchanan was also reimbursed for his "Expences fortifying Carlisle" and arms and ammunition sent him for its defense. His brother-in-law John Smith had similar accounts paid.[53]

The countryside was nearly deserted. Adam Hoops said that there were three thousand men fit to bear arms in Cumberland County in 1755, and a year later, exclusive of the provincial forces, "they did not amount to an hundred." Detachments protected farmers harvesting their crops, but, on a general alarm, the "farmers abandoned their Plantations, and left what Corn was not then stacked or carried into Barnes, to perish on the Ground." A writer in the *Pennsylvania Gazette* claimed that, from Carlisle to Virginia, "there is not an Inhabitant to be seen, a few in Shippensburg excepted."[54]

War temporarily disrupted the Cumberland County economy, with farmers afraid to harvest their crops and the fur trade stagnant; but for a few Carlisle merchants and traders, the war provided a larger commercial stage and a boost in capital formation. The necessities of moving troops and supplies in wartime caused roads to be built into the wilderness of western Pennsylvania and into Maryland that would make Carlisle the great thoroughfare to the backcountry.

In May 1757 Colonel John Stanwix arrived at Carlisle with the first five companies of his battalion of the Royal American Regiment and set them to constructing a fortified camp northeast of the town. The remaining six companies came in September. They were the advance guard of a major British advance planned for the following spring. Colonel John Armstrong received orders in March 1758 to hold his battalion in readiness "for Offensive Duty by the first of May." A few weeks later the governor ordered all the provincial forces to be ready to march to Carlisle. "With the assembly of the provincial troops at Carlisle and the arrival of British troops, the role of this post as a provincial defense came to an end."[55]

Command of the second expedition against Fort Duquesne fell to General John Forbes, but getting the army there and supplying them on the way was the responsibility of Swiss-born colonel Henry Bouquet. He was at Carlisle in May 1758 and at a dozen other places east of the Susquehanna arranging for wagons and teams and for flour, oats, beef, and pork. He ordered the Berks County magistrates, for instance, to send sixty wagons and teams "to Barney Hughes' and also to Thomas Harris' Mill" on Conewago Creek to load flour and oats and proceed with them to Carlisle.[56] Bouquet turned to Adam Hoops to organize much of this as an army contractor, strictly as Agent to the Contractors for Victualling His Majesty's Forces, since he represented Joshua Howell, who was in turn Philadelphia agent for Baker, Kilby, and Baker of London, who held the contract. Hoops made his headquarters at Carlisle and enlisted his son-in-law, Daniel Clark, and William Buchanan, among others, as his assistants.[57] General Forbes complained about the wag-

Richard K. MacMaster

ons, the pork, the bad flour, and the meal that Hoops supplied. He insisted "our men must not be poisoned." Supply wagons and droves of cattle continued to pass over the road to Carlisle all summer. "There is plenty of Cattle moving up with a large escort of wagons loaded with flour and pork."[58]

The army had to cut a new road and improve existing roads through more than two hundred miles of wilderness, slowing their advance. The British were poised to attack Fort Duquesne on November 24, 1758, when the French commander evacuated it and marched his men away in the night. The British army occupied the partially destroyed fort, and General John Forbes wrote a report to his superiors, dated from "Fort Duquesne, now Pittsbourg."[59]

The war was far from over, and the need to garrison and supply frontier outposts continued. Captain Robert Callender of Carlisle and Barney Hughes of Donegal Township had a contract to supply the army with packhorse trains in 1758–1759. In May 1759 Colonel Bouquet wrote General Stanwix: "I think it is now time to contract with Callendar and Barny Hughes for the 1000 packhorses to carry [supplies] from Bedford to Ligonier," but urged the general to "bring them down to reasonable terms." Bouquet evidently thought they charged too much, but Stanwix had already "contracted with Capt. Callendar & Mr. Bar. Hughes for 1000 packhorses" and "given them a Warrant for 2000 pounds Sterling." Stanwix was well enough satisfied to give them another contract for additional packhorses in July 1759.[60]

Victualing the army and supplying wagons and packhorses continued to be an important source of income for Scotch-Irish businessmen in Carlisle and their employers in Philadelphia and London through 1760. Early the next year, creditors were warned to present their claims before March 25, when the books would close, to representatives in Philadelphia and Lancaster or, for those west of the Susquehanna, to Adam Hoops at Carlisle.[61]

Army contracts proved invaluable in the upward trajectory from counting house or shop counter to city merchant and landed gentleman.[62] They clearly played a similar role in the careers of Adam Hoops and his colleagues in Carlisle. Hoops leased his house on the square in Carlisle in 1761 and moved his family to Philadelphia. He continued to take an interest in the Presbyterian church in Carlisle, but his business interests were now directed to importing dry goods and exporting flaxseed and flour to Ulster ports with his son-in-law Daniel Clark.[63] Two other daughters married Ulster-born merchants in the flaxseed trade. Isabel married James Mease of Mease and Caldwell, and Mary was the wife of Thomas Barclay of Carsan, Barclay, and Mitchell. Hoops took his family home to Belfast on his own ship *New Hope* in 1763 and returned the following year by way of Liverpool.[64] In later years he devoted time to his investments in Pennsylvania and Nova Scotia land and retired to his country home in Bucks County, where he died in 1771.[65]

Captain Robert Callender was typical of his generation of frontier merchants. "Although he continued to venture westward to the Ohio Valley to trade with the Indians into the 1770s, his domestic life in Carlisle took on many of the trappings of genteel respectability."[66] He, too, had a town house in Carlisle and a country house near the town. When his wife, Mary, died in 1765, the funeral procession moved from one house to the other.[67]

Carlisle was again the staging point for a British expedition and its supply base in 1763 when the Ottawa chief Pontiac united the western tribes and struck at frontier forts. Colonel Bouquet assembled another force of provincials and British regulars, won a decisive battle at Bushy Run, and relieved the siege of Fort Pitt in August.[68] During that summer, hundreds of settlers were killed, and many more took refuge in Carlisle. Indian traders, scattered throughout the west, were especially vulnerable.[69]

With the Indian wars at an end, Carlisle and the Cumberland Valley began to again flourish.[70] Carlisle was the hub of a network of roads leading into the western territory. The Forbes Road, constructed during the war, led from Carlisle through Shippensburg to Fort Pitt and soon became a thoroughfare for the Indian and backcountry trade. Another main road led from Carlisle to Baltimore. At McAllister's tavern, soon to be McAllister's Town, it intersected the Philadelphia Wagon Road that since 1745 led through western Maryland into the Shenandoah Valley of Virginia.

New towns sprang up along the main roads. Edward Shippen of Lancaster, one of the principal merchants in the Indian trade, began selling lots in his town of Shippensburg in February 1763. The 173 lots went mainly to Scotch-Irish buyers. The deeds described the lots as "within a certain new town called Shippensburg," but there had been a small settlement there before 1750.[71] Benjamin Chambers from County Antrim settled at the site of the Falling Spring by 1734, but he laid out the town of Chambersburg only in 1764.[72] Richard McAllister laid out his town, later called Hanover, in 1763 or 1764 to the great amusement of his German neighbors. He was the son of Archibald McAllister, an Ulster emigrant who settled near the Big Spring in Cumberland County in 1732.[73]

Shippensburg and Chambersburg were in many ways satellites of Carlisle. Both new towns would seem to have an even closer relation to Baltimore firms, since the distance there by road was so much less than to Philadelphia. Shopkeepers Samuel Jack and Robert Boyd of Chambersburg mortgaged real estate to Alexander McClure and William Goodwin, merchants of Baltimore, to secure payment of a bonded debt in 1773, but Samuel Jack mortgaged other property the same year to Caleb and Amos Foulke of Philadelphia.[74]

Richard McAllister's Hanover was the closest to Maryland of the new towns on the Carlisle-Baltimore road. McAllister was part of a business network reaching from Baltimore to Carlisle. His store records indicate customers in a wide circuit of (then) York County, including Littles Town, Abitstown (Abbotstown), and near Samuel Getuses (Gettysburg). His suppliers were all in Baltimore, including John Smith and sons, John and Alexander McClure, James Sterrett and son, William Neill, Joseph McGoffin, and David McClure. He also obtained goods from Robert Callender and John Montgomery in Carlisle.[75]

A Town of "People who keep Shops and Public Houses"

Colonel William Eyre, chief military engineer of the British army in America, wrote of Carlisle in 1762 as "mostly compos'd of People who keep Shops and Public Houses."[76] In 1763 the tax assessor counted eight merchants, five shopkeepers, and three traders in the town as well as eleven tavern keepers in a town with 182 inhabitants, so Colonel Eyre was not far off the mark.[77] Unlike York, Hanover, and the new towns east of the Susquehanna where many Germans settled, surnames on the tax lists suggest a fairly homogenous population with a high proportion of Ulster emigrants.[78] Among the earliest shopkeepers and tavern keepers were men who moved to the new town from the older Scotch-Irish settlement in Donegal Township, Lancaster County.

John Smith and William Lyon were the only ones listed as "merchant" on the 1759 tax assessment, but seven others on the tax roll were identified on later returns as either merchant or shopkeeper.[79] Smith was the son of Samuel Smith from Ballymagorry, County Tyrone, an Indian trader and one of Cumberland County's original justices. William Lyon from County Fermanagh was John Armstrong's nephew and, as an assistant surveyor, helped him in laying out the town of Carlisle in 1751.[80]

Three surviving buildings in Carlisle date back to the earliest development of the town and have associations with the Scotch-Irish pioneers. A one-story stone house located at 109 East Pomfret Street was built in 1759 by Stephen Foulk, a stone mason, for Captain William Armstrong, who lived there until 1766. He was the brother of Colonel John Armstrong. The William Trent house on East Street belonged to an Indian trader. The third, and possibly the oldest, is a stone house on East High Street owned before 1760 by William Buchanan, innholder. Buchanan and his extended family had much to do with the rise of Carlisle as a commercial center.

William Buchanan married Esther, daughter of Justice Samuel and Sidney Gamble Smith. He was living at Marsh Creek and keeping a tavern and store in 1752 when a sale of land was advertised to take place at his house.[81] The same year, the Buchanans moved to Carlisle. In August 1752, a local carpenter mortgaged his house and lot in Carlisle to "William Buchanan of Carlisle, innholder." Buchanan's tavern was located on Lot 109. In January 1760 William Buchanan of Carlisle, gentleman, and his wife, Esther, conveyed this property to James Pollock of Carlisle, tavern keeper, for the substantial sum of £1200 Pennsylvania currency, since the Buchanans were about to move to Baltimore. The price Pollock paid for the property is an indication that Pollock bought buildings erected by Buchanan as an inn. The tavern was described in a 1773 newspaper advertisement as a thirty-three-foot-square stone building with a twenty-five-foot-square stone addition that housed a kitchen and bar room on the first floor and lodging rooms on the second floor. Both buildings are still standing at 137 East High Street. Originally a handsome two-story Georgian house, the larger building had the roof raised and an additional story with a fashionable mansard roof added in the 1870s.[82]

During his years in Carlisle, Buchanan was more than an innkeeper. As early as 1753, he was associated with Callender and Taaffe in the Indian trade.[83] He was also a general merchant in Carlisle in the 1750s. Buchanan moved to Baltimore in 1760, where he was an important merchant, first in partnership with Barnabas Hughes and then with his own brother-in-law, John Smith.

Justice Samuel Smith's eldest son, John Smith, received Lot 125 in the first sale of lots in Carlisle in 1751 and subsequently recorded grants from the proprietor for Lot 125 in 1753, as well as Lots 116 and 85 in 1760.[84] John Smith had moved to Carlisle to set up as a general merchant. He would have built "a substantial dwelling house" on each property in order to qualify for a patent giving him title to the property, so he had a house on Lot 125 by July 1752, when his eldest son, Samuel, was born in Carlisle.

John Smith's wife was Mary Buchanan, daughter of Robert Buchanan of Donegal Township, who succeeded Samuel Smith as sheriff of Lancaster County. Buchanan, like Smith, was from County Tyrone. After his second term as sheriff ended in 1742, Robert Buchanan stood for the assembly in a bitter election; his Quaker opponent "trumpeted about the county that Robert Buchanan had two hundred acres of land given him by the proprietaries and that he and Samuel Smith had taken bribes to give up the liberties of the people."[85] He left Donegal Township for the Marsh Creek settlement (near present Gettysburg) and died there in 1748. William Buchanan was his son.

Ulster-born John Montgomery was another brother-in-law. He married Sidney Smith, John Smith's younger sister, in 1755. John Montgomery described himself as merchant and shopkeeper in deeds, although he is better remembered for his service in the Pennsylvania Assembly, the Pennsylvania Committee of Safety, the Continental Congress and as cofounder of Dickinson College. Unlike Smith and Buchanan, he remained in Carlisle.[86] The operations of a backcountry merchant were meticulously recorded in Montgomery's one surviving store ledger. He evidently relied on William West, James Fullton, Samuel Purviance Sr., and his own brother-in-law, John Smith, for his stock in trade and offered a bewildering variety of textiles and every other article from six-plate iron stoves to Philadelphia beaver hats. Customers of every social class appear to have demanded cloth of many different kinds, weaves, colors, and quality. They paid him in as many different ways: cash, credit for work performed, bills of exchange, cash paid to his creditors, turnips, cider, wheat, corn, whiskey, furs, and deerskins. Flaxseed was not a major item in his store credits, but he charged Robert Miller for "Carriage of Flaxseed to Phila. and goods back." Montgomery oversaw the Cumberland County interests of Philadelphia merchants Adam Hoops and James Fullton and of John Smith, merchant in Baltimore Town, paying taxes, collecting rents, keeping their Carlisle property in repair, and marketing their share of the tenants' crops on their plantations. Carlisle was still a frontier crossroads. John Boyd, who bought a "sett of Philadelphia china cups & saucers" and a "China pint bowl," settled his account with 397 pounds of fall deerskins. Joseph Spear, the Indian trader, sent furs to Philadelphia through Montgomery. The town was also a center for education. John Creigh, schoolmaster, was paid for schooling Montgomery's young daughters and charged for a copy of John Dickinson's *Letters of a Pennsylvania Farmer*. He also paid the Reverend John Steel for schooling his son Sammy and his nephew John Smith Jr. By 1773 the minister's school had become the Carlisle Grammar School, with John Montgomery as one of the original members of its board of trustees.[87] Mortgages of land on Shermans Creek to John Montgomery, merchant and shopkeeper of Carlisle, indicate his widespread custom.[88] He was also a man of influence in high places. John Wilkins complained that "Mr. MtGomery" had been able to obtain a lot on the square in Carlisle reserved for the proprietor, "although he had conveniant Lotts and houses in town," by using his connections in Philadelphia.[89] His political influence survived the American Revolution, and he served in the Pennsylvania Assembly in 1781–1782 and in the United States Congress in 1783.[90]

William Spear obtained a license to keep a tavern in Carlisle in 1756. The Spears came from Ulster with the Smiths and Sterretts and settled in Donegal Township. William Spear was assessed for land and an indentured servant there in 1750–1755.[91] He owned Lots 189 and 197 in the original distribution of Carlisle lots and, as William Spear of Baltimore, merchant, sold both in 1774 to his brother Joseph Spear Esq. of Carlisle. Joseph Spear was an Indian trader in 1763 and probably earlier. He sold Lot 189 a month later to John Wilkins of Carlisle, merchant.[92]

Wilkins, also a migrant from Donegal Township, was the grandson of a Welsh-born Indian trader and of a pioneer farmer from Ulster. He was born in Donegal Township and "educated in the principles of the Presbyterian church." In 1763 he sold his land and moved with his family to Carlisle, where he "entered into the line of Tavern and Store keeping, [and] continued the Store to the commencement of the Revolution." He also had a lumber yard and subscribed five thousand feet of dry pine plank toward building the stone Presbyterian church at Carlisle. ("I was the second subscriber and had the second choice of seats in the church. Mr. [John] Montgomery only higher, he subscribed £30.") In addition to an autobiography, Wilkins left correspondence with Randle and John Mitchell, Philadelphia merchants, giving a glimpse into his business operations between 1770 and 1775. He sent his own wagon with skins, iron, flaxseed, and hemp to Philadelphia once a month and ordered the usual variety of store goods, from cloth and boys' hats to scythes, rum, chocolate, and raisins. Wilkins himself went to the city on occasion to select a larger assortment of dry goods. Captain Robert Callender sent deerskins and fisher and fox pelts to the Mitchells in part payment for a large debt he owed Wilkins. Wilkins shipped furs on his own account to Robert Tuckness, a Quaker merchant long associated with Jeremiah Warder. The Wilkins store, like most in Carlisle, was a large room on the ground floor of his house. When William and John Holmes took over the business in 1775, Wilkins "Rented them my Shopp End of the house—the half of the Sellar and back Store house—the other End of the house and all up Stears I Reserve for my use togather with the Garden & Back buildings."[93]

John Fulton, younger son of Samuel Fulton of Donegal Township, whose house has been restored at the Ulster American Folk Park, was another early Carlisle tavern keeper. He moved to York in 1770.[94]

As early as 1757, William West, merchant of Philadelphia, sold Lot 108 on North High Street in Carlisle for a nominal sum to Francis West, merchant of Carlisle.[95] Other deeds shed light on Carlisle merchants' Philadelphia connections. Andrew Greer, Carlisle shopkeeper, mortgaged Lot 196 on North High Street to Daniel Clark, merchant of Philadelphia; and John Woods, shopkeeper of Carlisle, mortgaged his property to William Gough of Philadelphia, both to secure payment of money and goods advanced them.[96] John Glen, merchant of Carlisle, mortgaged land to cover book debts to John and Lambert Cadwalader, Philadelphia merchants, in 1767.[97]

They were not the only ones to "keep Shops and Public Houses" in Carlisle. James Fulton, another Philadelphia merchant, supplied ten wholesale customers in Carlisle with rum, wine, sugar, coffee, tea, and numerous other articles in 1760–1763. His ledgers show accounts with John Agnew, Captain Robert Callender, John Fulton, Robert Hanna, Robert Miller, John Montgomery Esq., James Parker, James Pollock, Joseph Spear, and John Trindle.[98]

Searching for Community

Thomas Penn's original plan for Carlisle provided for a central diamond where Hanover and High streets intersected, with a courthouse and market house on one side and lots set aside for Anglican and Presbyterian churches on the other. Two and a half centuries later, the market house is long gone, but a modern courthouse complex looks across the central square at eighteenth-century Presbyterian and Episcopal churches. Lots close to the square were at a premium and, as John Wilkins contended, granted only to those men with influence in Philadelphia. John Montgomery, John Smith, and William Buchanan owned the first three lots on High Street, adjoining the Presbyterian church on the square. Across the street, Francis West, John Smith, William West, and John Montgomery were the lot owners. On the other side of the square, adjoining the market house and the English church, Stephen Duncan, William Lyon, and William Spear owned the lots on High Street nearest the square. Captain Robert Callender and John Welsh owned the lots on Hanover Street adjacent to the courthouse and market house. Adam Hoops had the lot on the opposite side of the square facing the English church on Hanover Street. John Kinkead and John McKnight owned nearby lots on Hanover Street. Carlisle's most desirable building lots, in other words, went to the town's most prominent merchants and traders.

Carlisle's merchants were the recognized leaders of the community. Voters chose William West as their representative in the Pennsylvania Assembly in 1756 and sent John Smith there in 1759. John Montgomery represented the county continuously from 1763 through 1775. He also served as county treasurer from 1767 through 1776. Francis West, William's brother, and John and William Smith, both brothers-in-law of William Buchanan, were named justices of the county court in 1757.

Slaveholding was a mark of status in backcountry Pennsylvania, where the more genteel families owned one or more domestic servants. In 1769 John Kinkead, William Lyon Esq., and Joseph Spear were each taxed for one Negro and John Montgomery Esq. for two Negroes.[99]

These men took the lead in changing Carlisle from a frontier outpost to "a handsomely improved place." As Gregory Nobles observed, "Elites sought to shape the frontier to fit their social vision and economic interests." They provided important lines of social, economic, and political connection with the cultural centers of eastern Pennsylvania and the British Isles.[100]

As Carlisle became the commercial capital of the Scotch-Irish communities west of the Susquehanna, it also rapidly emerged as the cultural and intellectual capital. In 1765 George Croghan, Robert Callender, and Thomas Smallman petitioned for a lottery to build an Episcopal church on the square in Carlisle, where land was already set aside.[101] But Carlisle would be emphatically a Presbyterian community, reflecting the Scotch-Irish leadership of the town. William Buchanan and John Smith left Carlisle for Baltimore in 1760, but they continued to take an interest in the Presbyterian church there, as Adam Hoops did. The two Baltimore merchants were listed as managers of the Carlisle Presbyterian Church lottery in 1761, together with William Spear and John Montgomery of Carlisle.[102] The interest was reciprocal. Colonel John Armstrong of Carlisle joined Buchanan and Smith and four other Baltimore Presbyterians as managers of a lottery to build a church there.[103] Construction of the stone Presbyterian church on the square began in 1765, although it was not finished for several years.[104] John Montgomery paid carpenter James Ramsey in 1765 for "work done at ye Meeting house."[105] From 1773, the Presbyterian congregation sponsored the Carlisle Grammar School. John Armstrong and John Montgomery, both natives of Ulster, were the original trustees.[106] In 1782, Carlisle merchant and politician John Montgomery, assisted and inspired by his friend Dr. Benjamin Rush of Philadelphia, began to lobby the Pennsylvania legislature for the establishment of a Presbyterian college at Carlisle. It began the next year as Dickinson College.[107]

The merchants and shopkeepers of little Carlisle, as we have seen, were important links in the complex web of credit and goods that stretched through Baltimore and Philadelphia to Belfast and London and, in the other direction, to backcountry farms and Indian villages as far away as the Illinois Country. They brought their town and its rural hinterlands into the Atlantic world and the expanding consumer revolution and at the same time the intellectual currents that flowed through this British Atlantic world. It all came together when John Boyd came to John Montgomery's store in Carlisle to order an elaborate tea set from Philadelphia, perhaps originally from Britain, Holland, or China, and paid for it with 397 deerskins carried by packhorse from the Ohio Country or when schoolmaster John Creigh bought a copy of John Dickinson's *Letters of a Pennsylvania Farmer,* arguing the rights of British Americans.[108]

Notes

1. The "new town on Juniata," a tributary of the Susquehanna, was probably Bedford, then in Cumberland County. "Anglus Americanus," *Pennsylvania Chronicle,* March 27, 1769.

2. Thomas M. Doerflinger, *A Vigorous Spirit of Enterprise: Merchants and Economic Development in Revolutionary Philadelphia* (Chapel Hill: University of North Carolina Press, 1986), 76; William M. Swaim, "The Evolution of Ten Pre-1745 Presbyterian Societies in the Cumberland Valley," *Cumberland County History* 2 (Summer 1985): 3–30.

3. The problem was the Susquehanna River. Anyone in Britain looking at a map of Pennsylvania, like that made by Lewis Evans in 1749, would see a broad river flowing near the frontiers of the colony and emptying into Chesapeake Bay. Since it reached through its tributaries deep into New York and the western and southern parts of Pennsylvania, one might assume it would be a highway for the commerce of the interior. But that was not the case. As geographer Evans noted in 1753, in all the settled parts of the province the Susquehanna was "full of Falls which are all passable downwards by Rafts in Freshes," when heavy rains or melting snow brought the river to flood stage, "except one by great CONEWAGA mouth," near the Donegal settlement, which was always impassable. As a result, "there is no Navigation on this River, nor is the lower parts of it capable of any." Lawrence Henry Gipson, *Lewis Evans* (Philadelphia, 1939), 98. Despite these disadvantages, settlers did use the upper Susquehanna in season. In arguing "the great Advantage it would be to this Province having a Town somewhere on the Communication near the Frontier," specifically on the Juniata "where Fort Bedford is built," William Trent pointed out that "they are now preparing to build Battoes to carry Merchandise from there to John Harris's Ferry on Susquehannah & back." William Trent to William Peters, February 20, 1763, Penn Papers, Add. MSS, 1:110, Historical Society of Pennsylvania, Philadelphia (hereafter cited as HSP).

4. *Pennsylvania Gazette,* March 8, 1775.

5. James T. Lemon, *The Best Poor Man's Country: A Geographical Study of Early Southeastern Pennsylvania* (Baltimore: Johns Hopkins University Press, 1971), 29, 143.

6. Ibid., 133–34.

7. Judith Anne Ridner, "'A Handsomely Improved Place': Economic, Social, and Gender Role Development in a Backcountry Town, Carlisle, Pennsylvania, 1750–1815," PhD diss., College of William and Mary, 1994, 26–27. Ridner, *A Town In-Between: Carlisle, Pennsylvania, and the Early Mid-Atlantic Interior* (Philadelphia: University of Pennsylvania Press, 2010).

8. Indian trade was seen as the lifeblood of the new town. Governor James Hamilton wrote in 1752 that the trading partnership of George Croghan and William Trent "drew a great deal of trade to that part of the country, and made money circulate briskly," but their unexpected bankruptcy "will, I fear, retard the progress of the town." Hamilton to Thomas Penn, June 19, 1752, Penn MSS, Official Correspondence, HSP, V:183, as quoted in Nicholas B. Wainwright, *George Croghan Wilderness Diplomat* (Chapel Hill: University of North Carolina Press, 1959), 45.

9. Ridner, "A Handsomely Improved Place," 55–57. John Armstrong Business Papers, Dickinson College Library, Carlisle, Pa., shed light on his surveying business in the 1760s.

10. Lemon, *Best Poor Man's Country,* 104.

11. L. M. Cullen, "Merchant Communities Overseas, the Navigation Acts and Irish and Scottish Responses," in L. M. Cullen and T. C. Smout, *Comparative Aspects of Scottish and Irish Economic History 1600–1900* (Edinburgh: J. Donald, 1976), 172.

12. John Smail, *Merchants, Market, and Manufacture: The English Wool Textile Industry in the Eighteenth Century* (London: Macmillan, 1999), 2.

13. Doerflinger, *A Vigorous Spirit,* 88–94.

14. Smail, *Merchants, Market, and Manufacture,* 1–3.

15. T. H. Breen, "Narratives of Commercial Life: Consumption, Ideology, and Community on the Eve of the American Revolution," *William and Mary Quarterly,* 3rd ser., vol. 50 (July 1993): 471–501; Cary Carson, Ronald Hoffman, and Peter J. Albert, eds., *Of Consuming Interest: The Style of Life in the Eighteenth Century* (Charlottesville: University Press of Virginia for the United States Capitol Historical Society, 1994).

16. Thomas M. Doerflinger, "Farmers and Dry Goods in the Philadelphia Market Area, 1750–1800," in Ronald Hoffman et al., eds., *The Economy of Early America: The Revolutionary Period, 1763–1790* (Charlottesville: University Press of Virginia for the United States Capitol Historical Society, 1988), 166–95.

17. James Weston Livingood, *The Philadelphia-Baltimore Trade Rivalry, 1780–1860* (Harrisburg, Pa.: Pennsylvania Historical and Museum Commission, 1947), 4–6.

18. As early as 1763, Captain William Trent wrote from Carlisle that "Baltimore in Maryland, a new Town and likely to be a Place of considerable Trade, lays so that what Business they do must go through Bedford." William Trent to William Peters, February 20, 1763, Penn Papers, Add. MSS., HSP, 1:110.

19. LeRoy J. Votto, "Social Dynamism in a Boom Town: The Scots-Irish in Baltimore 1760 to 1790," MA thesis, University of Virginia, 1969, 1–4.

20. A Friend of Trade, "An Address to the Merchants and Inhabitants of Pennsylvania," Library of Congress, Pennsylvania Broadsides, fol. 143, as quoted in Livingood, *Philadelphia-Baltimore Trade Rivalry,* 6.

21. "Philo-Pennsylvaniensis," *Pennsylvania Chronicle,* February 17, 1772.

22. Petition of sundry inhabitants of Middleton and Allen Townships, January 1771, Road Petitions, Cumberland County Courthouse (hereafter cited as CCCH), as quoted in Ridner, "A Handsomely Improved Place," 249.

23. Cumberland County Deeds, CCCH, B-211, C-437, D-402.

24. The idea of a symbiotic relationship was proposed by Jo Hays for the nineteenth century, but it seems valid for the eighteenth as well. Cf. Jo N. Hays, "Overlapping Hinterlands: York, Philadelphia, and Baltimore, 1800–1850," *Pennsylvania Magazine of History and Biography* 116 (July 1992): 295–321.

25. Israel D. Rupp, *History and Topography of Dauphin, Cumberland, Perry, Bedford, Adams and Franklin* Counties (Lancaster, Pa.: Gilbert Hills, 1846), 382, 388.

26. D. W. Thompson, ed., *Two Hundred Years in Cumberland County* (Carlisle: Cumberland County Historical Society, 1951), 35.

27. Smith Family Genealogy, Tray 179, Smith-Carter Papers, Alderman Library, University of Virginia, Charlottesville.

28. Conrad Weiser to Governor James Hamilton, September 13, 1754, *Colonial Records* (Harrisburg and Philadelphia: State of Pennsylvania, 1838–1852), VI: 149; Charles A. Hanna, *The Wilderness Trail* (New York: G. P. Putnam, 1886), 176.

29. Ridner, "A Handsomely Improved Place," 248–50; Jerome Wood Jr., *Conestoga Crossroads: Lancaster, Pennsylvania, 1730–1790* (Harrisburg: Pennsylvania Historical and Museum Commission, 1979), 98–99.

30. Ridner, "A Handsomely Improved Place," 259.

31. Cumberland County Deeds, CCCH, 1-D-320; Merri Lou Scribner Schaumann, *A History and Genealogy of Carlisle, Cumberland County, Pennsylvania, 1751–1835,* (Dover, Pa.: the author, 1987).

32. Nicholas B. Wainwright, "An Indian Trade Failure: The Story of the Hockley, Trent and Croghan Company, 1748–1752," *Pennsylvania Magazine of History and Biography* 72 (October 1948): 344.

33. Ridner, "A Handsomely Improved Place," 256 citing Gratz Papers, HSP, case 14, box 19.

34. Among other mortgages to Mitchells and Lowerys, see Lancaster Deeds, NN-1–634. Lancaster County Courthouse (hereafter cited as LCCH).

35. *Pennsylvania Gazette,* December 10, 1771.

36. Jay Robert Stiefel, "Philadelphia Cabinetmaking and Commerce, 1718–1753: The Account Book of John Head, Joiner," *American Philosophical Society Library Bulletin* 1 (2001).

37. Robert D. Mitchell, "The Upper Shenandoah Valley of Virginia during the Eighteenth Century: A Study in Historical Geography," PhD diss., University of Wisconsin, 1969, 331.

38. Albert T. Volwiler, *George Croghan and the Westward Movement, 1741–1782* (Cleveland, Ohio: Arthur H. Clark, 1926), 41–42, 78–79; Wainwright, *George Croghan,* 29.

39. George E. Lewis, *The Indiana Company: A Study in Eighteenth Century Frontier Land Speculation and Business Venture* (Glendale, Calif.: Arthur H. Clark, 1970), 28–29.

40. Buchanan and Hughes were general merchants and accepted "merchantable Flour, Wheat, Hemp, &c." as payment at their Baltimore store. They announced the imminent dissolution of their partnership in 1763, but Buchanan and Daniel and Samuel Hughes, sons of Barnabas, advertised as his surviving partners for payment of debts due to Buchanan and Hughes and the Antietam Company in 1765. Hughes had diversified his interests to include ironworks in western Maryland. The major creditors of his estate were William Smith and James Sterrett, Baltimore merchants who had moved to Maryland from Donegal Township, Lancaster County, in 1761. Typical of the family ties that forged commercial ones, William Smith was married to William Buchanan's sister. *Pennsylvania Journal,* October 30, 1760; *Maryland Gazette,* January 21, 1762, March 3, 1763, February 21, 1765; Baltimore County Inventories, Maryland Hall of Records, Annapolis, 89:159-63.

41. Harris to Buchanan and Hughes, June 21, 1762, as quoted in Wainwright, *George Croghan,* 190–91.

42. "An Account of Losses sustained by William Buchanan, Barnabas Hughes & Thomas Smallman in Sundry Adventures of Trade to the Indian Countries by Indian Hostilities in the Year 1763," HSP, AM-2229.

43. Spear revoked the power-of-attorney in 1768. Cumberland County Deeds, CCCH, B-282.

44. Ridner, "A Handsomely Improved Place," 259–62. On Carlisle's role in the fur trade in the 1760s, see also Judith Ridner, "Relying on the 'Saucy Men' of the Backcountry: Middlemen and the Fur Trade in Pennsylvania," *Pennsylvania Magazine of History and Biography* 129 (April 2005): 133–62.

45. Cumberland County Deeds, CCCH, B-72, B-146, B-208, B-211, B-245, C-113, C-302, C-327, C-333, C-363, C-437, C-450, D-402.

46. Cumberland County Deeds, CCCH, 2A-128.

47. Volwiler, *George Croghan,* 92–94.

48. Ridner, "A Handsomely Improved Place," 91.

49. John Richard Alden, *General Gage in America* (Baton Rouge: Louisiana State University Press, 1948), 24–26. Governor Morris was outraged at the idea that "all that extensive and Rich Country which lies West of the Sasquehannah be abandoned and laid waste." Robert L. D. Davidson, *War Comes to Quaker Pennsylvania, 1682–1756* (New York: Columbia University Press for Temple University Publications, 1957), 150–51; Francis Jennings, *Empire of Fortune: Crowns, Colonies, and Tribes in the Seven Years War in America* (New York: W. W. Norton, 1988), 159.

50. William Buchanan to William Franklin, HSP, July 21, 1755.

51. William A. Hunter, *Forts on the Pennsylvania Frontier, 1753–1758* (Harrisburg: Pennsylvania Historical and Museum Commission, 1960), 171.

52. Ibid., 177. See also Jane T. Merritt, *At the Crossroads: Indians and Empires on a Mid-Atlantic Frontier, 1700–1763* (Chapel Hill: University of North Carolina Press, 2003), 176–81.

53. Hunter, *Forts on the Pennsylvania Frontier,* 200–202, 441, 447. Adam Hoops, a justice of Cumberland County, resided in present Franklin County, Pa. The career of this self-made man is sketched in Priscilla H. Roberts and James N. Tull, *Adam Hoops, Thomas*

Richard K. MacMaster

Barclay, and the House in Morrisville Known as Summerseat, 1764–1791, Transactions of the American Philosophical Society Held at Philadelphia for Promoting Useful Knowledge, Volume 90, Pt. 5 (Philadelphia: American Philosophical Society, 2000), 4–32.

54. Hunter, *Forts on the Pennsylvania Frontier,* 432; Pennsylvania Gazette, October 7, 1756. Armstrong provided detachments the following year "covering the People on this Frontier during the whole of their Harvest." *Pennsylvania Gazette,* October 13, 1757; see also Fred Anderson, *Crucible of War: The Seven Years' War and the Fate of Empire in British North America, 1754–1766* (New York: Alfred A. Knopf, 2000), 163–64.

55. Hunter, *Forts on the Pennsylvania Frontier,* 446–49.

56. Sylvester K. Stevens, ed., *The Papers of Henry Bouquet* (Harrisburg: Pennsylvania Historical and Museum Commission, 1951), vol. 2:31–32.

57. Roberts and Tull, *Adam Hoops,* 11–15.

58. Alfred P. James, ed., *Writings of General John Forbes Relating to his Service in North America* (Menasha, Wis.: Collegiate Press, 1938), 97–111, 178.

59. Ibid., 262.

60. Donald H. Kent, ed., *The Papers of Henry Bouquet* (Harrisburg: Pennsylvania Historical and Museum Commission, 1976), vol. 2:112–13, 289–91, 293–95, 429.

61. *Pennsylvania Gazette,* February 19, 1761.

62. This is one of the themes developed in David Hancock, *Citizens of the World: London Merchants and the Integration of the British Atlantic Community, 1735–1785* (Cambridge, U.K.: Cambridge University Press, 1995).

63. Clark's wife was Jane Hoops. Roberts and Tull, *Adam Hoops,* 17–22; Daniel Clark Letterbook, 1759–1761, HSP.

64. *Pennsylvania Gazette,* October 22, 1761; *Pennsylvania Journal,* November 15, 1763, June 14, 1764.

65. Roberts and Tull, *Adam Hoops,* 28.

66. Ridner, "A Handsomely Improved Place," 255, 59; Judith Ridner, "William Irvine and the Complexities of Manhood and Fatherhood in the Pennsylvania Backcountry," *Pennsylvania Magazine of History and Biography* 125 (January 2001): 15–17.

67. *Pennsylvania Journal,* October 3, 1765.

68. Howard H. Peckham, *Pontiac and the Indian Uprising* (Princeton, N.J.: Princeton University Press, 1947), 37ff.; Niles Anderson, *The Battle of Bushy Run* (Harrisburg: Pennsylvania Historical and Museum Commission, 1966), 5–6.

69. Croghan estimated two thousand killed or captured by Indians and thousands "drove to beggary." Wainwright, *George Croghan,* 199; Volwiler, *George Croghan,* 265–66.

70. Bitter memories of the war years prompted men of Cumberland County to block the shipment of guns and ammunition to the western tribes by the Philadelphia firm of Baynton, Wharton, and Morgan. The thinly disguised "Black Boys" captured a packhorse train at Sideling Hill and destroyed all of the trade goods. Volwiler, *George Croghan,* 178–80.

71. *History of Cumberland County, Pennsylvania* (Chicago: Beers, 1886), 257–61.

72. *Pennsylvania Gazette,* July 19, 1764; I. H. McCauley, *Historical Sketch of Franklin County* (Chambersburg, Pa.: D. F. Pursel, 1878), 9, 22.

73. John Gibson, ed., *History of York County, Pennsylvania* (Chicago: Beers, 1886), 574–75, 592.

74. Cumberland County Deeds, CCCH, C-399, C-436.

75. McAllister's 1771–1781 records were kept in a ledger stamped "Paul Zantzinger, Lancaster," so they were erroneously catalogued as Zantinger's in MG 2, Pennsylvania State Archives, Harrisburg.

76. Ridner, "A Handsomely Improved Place," 92.

77. The eight merchants were John Smith, John Montgomery, Francis West, Thomas Donnellan, William Spear, Stephen Duncan, Abraham Holmes, and William Lyon. John Vanlear, Elizabeth Ross, John Kinkead, Andrew Greer, and John McKnight were listed as shopkeepers. The traders, Robert Callender, Adam Hoops, and John Welsh, were among the wealthiest. Tax list in Schaumann, *History,* 174–75.

78. Conrad Bucher, a Swiss officer stationed at Carlisle, began holding Reformed services in German in 1763 and later made it his headquarters as a missionary pastor for a widely scattered flock. William J. Hinke, *Ministers of the German Reformed Congregations in Pennsylvania and Other Colonies in the Eighteenth Century* (Lancaster, Pa.: Evangelical and Reformed Historical Society, 1951), 138–43.

79. Stephen Duncan, Thomas Donnellan, William Spear, and Francis West, merchants, and Andrew Grier, John Montgomery, and Elizabeth Ross, shopkeepers. Tax List in Schaumann, *History,* 173–74.

80. Lyon's business records from 1759 are at the Cumberland County Historical Society, Carlisle, Pa.

81. *Pennsylvania Gazette,* February 11, 1752.

82. The Buchanans also owned Lot 117 from 1759 and sold it the following year. Schaumann, *History,* 196.

83. Robert Callender and Michael Taaffe to William Buchanan, September 2, 1753, *Colonial Records,* V:684.

84. Schaumann, *History,* 199. Smith had already built on Lot 125 on Market Street facing the central square by May 1751 (Ridner, *A Town In-Between,* 34).

85. Richard Peters to Thomas Penn, November 17, 1742, as quoted in Russell Sage Nelson Jr., "Backcountry Pennsylvania (1709–1774): The Ideals of William Penn in Practice," PhD diss., University of Wisconsin, 1968, 265–66.

86. Cumberland County Deeds, CCCH, B-45, C-304; "Smith Family Genealogy," 1729/179, Special Collections, Alderman Library, University of Virginia, Charlottesville.

87. John Montgomery, "Leger 3 1765–1771," Joseph Kent Collection, MS 092-31. Virginia Polytechnic Institute and University, Blacksburg; On the Grammar School, Schaumann, *History,* 213.

88. Cumberland County Deeds, CCCH, B-45, C-304.

89. John Wilkins to John Mitchell, June 2, 1772, Mitchell Papers, MG 92, Pennsylvania State Archives.

90. Schaumann, *History,* 214.

91. Richard K. MacMaster, *Donegal Presbyterians: A Scots-Irish Congregation in Pennsylvania* (Morgantown, Pa.: Donegal Society, 1995), 8, 41–43.

92. William Spear's tavern was probably on Lot 189. Joseph Spear lived on the other property at his death in 1781. Schaumann, *History,* 218; Lewis, *Indiana Company,* 45, 297–98.

93. John Wilkins to John Mitchell, October 13, 1772, June 14, 1774, July 20, 1774, April 3, 1775, Sequestered John Mitchell Papers, MG92, Pennsylvania State Archives, Harrisburg. Wilkins' autobiography, written in 1807, is in D. W. Thompson, *Two Hundred Years of Cumberland County* (Carlisle, Pa.: Cumberland County Historical Society, 1951), 54–58.

94. *Pennsylvania Gazette,* April 5, 1770.

95. Cumberland County Deeds, 2A-81.

96. Cumberland County Deeds, CCCH, 2A-102 (1761), 2A-128 (1762).

97. Cumberland County Deeds, CCCH, B-182.

98. James Fullton Papers, Historical Society of York County, York, Pennsylvania; see Richard K. MacMaster, "James Fullton: A Philadelphia Merchant and his Customers," *Familia* 17 (2001), 23–34.

99. Tax List in Schaumann, *History,* 174–77.

100. Gregory Nobles, "Breaking into the Backcountry: New Approaches to the Early American Frontier, 1750–1800," *William and Mary Quarterly,* 3rd ser., vol. 46 (October 1989): 642.

101. Volwiler, *George Croghan,* 24.

102. *Pennsylvania Gazette,* July 2, 1761.

103. *Maryland Gazette,* July 9, 1761.

104. Allan D. Thompson, *The Meeting House on the Square: Historical Sketch of the First Presbyterian Church of Carlisle, Pennsylvania* (Carlisle: First Presbyterian Church, 1964), 30–31.

105. Montgomery, "Leger No. 3," 84.

106. Schaumann, *History,* 213.

107. Ridner, "A Handsomely Improved Place," 398.

108. Montgomery, "Leger No. 3," 135, 158.

Searching for Peace and Prosperity: Opequon Settlement, Virginia, 1730s–1760s

Warren R. Hofstra

Winter was spreading its hoary frosts and deep, cold silences across the Shenandoah Valley late in 1731 when a party of sixteen families—perhaps one hundred men, women, and children—arrived at the Opequon Creek in the marchlands of Virginia's Shenandoah Valley. They were a mixed lot—young, old; German, Scots-Irish; seasoned pioneers and fresh arrivals off immigrant ships.[1] Most prominent and numerous among the Scots-Irish families were the Glasses. By family legend, they had only recently departed Banbridge, County Down, where patriarch Samuel Glass had supported this large family in the weavers' trade. With him were his wife, Mary Gamble; sons John, David, Robert, and Joseph; daughters Sarah and Elizabeth; and their spouses and children.[2]

This Ulster clan had followed Jost Hite from Pennsylvania to the settlement that took its name from the Opequon Creek. Hite was a German from the Kraichgau region of the upper Rhineland who had joined a band of German refugees from the continental wars in 1709. The charitable Queen Anne subsequently sent him and hundreds like him to labor in the wilds of New York at a Royal Navy tar works. Soon gaining his independence and later a Pennsylvania farm, this adventurer jumped at the offer of the Virginia government in the early 1730s for large grants of land west of the Blue Ridge to those who would organize a migration to this isolated region.[3]

Through Hite, Glass acquired nine hundred acres of some of the best-watered limestone land in the Shenandoah Valley. Combined with additional tracts obtained by sons and sons-in-law, this land provided a patrimony for generations of the family in the backcountry of Virginia. In all, the Glass kin group comprised eleven families. Each settled within a few miles of Samuel. Interlaced among them were various German, English, and Anglo-Virginia pioneers. By 1735 this larger group had engrossed close to thirty tracts of land.

An open-country neighborhood would eventually grow to incorporate sixty-four parcels covering about thirty-five square miles and including twenty-five Scots-Irish, thirteen German, and twenty-six English or Anglo-Virginia families with landholdings averaging three hundred and fifty acres. The settlement of Hite and Glass was one of about twelve similar open-country neighborhoods dispersed over a large region extending sixty miles south of the Potomac River in the Shenandoah Valley. Collectively, Pennsylvanians called this the "opickin Settlement" (see map 5.1).[4]

Isolation, dispersal, ethnic diversity, and mixed agriculture characterized Opequon. According to Hite, Opequon was "so far distant from any Settlment" that settlers "could scarcely procure any one thing necessary nearer than from Pennsylvania or Fredericksburg (which was near two hundred miles distant) and to which for the greatest and most difficult parts of the Way they were obliged to make roads." Between the northern Shenandoah Valley and the Susquehanna frontier lay a vast stretch of land unoccupied by Europeans, while the Blue Ridge and forty to fifty miles separated Opequon from Virginia's westward-advancing plantation frontier. Once in the Valley, however, Europeans "scattered for the Benefit of the best Lands," as one Virginia governor put it. Hite himself explained: "nothing but a prefference to the choice lands, would tempt men to become adventurers." Settlers clustered around springs or water courses. Miles of open space often separated neighborhoods. No towns organized this space, and even crossroad communities served few central-place functions. Thus Opequon emerged as a classic example of a dispersed, ethnically diverse settlement.[5]

Everyone farmed. A sample of twelve estates among the Scots-Irish families inventoried for probate between 1749 and 1768 reveals the diversity of farm activity. Most of these immigrant families had a full complement of livestock consisting of cattle, horses, swine, and sheep. Field crops included rye, oats, barley, and corn, but wheat was the most common. Nearly every Scots-Irish family at Opequon produced yarns or textiles of linen or wool. The efforts of James Vance to provide for his family present an excellent example of how varied life was on a pioneer farm. Livestock constituted 32 percent of his inventoried wealth, and stocks of barley, oats, wheat, rye, hay, and "Ingin Corn" another 13 percent. Hemp and flax also grew in his fields, and the tools necessary to transform them into cloth such as cards, spools, wheels, and pounding tubs filled his house. An excess of twenty pounds due his estate as book debts or notes of hand and about half that in other obligations to be paid indicates that the Vance family made up in trade with neighbors for whatever they lacked.[6]

Warren R. Hofstra

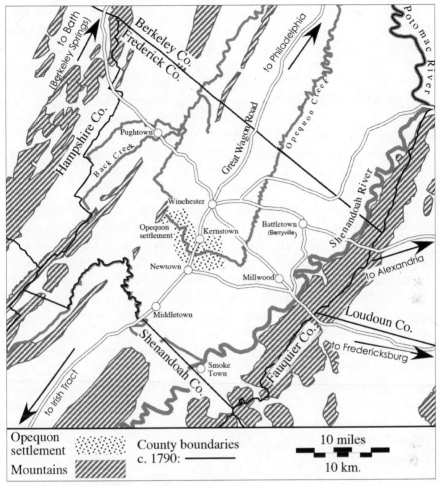

Map 5.1. *The Opequon settlement, 1730s to 1760s.*

What is missing on the Vance farm and from the family's circle of kin and neighbors were the slaves and tobacco that had defined life in Virginia for more than a century. Whereas plantation culture, Anglo-American conformity, and the Anglican communion characterized Old Virginia; mixed farming, ethnic diversity, and religious pluralism had sprung up west of the Blue Ridge. Explaining why two so vastly different ways of life divided the colony along this ridge illuminates the meaning of peace and prosperity for the Scots-Irish of the Opequon settlement.

Scots-Irish folklore has long claimed that Ulster immigrants were rest-less strivers after wild space and unrestrained opportunity on the American frontier. They were people on the go, on the make, and always on the edge of settlement. Mobile, ambitious, and ungovernable, these people presum-ably would have eventually pushed into the Shenandoah Valley in a relentless quest for land. But the fact that they leapfrogged over miles of excellent prop-erty on their way to a colony in which a powerful planter elite had always coveted land for its own benefit belies this image. The forces motivating Ul-ster men and women to make a life in the Virginia backcountry were much larger than their own volition would indicate. These were the forces un-leashed by imperial conflict, Native American warfare, colonial expansion, and African enslavement that were reshaping the entire Atlantic world in the eighteenth century.[7]

By the late 1720s and early 1730s, there were a number of reasons why English authorities in London and Williamsburg wanted Virginia's frontiers occupied by just such Protestant yeoman farmers as the Scots-Irish and Ger-mans. Leaders in these imperial capitals were acutely aware of France's grow-ing power throughout a broad arc of inland settlements connecting Canada to Louisiana along the Ohio and Mississippi rivers. Fears of French encircle-ment came to shape the expansionist policies of these men. The extension of English-sponsored settlement into contested interior territories would also secure a region destabilized by Indian conflicts. Although the Shenandoah Valley served as a home for only small, scattered groups of Native Americans during the first half of the eighteenth century, the constant and sizeable movement of native peoples through this area connecting northern centers of Iroquois power with Cherokee, Catawba, and Creek towns in the south provided persistent provocation for violence with Virginia Indians and fron-tiersmen. "As our Frontier Inhabitants lye at the same time exposed to the barbarous Insults of these Indians, and the foreign Nations they call in to their aid," observed one Virginia governor, "this in all probability will involve us in continual Skirmishes & Alarms."[8]

Other tensions argued for organized backcountry settlement. Through-out much of the first half of the eighteenth century, Virginia struggled with Thomas, Lord Fairfax, Proprietor of the Northern Neck, over conflicting claims to land northwest of the Blue Ridge. Nationality aside, settlers in the region holding Crown grants would help secure it to Virginia, not Fairfax. A similar rationale justified the settlement of the region by non-plantation peoples. Due to an ample supply of indentured servants, Virginia's tobacco

Warren R. Hofstra

economy had created only a modest demand for slaves in the seventeenth century. Declining numbers of available servants, a huge expansion of the British-led African slave trade, and a sharp increase in the European craving for tobacco during the early eighteenth century led to a burgeoning slave population in eastern Virginia. Fears of slave rebellion gripped many planters, while hopes for freedom impelled several parties of runaways to seek maroon havens in the mountains. Allowing plantation society to overspread the valleys would only increase the danger.[9]

All of these forces and fears were on the mind of William Gooch as he assumed the powers of colonial governor in 1727. The London-based Board of Trade, the British advisory body on colonial affairs to whom Gooch owed his authority, had only a few years earlier called publicly for "making ourselves considerable at the two heads of your Majesty's Colonies north and south; and by building of forts, as the French have done, in proper places on the inland frontiers." Worried that the Appalachian Mountains would become a barrier to imperial expansion, the board also proclaimed that "British settlements might be extended beyond them and some small forts be erected on ye great lakes."[10]

Thus between 1730 and 1732, Governor Gooch and the Virginia Council issued nine grants totaling 385,000 acres for lands west of the Blue Ridge. Conditions in these grants, which went to Jost Hite and others, were designed to implement the policies of the Board of Trade at the same time they addressed the issues confronting Virginia. Orders for up to one hundred thousand acres obligated grantees to recruit and settle one family per every one thousand acres within two years. Because all these grantees with one exception were men from northern, non-plantation colonies, colonial authorities were well aware that they were touching off a migration of yeoman farmers to the Virginia frontier. As Jost Hite promised, "Families to the number of one hundred are desirous to remove from thence [Pennsylvania] & seat themselves on the back of the great Mountains." More than 160 patents either issued or pending by 1735 indicated that at least 800 people were living and developing farms where few Europeans had been only four years previously. That all these men, women, and children served the interests of imperial expansion and colonial security in a western buffer against the French, the Indians, Lord Fairfax, and black maroons was made clear by Gooch when he boasted to "your Lordships [about] how soon that part of Virginia on the other side of the great Mountains may be Peopled, if proper Encouragements for that Purpose were given . . . for by this means a strong

Barrier will be Settled between us and the French . . . and thereby so much weaken the Power of the French as to have little to fear from that Quarter hereafter."[11]

Just as London authorities had planted Scottish and European Protestants in the north of Ireland during the seventeenth century to secure England from the threat of Catholic power and the "barbaric" Irish, their eighteenth-century counterparts organized the plantation of western Virginia by Ulster and German farmers to shield the colony from multiple threats by both French Catholics and various "heathen" peoples. Because their interests in acquiring land coincided with imperial purposes for granting land, families such as the Glasses and Hites led the western migration. Their security and independence relied upon peaceful coexistence with all peoples; but lying behind the strategic interests they served, ironically lurked the violence of colonial conflict.

The first quarter century of developing farms, families, and communities in the Virginia backcountry was undisturbed by warfare. Only a few exceptions—"dangers" in 1736, twelve deaths due to misunderstandings with Native Americans in 1738, and a 1742 skirmish that cost the lives of more than twenty Indians and whites—broke the peace. And significantly in each case the threat of wider warfare was squelched by careful negotiation across cultures. In contrast to a popular culture of frontier violence in America today, the memory of the Shenandoah Valley frontier that survived into the nineteenth century stressed peace and accommodation. "Tradition informs us, and the oral statements of several aged individuals of respectable character confirm the fact," wrote one of the region's first historians in the 1830s, "that the Indians and white people resided in the same neighborhood for several years after the first settlement commenced, and that the Indians were entirely peaceable and friendly." The long period of peace, furthermore, had allowed the settlement generation the "opportunity of acquiring considerable strength as to numbers, and the accumulation of considerable property and improvements, before Indian hostilities commenced."[12]

Peace and prosperity thus went hand in hand. And land itself meant substantial wealth for a generation of immigrants who, to a family, would have lacked hope for landowner status had they stayed in Europe where feudal tenures and aristocratic supremacy prevailed. The average landholding among the Scots-Irish at Opequon practically equaled the size of an Irish townland, and landowning meant that profits from labor on the land could not be extracted as rent. Anyone could sell, subdivide, or will property for present speculation or as patrimony for future generations. Land also bound family and kin to communities. Within the eleven interrelated families surrounding Samuel Glass, nineteen of twenty-five second-generation marriages were to kinfolk. Nineteen men and women in these first two generations also acquired twenty-five tracts of land totaling more than eight thousand acres, 95 percent of which passed to sons, sons-in-law, or other Opequon kin.[13]

Land to the men and women at Opequon meant the same security that wealth brings today as a hedge against retirement or ill health. Take the case of Elizabeth Vance, wife to James Vance and daughter of Samuel Glass. Not only could she turn to three brothers and a sister for support when her husband died in the 1750s, but she was also allied to every other Scots-Irish family at Opequon. A brother and brother-in-law served as executors of her husband's will in which he further stipulated that the children provide for her as they came of age. Each of these five children married, remained within the community, and received land from their mother when she died in the 1780s. Not wealthy perhaps, the Vances were clearly prosperous people.[14]

William Hoge provides another example of landed prosperity. When he died in 1749, he lived in a single-room cabin with possessions worth only £44, near bottom in the rank order of inventoried wealth at Opequon. Debts against his estate, moreover, exceeded £78. But at age eighty-eight, he had eight children and twenty-nine grandchildren. Land went to each of his five sons and two sons-in-law. A son and grandson served on the county court, and another grandson later sat in the first federal Congress. Hoge, furthermore, was the principal benefactor of the Opequon Presbyterian Church, where grandson John Hoge became the congregation's first regular pastor. What prosperity he lacked in possessions, he made up for in stature and status within his community.[15]

Prosperity derived from land assumed other forms as well at Opequon. Citizens today surrender a portion of their wealth annually as taxes to support institutions such as courts and police forces that provide for security of person and property. At the early Opequon settlement, the nexus of land, family, kin, and congregation not only secured possessions but also life and limb. David Vance, James's brother, served as a justice of the peace during the 1740s and 1750s. Justices settled small claims and resolved other disputes arising in their neighborhoods. By certifying accounts and initiating debt suits, they also protected private property. Their powers included bonding scofflaws to keep the peace or slanderers to keep silent. Vance had the authority of the common law and the county court behind him, but many disputes were resolved informally through other community institutions. When Evan Thomas and William Joliffe, for instance, broke the peace and "suffered

ourselves to be so far overcome with passion & anger which tended to fighting & quarreling with each other," the members of the Hopewell Quaker
Meeting intervened and convinced them "to be more careful & circumspect
in our lives."[16]

The bartering of goods and services out of necessity at Opequon was, in
itself, not a badge of poverty but a sign of the community's prosperity. Today,
wealth means possessing money enough to acquire the necessities of life in
abundance. Much the same can be said about what the exchange economy
accomplished at Opequon. Money was admittedly in short supply. Philip
Windle, for instance, paid Jost Hite for land acquired from him at the rate of
three pounds per one hundred acres not in any currency of the realm but in
the wagon wheels he was skilled in making. When John Russell came to settle with John McCormick for tobacco, handkerchiefs, shoes, shirts, and other
items, he could cite his services in threshing six bushels of wheat, breaking
thirty-three pounds of flax, and mowing for three days. Robert Eadmeston
helped balance his debt to Mary Ross for seven months' board with weaving
twenty-five yards of cloth and making a ladder.[17]

Networks of debt and credit bound Robert Allen firmly into the Scots-
Irish kinship community at Opequon. Allen owned a sizeable tract of land
along the creek about halfway between Samuel Glass and Jost Hite, where he
raised sheep, grew wheat and rye, and distilled liquor. When he died in the
early 1770s, fifty-one individuals were in his debt, most notably David Vance
and Joseph Glass. Also obligated to him, however, were numerous German
neighbors, including Stephen Hotsinpiller. A blacksmith, Hotsinpiller owed
Allen the considerable sum of £10 presumably for whiskey. Others in the
Scots-Irish community, including William Hoge, were indebted for various
sums to Hotsinpiller in turn.[18]

Networks of exchange among all these families—Scots-Irish and German alike—demonstrate how a dense web of economic interdependency
throughout the community made the small surpluses of one household available to others. If wealth today means the ability to shop and consume, the
men and women at Opequon could do their marketing regularly at the "dispersed general store" of their community. Trading a little extra wheat, some
eggs, a sow or a calf, or a day's work at harvest for someone else's corn, wool,
linen, whiskey, or a little blacksmithing or weaving here and there spread the
wealth of the community around. What made this system work were book
accounts. The ability to track what one received from others and recipro-
cated in kind—even if miles, years, or third parties intervened—substituted
for money as the medium of exchange. Single- or double-entry accounting

Warren R. Hofstra

and the logic of recording transactions as debit and credit had evolved since the early Italian Renaissance to order and rationalize commerce throughout the Atlantic world. Whether executed formally in the multiple journals and ledgers of merchants or simply on scraps of paper by neighbors, the system permitted goods and services to flow in the absence of money throughout dispersed communities. If the prosperity of a community is related to the liquidity of exchange—more money in circulation means greater wealth—then Opequon, where keeping book substituted for money, was indeed prosperous. A common sense of the just value of things, moreover, suppressed inflation, and the elasticity of debits and credits insured that wealth was distributed broadly.[19]

Insofar as culture comprises learned behaviors adapted to natural and social environments, then cultural resources are those customary acts or shared ideas that equip a people to thrive and prosper. Flexibility in adjusting to new and unfamiliar conditions would be an important resource for any group developing households and communities on a frontier. This quality among the Scots-Irish at Opequon proved to be a significant source of prosperity. The shift from stone to wood and log for construction is well known as a means for taking advantage of available building materials. Other architectural practices also displayed this type of adaptability. William Hoge's single-room cabin, for instance, served not as an emblem of impoverishment but as a signifier of the inventiveness necessary for making the most out of altered conditions. The single-unit house was fast becoming the most common contemporaneous house type in the north of Ireland as the pressures of population growth diminished the land and resources essential for survival. Under the stress of reduced circumstances, Ulster peoples were constricting living space unit by unit to a multipurpose, one-room dwelling. On the American frontier, the demands of farm building prompted a similar response from a people accustomed to cultural accommodation and creativity. As investments in improving land bore fruit by the end of the eighteenth century, these same people adapted the unit-by-unit approach to housing to add rooms horizontally and vertically within the strictures of Georgian symmetry to produce the classic I-house as a statement of American success and prosperity. The well-ordered I-house then proved a powerful cultural resource in the conquest of trans-Appalachian frontiers.[20]

The long period of peace that brought prosperity to Opequon landowners crashed to a bitter end in 1755. Indian raids that fall terrorized and depopulated the Anglo-American frontier across Pennsylvania and Virginia. The Scots-Irish and other settlers, according to one observer, were "abandoning their Dwellings, and flying with the utmost Precipitation." The destruction of General Edward Braddock's army near the Forks of the Ohio by French and Indian fighters that previous July precipitated the violence, but the French and Indian or Seven Years' War resulted from the larger collision of peoples and the forces of empire in the Ohio Valley. Depopulated in the Iroquois Wars of the eighteenth century, the Ohio Country became the homeland of Shawnees, Delawares, and related groups beginning in the 1720s. Two decades later, settlement schemes impelled by Virginia land speculators with the backing of imperial authorities threatened the lifeways of these Indians as did the expansion of French forces along the Ohio Valley. To Native Americans, the Seven Years' War represented an effort to defend their homes, but to the British and French it was an imperial war of territorial conquest. Ironically, the same strategic forces that had brought Scots-Irish peoples to the Shenandoah Valley in a search for peace and prosperity produced a cataclysmic conflict that threatened all they had achieved in two decades of hard work.[21]

Not surprisingly, the war revealed a conflict of values between its perpetrators and its victims. The precocious George Washington commanded the Virginia Regiment charged with the defense of Virginia frontiers behind a chain of forts. To supply and supplement his regular forces, Washington turned to the people of Opequon. "Had they acted as becometh every good Subject," Washington quipped, they "would have exerted their Utmost abilitys to forward our just designs." The wagons they supplied, however, were "so illy provided with Teams that we could not travel with them without the Soldiers assisting them up the Hills when it was known they had better Teams at home." Worse still, they refused militia duty even in emergencies. From 1755 to 1763, 675 militiamen were charged with 1,330 offenses for refusing to muster under Washington's orders. "You may, with almost equal success, attempt to raize the Dead to Life again, as the force of this Country," Washington grumbled. Their behavior was incredible to him: "I could [not] believe did I not see it, that these are the people of a country whose bowels are at this juncture torn by the most horrid devastations of the most cruel and barbarous enemy."[22]

Concealing precious resources and rejecting service to the Crown, however, was entirely consistent with the way of life the Scots-Irish and others had created on the frontier. As Lord Fairfax's secretary explained to Washington, they "absolutely refus'd to stir, choosing as they say to die with their Wives and Family's." A militia captain ordered "to repair with his Company forthwith to Winchester" was blunter with this commander: "his Wife, Family,

Warren R. Hofstra

and Corn was at stake, so were those of his Soldrs therefore it was not possible for him to come." The imperial interests that Washington represented contradicted their interests in the safety and prosperity of families and communities, which only peace could serve.[23]

Sporadic violence persisted in the Shenandoah Valley until 1765 and the collapse of Indian resistance concluding Pontiac's War. Peace finally and fortunately brought new forms of prosperity to the region. Due partly to imperial wars and partly to population increase and industrialization, wheat prices on the Atlantic market had been rising since the 1740s. The military demand for provisions, moreover, had enlarged the Philadelphia market area to include the Shenandoah Valley by the late 1750s. Thus, when flour prices reached the point one decade later at which returns to farmers exceeded production and shipping costs from inland areas as distant as the Shenandoah Valley, the grain trade in the region took off. Familiarity with wheat cultivation as part of the mix of agricultural activities the Scots-Irish brought to Opequon once again positioned them to take advantage of new sources of commercial profit.[24]

Farm profits, combined with the so-called consumer revolution flooding the late eighteenth-century Atlantic world with British goods, made the decades following the American Revolution remarkably prosperous throughout the old Opequon settlement. Demand in the countryside encouraged the rapid rise of the retail trade in area towns. Rural consumption and urban commerce both boomed during the 1790s and the Napoleonic Wars as American merchants captured the trans-Atlantic shipping trade. Peace, of course, would never be permanent, but war would not darken the prospects of the Shenandoah Valley and subsequent generations of Opequon settlers until the Civil War, when the region was justly known as the breadbasket of the Confederacy and its prosperity so renowned that Union victory could only be achieved by the wholesale burning of its fields, barns, and mills. By 1870, however, Valley farmers were producing more wheat and flour than they had at the outset of the conflict, in testimony to the continuing power of the search for peace and prosperity.[25]

Notes

1. Because the term "Scots-Irish" has no tradition of historical usage, it has been widely adopted in American writing and publishing as a standard that evades partisan association or affiliation. It is for this reason that I employ it in my article.

2. In local historical writing on the European settlement of the Shenandoah Valley, the sixteen families reported to have accompanied Jost Hite have been celebrated as the region's first pioneers. According to Thomas Cartmell, "the first families to settle in the Lower Shenandoah Valley, were generally known as the *sixteen families* who came with Joist Hite." See Thomas K. Cartmell, *Shenandoah Valley Pioneers and Their Descendants: A History of Frederick County, Virginia* (1909; rpt. Bowie, Md.: Heritage Books, 1989), 1. See also Samuel Kercheval, *A History of the Valley of Virginia,* 5th ed. (Strasburg, Va.: Shenandoah Publishing House, 1973), 49. That the Glass family came from Banbridge, County Down, has never been substantiated in the genealogical or documentary record. A number of authors, however, have made this assertion on the strength of tradition and the size of the Glass family in the Banbridge area from the eighteenth century to the present day. See Cartmell, *Shenandoah Valley Pioneers,* 413–16; William H. Foote, *Sketches of Virginia, Historical and Biographical,* 2 vols. (Philadelphia: J. B. Lippincott, 1856), vol. 2:24.

3. Biographical information on Jost Hite can be found in Henry Z. Jones, Ralph Conner, and Klaus Wust, *German Origins of Jost Hite: Virginia Pioneer, 1685–1761* (Edinburg, Va.: Shenandoah History, 1979); Philip Otterness, "The New York Naval Stores Project and the Transformation of the Poor Palatines, 1710–1712," *New York History* 75 (April 1994): 133–56; Otterness, *Becoming German: The 1709 Palatine Migration to New York* (Ithaca and London: Cornell University Press, 2004), 138–39, 145. For documentation on Hite's grant, see H. R. McIlwaine, Wilmer L. Hall, and Benjamin J. Hillman, eds., *Executive Journals of the Council of Colonial Virginia,* 6 vols. (Richmond: Virginia State Library, 1925–1966), vol. 4:253; for additional grants he purchased from the Van Meter family, see *Executive Journals* 4:223–24.

4. Reference to the "opickin Settlement" appears in *Bringhurst v Blackburn,* May 1744, Ended Causes, 1743–1909, Frederick County Court Papers, Library of Virginia, Richmond. Samuel Glass purchased nine hundred acres from Jost Hite in November 1742; see Deed of Hite to Glass, November 26, 1742, Orange County Deeds, Orange County Courthouse, Orange, Va. The eleven families of Samuel Glass's kin group include those of Robert Allen and his wife, Sarah; John Beckett and Sarah Glass; Joseph Colvill and Elizabeth; William Hoge and Barbara Hume; William Marquis and Margaret Colvill; William Reid and Mary Allen; Andrew Vance and Elizabeth Colvill; John Wilson and Mary Marquis; Robert Wilson and Garrata Hoge; and Thomas Wilson and Mary. Conrad Arensberg was the first scholar to describe dispersed frontier farm communities as "open-country neighborhoods"; see "American Communities," *American Anthropologist* 57 (December 1955): 1143–62. William Foote provided the best description of the open-country neighborhood emerging along the drains of the upper Opequon Creek in the 1730s: "Samuel Glass took his residence at the head-spring of the Opecquon. . . . A son-in-law,

Warren R. Hofstra

[John] Becket, was seated between Mr. Glass and North Mountain; his son David took his residence a little below his father, on the Opecquon, at Cherry Mead . . . ; his son Robert was placed a little further down at Long Meadows, now in possession of his grand-son Robert. . . . Next down the creek was Joseph Colvin and family. . . . Then came John Wilson and the Marquis family, with whom he was connected. . . . Next were the M'Auleys, within sight of the church here; and then William Hoge had his residence on that little rising ground near by us to the west. He gave this parcel of land for a burying-ground, a site for a church and a school-house. Adjoining these to the south were the Allen family. . . . A little beyond the village, on the other side of the paved road, lived Robert Wilson. . . . A little further down the stream lived James Vance, son-in-law of Samuel Glass, and ancestor of a numerous race, most of whom are to be found west of the Alleghenies. These were all here as early as 1736, or '37. Other families gathered around these, and on Cedar Creek, charmed with a country abounding with prairie and pea vines, and buffaloe and deer." See Foote, *Sketches of Virginia,* 18–19.

5. *John Hite et al. v Lord Fairfax et al.,* Additional Manuscript 15317, British Museum, London, England, transcript by Hunter Branson McKay, 1521; Robert A. Brock, ed., *The Official Records of Robert Dinwiddie, Lieutenant-Governor of the Colony of Virginia,* 2 vols. (Richmond: Virginia Historical Society, 1883), vol. 1:389; Transcript of the Record in the Case, *Jost Hite and Robert McCoy v Lord Fairfax 1749–,* folio 713, folder 100, Clark-Hite Papers, Filson Historical Society, Louisville, Ky.

6. Inventory of James Vance, February 12, 1752, Frederick County Wills (hereafter FCW), 2:17, Frederick County Courthouse, Winchester, Va. The remaining eleven inventories can be found in FCW 1:428, 487–88; 2:44–45, 125–27, 160–62, 202–4, 311–13, 492–93; 3:28–29, 121, 435.

7. At the time Europeans first occupied the Shenandoah Valley, a variety of environmental and political factors were discouraging the settlement of western Maryland and Pennsylvania, including high land prices, land speculation, the closing of the Pennsylvania land office, and a conflict between the two colonies over rights to land west of the Susquehanna River. See James T. Lemon, *The Best Poor Man's Country: A Geographical Study of Early Southeastern Pennsylvania* (1972; New York: W. W. Norton, 1976), 56–57; John J. McCusker and Russell R. Menard, *The Economy of British America, 1607–1789* (Chapel Hill: University of North Carolina Press, 1985), 202–4; Frank W. Porter III, "From Backcountry to Country: The Delayed Settlement of Western Maryland," *Maryland Historical Magazine* 70 (Winter 1975): 329–49. On the control of planter elites over land granting, see Sarah S. Hughes, *Surveyors and Statesmen: Land Measuring in Colonial Virginia* (Richmond: Virginia Surveyors Foundation and Virginia Association of Surveyors, 1979), 84–85, 107; Turk McCleskey, "Rich Land, Poor Prospects: Real Estate and the Formation of a Social Elite in Augusta County, Virginia, 1738–1770," *Virginia Magazine of History and Biography* 98 (July 1990): 449–86; Charles S. Sydnor, *Gentlemen Freeholders: Political Practices in Washington's Virginia* (Chapel Hill: University of North Carolina Press for the Institute of Early American History and Culture, 1952); Manning C. Voorhis, "Crown Versus Council in the Virginia Land Policy," *William and Mary Quarterly,* 3rd ser., vol. 3 (October 1946): 499–514.

8. William Gooch to Board of Trade, March 26, 1729, C.O. 5/1321, Colonial Office Papers, Public Records Office, London. The struggle among European powers over the North American interior is treated in a variety of works including Charles M. Andrews, *The Colonial Period of American History,* vol. 3, *The Settlements, III* (New Haven, Conn.: Yale University Press, 1937), 235–36; Verner W. Crane, *The Southern Frontier, 1670–1732* (1928; New York: W. W. Norton, 1981), 47–70; W. J. Eccles, *France in America* (East Lansing: Michigan State University Press, 1990), 107–9; Daniel H. Usner Jr., *Indians, Settlers, & Slaves in a Frontier Exchange Economy* (Chapel Hill: University of North Carolina Press for the Institute of Early American History and Culture, 1992); David J. Weber, *The Spanish Frontier in North America* (New Haven, Conn.: Yale University Press, 1992), 147–58. For studies of Native Americans and imperial conflicts, see Richard Aquila, *The Iroquois Restoration: Iroquois Diplomacy on the Colonial Frontier, 1701–1754* (Detroit, Mich: Wayne State University Press, 1983), 205–45; Warren M. Billings, John E. Selby, and Thad W. Tate, *Colonial Virginia: A History* (White Plains, N.Y.: KTO Press, 1986), 175–76; Gregory Evans Dowd, *War under Heaven: Pontiac, the Indian Nations, & the British Empire* (Baltimore: Johns Hopkins University Press, 2002); Eric Hinderaker, *Elusive Empires: Constructing Colonialism in the Ohio Valley, 1673–1800* (New York: Cambridge University Press, 1997); Francis Jennings, *The Ambiguous Iroquois Empire: The Covenant Chain Confederation of Indian Tribes with English Colonies from Its Beginnings to the Lancaster Treaty of 1744* (New York: W. W. Norton, 1984), 210–12; Michael N. McConnell, *A Country Between: The Upper Ohio Valley and Its Peoples, 1724–1774* (Lincoln: University of Nebraska Press, 1992), 15–17; James H. Merrell, *The Indians' New World: Catawbas and Their Neighbors from European Contact through the Era of Removal* (Chapel Hill: University of North Carolina Press for the Institute of Early American History and Culture, 1989), 25, 41–42, 78, 89, 97–98, 113–22, 135–36, 149–67, 244–45; Merrell, *Into the American Woods: Negotiators on the Pennsylvania Frontier* (New York: Norton, 1999); Jane T. Merritt, *At the Crossroads: Indians and Empires on a Mid-Atlantic Frontier, 1700–1763* (Chapel Hill: University of North Carolina Press, 2003); Daniel K. Richter, *The Ordeal of the Longhouse: The Peoples of the Iroquois League in the Era of European Colonization* (Chapel Hill: University of North Carolina Press for the Institute of Early American History and Culture, 1992), 32–38, 236–80; Ian K. Steele, *Warpaths: Invasions of North America* (New York: Oxford University Press, 1994), 148–50, 166–67.

9. Seventeenth-century royal charters had established the Northern Neck Proprietary between the Potomac and Rappahannock rivers and a line connecting their headwaters. By the early 1720s, control over Proprietary land rights had devolved upon Thomas, sixth Lord Fairfax, who claimed that these rights extended across the Blue Ridge and Shenandoah Valley to incorporate much of the Potomac highlands. Asserting that the Potomac commenced at its confluence with the Shenandoah River, the colony of Virginia laid claim to all land west of the Blue Ridge. Histories of the Northern Neck Proprietary can be found in Stuart Brown, *Virginia Baron: The Story of Thomas 6th Lord Fairfax* (Berryville, Va.: Chesapeake Book Company, 1965), 26–100; Douglas Southall Freeman, *George Washington: A Biography,* 7 vols. (New York: Charles Scribner's Sons, 1948–1957), vol. 1:447–525; Edmund S. Morgan, *American Slavery, American Freedom: The Ordeal of*

Colonial Virginia (New York: W. W. Norton, 1975), 244–45. Worries for the security of plantation Virginia if slaves could escape to mountain strongholds to the west and establish maroon colonies escalated in June 1729 "when a number of Negroes about fiftenn belonging to a new plantation, on the head of James River formed a design to withdraw from their master and to fix themselves in the fastnesses of the neighbouring mountains." This was, according to the Virginia governor, a "design which might have proved as dangerous to this country, as is that of the negroes in the mountains of Jamaica to the inhabitants of that island." The threat called for "some effectual measures for preventing the like hereafter, it being certain that a very small number of negroes once settled in those parts, would very soon be encreas'd by the accession of other runaways." See William Gooch to Board of Trade, June 29, 1729, C.O. 5/1322, Colonial Office Papers.

10. The thinking of the Board of Trade on important issues of colonial security can be found in the board's Report of 1721, which had been prompted by negotiations with France over colonial boundaries and by a need for greater information about colonial circumstances and defenses. See Board of Trade to the king, September 8, 1721, C.O. 324/10, Colonial Office Papers.

11. McIlwaine et al., *Executive Journals* 4:253; Gooch to Board of Trade, May 24, 1734, C.O. 5/1323, Colonial Office Papers. Grants in the Shenandoah Valley can be found in McIlwaine et al., *Executive Journals* 4:223–24, 229, 249–50, 253, 270, 295. For information about land patents and settler families, see Land Patent Books 15, 16, 17, Library of Virginia, Richmond; Brown, *Virginia Baron,* 74, 163, 166–67; *Hopewell Friends History, 1734–1934* (Strasburg, Va.: Shenandoah Publishing House, 1936).

12. McIlwaine et al., *Executive Journals* 4:370; Kercheval, *History of the Valley,* 53. For information about Anglo-Indian conflict between 1736 and 1742, see William Gooch to Board of Trade, September 20, 1738, C.O. 5/1324, Colonial Office Papers; Samuel Hazard, ed., *Minutes of the Provincial Council of Pennsylvania,* 16 vols. (Harrisburg, Pa.: Theo. Fenn, 1838–1853), 4:93–95, 203–4, 630–46, 644; McIlwaine et al., *Executive Journals* 4:383, 398, 404, 414; H. R. McIlwaine, ed., *Journals of the House of Burgesses of Virginia, 1727–1734, 1736–1740* (Richmond: Virginia State Library, 1910), 320–21; H. R. McIlwaine, ed., *Legislative Journals of the Council of Virginia* (Richmond: Virginia State Library, 1918–1919, 1979), 864–65; Edmund Bailey O'Callaghan and Berthold Fernow, eds., *Documents Relative to the Colonial History of the State of New-York,* 15 vols. (Albany: Weed, Parsons, 1853–1887), vol. 4:230–42; James Patton to Gooch, December 18, 23, 1742, enclosure in Gooch to Board of Trade, February 14, 1743, C.O. 5/1325, Colonial Office Papers; *Pennsylvania Gazette,* January 27, March 31, 1743; *Virginia Gazette,* April 7, June 30, July 21, 1738.

13. For more on marriage, land, and family at Opequon, see Warren R. Hofstra, "Land, Ethnicity, and Community at the Opequon Settlement, Virginia, 1730–1800," *Virginia Magazine of History and Biography* 98 (July 1990): 423–48.

14. Will of James Vance, February 26, 1750, FCW, 1:495; Will of Elizabeth Vance, November 12, 1781, FCW, 5:110; Grant from Thomas, Lord Fairfax, to Elizabeth Vance, August 7, 1752, Northern Neck Land Grants, 1690–1874, H:191, Library of Virginia, Richmond.

15. Will of William Hoge, November 15, 1749, FCW, 1:338; Inventory of William Hoge, February 12, 1751, FCW, 1:428; Deed from William Hoge to David Vance et al., February 19, 1745, Frederick County Deeds, 1:275, Frederick County Courthouse, Winchester, Va.

16. *Hopewell Friends History,* 52

17. Deposition of Christopher Windle, February 8, 1787, *Christopher Windle v. Rep. of Jost Hite et al.,* 1787–1790, folio 742, folder 175, Clark-Hite Papers; Account of John Russell with John McCormack, n.d., *McCormack v. Russell,* August 1748, Ended Causes, 1743–1909, Frederick County Court Papers; Account of Robert Eadmeston with Mary Ross, n.d., *Ross v. Eadmeston,* May 1745, Ended Causes, 1743–1909, Frederick County Court Papers.

18. Inventory of Robert Allen, October 17, 1757, FCW, 2:294; Inventory of Stephen Hotsinpiller, August 6, 1776, FCW, 4:327.

19. The term "dispersed general store," has been used by historical geographer Joseph S. Wood to describe the rural exchange economy of early New England. See Wood, "Elaboration of a Settlement System: The New England Village in the Federal Period," *Journal of Historical Geography* 10 (October 1984): 331–56 (quote on 338); Wood, "Village and Community in Early Colonial New England," *Journal of Historical Geography* 8 (October 1982): 333–46. The literature on accounting history and bookkeeping in early America is sparse but does include W. T. Baxter, "Accounting in Colonial America," in A. C. Littleton and B. S. Yamey, eds., *Studies in the History of Accounting* (New York: Arno Press, 1978), 272–87; Stuart Bruchey, "Success and Failure Factors: American Merchants in Foreign Trade in the Eighteenth and Early Nineteenth Centuries," *Business History Review* 32 (Autumn 1958): 272–92; Bruce G. Carruthers and Wendy Nelson Espeland, "Accounting for Rationality: Double-Entry Bookkeeping and the Rhetoric of Economic Rationality," *American Journal of Sociology* 97 (July 1991): 31–69; Michael Chatfield, *A History of Accounting Thought* (Huntington, N.Y.: Robert E. Krieger, 1977), 32–43; Peter A. Coclanis, "Bookkeeping in the Eighteenth-Century South: Evidence from Newspaper Advertisements," *South Carolina Historical Magazine* 91 (January 1990): 23–31; Barry E. Cushing, "A Kuhnian Interpretation of the Historical Evolution of Accounting," *Accounting Historians Journal* 16 (December 1989): 1–41; A. C. Littleton, *Accounting Evolution to 1900* (1933; New York: Garland, 1988), 41–122; McCusker and Menard, *Economy of British America,* 344–46; Gary John Previts and Barbara Dubis Merino, *A History of Accountancy in the United States: The Cultural Significance of Accounting* (Columbus: Ohio State University Press, 1998), 25–27; Winifred Barr Rothenberg, *From Market-Places to a Market Economy: The Transformation of Rural Massachusetts, 1750–1850* (Chicago: University of Chicago Press, 1992), 61–65; Basil S. Yamey, "Scientific Bookkeeping and the Rise of Capitalism," *Economic History Review,* 2nd ser., vol. 1 (1949): 99–113; and Yamey, "Accounting and the Rise of Capitalism: Further Notes of a Theme by Sombart," *Journal of Accounting Research* 2 (Autumn 1964): 117–36.

20. On the single-unit house in the north of Ireland, see Alan Gailey, *Rural Houses of the North of Ireland* (Edinburgh: J. Donald, 1984), 35–40, 148; Gailey, "The Housing of

the Rural Poor in Nineteenth-Century Ulster," *Ulster Folklife* 22 (1976): 34–58; Warren R. Hofstra, "Adaptation or Survival? Folk Housing at Opequon Settlement," *Ulster Folklife* 37 (1991): 36–61; Caoimhín Ó Danachair, "Traditional Forms of the Dwelling House in Ireland," *Journal of the Royal Society of Antiquaries of Ireland* 102 (1972): 81. The I-house, its form, evolution, and diffusion, is treated in Edward A. Chappell, "Acculturation in the Shenandoah Valley: Rhenish Houses of the Massanutten Settlement," *Proceedings of the American Philosophical Society* 124 (1980): 55–89; Henry Glassie, "Eighteenth-Century Cultural Process in Delaware Valley Folk Building," *Winterthur Portfolio* 7 (1972): 29–95; Fred Kniffen, "Folk Housing: Key to Diffusion," *Annals of the Association of American Geographers* 55 (December 1965): 549–77; Richard Pillsbury "Patterns in the Folk and Vernacular House Forms of the Pennsylvania Culture Region," *Pioneer America* 9 (1972): 13–31.

21. George Washington to Robert Dinwiddie, October 11, 1755, *The Papers of George Washington,* Colonial Series, ed. W. W. Abbot et al., 10 vols. (Charlottesville: University Press of Virginia, 1983–1995), vol. 3:1. On the Seven Years' War, see Fred Anderson, *Crucible of War: The Seven Years' War and the Fate of Empire in British North America, 1754–1766* (New York: Vintage Books, 2001); Lawrence Henry Gipson, *The British Empire before the American Revolution,* 15 vols. (Caldwell, Idaho: Caxton Printers, 1936–1970).

22. Washington to Dinwiddie, April 25, 1754, *Washington Papers,* Colonial Series, vol. 1:88–89; Washington to John Augustine Washington, May 28, 1755, vol. 1:289; Washington to Dinwiddie, October 9, 1757, vol. 5:12. On militia offenses, see Raymond Chester Young, "The Effects of the French and Indian War on Civilian Life in the Frontier Counties of Virginia, 1754–1763," PhD diss., Vanderbilt University, 1969, 57–58.

23. Washington to Dinwiddie, October 11, 1755, *Washington Papers,* Colonial Series, vol. 2:101, 104.

24. Thomas M. Doerflinger, *A Vigorous Spirit of Enterprise: Merchants and Economic Development in Revolutionary Philadelphia* (Chapel Hill: University of North Carolina Press for the Institute of Early American History and Culture, 1986), 108–14; Carville V. Earle and Ronald Hoffman, "Staple Crops and Urban Development in the Eighteenth-Century South," in *Perspectives in American History* 10, ed. Donald Fleming and Bernard Bailyn (Cambridge: Harvard University Press, 1976), 7–78; Marc Egnal, *New World Economies: The Growth of the Thirteen Colonies and Early Canada* (New York: Oxford University Press, 1998): 25–77; Paul W. Gates, *The Farmer's Age: Agriculture, 1815–1860,* Economic History of the United States, vol. 3 (New York: Holt, Rinehart & Winston, 1960), 159; Lewis C. Gray, *History of Agriculture in the Southern United States to 1860,* 2 vols. (1933; rpt., 1 vol., New York: Augustus M. Kelly, 1973), 161–66, 881, 908; David Klingaman, "The Significance of Grain in the Development of the Tobacco Colonies," *Journal of Economic History* 29 (June 1969): 268–78; Jacob Price, "Economic Function and the Growth of American Port Towns in the Eighteenth Century," in *Perspectives in American History* 8, ed. Donald Fleming and Bernard Bailyn (Cambridge, Mass.: Harvard University Press, 1974), 151–56.

25. The consumer revolution is treated in T. H. Breen, *The Marketplace of Revolution: How Consumer Politics Shaped American Independence* (Oxford, U.K.: Oxford University

Press, 2004); Breen, "An Empire of Goods: The Anglicization of Colonial America, 1690–1776," *Journal of British Studies* 25 (October 1986): 467–99; Cary Carson, Ronald Hoffman, and Peter J. Albert, eds., *Of Consuming Interests: The Style of Life in the Eighteenth Century* (Charlottesville: University Press of Virginia, 1994); Thomas M. Doerflinger, "Farmers and Dry Goods in the Philadelphia Market Area, 1750–1800," in Ronald Hoffman, John J. McCusker, Russell R. Menard, and Peter J. Albert, eds., *The Economy of Early America: The Revolutionary Period, 1763–1790* (Charlottesville: University Press of Virginia, 1988), 166–95; Jack P. Greene, *Pursuits of Happiness: The Social Development of Early Modern British Colonies and the Formation of American Culture* (Chapel Hill: University of North Carolina Press, 1988), 108–9; Neil McKendrick, John Brewer, and J. H. Plumb, *The Birth of a Consumer Society: The Commercialization of Eighteenth-Century England* (Bloomington: Indiana University Press, 1985); Carole Shammas, "Consumer Behavior in Colonial America," *Social Science History* 6 (Winter 1982): 67–86. On economic growth and prosperity in the 1790s, see Cathy Matson, "The Revolution, the Constitution, and the New Nation," in Stanley L. Engerman and Robert E. Gallman, eds., *The Cambridge Economic History of the United States,* vol. 1: *The Colonial Era* (Cambridge, U.K.: Cambridge University Press, 1996), 388–401. For a definitive study of grain and flour production in the Shenandoah Valley, see Kenneth E. Koons, "'The Staple of Our Country': Wheat in the Regional Farm Economy of the Nineteenth-Century Valley of Virginia," in Kenneth E. Koons and Warren R. Hofstra, *After the Backcountry: Rural Life in the Great Valley of Virginia, 1800–1900* (Knoxville: University of Tennessee Press, 2000), 3–20.

Searching for Status: Virginia's Irish Tract, 1770s–1790s

Katharine L. Brown
Kenneth W. Keller

The first major literary depiction of the Scotch-Irish in the southern United States was the 1824 novel *The Valley of the Shenandoah* by George Tucker. In this landmark novel, a gentleman from a bankrupt coastal Virginia family travels to the interior of the commonwealth, searching for a way to improve his declining family's fortunes. He travels about the Valley of Virginia, being introduced to characters the likes of which he has never encountered, including many people of German and Scotch-Irish descent, most of them having migrated up the Valley of Virginia from Pennsylvania to the north. The story gives author Tucker the opportunity to develop ethnic stereotypes of the Germans and Presbyterians from the north of Ireland, the latter of whom the Americans were beginning to call the "Scotch-Irish." In Tucker's depiction, the Germans were generally hard working but culturally impoverished, dull, phlegmatic, small minded, selfish, plodding farmers; the "Scotch-Irish," who were clearly Tucker's favorites, were civic minded, impulsive, bold, daring, restless, outgoing, imaginative, ardent, decisive, proud, enterprising, and, though upstarts to the old families of the coast, were likely to rise to elevated station in public life. They were given to extremes. While some would waste their resources on extravagant projects and luxury, others of them may be engaged "in a course of rapid and adventurous speculation."[1] Plainly, according to the novelist, what distinguished the Scotch-Irish from their neighbors on the Virginia frontier is that they were constantly striving, sometimes recklessly, to secure their position in the society of the backcountry. They had recently arrived on the land, sacrificed, and now were willing to take risks to provide a place for themselves and their posterity in an ordered republican society that they would build, free of unmerited privilege and status.[2]

Like many literary stereotypes, this portrait of the Scotch-Irish on the American frontier has some truth in it, especially in an area of the Valley of

Virginia known as the Irish Tract, a region of about four hundred square miles between Rockbridge and Augusta counties that straddles the upper James and the upper Shenandoah river valleys (see map 6.1). It is most certainly true that, in this region, the Scotch-Irish were able to establish themselves so that they and their families led the cultural, economic, and political institutions of this part of Virginia. Today the Irish Tract contains one of the highest concentrations of Presbyterian churches in the United States, and the landscape is dotted with colleges and universities founded and supported by the Scotch-Irish, and with businesses and professional interests that families have maintained and prospered from for generations. In the Irish Tract, a Scotch-Irish elite formed early in its history and is still in evidence. Although Virginians to the east identified with the culture and history of the Old Dominion's motherland of England, the leaders of the Irish Tract looked to a republican and dissenting culture as they strove to build their lives in the New World. The republican society they searched for was one where men would live without a king and without artificial distinctions imposed by aristocratic privilege and an established church, but they lived with limited government and political institutions they controlled through frequent elections. Such a society was supposed to be one where hard work, frugality, honesty, austere dissenting piety, avoidance of luxury, social harmony, and the opportunity to own land and slaves would reward white people like themselves.

Recently historians have told the story of the formation of this Scotch-Irish elite. Studies by the historians Turk McCleskey and Albert H. Tillson Jr. have documented how before 1790 the early Scotch-Irish of the region accumulated real estate, began to build their fortunes, and created a power structure that maintained their dominance in their region of the upper Shenandoah Valley.[3] In the Irish Tract of the upper Valley, the initial landholders were not Ulstermen, but the land quickly fell under the control of the Scotch-Irish. In the late 1730s the Crown disposed of the land by deeding it over to two landholders who were not of Scotch-Irish descent. They were William Beverley, who lived in coastal Virginia, an area known as the Tidewater, and Benjamin Borden Sr., who was from New Jersey and served as a land agent of the only resident English peer in the American colonies, Lord Fairfax.[4] Beverley and Borden selected as resident land agents to sell their properties two Ulstermen whose families were related to each other before they emigrated to America, John Lewis and John McDowell. Both Lewis and McDowell were the first settlers as well as land speculators in different sections of the Irish Tract.[5] John Lewis's son Thomas became the county surveyor of Augusta County, in the northern part of the Irish Tract,

Katharine L. Brown and Kenneth W. Keller

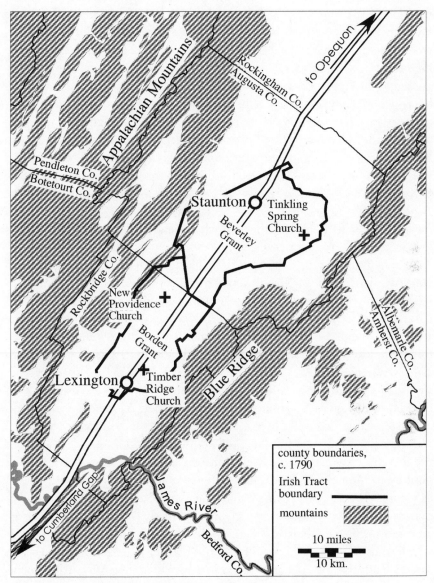

Map 6.1. *Virginia's Irish Tract, 1770s to 1790s.*

while John McDowell's son James held the same appointment in Rockbridge County, which was created from Augusta County in the southern Irish Tract in 1778.[6] In the county to the south of Rockbridge, Thomas Lewis's relative William Preston served as county surveyor of Botetourt County until 1772, when Thomas Lewis's nephew got the position.[7] As county surveyors, these men controlled who had access to landownership in the Irish Tract and consequently the right to vote and hold office. In addition, as the exploration of the region to the west of the Alleghenies took place, these men invested in optimistic land speculation schemes involving vast tracts of land in the region between the Allegheny Ridge of the Appalachians and the Ohio River.[8] Those persons who obtained surveys from these men and secured their titles would then find doors open to political power through commissions of the peace, positions in the militia, and seats on the grand jury. By the time of the American Revolution, although the Scotch-Irish did not exclude others from the land they settled, most of the men who received title from them were fellow Scotch-Irish or their descendants.

Among the Scotch-Irish of the Irish Tract, the drive to purchase western lands was part of their effort to establish their status as leaders. Numerous settlers of the Irish Tract saw speculative opportunities on the Holston and Clinch rivers of southwest Virginia, in Kentucky, and beyond. Men like John and Arthur Campbell and William Christian took up land there before American independence. Such property was a safety net against financial reverses in the Irish Tract, but it could be subject to threats from other speculators who organized land companies to acquire thousands of acres of land in southwestern Virginia and the Ohio Valley. As the historian of this early speculative activity, Thomas Perkins Abernethy wrote that these men were not poor squatters but "men of position and education."[9] They were not driven by poverty to the West, but by the hope of strengthening their position in the western elite. There were risks involved in such enterprises, as George Tucker's Scotch-Irish character, Mr. McCulloch, reveals. Tucker portrayed Mr. McCulloch as extravagant in his spending, and the debts he incurred in his speculative adventures led him and his wife to worry constantly about debt and the loss of his land and slaves. According to Tucker, Mr. McCulloch's experience was a common one among Virginia's Scotch-Irish, who would find land, buy it, have it surveyed and registered, and lose it through bad financial management. Tucker's character eventually is forced to sell his Valley land and move to Kentucky, where he accumulates more debts and dies within two years of his arrival.[10] Such management allowed

Katharine L. Brown and Kenneth W. Keller

many a Scotch-Irish estate to pass into the hands of others, especially the less-adventurous Germans.

Beyond the mere accumulation of real property and wealth, by the last decade of the eighteenth century, the Scotch-Irish gentry of the upper Valley cemented their leadership through intermarriage with other Scotch-Irish people and through establishing governmental and cultural institutions to consolidate the social order of their communities. After 1790, these *arrivistes'* search for status and social standing continued as they achieved their goals in a republican political environment based upon a stratified society led mostly by descendants of the first Scotch-Irish settlers.

The Scotch-Irish of the upper Valley formed an extended cousinage, not only because many of them were related to each other before they emigrated but also because, once they arrived, their families continued to intermarry. While the tie between the two principal surveyor families on the Irish Tract, the Lewises and the McDowells, was a Virginia extension of an Ulster reality, an equally close kinship seems to have existed between the Lewises and James Patton, a frontier explorer and sea captain who imported numerous Ulster settlers for the Irish Tract. John Lewis's wife and James Patton may have shared descent from the Pattons, who were richly rewarded with County Donegal lands for their part in the Williamite war.[11] The Croghan and Springfield estates, with their lands and the fine houses erected on them, qualified the Pattons and a few other Scotch-Irish families as gentry in early eighteenth-century Donegal. In their new Virginia home, they certainly did not aspire to a lower status than they had left behind in Ulster. Their thirst for power and prestige was not lost upon their minister, the Reverend John Craig, a native of Donegore Parish, County Antrim. He labeled them "proud, Selfinterested, Contentious, & ungovernable, all of them Close handed about providing necessary things for pious or religious uses."[12] Certainly the Reverend Mr. Craig's sketch of his parishioners was one with which George Tucker would have agreed.

James Patton's sister Elizabeth had married a shipbuilder, John Preston, in Ulster. Their Londonderry-born son, William Preston, was nephew to Patton. The enterprising Patton, who had only two daughters, saw to the nephew's education. It is scant surprise to find the young man rising rapidly in the militia and moving into the lucrative post of surveyor. The Lewis-McDowell-Preston-Patton linkage connected themselves through marriage to the Moffetts, the McClungs, the McGavicks, the McClanahans, the Stuarts, the Browns, the Humphreys family, the Campbells, the Montgomerys, the

Finleys, and even an occasional person of English descent or, more rarely, a person of German background.[13] A good illustration of the interconnections the Scotch-Irish of the Irish Tract formed is the family linkages of one especially well-known leader of the Scotch-Irish communities of the upper Valley, the Reverend John Brown.

John Brown, a Londonderry-born lad who was educated in Pennsylvania and graduated with the second class of the College of New Jersey (later Princeton), came to the Irish Tract as a New Light preacher and was called as minister to the New Providence and Timber Ridge congregations, both in present Rockbridge County. Brown married Margaret Preston, thus joining the Lewis-Patton-Preston circle, the most powerful extended family of colonial Augusta County. This alliance, perhaps the first of what became a pattern among Presbyterian ministers in western Virginia, placed the young man in a position to launch a stunningly successful family. Brown's brother-in-law and close friend, William Preston, a militia leader in the French and Indian War, frontier surveyor, and officer in the Revolution, became a major landholder in Augusta, Botetourt, and Montgomery counties. At present-day Blacksburg, where his uncle and mentor, James Patton, was killed by Indians, Preston built Smithfield, a handsome plantation house in the eastern Virginia style, from which he and his sons played a leading role in the political and economic development of southwestern Virginia. His sons and grandsons include Francis Preston, a congressman in the 1790s; James Patton Preston, governor of Virginia; and James Floyd, also governor of Virginia. Another sister of William Preston and Margaret Preston Brown was Letitia Preston, who married Robert Breckinridge, one of the first justices of Augusta County. Their son, James Breckinridge (1763–1833), fought in the American Revolution under his uncle William Preston; studied law with Jefferson's mentor, George Wythe; served in the Virginia legislature and as a United States congressman from Virginia; and became a brigadier general in the War of 1812.[14]

Every branch of this interconnected family that John Brown married into rose rapidly to the top of the socioeconomic heap on the Virginia frontier and its later Kentucky extension. Brown educated his children at his academy near Timber Ridge. This became Liberty Hall Academy and was a forerunner of present Washington and Lee University. One daughter married a Presbyterian minister, keeping in the forefront of the most influential Scotch-Irish institution on the frontier. Another daughter married Alexander Humphreys, an Edinburgh-educated physician who trained young doctors at his own medical practice in Staunton, the seat of Augusta County. Three

Katharine L. Brown and Kenneth W. Keller

of the Brown sons became physicians. One of them, Samuel Brown, studied under Benjamin Rush in Philadelphia and at Edinburgh and Aberdeen, and he held the chair of medicine at Transylvania University in Kentucky. The two remaining sons, John and James, studied law and forged brilliant careers in politics and public service on the next Scotch-Irish frontier—that in Kentucky. John Brown Jr. (1757–1837), a vigorous advocate of Kentucky statehood, built an elegant plantation house, Liberty Hall, and served in the Confederation congress, the House of Representatives, and then as United States senator from Kentucky. James Brown (1766–1835) married a sister of Henry Clay's wife, was secretary of state for Kentucky, and then moved to New Orleans, where he became secretary of the Louisiana Territory, district attorney, and United States senator. In 1823, President James Monroe appointed him United States minister to France.[15] As examples of a Scotch-Irish gentry in the emerging American West, these sons and daughters of Ulster proved themselves unparalleled in their successful search for status, rivaling landlords from their homeland and eastern Virginian planter elite of an earlier generation such as Robert "King" Carter and William Byrd II. Subsequent generations of these people moved beyond the Mississippi to become political leaders. In the western state of Missouri, for example, three descendants of the Ulster Tract Scotch-Irish, Thomas Hart Benton, Francis Preston Blair Jr., and B. Gratz Brown, established their political careers and entered national politics.[16]

The rise to political power and social respectability among the Scotch-Irish could not have been achieved without women, who maintained domestic order in the Irish Tract. Some Scotch-Irish women remained single, but most women had a marriage-centered future. Men prescribed the role that married women were to play, and there is little evidence of any resistance to it from women. In the case of Tucker's fictional Scotch-Irish characters, relations between spouses were affectionate, but husbands dominated their wives. McCulloch , a jocular man who was not given to introspection, thoughtlessly referred to his wife as "my old woman," and in the novel she usually responded in silence. Faced with his bumptious joking, she remained meek and placid. Such a response, according to the novelist, showed her to be "ideal in the character of a companion or a wife." Mr. McCulloch patronizingly referred to a pretty, younger, single woman as "my lily of the valley."[17] These literary characters were inevitably expressions of the author's biases, but common attitudes among the Valley Scotch-Irish shaped the outlines of their relationship. The great-granddaughter of John Lewis, Ann Montgomery Lewis, illustrates this conformity and the accolades it brought in the Irish Tract to a real member of the elite. According to a published memorial about her, after studying with a teacher in western Virginia, she moved to Staunton, where she married the attorney and editor John Howe Peyton. Ann Lewis fulfilled the duties of wife and mother well: she bore ten children, attended her husband's slaves, served the poor, used medicinal herbs, welcomed guests, read widely, prayed and studied the Bible, loved animals, practiced what her husband called "good housewifery," supported the education of young women, listened patiently to her husband's patronizing advice, traveled to the springs, visited relatives—all of which were consistent with the role prescribed for women of her status. Her husband's instructions to their daughter Susan Madison Peyton, who was to give up her goal of becoming a teacher to marry the attorney John B. Baldwin, prepared her for submissiveness. Susan Peyton was to be circumspect, dignified, cheerful, sensible, agreeable, an attentive listener, and good-humored at all times.[18]

There were other women among the Scotch-Irish who were more involved in their families' pursuit of landed wealth. A good example is Mary McDowell Greenlee, who settled with her husband on Benjamin Borden's grant in southern Augusta and northern Rockbridge counties. Mary Greenlee's family came to the Borden Grant in 1737; almost seventy years later, she keenly remembered many details of her and other families' rise by the accumulation of land on the grant, including who married whom and what lands families and their children occupied and sold. She reported somewhat admiringly in a deposition of 1806 that one woman did accumulate property on her own, sometimes by stretching the law. One enterprising Scotch-Irish servant woman she knew dressed herself in men's clothes and applied for rights in numerous places in the Irish Tract, accumulating hundreds of acres. Mary Greenlee was no passive observer of the settlement of the tract, making her wishes very clear to the men in her family who built early settlements there. When her husband built a cabin in a spot to which she objected, she compelled him to move and build another elsewhere. She knew of other women in the tract who carefully sized up prospective mates' economic potential before tying the knot. Mary Greenlee made economic decisions as well. She chose property to acquire in the tract when her husband was away and noted that, since cash was scarce, the people of the tract sent butter to Williamsburg and New Castle to pay their debts. Farm women customarily made dairy products like the butter the tract residents used for cash. Women like Mary Greenlee well knew the details of their husbands' activities in their rise to prominence and wealth.[19]

Katharine L. Brown and Kenneth W. Keller

Another example of attainment of power and status by a handful of the Scotch-Irish settlers on the Irish Tract can be found in their leadership role in the established Anglican Church. For a group of Presbyterian dissenters from the north of Ireland, this was no mean feat. When the established church was organized in Augusta County by Governor William Gooch's 1746 order to the sheriff of Augusta County to hold an election for vestry, at least eight of the twelve men elected were Scotch-Irish Presbyterians. James Patton, Robert Alexander, John Buchanan, Patrick Hays, John Christian, Thomas Gordon, James Lockhart, and John Buchanan Jr., son-in-law to Patton, were Presbyterians.[20] The important secular duties of a Virginia vestry included the care of the infirm, impoverished, and the aged; the foster care and education of orphans and illegitimate children so that they could become self-supporting adults; and the processioning of, or walking around, land boundaries to prevent quarrels and litigation. The vestry levied the taxes to underwrite these secular activities as well as the minister's salary and the construction and upkeep of churches and chapels. Such a position of power and authority had appeal to the leaders who had emerged among the Scotch-Irish on the Virginia frontier. Consequently, doctrinal and liturgical differences between the church in which they were raised and to which they still belonged and the established church could not be allowed to interfere with the exercise of power and authority that was rightfully theirs. In the words of nineteenth-century Augusta County historian John Lewis Peyton, these men were "politically Episcopalians and doctrinally Presbyterians."[21] When a handful of established church members in Augusta Parish complained about dissenters on the vestry and requested the government in Williamsburg to order a new election, they were ignored. Crafty Williamsburg politicians recognized the value of having the local leadership to whom the Scotch-Irish settlers turned.

As settlers on the edge of the eighteenth-century Virginia frontier, the 150 Scotch-Irish inhabitants of the Irish Tract had to take up the rifle and defend their farmsteads from attack by Native Americans, who objected to the settlers' intrusion upon Indian hunting lands and the more-than-occasionally sharp trading practices of Virginia Indian traders. In doing so, they found a way to assert their status as public leaders. Although the 1744 Treaty of Lancaster with Native Americans allowed new settlers to traverse the Valley of Virginia, tribesmen who were not party to the treaty and settlers who were unwilling to stay contained in the boundaries it established frequently clashed in violent attacks along the western frontier. The major white–Native American conflicts in the Irish Tract ended by 1764, but by the 1770s Virginians pushed west across the Appalachians into the Kentucky Bluegrass region, and the violence continued. As a result, the commonwealth of Virginia called upon male Ulster settlers to serve in local militia to defend frontier settlements. Militia service gave Ulstermen the chance to occupy positions of leadership and high status in western communities, including those of the Irish Tract. Under British colonial rule, only aristocrats could be officers in the British professional army, but with American independence the doors were opened to men of less-elevated status to distinguish themselves by rank. Frontier troubles leading to the Revolution gave Scotch-Irish settlers like the Lewis brothers their first opportunities to demonstrate military leadership in campaigns against the Indians of the Ohio Valley in Lord Dunmore's War of 1774.[22] Then once more, with the coming of the American struggle for independence, Irish Tract men fought in battles from the Carolinas to Pennsylvania and established their reputations as American patriots who could be counted upon to resist the British.

People of the Irish Tract believed that a local militia was the key to the survival of their settlement, and Augusta's freeholders resolved at a public meeting at the courthouse on February 22, 1775, that "a well regulated militia is the natural strength, and staple security, of a free government" and that Augusta men should make themselves "masters of the military exercise" to preserve America as "happy, virtuous, and free."[23] While doing so, they would develop a class of local militia veterans who would dominate local society and government for decades after the winning of independence. Service in the revolutionary armies became a mark of status in the entire early American republic, but according to one observer, especially in the heart of the Irish Tract. According to Isaac Weld, a British traveler in the 1790s whose opinions of the new republic were not always favorable, Staunton had a remarkable "superfluity of these military personages." According to Weld, there was "hardly a decent person in it [Staunton], excepting lawyers and medical men, but what is a colonel, a major, or captain. . . . In Staunton there are two or three corps, one of cavalry, the other of artillery. These are formed chiefly of men who find a certain degree of amusement in exercising as soldiers, and who are induced to associate, by the vanity of appearing in regimentals . . . and if a man has been a captain or a colonel but one day either in the one body or the other, it seems to be an established rule that he is to have nominal rank the rest of his life."[24] The veterans of the Irish Tract enthusiastically displayed the marks of their status as they paraded in their regalia at militia musters.

For those men of the Irish Tract who could not take up arms, there were many opportunities to assume roles as political leaders in the Americans' new system of republican government. Irish Tract inhabitants called upon the sons of the first Scotch-Irish emigrants to the tract to represent them in Virginia's extra-legal revolutionary conventions, which patriots held in place of the meeting of the colonial legislature, the House of Burgesses, when George III's royal governors dissolved it to keep it from meeting.[25] In this way, leading families of the tract gained political experience that they would pass to their progeny. Both of the Irish Tract's representatives in the Virginia conventions of 1775–1776 had been born in Ulster. Thomas Lewis, son of John Lewis, first European settler at Staunton, was born in County Donegal, became Augusta County surveyor in 1746, and laid out the town of Staunton. Augusta County voters chose him to represent them in the Virginia conventions. Sent with him to Richmond was Samuel McDowell, a relative of the Lewis family, who had been brought as an infant from Ulster to the Borden Grant by his father. He had served in the disastrous expedition of General Sir Edward Braddock to western Pennsylvania during the French and Indian War, in the House of Burgesses in 1772, and then again with his Lewis family relatives in Lord Dunmore's War. These men probably had no significant role in the revolutionary conventions, but they were there and were elected to the Virginia House of Delegates under Virginia's constitution of 1776. Thomas Lewis became the largest landholder in Rockingham County when it was cut off from Augusta in 1777; he also served as commissioner to negotiate for the revolutionary government with western Indians and continued to serve as a representative of western Virginia in the movement to ratify the United States Constitution in 1788. Samuel McDowell served as one of the first justices of Rockbridge County, which the legislature separated from Augusta in 1778, and moved to Kentucky, where he also led the movement to ratify the Constitution.[26] These two men had long political careers based upon their families' early settlement and status in the Irish Tract and their assumption of public offices that the tract's inhabitants bestowed upon them in election after election.

The republican society the Scotch-Irish sought to create was based on legal but not social equality. They had supported independence and the end of hereditary privileges, but what they did not favor was social leveling and what they saw as "anarchy." When after 1793 the French revolutionaries experimented with creating an egalitarian society, the Valley Scotch-Irish recoiled from abandoning social order completely. A republic that maintained harmonious mutual interdependence of social classes was their ideal. Although Irish Tract leaders of the late eighteenth century supported the political organization and ideas of Thomas Jefferson, the Scotch-Irish in the Valley increasingly voted for candidates of the conservative Federalist Party after the French Revolution became bloody. Federalists stood for an ordered, deferential society, a powerful federal government, and an alliance among wealthy people to secure frontier defense, banking, corporate monopolies, and economic development. Natives of Augusta County such as the land speculator Arthur Campbell, who moved up the Great Valley on the eve of the American Revolution, believed that, because of the uproar in France, "our liberties are in danger." He favored "representative or mixed government" in which both the rich and the poor had a voice. In such a balance of interests, "if one of them have a just demand for submission and obedience, for honor and respect, for convenience and ease, the other have a just claim for protection and defence, for the administration of justice, and the preservation of equal liberty for the supply of their wants, and the relief of their distresses, for *instruction* and *good example*." Concord and harmony, not conflict and class antagonism should be the result of such an ordered society, Campbell believed, but common folk should learn from the privileged and the educated. In every social body, he concluded, "there must be superiors, inferiors, and equals," and all parts of society were mutually dependent upon each other as were the organs of the human body. Ordinary citizens owed "obedience and submission," while leaders provided "justice and disinterested zeal, for the public good." This condition was, in his view, *"real republicanism,"* removed from both "furious jacobinism" and "chilling aristocracy."[27] Studies of Irish Tract voting show it was shifting toward the Federalists. Staunton became the headquarters of the Virginia Federalists; and after the Federalist Party died around 1816, the voters of the tract voted for the Whigs, who succeeded the Federalists. By the 1830s–1840s, the Scotch-Irish Presbyterians in the Valley of Virginia were, according to political historian William G. Shade, "overwhelmingly Whig."[28] Even George Tucker's characters recognized the shift. In his novel, Mr. McCulloch abandoned the Jeffersonians to oppose the guillotine and "Jacobinism."[29]

The prime institution of special privilege in the commonwealth of Virginia was the established church. The elite leaders of the upper Valley took aim at the legally established Anglican Church—or as Anglicans somewhat presumptuously called it, "The Church"—in Virginia. Since the founding of the colony, Virginia's government provided for the establishment of the Church of England in the colony. Anglican priests and parishes received pub-

Katharine L. Brown and Kenneth W. Keller

lic assistance from the colony's treasury, accepted glebe land from the colonial government, and exercised some of the functions of civil government, especially on the local level, in each county. With the coming of the American Revolution, non-Anglican dissenters, who outnumbered Anglicans in the colony by the mid-eighteenth century, demanded that the Anglican Church be stripped of its religious monopoly. Presbyterians, who were the second-largest religious group in the colony by 1776, were leaders in this crusade for recognition of their religious rights; and in the Valley, Scotch-Irish Presbyterians from the Irish Tract were in the forefront of that campaign, although they were quite willing to form coalitions with other religious denominations that felt similar discrimination.[30]

One representative of the Irish Tract who played a particularly important role in the move from established church to freedom of religion as a member of the Virginia legislature was Zachariah Johnston. The son of Ulster emigrants who proved their importation into Virginia in 1740, Johnston was baptized at Tinkling Spring Presbyterian meetinghouse near present Fishersville, Augusta County, in September 1742 and was educated by the Reverend John Brown of the Timber Ridge and New Providence meetings in the Irish Tract. Johnston served in the militia in the French and Indian War, farmed and raised his large family near Fishersville, served on the Augusta County Committee of Safety as the Revolution brewed, was an ensign in a 1776 expedition against Indian settlements on the French Broad River, and the following year became a captain in the county militia, seeing active duty on the West Fork of the Monongahela River in fall 1779. In 1778 the voters of Augusta County elected Johnston to the legislature. He and Samuel McDowell were chosen to present the petition of the Presbytery of Hanover, representing all Virginia Presbyterians, to the legislature in 1780 in opposition to a general tax assessment for the support of all denominations. In 1785 Johnston was chosen chairman of the Committee on Religion in the House of Delegates. This was the body that deliberated and recommended Jefferson's landmark Bill for Establishing Religious Freedom; and Johnston, who had worked closely with Madison on the bill, spoke eloquently as a Presbyterian in its behalf.[31]

Once the Virginia General Assembly in 1786 passed a bill granting religious freedom to Virginians and disestablishing the Anglican Church, the Scotch-Irish of the Valley did not rest, for the clergy of the former state church still enjoyed the use of glebe land—about two hundred acres of farmland and a house—that the law guaranteed each minister of the established church. Scotch-Irish Presbyterians promoted a campaign to strip the Anglican clergy of their glebes and to sell the land for revenue for public use. The animosity Augusta County's Presbyterians felt to the once-privileged Church of Virginia came through clearly in a remonstrance to the legislature, signed by many of the elders of local congregations and received December 4, 1786. This document complained that the glebe land "(under the former government) was extorted from all, by the hand of arbitrary power" and that a recent bill incorporating the Protestant Episcopal Church, as the Anglican Church called itself in the newly independent United States, had received "an immediate a[nd] dangerous and unwarrantable connection between the legislature and that church." The proposed bill made the legislature "the head of that church and peculiarly interested in its welfare for from the Assembly it receives its authority to act." The petitioners concluded that Virginia should "dispose of the glebes which were purchased at common expense towards the lessening of our common debt."[32] An even more indignant petition against incorporation of the Protestant Episcopal Church and a proposal that all Virginians be taxed to support any church came from Rockbridge County Presbyterians, who asserted that such proposals would fill up the ministry with "Fools, Sots, and Gamblers."[33] The campaign eventually succeeded in defeating the incorporation of the Episcopal Church, and Presbyterians continued their attacks on the last of the old established church's privileges, the glebe lands.

With the termination of Anglican privileges, local Scotch-Irish leaders could work to build a new set of republican institutions that would provide young people with a liberal education. These institutions would be republican because an elected republican legislature created them by giving local leaders the right to govern themselves. In Augusta and Rockbridge counties, the primary organizations that would serve to create a new class of leaders for the backcountry would be academies for the education of young men. The most important of these efforts took place in Lexington, a village that always seemed to aspire to develop an intellectual culture. Like many other Presbyterian clergy in Pennsylvania and New Jersey, the Scotch-Irish Presbyterian ministers of the Irish Tract began teaching boys by tutoring them in their homes. The Reverend Robert Alexander, who settled on the tract in 1746, started instruction in his home in 1749. Other Presbyterian clergy succeeded him after he left the area. The Reverend John Brown and the Reverend William Graham, both graduates of Princeton, led the school, which called itself Liberty Hall Academy, possibly in recognition of Brown's family home in Ulster.[34] The founders of the school constructed a building to house it by 1776. The coming of the American Revolution drew students away

Katharine L. Brown and Kenneth W. Keller

into the patriot armies, fires destroyed the structure and its collections, and financial reverses led to operating difficulties; but its supporters succeeded in convincing the Virginia legislature to incorporate the institution in 1782.[35] Following a generous gift of stock from George Washington, the premier symbol of the early American republic, the school changed its name to Washington Academy. Although its direct ties with the Presbyterian Synod of Virginia declined, Presbyterian clergy were always deeply involved in the work of the school. Moreover, its curriculum was never narrowly focused on religious training but instead centered on studies meant to equip young men for leadership in a variety of professions, with strong emphasis on the sciences, classical languages, philosophy, political thought, and *belles lettres*.

In 1792 the campaign to establish an academy for young men also spread to Augusta County, and it became another opportunity for the local Presbyterians of Ulster descent to attack the remaining privileges of the old Virginia Anglican elite. Seventy-eight citizens led by other Presbyterians in Staunton petitioned the legislature for the incorporation of an academy in that town.[36] Maintaining that the "spirits of fame and prosperity might be attributed to the education bestowed by the state upon the youth with more propriety than to any other or indeed every other institute of Lycurgus. That ignorance is favorable to despotism is not a novel discovery and perhaps it is equally certain that science is the parent of liberty," the Staunton petitioners requested permission to sponsor a lottery to raise five hundred pounds to support the institution. They also asked that the legislature name trustees to administer it. More than half of the proposed trustees were town leaders of Scotch-Irish descent, including Alexander St. Clair, Archibald Stuart, Alexander Humphreys, Robert Grattan, William Lewis, Robert Gamble, Sampson Mathews, William Bowyer, and John Tate.[37] The legislature responded by establishing the academy; but since it did not provide adequate financial support, in 1793 the petitioners again addressed the legislature, emphasizing that Williamsburg's College of William and Mary, which had been under the administration of Anglicans, had received liberal assistance from Virginia but was too far away and in too unhealthy an environment for the benefit of Augusta students. Since there were so few Episcopalians in Augusta County, the glebe lands of that denomination, which had not yet been confiscated by the state of Virginia, should be given to the Staunton Academy for its support, along with income from one-sixth of the surveyors' fees and all fines and forfeitures. The petitioners also pointedly observed that since there were so few Episcopalians in the county, the glebe lands of the old established church had been applied to the county levy of taxes since the disestablishment of the Anglican Church in 1786.[38] The legislature eventually confiscated the glebes in 1802 but did not answer the financial pleas of the supporters of the academy, so Augusta Countians sent another petition to the legislature in 1807. After the general assembly failed to satisfy that demand, 750 inhabitants of the county addressed the legislators in 1812, reminding them that "no statesman will deny [that] the promotion of literature . . . was [essential] to the prosperity, respectability, and permanent happiness of a republic." [39] Nevertheless, no further aid came from Richmond, which favored the interests of eastern Virginia over those of the West. It took another generation of effort to place the Staunton Academy on a stable foundation; and in that struggle, local Presbyterians of Ulster descent played an important part.

Ulstermen and their descendants were also key leaders in the founding of fraternal institutions that bound together gentlemen of their communities in sociability and public-spirited deeds. In the Irish Tract, the primary local fraternal institution of the late eighteenth century was the Staunton lodge of Freemasons, founded in 1786. The upper-class gentry of Tidewater Virginia founded the first Virginia Masonic lodges as early as the 1740s. These semi-secret organizations had gathered local elites in the towns of Norfolk, Port Royal, Blandford, Fredericksburg, Hampton, and Williamsburg by the eve of the American Revolution. The first Virginia lodge west of the Blue Ridge appeared in Winchester in 1768; it was soon followed by another western lodge, in Botetourt County, south of the Irish Tract, in 1773. Not until 1786 was a lodge established in the Irish Tract itself, in Staunton.[40] Potential members of the lodge had to be proposed by other members and underwent a thorough screening process to assure that they conformed to Masonic ideals of respectability, honor, order, gentility, morality, philanthropy, sound reputation, and devotion to God and religion. They were to have a trade or craft and a sufficient livelihood to support their families and were not to be deformed or dismembered.[41] Masons took pride in the fact that their members, whom they called "brothers," were gentlemen of high regard in their communities and that membership in the lodge had the blessing of clergymen in the Presbyterian, Episcopalian, and Methodist denominations. Once the new brothers had been initiated into the mysteries and rituals of the lodge, they were to progress upward through a series of ordered "degrees" that admitted them to higher secrets and a rigidly hierarchical leadership with responsibilities based on their passing further tests of good character and doing charitable deeds that benefited the public. In the Irish Tract, the Scotch-Irish and their descendants became leaders of the early lodge, and some were

Katharine L. Brown and Kenneth W. Keller

elevated to serve as Grand Master, or the chief official of the local lodge. Dr. Alexander Humphreys, Robert Grattan, William Christian, and Robert McClenachan were grand masters or other officials of the Staunton Lodge at various times before 1830.[42] The emphasis on order, hierarchy, and reputation in the Masonic organization provided reinforcement for searching for status in backcountry communities like those of the Irish Tract.

While the leaders of the Irish Tract worked to remove the last privileges of the old established church, build educational institutions designed to produce a new group of well-educated republican young men, and promote private virtue and order, they also sought to consolidate their power, incorporating the communities in which they lived so that resident elites like themselves might govern local affairs rather than depend upon the distant legislature in Richmond. Local self-government was the cornerstone of republican politics, and if leaders were needed to establish self-government, Scotch-Irish people would provide them. Initially, the drive for local self-government took the form of establishing towns and eventually incorporating them. When the inhabitants of the Irish Tract secured local government for themselves, the legislature assured their domination of the new communities they formed by naming mostly men of Scotch-Irish background to serve as town trustees or by providing for their election by town residents, a majority of whom were of Scotch-Irish background. In 1761, Staunton was the first town to be established in the Irish Tract, and its early trustees included Prestons, Stuarts, Browns, Lewises, McClanahans, and Brackenridges, all of whom bore Scotch-Irish names.[43] Ulstermen such as the Browns, McKees, Campbells, Houstons, Pattons, Finleys, and Steeles were designated "gentlemen, trustees" by the legislature in 1793, when it established the town of Brownsburg. When the legislature named trustees for the already-established town of Lexington in 1799, members of the Caruthers and Blair families received the appointments, and the statute specifically called them "gentlemen."[44] Other Ulstermen, including McDowells, McClungs, Paxtons, and Scotts, all also designated by the statute as "gentlemen," got positions as trustees of the new town of Fairfield, which the general assembly established in 1800. The establishment of Waynesboro and Greenville in 1801 gave the jobs of trustees to Patricks, Stuarts, Steels, Fultons, Finleys, and Mitchells, although, in the latter community, two persons of German background were also named. In both new communities, by vote of the legislature, the trustees were christened "gentlemen."[45] In Staunton, once the town had been legally established, 108 inhabitants of the town, complaining that the powers of the trustees were "inadequate to produce the desired effects," requested the vesting of corporate powers in the hands of the elected local leaders by petitioning the legislature for Staunton's incorporation and the right of self-government. These local burghers included representatives of the Bell, Bowyer, Breckenridge, Gamble, Humphreys, McCausland, McClenachan, McCue, McCulloch, McDowell, McPheeters, Moffett, and Stuart clans. They secured the legislature's consent to the election of the officers of town government and members of the city council. The town also received "perpetual succession" to its rights of self-government.[46] By the late eighteenth century, local government was clearly in the hands of local men of largely Scotch-Irish background, who all had the status of "gentlemen" by vote of the commonwealth's legislature.

In the case of Staunton, the principal commercial center for the Irish Tract and the upper Shenandoah Valley, the growth and expansion of the town was kept well under the wings of the elite of the town's Scotch-Irish community. In 1786, the Beverley heirs added a tract of their land to the east of the town for sale. Not to be outdone by the Tidewater family, in 1787 Alexander St. Clair, a leading Staunton merchant of Ulster background and spokesman for local Presbyterians, made his move. By permission of the legislature, a tract of twenty-five acres that St. Clair owned was added to Staunton and called Newtown. In a clear sign of the strong commitment that St. Clair and so many others in town had to the ideals of the Revolution and the emerging republic, each of the streets bore the name of a revolutionary military or political leader. Washington, Greene, St. Clair, Montgomery, and Fayette streets pay tribute to the military effort, while Madison and Federal streets point to the political outcome so ardently supported on the Irish Tract. Johnston Street recognizes the local delegate's role in bringing about religious freedom. Purchasers of the lots included prominent local Scotch-Irish figures such as Dr. Alexander Humphreys, Robert and Hugh McDowell, Robert McClenachan, and clerk of court James Lyle.[47] Archibald Stuart, grandson of an Ulster immigrant and then a rising young lawyer who had studied with Jefferson, bought one of the larger lots. Within three years, Stuart built there one of Virginia's first Classical Revival mansions, clearly influenced by Jeffersonian architectural concepts. In 1804, Stuart, by then a judge, had lands that he had accumulated to the north of town added to Staunton in what was named Stuart Addition. Like Newtown, the streets were laid out in an orderly fashion, and the lots were sold by Stuart and his wife, Frances.[48]

The Scotch-Irish network of influence continued to expand as these local leaders of the Irish Tract developed cultural, religious, and economic institutions that assured their status as community leaders. Early in the nineteenth century, inhabitants of Lexington, led by Scotch-Irish members of

Katharine L. Brown and Kenneth W. Keller

the Alexander, Campbell, Caruthers, Leyburn, Preston, and Shields families, founded literary and debating societies and libraries.[49] They also established a Lexington Volunteer Fire Company after a disastrous fire in 1796.[50] Presbyterians created local Presbyterian congregations and incorporated them by the early nineteenth century, and congregants built church buildings to eliminate the earlier practice of sharing common meetinghouses with Episcopalians.[51] The first Presbyterian meetinghouse in Staunton resembled an appropriately classical republican temple. In Staunton, local worthies were also interested in making money as well as promoting literature, so they petitioned the legislature for lotteries to support the erection of paper and woolen mills, the completion of a church, the channeling of watercourses through the town, and the extension of the charter of the Bank of Alexandria. To protect the town from fire, the same leaders organized a local fire company. The gentlemen of Staunton also complained of hogs running wild and of having to repair the streets themselves, because the inhabitants of the town were unaccustomed to manual labor and preferred that the town government hire workers to perform chores they did not wish to do.[52] The respectable inhabitants of the town required an orderly and dignified community that befit merchants and professional men. By 1800 such Scotch-Irishmen and their descendants led nearly every institution of importance in the Irish Tract.

The last step in the development of a Scotch-Irish elite in the tract brought the demise of the initial landowners, the Beverleys and the Bordens. Resentment against the Beverley and Borden proprietors' monopoly of large tracts of land boiled up during the years of the American Revolution, when people who had settled upon these lands demanded that the proprietors pay taxes on the lands or else convey the lands to people actually settled upon them.[53] Even as late as the beginning of the nineteenth century, the proprietors continued to own the largest landholdings in either county, but their proprietorships were troubled and their lives short. After William Beverley died in 1756, his young son Robert inherited his properties. Robert died near the end of the eighteenth century, when his son Carter Beverley came to Staunton and attempted to live a life of high style in a fashionable brick mansion called "Kalorama." His tastes got the better of him, however, and he sank into such debt that the sheriff had to seize and sell his personal property to pay his creditors. He, and the Beverley family, left Staunton for good by around 1810.[54] The Borden family fared even worse. Benjamin Borden Sr. had died in the middle of the eighteenth century, and his son Robert was embroiled in litigation with people living on his lands. The Borden heirs quarreled among themselves and sued each other repeatedly during the late eighteenth and early nineteenth centuries. The heirs multiplied, thus complicating the tangled inheritance disputes. Some left Virginia while the litigation became even more complicated. It was not ended until the late nineteenth century, when funds in the custody of the Augusta County courts were distributed to the remaining heirs and the case was removed from the docket. Only one member of the Borden family had ever lived on the Borden grant. Like the Beverleys, almost all of the Bordens were absentee owners.[55] Those Scotch-Irish settlers and their descendants who were actual settlers on the land were confirmed in their titles.

Certainly by 1830 a Scotch-Irish elite was installed as the gentry of the Irish Tract. It had not established its status by inherited titles, except through real estate. It did not benefit by the privileges of an established church but benefited by destroying them. It did not exclude other white men from its councils but included an occasional person of German or English descent, while it maintained its political and institutional leadership in the tract. The republican elite of the Irish Tract did not win its status through rank in any standing army or professional officer class but rather established its position through service in the militia, a citizen army. Such an elite kept its position of leadership through the consent of those whom it directed and the blessing of the people's representatives in the legislature. An elite on such a foundation was republican yet a subject of the deference of those upon whose sufferance it depended.

Notes

1. George Tucker, *The Valley of the Shenandoah, or Memoirs of the Graysons* (Chapel Hill: University of North Carolina Press, 1970), 54–57.

2. The most widely and commonly used term that the emigrants from the north of Ireland and their descendants in North America applied to themselves was "Scotch-Irish." It is for this reason that we have adopted "Scotch-Irish" in our article. "Scots-Irish" is of more recent usage, and "Ulster Scots" is employed primarily in Northern Ireland today.

3. Turk McCleskey, "Rich Land, Poor Prospects—Real Estate and the Formation of a Social Elite in Augusta County, Virginia, 1738–1770," *Virginia Magazine of History and Biography* 98 (July 1990): 449–86; Albert H. Tillson Jr., *Gentry and Common Folk—Political Culture on a Virginia Frontier, 1740–1789* (Lexington: University of Kentucky Press, 1991).

4. McCleskey, "Rich Land, Poor Prospects," 469.

5. John McDowell's father had fought with Protestants in Ulster in 1689. Local historians believe the Lewis family of Donegal was descended from Huguenots who had immigrated to Ulster. John Lewis's relative and business partner was James Patton, who

had also done so. See McCleskey, "Rich Land, Poor Prospects," 475; n99, 486. Among the first persons to obtain title in the Irish Tract from Robert Beverley, landholders with common Scotch-Irish names who received titles in 1738 and 1739 included the Lewises, Caldwells, Wilsons, Davisons, McClures, Moffetts, Breckenridges, Kirkpatricks, Hutchesons, Campbells, Reids, Pattersons, McClenachans, Crocketts, Pattons, Doags, Reeds, McCullochs, Craigs, Cunninghams, Thompsons, and Youngs. See J. Lewis Peyton, *History of Augusta County, Virginia,* 2nd edition (Harrisonburg, Va.: C. J. Carrier Press, 1953), 327–28. The early families in the Borden grant included the Alexanders, Allisons, Buchanans, Campbells, Ca256rutherses, Edmistons, Erwins, Halls, Houstons, Lowrys, Lyles, Martins, McChesneys, McClungs, McClures, McCroskeys, McDowells, Montgomerys, Moores, Pattersons, Paxtons, Poagues, Steeles, and Wallaces. See Oren F. Morton, *History of Rockbridge County Virginia* (Baltimore: Clearfield Company, 2002), 343–50.

6. Morton, *History of Rockbridge County, Virginia,* 564. John Lewis was a distant relative of Ephraim McDowell, the father of John McDowell. See Morton, *History of Rockbridge County, Virginia,* 507; McCleskey, "Rich Land, Poor Prospects," 472.

7. Tillson, *Gentry and Common Folk,* 21–22. William Preston was James Patton's nephew.

8. On the tangled history of land speculation schemes in what was to become the state of West Virginia, see Barbara Rasmussen, *Absentee Landowning and Exploitation in West Virginia, 1760–1920* (Lexington: University of Kentucky Press, 1994), 17–44.

9. Thomas Perkins Abernethy, *Western Lands and the American Revolution* (New York: Russell & Russell, 1959), 79–80, 124, 222, 249–50, 274–87.

10. Tucker, *Valley of the Shenandoah,* 41, 55, 169, 319–20.

11. Patricia Givens Johnson, *James Patton and the Appalachian Colonists* (Radford, Va.: Edmunds Printing, 1973). The loss of so many Irish records generally leaves great gaps in seventeenth- and eighteenth-century genealogies, but the conjectural aspects of some family lines would appear to have a strong likelihood of reality. See also Richard K. MacMaster, "Captain James Patton Comes to America, 1737–1740," *Augusta Historical Bulletin* 16 (Fall 1980).

12. John Craig Autobiography in Kerby A. Miller, Arnold Schrier, Bruce D. Boling, and David N. Doyle, *Irish Immigrants in the Land of Canaan: Letters and Memoirs from Colonial and Revolutionary America, 1675–1815* (New York: Oxford University Press, 2003), 392.

13. An excellent record of the extensive interconnections among these Scotch-Irish families can be found in Irvin Frazier et al., *The Family of John Lewis, Pioneer* (San Antonio, Texas: Fisher Publications, 1960).

14. Mary D. Robertson, ed., *Lucy Breckinridge of Grove Hill: The Journal of a Virginia Girl, 1862–1864* (Kent, Ohio: Kent State University Press, 1979), 2–5.

15. Allen Johnson, ed., *Dictionary of American Biography* (New York: Charles Scribner's Sons, 1929), vol. 3:126. Rich material on the relationship between John Brown and his brother-in-law, William Preston, is to be found in letters between the two in the Draper Papers at the Wisconsin Historical Society and available on microfilm. Philip Fithian, the

young Presbyterian theology student and diarist, visited in John Brown's household and has interesting observations to offer about Margaret Preston Brown and her daughters. Philip Vickers Fithian, *Journal, 1775–1776, Written on the Virginia-Pennsylvania Frontier and in the Army around New York,* ed. Robert G. Albion and Leonidas Dodson (Princeton, N.J.: Princeton University Press, 1934), 141–44.

16. Peyton, *History of Augusta County,* 306–8.

17. Tucker, *Valley of the Shenandoah,* 59, 151, 158, 166, 168.

18. J. Lewis Peyton, *Memoir of John Howe Peyton in Sketches by His Contemporaries* (Staunton, Va.: A. B. Blackburn, 1894), 8, 14, 37, 45, 54, 72–73, 78–79, 90–91, 108, 113.

19. Peyton, *History of Augusta County,* 69–74.

20. Augusta County Vestry Book, April 6, 1747, Augusta County Courthouse.

21. Peyton, *History of Augusta County,* 97.

22. The story has been told from a clearly American point of view in Howard McKnight Wilson, *Great Valley Patriots—Western Virginia in the Struggle for Liberty* (Verona, Va.: McClure Press, 1976).

23. The Augusta freeholders' statement of February 22, 1775, known to local historians as the "Augusta Resolves," is published in its complete form in William J. Van Schreeven and Robert L. Scribner, eds., *Revolutionary Virginia—The Road to Independence,* vol. 2: *The Committees and the Second Convention, 1773–1775—A Documentary Record* (Richmond: University Press of Virginia for the Virginia American Revolution Bicentennial Commission, 1975), 300. John Lewis Peyton's *History of Augusta County* gives a shortened version of the Augusta resolutions that leaves out a reference to show that Augusta Countians were responding to an earlier similar protest from Fairfax County, Virginia, thus indicating that the Augusta Resolves were not the first call for resistance in Virginia. See Peyton, *History of Augusta County,* 173–74.

24. Isaac Weld, *Travels through the States of North America,* ed. Martin Roth (New York: Johnson Reprint, 1968), vol. 1:237–38.

25. Robert L. Scribner et al., eds., *Revolutionary Virginia—The Road to Independence* (Charlottesville: University of Virginia Press, 1973–1983), volumes 1–7, indicate the Irish Tract representatives attended sessions of all of the revolutionary conventions except the first.

26. Van Schreeven and Scribner, *Revolutionary Virginia,* vol. 2, 301; Peyton, *History of Augusta County,* 285–86, 302, 333–35; Wilson, *Great Valley Patriots,* 210, 211, 212, 215; Frazier et al., *Family of John Lewis,* 23–33.

27. Arthur Campbell's statement of his political philosophy appears in David Hackett Fischer, *The Revolution of American Conservatism* (New York: Harper & Row, 1965).

28. Norman K. Risjord, *Chesapeake Politics, 1781–1800* (New York: Columbia University Press, 1978), 45; Fischer, *Revolution of American Conservatism,* 79; William G. Shade, *Democratizing the Old Dominion—Virginia and the Second Party System, 1824–1861* (Charlottesville: University of Virginia Press, 1996), 120, 138–39. Shade calls Augusta County "the premier western Whig constituency" in Virginia. Virginia did not have universal white male suffrage until 1851. Prior to that time, voters had to be freeholders to qualify.

29. Tucker, *Valley of the Shenandoah,* 44.

30. Thomas E. Buckley, *Church and State in Revolutionary Virginia, 1776–1787* (Charlottesville: University Press of Virginia, 1977), 12–14, 53–54, 137–38.

31. Howard McKnight Wilson, "Zechariah Johnston, A Virginia Champion of Freedom," *Augusta Historical Bulletin* 8 (Spring 1972): 29–45.

32. Remonstrance of a Number of Inhabitants of Augusta County, Legislative Petitions, Augusta County, December 4, 1786, Box 15, Folder 52, Virginia State Archives, Library of Virginia, Richmond.

33. Buckley, *Church and State,* 97–98. See also petition of John Davidson et al., December 1, 1784, Rockbridge County Petitions, Virginia Legislative Petitions, Box 221, Folder 13; petition of November 2, 1785, Box 221, Folder 14, Virginia State Archives, Library of Virginia, Richmond.

34. John M. McDaniel, Charles N. Watson, and David T. Moore, *Liberty Hall Academy—The Early History of the Institutions Which Evolved into Washington and Lee University* (Lexington, Va.: Liberty Hall Press, 1979), xi–24.

35. See petitions of November 24, 1794, Box 221, Folder 30; December 9, 1797, Box 221, Folder 34; December 19, 1799, Box 221, Folder 40; December 15, 1807, Box 221, Folder 54, Rockbridge County Petitions, Virginia Legislative Petitions, Virginia State Archives, Library of Virginia, Richmond.

36. Petition of October 10, 1792, Augusta County Petitions, Virginia Legislative Petitions, Virginia State Archives, Library of Virginia, Richmond.

37. Peyton, *History of Augusta County,* 214, 308, 311, 312, 317.

38. Petition of November 2, 1793, Legislative Petitions, Augusta County, Virginia State Archives, Library of Virginia, Richmond.

39. Petition of citizens of the County of Augusta, December 4, 1812, Legislative Petitions, Augusta County, Virginia State Archives, Library of Virginia, Richmond.

40. Richard A. Rutyna and Peter C. Stewart, *The History of Freemasonry in Virginia* (Lanham, Md.: University Press of America, 1998), 33, 45; Steven C. Bullock, *Revolutionary Brotherhood—Freemasonry and the Transformation of the American Social Order, 1730–1840* (Chapel Hill: University of North Carolina Press, 1996), 50–169.

41. John Dove, *Virginia Text Book Containing "The Book of Constitutions,"* 19th edition (Highland Springs, Va.: Masonic Home Press, 1944), 10–17. This work contains the rules for admitting members to the fraternity in Virginia that were compiled in 1790.

42. William Moseley Brown, *Freemasonry in Staunton, Virginia* (Staunton, Va.: McClure Printing, 1949), 29, 90.

43. William Waller Hening, ed., *The Statutes at Large; Being a Collection of All the Laws of Virginia from the First Session of the Legislature in the Year 1619* (Richmond, Va.: Franklin Press, 1820), vol. 7:475.

44. Samuel Shepherd, ed., *The Statutes at Large of Virginia, from October Session 1792, to December Session 1806, Inclusive . . .* New Series (New York: AMS Press, 1970), vols. 1:266, 2:216.

45. Ibid., vol. 2:262, 270.

46. Ibid., 335–36. See also Petition of the Freeholders of the Town of Staunton, 1801, Legislative Petitions, Augusta County, Virginia State Archives, Library of Virginia, Richmond.

47. The plat of Newtown is found in the first land tax book for Staunton at the clerk's office, Staunton Courthouse. Deeds for the sale of the lots are recorded in Augusta County, with Alexander St. Clair as grantor, until 1801. After the formation of the Court of Hustings for Staunton, deeds are recorded in Staunton deed books one and two with St. Clair as grantor.

48. All Stuart addition sales are recorded in Staunton deed books, with the Stuarts as grantors.

49. Morton, *History of Rockbridge County*, 215.

50. David R. Rossi, "History of the Lexington Fire Department, 1796–1899," *Proceedings of the Rockbridge Historical Society* 12 (1995–2002): 434.

51. Petition of the Tinkling Spring Congregation, October 15, 1792; Petition of Inhabitants of Augusta County and Members of the Presbyterian Church Usually Denominated Augusta Church, December 10, 1805, Legislative Petitions, Augusta County, Virginia State Archives, Library of Virginia, Richmond.

52. Petition of William Bowyer et al., October 28, 1789; petition of Gideon Morgan, Peter Burkhart, et al., November 13, 1790; memorial of Thomas Douthat, October 28, 1793; petition to extend the charter of the Bank of Alexandria, December 19, 1799; petition for the general benefit of Staunton, December 24, 1807, Legislative Petitions, Augusta County, Virginia State Archives, Library of Virginia, Richmond.

53. Petition of the Inhabitants of the Countyes [sic] of Augusta and Rockbridge, June 13, 1783, Legislative Petitions, Augusta County, Virginia State Archives, Library of Virginia, Richmond.

54. Joseph A. Waddell, *Annals of Augusta County, Virginia, from 1720 to 1871*, 2nd ed. (Harrisonburg, Va.: C. J. Carrier, 1986), 29.

55. Morton, *History of Rockbridge County*, 21–32.

Searching for Security: Backcountry Carolina, 1760s–1780s

Michael Montgomery

What images come most readily to mind when we think of early American colonies? Beyond the dockside where ships unloaded their cargoes and emigrant passengers (such as the one for Philadelphia recreated at the Ulster American Folk Park in Northern Ireland today), what was the landscape to be found really like? Textbooks and standard histories, especially in the United States, more often than not portray the European settlement of America as the steady growth and spread of well-ordered communities, particularly small villages centered upon a local school, church, or inn.

At best, however, this picture is a partial and often misleading one, according to Jack P. Greene, an eminent historian of the American colonies, who argues that it is an unfortunate legacy of nineteenth-century New England historians, most prominently George Bancroft (1808–1891).[1] In his book *Pursuits of Happiness,* Greene concludes that such a view may faithfully reflect life in Massachusetts and nearby Puritan colonies but not that in the Chesapeake colonies of Virginia and Maryland, with their more fluid, often undisciplined, societies, or in the rest of British North America both on the mainland and in the Caribbean. He writes that, "far from having been a peripheral, much less a deviant, area, the southern colonies and states were before 1800 in the mainstream of British-American development. Indeed, perhaps as much as any of the several distinctive regional entities that emerged in colonial British America during the early modern era, they epitomized what was arguably the most important element in the emerging British-American culture: the conception of America as a place in which free people could pursue their own individual happinesses in safety and with a fair prospect that they might be successful in their several quests."[2]

Nowhere in the American South was this description more fitting than in South Carolina, founded in Charles Town (now Charleston) at the confluence of the Ashley and Cooper rivers in 1670 as an extension of Barbados and the only mainland British colony not settled directly from Britain. Not far upriver from that colonial capital lay a rough hinterland that officials in the capital only sometimes and with middling success sought to govern over the next century. Across the Savannah River, the Georgia colony (established in 1733) formed an even more unsettled western and southern frontier, with native tribes having interests of their own and acting in league with other European powers, threatening to do so, or feared to do so (see map 7.1). The Spanish in Florida posed a danger to South Carolina until the Georgia colony provided a buffer. The larger tribes to the north, northwest, and west included the Creeks, the Chickasaws, the Choctaws, the Cherokees, and the Catawbas. They contended with one another and were also players in larger struggles, first between Britain and France, and then between Britain and the united colonies of America, and finally against the new nation itself. Their presence, along with large numbers of enslaved Africans from many different areas of that continent, made South Carolina the most fluid and heterogeneous part of North America in the eighteenth century. To grasp fully how the early interior South developed, one must understand how diverse peoples from each of three continents came to negotiate a shared but highly varied landscape in places like South Carolina.

The earliest Europeans permanently in South Carolina were English by way of the Caribbean. But soon there were Scots, Swedes, Jews, Germans, Welsh, and French. Two years after revocation of the Edict of Nantes in 1685, six shiploads of French Huguenots sailed for America, bound mainly for Charles Town, which became a haven and remains a center for Huguenot heritage to this day. By the early 1700s, emigrants from Ireland, especially from Ulster, also arrived, some through the port of Charles Town, to populate a terrain not well ordered by rivers or valleys, others down the Great Wagon Road from North Carolina and Virginia. These two streams of migrants converged in the Carolina interior (or backcountry) by the early 1750s.

Its fertile soils and its situation on trade routes both along the Atlantic and into a vast area as far west as the Mississippi River made South Carolina an inviting place for anyone seeking immediate economic opportunities, especially the acquisition of land. But the price to pay was sometimes great, for the mortality rate from malaria and other diseases was fearfully high, making it uncertain whether the resident white population, long in a minority, could reproduce itself. Then, too, there was the insecurity of life in a colony under threat posed by Indian war (such as the disastrous conflict with the Yamassee in 1715) and slave insurrection (such as the Stono Rebellion in 1739).

Michael Montgomery

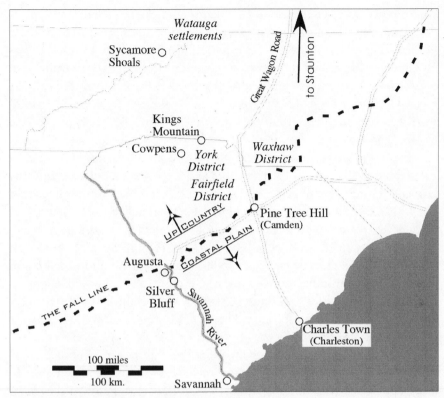

Map 7.1. *Backcountry Carolina, 1760s to 1780s.*

In the early days, ranching and producing naval stores were important economic activities in the colony, replaced in the eighteenth century by agricultural products, especially rice in coastal areas after 1720. Before long, slave traders were actively seeking skilled Africans from the Senegambia coast, famed for its rice cultivation, to tend the fields along South Carolina's two-hundred-mile coast.[3] It was exports of rice that placed South Carolina among the wealthiest of the thirteen rebelling colonies by 1776.

Although the Church of England had official status in South Carolina, in the hinterland there was little practical conformity to it. Its representatives were few on the ground, and religious toleration was de facto the order of the day just as adherence to other authority was haphazard. The Englishman Charles Woodmason, one clergyman who was sent circa 1760 to Pine Tree Hill (present-day Camden), a difficult hundred miles from the coast, to bring backcountry folk into the Anglican fold, had a particularly trying experience with settlers of Ulster extraction who had migrated from the northern parts of Ireland, and whose qualities he described thus in his journal: "a finer Body of Land is nowhere to be seen—But it is occupied by a Sett of the lowest vilest Crew breathing—Scotch Irish Presbyterians from the North of Ireland. . . . These people are all from Ireland, and live wholly on Butter, Milk, Clabber, and what in England is given to Hogs and Dogs . . . Ignorant, mean, worthless, beggarly Irish Presbyterians, the Scum of the Earth, the Refuse of Mankind."[4]

Toleration was a simple, direct byproduct of land settlement. To create a geographical buffer against native tribes and a population buffer against the burgeoning numbers of Africans (estimates are that 40 percent of African slaves in North America were brought through Charles Town), the South Carolina government sought to attract "poor Protestants" from Britain and Ireland. First it granted bounties of land outright. Then in the 1730s it laid out a series of eleven "townships" sixty miles or more inland and issued cheap land grants on favorable terms to Swiss, Germans, and others.[5] The opportunities that townships and other settlement arrangements presented were advertised abroad. After one appeal appeared in the October 21, 1763, issue of the *Belfast Newsletter,* 170 passengers in Belfast took sail on the *Prince of Wales* for Charles Town the following month.[6] After the arrival of such ships, dissenters came rapidly to outnumber members of the established church, and South Carolina formed a southern counterpart to Pennsylvania in its reception of non-Anglicans.

For three generations, plantation agriculture, based on chattel slavery, was concentrated in coastal areas, while farming units in the interior were usually small family homesteads. Agriculture was only one of the economic engines of colonial South Carolina, however. The greatest potential for prosperity lay in the Indian trade, first established in 1674. Quick profits made in that early period were what enabled many Charles Town families to acquire the capital for purchasing slaves and developing plantations. For the better part of a century, rapid fortunes were to be made in the Indian trade. Indeed, one observer commented in 1709 that traders "soonest rais'd themselves of any People I have known in Carolina."[7] It was always and probably inevitably a ruthless, cutthroat, and unpredictable business. Not until more than thirty years after the trade was founded were steps first taken to regulate it with the establishment of the Commission of the Indian Trade in 1707, and not until after recovery from the Yamassee War eight years later did these steps begin to take hold, whereby traders were required to be licensed and were forbidden to deal in rum or to take captives for nonpayment of debts. However, the system long remained riven with abuse, most tragically in the trafficking of native slaves sold to other colonies.

In particular, the Indian trade lured unmarried men, either singly or in small companies, into the interior in search of the economic independence and security that could come from prospecting for the unlimited skins of white-tailed deer. The work was dangerous and intensely competitive among traders serving the British, the French, or the Spanish. For it to function on the colonial side required the coordination of a network of traders, politicians, bankers, merchants, and servants of all kinds. Trading companies themselves often had a hierarchy of one or two "master traders" at the top, down to many hirelings (packhorsemen and servants of all kinds). On the workaday level the trade involved the exchange of such European goods as clothing, blankets, firearms and ammunition, cooking utensils, and other metal wares for furs and especially deerskins destined for the markets of London and Amsterdam. On a much broader level, the trade intermeshed with British imperial interests in the vast territory between the Savannah River and the French empire to the west, i.e., from what is now Tennessee south to the lower Mississippi Valley and the Gulf of Mexico.

Backcountry traders were by and large the key to stable management of relations between indigenous peoples and the British. They were the vital link in the flow of commodities and, just as important, information for the security of the South Carolina colony. They were the de facto monitors of all activity and intelligence in the hinterland, and their dealings were no less than "the basis of white-Indian relations" in colonial America.[8] But they were also in business for themselves, always dealing with unscrupulous competitors. Hundreds of men worked the trade in South Carolina after the defeat of the Yamassee began opening up the interior territory to trade, though its relative importance to the colony's economy declined after midcentury. Although trading went back to the first days of the colony, by the 1730s men from Ireland had begun to dominate the trade through superior organization and networking, and they often preferred to hire compatriots. This can be surmised from their surnames as found in newspaper accounts, correspondence kept by the colonial government, and occasionally other sources.[9] Many had come to the colony as indentured servants. Though at first few had money to their name, they were often able to apprentice themselves in a firm operated by a fellow countryman or kinsman or to receive a small line of credit through such a person.[10]

The man who became the most prominent and successful of all South Carolina Indian traders was George Galphin, who in 1737 emigrated to Savannah from north County Armagh, an area of Ulster mainly populated by descendants of settlers from the southwest and from the northwest Midlands of England in the plantation period a century earlier.[11] Born around 1710, he was one of six children of Barbara and Thomas Galphin, a linen weaver whose economic prospects had been severely limited because of British restrictions on the exportation of linen from Ireland.[12] By the early 1740s, Galphin joined the Augusta Company, a trading firm founded by Patrick Brown and John Rae headquartered in Augusta, Georgia, and licensed to trade with the Creeks. Galphin soon procured a license himself. Brown, from southern Ireland, and Rae, from near Ballynahinch in County Down, were already prosperous men who were gaining near-monopolistic control over the fur and deerskin trade near modern-day Augusta. Before long Galphin obtained his own license and established a trading post or store at Silver Bluff, on the South Carolina side of the Savannah River, thirteen miles southeast of Augusta, and began looking for land. By 1752 he had been successful enough that he could purchase a nearby plantation, scale back his own travels into Indian territory, and hire others to do the harder work of the business.

From Silver Bluff, Galphin developed an extensive network to deal with the Creeks and other tribes in modern-day Georgia and Alabama, one that he maintained for nearly three decades. In his career we see in especially dramatic fashion that contacts with the natives were more often symbiotic and mutually dependent than confrontational and how thoroughly the lives of Europeans and indigenous peoples were intertwined in colonial America. Galphin's abilities were unparalleled as a diplomat, interpreter, businessman, spy, and quite possibly a double-dealer. As a result, he became one of the wealthiest men in the South Carolina backcountry and presided over a personal trading empire that stretched westward for hundreds of miles. The continuous flow of all ranks of Indians, traders, and officials through his Silver Bluff estate made it one of the chief intelligence points in the backcountry, a nerve center as much as an outpost. He entertained colonial dignitaries and organized parties of Creeks to visit Charles Town to confer with the governor of the colony, all the while strengthening his own position in the trade.

Early in his career, Galphin took a Creek wife,[13] which no doubt aided his becoming, in the terminology of the day, a "linguister," or interpreter. The intimate knowledge he gained of the customs and habits of several peoples whose cultures were very different from his own brought an economic advantage that few could rival. His negotiating talents and his careful finger

Michael Montgomery

on the pulse of tribal sentiments and activities made him indispensable to the British in the Seven Years' War in countering attempted French provocations of tribes in the interior. He proved equally valuable to the colonials when in 1775 the Continental Congress appointed him its commissioner of Indian affairs in the South.[14] Having secured his own financial independence, he cast his lot to defend those who sought political independence, investing decades of trust to persuade the Creeks to stay neutral despite British efforts from their base in Florida to enlist them in opening a rear southwestern front in the war.

While the Indian trade in which Galphin played a major role brought quick wealth to a few, most traders left only a name, if that much, in colonial records or in newspapers and never rose above the level of hireling. But the trade remained both lucrative and instrumental in South Carolina's security and prosperity. At its peak around 1750, 150,000 deerskins a year were shipped from Charles Town, accounting for 20 percent of the colony's exports. Other than perhaps land speculation (in which he was also engaged), the Indian trade in Galphin's day provided the "get-rich" opportunity par excellence to young men of middling or lower ranks of society, especially emigrants from Ulster and elsewhere in Ireland who sought enough money to buy land and settle down. As a pathway to upward social mobility and respectability, the trade epitomized the quest for economic independence.

Letters from such contemporaries as the merchant Henry Laurens and the naturalist William Bartram, who were guests at his table, indicate that Galphin's Silver Bluff estate was, in Bartram's terms, "a very celebrated place." With income from the deerskin trade and the labor of slaves this income afforded, Galphin had transformed a simple trading station on the edge of European settlement into a large plantation growing indigo, maize, and other crops and enjoyed a lifestyle of near-legendary scale by backcountry standards. His estate became a meeting ground where peoples of three worlds—diverse groups of Europeans, Indians, and Africans—came together, where one could witness a new, multi-ethnic society being formed and all kinds of cultural exchange taking place. One and all came and went to Silver Bluff. On his property and under his auspices, African Americans first worshiped at their own church in South Carolina. Silver Bluff Baptist Church, founded in 1773 as an offshoot of Emmanuel Baptist Church in Savannah, was one of the birthplaces of organized African American religion.[15] In 2001 the congregation received a grant of $250,000 to restore the building to its 1873 state, and a historical marker erected at the site states: "This church, one of the first black Baptist churches in America, grew out of regular worship services held as early as the 1750s at 'Silver Bluff,' the estate of Indian trader George Galphin. At first a nondenominational congregation with both white and black members, it was formally organized as Silver Bluff Baptist Church in 1773, with Rev. Walt Palmer as its first preacher."

There is no method to calculate Galphin's wealth, but at his death in 1780 he owned at least fourteen thousand acres of land and perhaps as many as fifty thousand, and two of the three houses cited in his will were of brick, not the "post-in-the-ground frame dwellings and log cabins" usually found in the backcountry.[16] On his property were three mills, considerable livestock, numerous outbuildings, warehouses, slave quarters, and, as noted, at least one church. Among other things, Galphin's detailed will made provision for children by an African American woman, a native woman, and a European woman. Five years after his death, a wife he apparently had left in Ireland a half-century earlier filed claim for part of his estate.[17] His will, reproduced in Appendix 1, shows that he was generous to relations, friends, and strangers alike, leaving fifty pounds sterling to "all the poor widows and fatherless children within thirty miles of where I live in the Provinces of South Carolina and Georgia" and same amounts "to be shared among the poor of Eneskilling and . . . among the poor of Armagh in Ireland."

In 1996 archaeologists at the Savannah River Archaeological Research Project began surveying and excavating the foundations on Galphin's Silver Bluff compound.[18] The dig at an initial one-hundred-by-one-hundred-meter plot revealed six structures, including two brick buildings, the "main trade house or store where business was conducted," and three other buildings that were most likely residences.[19] One brick building had a stone chimney similar in construction to ones found in Ireland.[20] Other remains suggest a cellar and a kitchen, and researchers were still tracing the one side of a palisade that they located. The excavation promised to continue into the foreseeable future and provide a perspective on backcountry life in South Carolina to complement and balance what is the most famous (if not also infamous) account, Woodmason's journal.[21]

Galphin made his mark in what was a little-populated part of the South Carolina colony, where settlers were relatively few on the ground and their impact was individual more than collective. This was in contrast to an area a hundred miles away, along South Carolina's border with North Carolina. Here from the 1750s other settlers, mainly family groups who were the children of Ulster emigrants, spread down from points north and began rapidly to establish farmsteads, churches, and dispersed rural communities. Few of

Michael Montgomery

these settlers could have imagined or aspired to Galphin's vision of becoming members of an emerging elite of prosperous backcountry planters. They came as commoners with modest hopes and prospects, seeking the security and self-sufficiency of dispersed rural settlements, quite different from the orderly town life of New Englanders.

While Galphin left at least sixteen letters, these were business documents to colonial officials presenting details of the negotiations, misfortunes, encounters, and challenges of running a precarious trade involving very different parties constantly seeking an advantage over one another. The letter reproduced below in Appendix 2, written in his capacity as Southern Indian Commissioner to Henry Laurens, secretary of the Continental Congress, gives a close view of Galphin's efforts to keep the western periphery of the colony pacified in 1778. It was also a potent reminder to the Congress, as his earlier service had been to colonial authorities, of Galphin's statesmanship and his importance to their well-being. Collectively his letters tell us much about his activities but ultimately reveal little about the person. Galphin's will does much more of the latter.

We know more about the more numerous settlers in the South Carolina "upcountry," to the north of Silver Bluff, than about Indian traders because of the roles the former played in the impending struggle to free the colonies from British rule. They had come to America singly and in families for land and for stability, self-sufficiency, self-determination, and independence from Old World authority. For these reasons many of them joined the American rebellion that commenced in 1776 in that spirit.[22] Indeed, they appeared not only in contemporary records and sketches, but also in accounts that have been passed down to later generations and in events that are reenacted annually.

In South Carolina the conflict between 1775 and 1780 became as brutal as anywhere. Officials in Charles Town were fiery for rebellion, but their long neglect of the backcountry in not providing constables and in refusing to permit or allow many legal proceedings beyond the capital had bred much resentment against them. These mistreatments meant that the inherently less disciplined nature of backcountry life could easily descend into lawlessness. That the backcountry was often a chaotic place became evident with the rise of the Regulator movements, a revolt against the colonial government in North Carolina in the early 1770s. Similar tendencies threatened stability in the South Carolina interior throughout the decade. When war finally came, many there wavered in their allegiance, using circumstances to settle personal grievances against fellow citizens, shifting their partisanship according to the fortunes of one side or another, or opposing the cause for independence altogether. Families were split, and vigilantism was all too frequently the order of the day, as reprisals and depredations followed one another.

In 1780, the most critical year of the American Revolution, the upcountry settlements of York District and Fairfield District were being severely pressed by British forces headquartered in Charles Town, which they had captured two years earlier. Engagements across a wide swath of the backcountry climaxed in two confrontations that turned the very tide of the conflict: on October 7, 1780, at Kings Mountain (now a national military park) and on January 17, 1781, at Cowpens (a national battlefield). At Kings Mountain, the Continental victory was its most decisive and significant in the South. By one account eight hundred patriot soldiers, twenty-eight were killed and sixty-two wounded. The battle destroyed the left wing of the main British army in the Carolinas (composed of American loyalists), which had 225 killed (including Scotsman Major Patrick Ferguson, its commander), 163 wounded, and 716 taken prisoner. General Lord Cornwallis was forced into a slow retreat from the South that culminated in surrender at Yorktown. According to British commander-in-chief General Sir Henry Clinton, the battle of Kings Mountain "unhappily proved the first link in a chain of events that followed each other in regular succession until they at last ended in the total loss of America" only twelve months later.[23]

The battle of Kings Mountain achieved legendary status within two generations, as evidenced by Lyman Draper's tireless travel in the 1840s compiling accounts from veterans of the engagement and their descendants,[24] not only because it reversed colonial fortunes in a war that ended only a few months later but also because a large proportion of its combatants were the sharpshooting "overmountain" men who had undertaken a dramatic march from the Watauga settlements of North Carolina (present-day Tennessee) and from Virginia to meet the British off-guard.[25] As generations have passed, their status has become more heroic. Writing to Clinton, his superior, about the ignominy, British general Lord Cornwallis admitted that "a numerous and unexpected enemy came from the mountains; as they had good horses their movements were rapid" and about the impending confrontation in Virginia stated with foreboding that "after everything that has happened I will not presume to make your Excellency any sanguine promises."[26]

Many other South Carolinians having Ulster roots were caught up in the struggle as well, none more famous than Andrew Jackson, born in 1767 in the Waxhaw District near the North Carolina border, the son of emigrants who left from near Carrickfergus in 1765.[27] The mustering of the Overmountain Men at Sycamore Shoals on the Long Island of the Holston River and their march to South Carolina continue to be reenacted every year and are now recognized in the Overmountain Men National Historic Trail.[28] In 1785 many of these participants led the movement (ultimately unsuccessful) to establish the state of Franklin, the first self-governing entity west of the mountains in what is now Tennessee. Jackson soon removed to the area himself and participated in founding the new state of Tennessee in 1796.

By the end of 1780, George Galphin was dead. His stockade at Silver Bluff, which had become Fort Galphin during the war before being abandoned in 1778 because of its exposed position, was taken by the British in December 1780 and renamed Fort Dreadnought.[29] Five months later, the site was destroyed when American general Harry Lee retook it. Nonetheless, Galphin's hand in ensuring patriot victories in South Carolina was indispensable. A little-known prelude to the engagements to come was a conference in Georgia in June 1777 between George Galphin and his old friends, the Creeks.[30] Lacking funds from a cash-strapped colonial government, he used much of his wealth and stores over a period of two and one-half years to supply goods to the Creeks and keep the trade alive (the amounts designated in his will to heirs were still prodigious). This, along with his diplomacy, kept them neutral and the unprotected western flank of the southern colonies safe.

Thus, emigrants from Ireland, especially the Scotch-Irish from Ulster, played a pivotal role in the war's success in the southern theater and ultimately in securing the cause of independence. Though their actions were often heroic and they well understood the need for sacrifice, we must be careful not to romanticize or overgeneralize about them. The conflict in which they were engaged often took the character of a civil war, with many South Carolinians of Ulster ancestry, even in the backcountry, opposing the rebellion rather than joining it, as a way of resisting an authoritarian government closer to hand in Charles Town than the one in London and in expressing their desire for autonomy. The dramatic, larger-than-life figures of rough-and-ready volunteers firing in Indian style formation as they wrested control of Kings Mountain from bewildered Tory forces and the career of George Galphin can easily obscure the conflicting and sometimes ambivalent motivations of people and their descendants whose lives grappled with sectionalism, social and economic dislocation, racial diversity, constant threat of insecurity, and other forces that made the struggle for independence especially uncertain and often bloody there.

At first the Indian trade directed from Charles Town and the peopling of the South Carolina backcountry through migration from more northerly colonies may seem to be two unrelated processes. Both frontier outposts and settled communities were originally motivated by the search, often by emigrants from Ulster, for economic security on only a personal scale. But Galphin and the revolutionaries had a fundamental commonality, in that they recognized that individual economic security was not without its obligations. Their willingness to bind together and to put their livelihood at risk was what turned out to be crucial in achieving political security and independence for the colonies with the Treaty of Paris in 1783. As elsewhere, the search for "individual happinesses" grew into a larger, collective quest for security, but it had the personal angle of sacrifice. The common denominator is that individual economic security has minimal value without sacrifice. These two sentiments are seen most clearly in the person of George Galphin, entrepreneur and patriot, a man of humble beginnings but unquestioned generosity and willingness to serve. It was his efforts, his contacts, and the willingness to exhaust his personal treasure to keep good relations with the Creeks that gave the colonials much-needed breathing space and played a part too rarely acknowledged or celebrated in winning the American cause.

Appendix 1

Will of George Galphin

Will dated April 6, 1776. Exrs: James Parsons, John Graham, Lauchlin McGillvery, Esq., John Parkinson *Merc.* Wit: Michael Meyer, John Sturzenegger, David Zubly. Ment: Lived in 96 Dist. Will that my mulatto girl named Barbara be free. I give to my mulatto girls Rachael and Betsy (daughters of a mulatto woman named Sapho) their freedom. Give to my halfbreed Indian girl, Rose (daughter of Nitehuckey) her freedom. I Give to Thomas Galphin, son of Rachel Dupee, and his sister, Cowpen, in Ogechee, horses, cattle, etc. Also grist mill and saw mill situated on the north side of Town Creek. Also land from Mr. Shaw's lower line upon Savannah River at the Spanish Cutoff, down the said river to Mr. McGillvery's lower line, containing about 1300 acres in the Province of Georgia. Also 350 acres of acres upon Ogechee, which I bought of Patrick Dennison. Give to Martha Galphin, daughter of Rachel Dupee, 500 acres of land above Augusta, in Georgia. Also cattle, etc. at Ogechee. Give to George, son of Metawney (an Indian Woman), stock of cattle with his own, his sister Judith's and brother John's mark and brand. Also the old brick house, in S. C. land above the Spanish Cutoff on Savannah River in Georgia. Give to John, son of Metawney, cattle with his own, his sister Judith's and brother George's mark. Also land upon Ogechee, in Georgia, called the Old Town. Give unto Judith, daughter of Metawney, land and dwelling at Silver Bluff, where she now lives, in S. C. Give unto Barbara, daughter of Rose, decd., land at Silver Bluff in S. C. Give unto Thomas slaves, etc. Give to David Holms land in Georgia. Give to Judith Galphin, my sister, 150 pounds sterling. I leave Catherine Galphin, living in Ireland, 150 pounds sterling. To my sister, Margaret Holms, 50 pounds sterling. To each of her children, now in Ireland, 50 pounds sterling. To her son Robert, now living here, 50 pounds sterling. Give to Mrs. Taylor 50 pounds sterling, etc. To my cousin George Rankin, in Ireland, 70 pounds sterling, to him or his children. Leave to George Nowlan 50 pounds sterling. I leave to my Aunt Lennard's daughter in Ireland, to her and her children, 50 pounds sterling. Leave to my cousin John Trotter, 50 pounds, to him and his children. I leave to Rachel (daughter of Sapho) two negro men and two negro women to be bought out of the first ship that comes in with negros. Give to Thomas, son of Rachel Dupee, and his children to be maintained and schooled on the plantation. Leave to Betsey Callwell, daughter of Mary Callwell, land at the Three Runs, at the Old Stomp, above Tims Branch. Also 50 pounds Carolina currency. I leave to all the poor widows and fatherless children within thirty miles of where I live in the Provinces of South Carolina and Georgia 50 pounds sterling. I leave 50 pounds sterling to be shared among the poor of Eneskilling and 50 pounds sterling to be shared among the poor of Armagh in Ireland. Leave to Timothy Barnard 200 pounds sterling. Leave to all the orphan children I brought up 10 pounds sterling each and Billey Brown to be bound out to a trade. I leave John McQueen and Alexander, his brother, each a good riding horse. Leave to Mr. Netherclif and his wife each a ring. Leave to Mr. and Mrs. Wylly each a ring. Leave to their daughter Sucky Wylly 50 pounds. Leave to Mrs. Campbell a ring. Leave to Mr. Carlan a ring. Leave to Mrs. Fraisier a ring. Leave to Mr. Newman a ring. Give to the widow Adkins, 20 pounds sterling. To her son William, a riding horse. Give to Parson Seymour and his wife, each a ring. Give to George Parsons, a likely negro boy to be bought him out of the first ship that comes in. Leave to Quintin Tooler 500 acres of ceded land and to all the rest of my Cousin Toolers (men and women) each a ring. I leave my sister Young, in Ireland, 50 pounds sterling, and to each of her children 50 pounds. Give to

Clotworthy Robson 500 acres, to his and his heirs. Give to my sister Martha, wife of William Crossley, slaves, etc.

From Willie Pauline Young, *Abstracts of Old Ninety-Six and Abbeville District Wills and Bonds: as on File in the Abbeville, South Carolina, Courthouse* (Easley, S.C.: Southern Historical Press, 1977), 128–29.

Appendix 2

Letter from George Galphin to Henry Laurens
November 11, 1778

My Dear Sir

I wrote you the other Day InClosg you Some talks the white men I Sent to the Creek[s.] to Demand Sattisfation Sent me the InClose[d] talks by an Indian I find our frind[s.] Can not give us the Satisfattion we Demande[d] a warr is unavodable with our Enemis but it is our Enterest to keep them Divide[d] till we are redey for them I beLeve we have Lost Some groun[d] In the Creek[s.] by Stoping the trade I noe[d] it was ronge at the Same time but the people upon the frontier[s] thret[d] to kill me & the Indian[s.] two if I Seply[d] them InClose[d] is a Cop[y.] of an affadav[d.] you will Se what it Say[s.] it is har[d] a man[s] Livi[g] Shoul[d] be threten[d] for Doing all in his power to Serve his Contry & our Enemis ofering a Large rewar[d.] for me De[d] or aLive the Cede[d] Lan[d] people may thanke them Selves for the Creeke warr as [it] never w[d] been in Stuart[s] power to have Set them on us I beleve I menti[d] to you before there was 5 Indian[s] kill[d] before one white man was kill[d] upon the frontiers it will be an Exepensef warr but there may be Land[s] got from them to pay a great part of it numbers of people in the Cede[d.] Lan[d] has run a great Deale of the Indian Land out that was a neff to Set them on us I thinke them that run it ought not to get a foot of it when it is got from the Indian[s.]

it is reporte[d] hear the king[s] troop[s] has Left Neue Yourke god Sen[d] it may be true and that the french has tacke two Island[s.] from the Englissh

My Complimt[s.] to your Son I am Dear Sir
Your Excell[y.] most Obed & Oblige[d] humble / Servant

George Galphin

From David R. Chestnut and C. James Taylor, *The Papers of Henry Laurens,* vol. 14. (Columbia: University of South Carolina Press for the South Carolina Historical Society, 1994).

Notes

1. See especially his *History of the United States of America, from the Discovery of the Continent* (New York: Appleton, 1892).

2. Jack Greene, *Pursuits of Happiness: The Social Development of Early Modern British Colonies and the Formation of American Culture* (Chapel Hill: University of North Carolina Press, 1988), 5.

3. Charles W. Joyner, *Down by the Riverside: A South Carolina Slave Community* (Urbana: University of Illinois Press, 1984); Daniel C. Littlefield, *Rice and Slaves: Ethnicity and the Slave Trade in Colonial South Carolina* (Baton Rouge: Louisiana State University Press, 1981).

4. Charles Woodmason, *The Carolina Back Country on the Eve of the Revolution,* edited with an introduction by Richard J. Hooker (Chapel Hill: University of North Carolina Press, 1949), 14, 34, 60; for discussion of the term *Scotch-Irish* for emigrants from Ulster, see Michael Montgomery, "Nomenclature for Ulster Emigrants: *Scotch-Irish or Scots-Irish?*" *Familia* 20 (2004): 16–36.

5. Walter S. Edgar, *South Carolina: A History* (Columbia: University of South Carolina Press, 1998), 42–50.

6. R. W. Dickson, *Ulster Emigration to Colonial America, 1718–1775* (London: Routledge Kegan Paul, 1966; reprinted Belfast: Ulster Historical Foundation, 1987), 165.

7. John Lawson, quoted in Edgar, *South Carolina,* 135.

8. Kathryn E. Holland Braund, *Deerskins and Duffels: The Creek Indian Trade with Anglo-America, 1685–1815* (Lincoln: University of Nebraska Press, 1993).

9. Eirlys M. Barker has identified 694 traders from colonial South Carolina and Georgia. See her "Indian Traders: Charles Town and London's Vital Link to the Interior of North America, 1717–1775," paper presented to the College of Charleston Program for the Study of the Lowcountry and the Atlantic World, 1995; Barker, "'Much Blood and Treasure': South Carolina's Indian Traders, 1670–1755," PhD diss., College of William and Mary, 1993; William L. McDowell Jr., *Documents Relating to Indian Affairs,* 3 vols. (Columbia: South Carolina Department of Archives and History, 1970).

10. Barker, "Much Blood and Treasure."

11. John Braidwood, "Ulster and Elizabethan English" in G. B. Adams, ed., *Ulster Dialects: An Introductory Symposium* (Holywood: Ulster Folk Museum, 1964), 5–110; Philip Robinson, *The Plantation of Ulster: British Settlement in an Irish Landscape* (Dublin: Gill and McMillan, 1984). The surname "Galphin" is apparently a variant on "Gilpin," the better-known form in County Armagh today.

   In being most likely of Ulster-English rather than Ulster Scot ancestry (i.e., a descendant of English settlers who came to the province in James I's plantation in the early seventeenth century), Galphin exemplified the fact that not all those who have come to be known as "Scotch-Irish" have had ultimately Scottish lineage. The label "Scotch-Irish" has been found two dozen times in eighteenth-century usage. It seems normally if not exclusively to have referred to Presbyterian emigrants from Ulster, but its exact denotation has yet to be pinned down in all instances that have come to light. Nonetheless, by at least the mid-nineteenth century, many descendants of pre-Revolutionary arrivals from Ulster in North America, especially those of Protestant tradition, were apt to be lumped together under the general rubric "Scotch-Irish." In the nineteenth century "Scotch-Irish" came to mean primarily two things: first, having or being perceived to have a certain cultural (i.e., Protestant and in some sense Scottish—or in the usage of the day, "Scotch") affinity; and second, a chronological (i.e., eighteenth-century) background from the northern part of Ireland. Its usage in contrast to "Irish," both in self-reference and in reference to such emigrants and their descendants, grew in currency and was well established by the mid-nineteenth century. But for countless Americans the term has been an inherited, chronologically based label whose usage made no inherently political statement, much less a partisan or sectarian one. Rather, it has been a simple marker of traditional family affiliation. It is for that reason that I employ "Scotch-Irish" in my essay. For more on this subject, see Michael Montgomery, "*Scotch-Irish* or *Scots-Irish:* What's in a Name?" *Tennessee Ancestors* 20 (2004): 143–50.

12. See George Galphin folder, MacDowell Geneaologies, South Caroliniana Library, University of South Carolina, as summarized in Frederick Hamer, "Indian Traders, Land, and Power: A Comparative Study of George Galphin on the Southern Frontier and Three Northern Traders," master's thesis, University of South Carolina, 1982.

13. This was far from unusual. The Scotsman Lachlan McGillivray is another well-known example. For their Caucasian husbands, Indian women often worked as interpreters of both their native language and their native culture. See Barker, "Much Blood and Treasure," 149ff.

14. Hamer, "Indian Traders."

15. Before this time, they were required to stand in the balcony at services for whites. See Walter H. Brooks, "The Priority of the Silver Bluff Church and Its Promoters," *Journal of Negro History* 7 (1922): 172–96; Frank G. Roberson and George H. Mosley, *Where a Few Gather in My Name: The History of the Oldest Black Church in America—the Silver Bluff Baptist Church* (North Augusta, SC: FGR Publications, 2002).

16. Tammy Forehand, Mark C. Groover, David C. Crass, and Robert Moon, "Bridging the Gap between Archaeologists and the Public: Excavations at Silver Bluff Plantation, the George Galphin Site," *Early Georgia* 32 (2004): 51–73.

17. See the Catherine Galphin Claim, 1786, Chatham County Deeds, Georgia, 1E-1F, 306–7, microfilm copy deposited in Georgia State Archives, as summarized in Hamer, "Indian Traders," 13–14.

18. Forehand et al., "Bridging the Gap."

19. Ibid., 58.

20. Robert Moon, personal communication, June 2003.

21. Developments at the site can be tracked at the project's website, www.srarp.org.

22. Henry Lumpkin, *From Yorktown to Savannah: The American Revolution in the South* (New York: Paragon, 1987); Walter S. Edgar, *Partisans and Redcoats: The Southern Conflict*

that Turned the Tide of the Revolution (New York: Morrow, 2001); Bobby Gilmer Moss, *Patriots at Kings Mountain* (Gaffney, SC: Scotia-Hibernia, 1990); J. David Dameron, *King's Mountain: The Defeat of the Loyalists, October 7, 1780* (Cambridge, Mass.: Da Capo, 2003).

23. Dameron, *King's Mountain,* 88.

24. Lyman Copeland Draper, *King's Mountain and Its Heroes: History of the Battle of King's Mountain, October 7th, 1780, and the Events Which Led to It* (1881; Johnson City, Tenn.: Overmountain Press, 1996).

25. Pat Alderman, *The Overmountain Men: Early Tennessee History, 1760–1785* (Johnson City, Tenn.: Overmountain Press, 1970).

26. Dameron, *King's Mountain.*

27. D. J. McCartney, *The Ulster Jacksons: From Cumbria to the White House, Shenandoah and Australia* (Carrickfergus: Carrickfergus Borough Council, 1997).

28. See www.nps.gov/ovvi.

29. Forehand et al., "Bridging the Gap," 54.

30. Robert Scott Davis Jr., "George Galphin and the Creek Congress of 1777," typescript on deposit at the Georgia Historical Society, Savannah, 1981.

Searching for "Irish" Freedom—Settling for "Scotch-Irish" Respectability: Southwestern Pennsylvania, 1780–1810

Peter Gilmore
Kerby A. Miller

Most histories of Scots-Irish[1] settlement in the New World end triumphantly with the American Revolution. In the half-century or so after the Revolution, however, many more Ulster Presbyterians (with other Irish immigrants) left Ireland for the United States than had journeyed to Britain's North American colonies in the one hundred years prior to 1776. More important, it is arguable that the three decades following the achievement of American independence comprised a crucial, formative era of Scots-Irish social, political, and cultural development.

Between 1780 and 1810, various groups of Ulster Presbyterians contended with each other to achieve social control, political power, and cultural hegemony over the Ulster American community and to define its relationships with Anglo-America's social and political hierarchies. This contest paralleled a similar struggle within northern Ireland itself, where the same decades saw the flowering and collapse of the radical, republican strains in Ulster Presbyterianism, as the euphoria engendered by the Irish Volunteers and the French Revolution was destroyed in 1798 by the failure of the United Irish Rebellion and in 1800 by the Act of Union. Indeed, events in Ulster were intimately related to developments in the United States, for northern Presbyterians who migrated to the New World to fulfill "Irish" dreams of "freedom" often discovered that, in an increasingly stratified and fragmented Ulster American society, the best they could achieve was a newly defined "Scotch-Irish" respectability.

Many readers may find alleged associations between Ulster Presbyterians and "Irish" nomenclature and characteristics to be startling or even discomfiting. The reason, of course, is that by the late nineteenth century Americans of Ulster Presbyterian birth or ancestry had become known as "Scotch-Irish," whereas the "Irish" label in the United States was now almost exclusively confined to Catholic immigrants and their descendants. Indeed, by the late 1800s, the meaning of "Scotch-Irish" had expanded informally to include all Protestants of Irish birth or background. Equally important, this ethno-religious dichotomy was also a hierarchy, since all but Irish American Catholics themselves regarded the "Scotch-Irish" as the socially, culturally, and even morally superior group. In the eighteenth century, however, and well into the nineteenth, the "Irish" label, with or without a religious qualification, was the term most commonly employed to designate Ulster Presbyterians (and other Irish Protestants) on both sides of the ocean; this was true of Ulster Presbyterians themselves as well as of contemporary observers, whether sympathetic or hostile. By contrast, according to historian James Leyburn, the term "Scotch-Irish" was rarely employed, either before or immediately after the American Revolution.[2]

Arguably, in the early 1700s, the term "Irish," when applied to Ulster Presbyterians of Scottish ancestry, had merely geographic connotations, referring to domicile or birthplace or, in the case of Ulster immigrants in America, to their immediate country of origin. By the last quarter of the eighteenth century, however, among many Ulster Presbyterians (and other Irish Protestants) a new "Irish" identity had acquired broad, positive, and "patriotic" political and other associations. Unlike the previous century, it was no longer confined to Ireland's defeated and degraded Catholics, and so it no longer signified only the negative characteristics (savagery, superstition, ignorance, poverty, and so on) generally ascribed to that group in Anglo-American Protestant culture. In America the new "Irish" label, with its favorable associations, was for a time even fashionable. In the merchant communities of colonial American seaports, for instance, Ulster Presbyterians and other Irish immigrants of all religions found it socially advantageous to club together in distinctively "Irish" organizations. Moreover, as James Caldwell, an Ulster-born member of Philadelphia's St. Patrick's Society, proudly attested, by 1774 those he called "the Irish" in America (comprised overwhelmingly of northern Presbyterians, like himself) were widely admired for their devotion to the political principles that soon produced the American Revolution.[3] That devotion was in turn a reflection of similar developments taking place in Ireland itself, as Ulster's Presbyterians were disproportionately prominent in the liberal Patriot and Volunteer movements of the 1770s and 1780s and in the radical and, eventually, revolutionary Society of United Irishmen in the 1790s. Inspired by the American Revolution and, after 1789, by the French

Peter Gilmore and Kerby A. Miller

Revolution, both movements sought to unite Protestants and Catholics under the common name of "Irishman" and to achieve at least some degree of "Irish freedom" from British political control.

Thus, the emergence of a positive, ecumenical, and politicized sense of "Irishness" was a trans-Atlantic phenomenon; trends and events on each side of the ocean were mutually reinforcing. Indeed, it is arguable that the final flowering of Ulster Presbyterians' radical "Irishness" took place in the United States, as during the 1790s and especially after the 1798 rebellion, thousands of embittered emigrants from northern Ireland flocked to American shores. There they joined with most of the earlier Ulster Presbyterian immigrants in enthusiasm for Thomas Jefferson's "republican principles" and in opposition to the allegedly "aristocratic" leaders and pro-British policies of those they condemned as "Anglo-Federalists." Exiled United Irishmen, especially, feared that American Federalists, in alliance with British "monarchists," endangered the future of republicanism on both sides of the ocean and thus threatened to thwart the immigrants' quest for "freedom" on American shores.

For the newcomers from Ulster, as for their predecessors, "Irish" understandings of "freedom" had social as well as political connotations. Long before the American and French revolutions, Ulster Presbyterians had characterized emigration as "escape" from "slavery": from rack-rents and submission to the "tyranny" of Anglican landlords and to the tithes and petty persecutions imposed by a legally established church that anchored and sanctified the gentry's and the government's interests. Heavy Ulster emigration since the 1710s, as well as the violent agitations by the Oakboys in the 1760s and the Steelboys in the early 1770s, reflected Ulster Presbyterians' specific economic grievances as well as their general alienation. In the late 1700s the Patriot and United Irish movements broadened and politicized both particular and generalized resentments, giving them a radical, egalitarian tone, while between 1793 and 1815 government repression, heavy wartime taxes, and, after 1815, severe economic depression stimulated unprecedented levels of Ulster emigration. Despairing of economic improvement or political reform, growing numbers of northern Presbyterians sought the "freedom" denied at home in the new, idealized American republic. Thus, after reading many of his countrymen's letters from the United States, John Gamble of Strabane, County Tyrone, observed that "scarcely with an exception, the comfort" on which Ulster Presbyterians "most insisted," and which urged them to emigrate, was that in America, unlike Ireland, "they could . . . speak to man as man" and would not be "obliged to uncover the head, or to bend the knee, to any stern Lord, arrogant squire, proud vicar, or above all, upstart agent."[4]

Nurtured in Ireland, these yearnings commonly found expression in the immigrants' desire to achieve in America what they called "independence." In socioeconomic terms, for Ulster's struggling tenant farmers "independence" signified the security and "comfortable self-sufficiency" that could only be gained through landownership. Likewise, for the North's innumerable cottage-weavers, "independence" meant that in America, as one immigrant put it, they would not have to grovel for work, at starvation wages, before the doors of wealthy manufacturers.[5] Yet these mundane ambitions also had inseparable political connotations, for Ulster immigrants believed that only in a "free republic," like the United States, could universal ownership (for white men) of land or of craftsmen's shops be achieved and protected against the high taxes, monopolistic practices, or elite machinations that otherwise might force them back into "slavish dependence." Thus, their quests for land or artisanal "independence" should not be confused with the capitalist acquisitiveness of later decades.[6] In late 1787 during debate in the Pennsylvania legislature over bank incorporation, a leading proponent of banks, the fabulously affluent Robert Morris, accused his political opponent, the Ulster immigrant William Findley, of being just as avid in pursuing wealth as was Morris himself. Findley's reply, however, made a clear distinction between the two men's ambitions and outlooks: "Doubtless I do," Findley rejoined; "I love and pursue it," but "not as an end" in itself, but rather only "as a means of enjoying happiness and independence."[7]

Presbyterian society in both Ulster and the United States, however, was always economically diverse and socially stratified. The various waves of Scots-Irish immigrants comprised varying mixtures of farmers rich and poor, of weavers and laborers, and of those whose superior positions in Ulster had already conditioned them to seek "independence" in a more "modern" sense: as individual upward mobility in the competitive marketplace, rather than as security or "comfortable self-sufficiency" in communities of relative equals. Moreover, all entered an America that had a dynamic, expansive, but by no means egalitarian, economy; and its operations and political manipulations often ratified or exacerbated status distinctions brought from Ireland or created new kinds of hierarchy and fragmentation in Ulster American society. These, in turn, had both political and cultural consequences, as rising members of a nascent Ulster American bourgeoisie sought to "uplift," "tame," and "civilize" ordinary frontier farmers and village craftsmen and to mobilize them for political or religious advantage. The ultimate result was a kind of "Americanization" characterized by individual acceptance of, and group identification with, middle-class social and cultural norms that were—per-

Peter Gilmore and Kerby A. Miller

haps inevitably, given power relationships in the Anglo-American world—intimately associated with Protestantism and with "British" origins. This form of Americanization, therefore, required rejection of the rambunctious social and "licentious" political behavior that Anglo-American Protestants had traditionally associated with Irish Catholics and other "inferior" groups, and that conservatives now conflated with the supposed "dangers" to "social order" posed by the democratic ideals and "excesses" of the American and the French revolutions and by the threats that the latter's "Irish" admirers, in Ireland and America alike, allegedly represented to hierarchy, property, and religion. Thus began a process of assimilation by which Ulster Presbyterians in the United States—once the quintessential "Wild Irish" Jacobins of Federalist nightmares—eventually became socially respectable and politically conservative "Scotch-Irish."

Ulster Presbyterians' journey from a late eighteenth-century "Irish" to a nineteenth-century "Scotch-Irish" identity would be long and tortuous, as reflected, for example, by the shape-shifting ethnic identities variously ascribed to Andrew Jackson by friend and foe alike. Similarly, in Ulster itself, earlier "Irish" traditions of opposition to political, social, and religious establishments were not so much "naturally" or "inevitably" abandoned, as many historians contend, as they were transported overseas. As late as the 1850s, at least some Ulster Presbyterian emigrants, such as the Kerr and McElderry brothers, still expressed hopes for "Irish" revolution against landlordism and British rule.[8] To be sure, some Presbyterians in Ulster and America had never experienced a radical or even a liberal "Irish" interlude, even during the headiest days of the late eighteenth century, when it had seemed for a time that the world might be made anew. Even in the 1780s and 1790s, the seeds of reaction had germinated, as Ulster Presbyterians began the slow, uneven, but eventually wholesale transformation to "Scotch-Irish" respectability and, in Ireland, to "British" loyalism.

In the United States, perhaps the most important crucible for these developments was the southwestern corner of Pennsylvania, together with adjacent areas in Ohio, Kentucky, and what is now West Virginia. In the late eighteenth century, an extensive network of Irish communities played a major role in shaping society and political culture in southwestern Pennsylvania, a region transformed in this Early National Period by rapid growth and social conflict. Here, where Pittsburgh grew from frontier trading post to "smoky citadel of Scotch-Irish enterprise,"[9] a critical mass of Ulster immigrants and their children allowed for contests over political, economic, and cultural hegemony that defined and redefined party allegiance and ethnic identity (see map 8.1). Among the contestants were Revolutionary War veterans whose leadership role in that conflict positioned them to guide the region's economic and political development. Others included the war's less successful participants, as well as newcomers from the north of Ireland. The failure of many members of these groups to find Eden on this terrain would eventually propel them farther westward.

* * *

It was William Findley's quest for "happiness and independence" that led him and other Scots-Irish across the mountains. In the final decades of the eighteenth century, the hills and valleys of Pennsylvania west of the Allegheny Mountains experienced an explosive growth of Scots-Irish and other European populations.

Little European settlement occurred prior to the Treaty of Fort Stanwix in 1768. A royal proclamation promulgated at the formal conclusion to the French and Indian War sought to forestall frontier hostilities by containing settlement east of the Appalachians. The Proclamation Line of 1763 slowed westward movement but could not cure land fever among Europeans seeking a "competence," among them families from Ulster. (Illegal settlements by Scots-Irish squatters in mountain valleys later became formalized as "Belfast" and "Colerain [sic].") The Treaty of Fort Stanwix opened transmontane Pennsylvania to extensive migration by moving the official frontier irrevocably beyond the spine of the mountain chain. Also, through a separate "New Purchase" from the Iroquois, the Penn family acquired much of western Pennsylvania for legal settlement.[10]

By 1774 some fifty thousand whites had settled west of the Alleghenies; by 1798 perhaps seventy-five thousand whites had made their homes in southwestern Pennsylvania alone. By 1810 that number had risen to approximately 126,000, with the total population of Pennsylvania west of the mountains estimated as 210,000. In 1790 transmontane Pennsylvania could claim just four counties—Allegheny, Fayette, Washington, and Westmoreland. By 1800, however, the area had been subdivided into thirteen counties, and another six counties were created during the following decade.[11]

Population grew most rapidly along the valleys of the principal rivers—the Monongahela, the Allegheny, and the Ohio—and of tributaries like Chartiers Creek. Market towns such as Washington and Canonsburg, Pittsburgh and Brownsville, were built along these waterways. The locus of population in Pennsylvania west of the mountains lay in the state's far southwest—

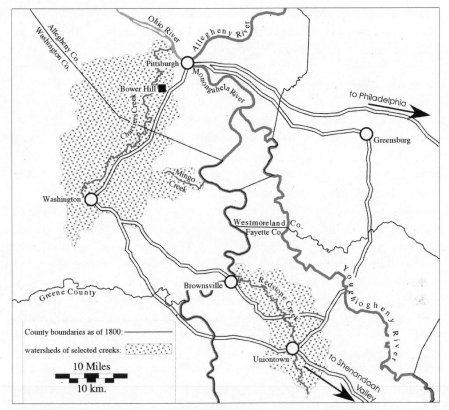

Map 8.1. *Scots-Irish settlement in western Pennsylvania, 1780–1810.*

within or adjacent to modern Allegheny, Washington, and Westmoreland counties. This region remained overwhelmingly rural, yet, like contemporary Ulster, it was also heavily industrial, as residents combined agriculture with weaving, distilling, and ironworking. The town of Washington, laid out (and owned) by an Ulsterman, had such a large collection of artisans and tradesmen that it was presumed to be a rival to Pittsburgh. The latter town (later dubbed the "Belfast of America") early developed metalworking, glass-making, shipbuilding, and textile industries. Despite Pittsburgh's rapid rise, from 376 inhabitants in 1790 to 7,250 in 1820, not until 1830 did the population of Allegheny County (including Pittsburgh) exceed that of largely rural Washington County.[12]

With the elimination of an Indian threat in 1794 and the ratification of Pinckney's Treaty the following year, the farmers, artisans, and merchants of southwestern Pennsylvania gained access to the Ohio and Mississippi waterways and increasingly became enmeshed in a considerable national (and even international) commercial network. The Louisiana Purchase of 1803, by further opening the West to trade and settlement, accelerated the pace of commercial, industrial, and agricultural development, thus extending the reach of the market. Rivers and transmontane trails connected southwestern Pennsylvania farmers to a vast commercial network involving the Mississippi and Ohio valleys, the eastern seaboard, and beyond. Nodal points included the Chartiers Valley market towns of Washington and Canonsburg (in Washington County) and the flour and wool-carding mills along Miller's Run, Robinson's Run, and Montour Run (in Allegheny and Washington counties), with exchange centered on the regional entrepôt, Pittsburgh. Whiskey, flour, and other rural products came by canoe down creeks to be transferred to keelboats for shipment on the Ohio River. Pittsburgh's position as "gateway to the West" placed its shopkeepers in a unique position to outfit westward migrants and supply the needs of the Ohio River trade.

Despite the growth of the market, many Scots-Irish farmers—particularly but not exclusively among the earlier and now older immigrants—long continued to pursue a strategy of household production designed primarily to ensure self-sufficiency while also producing a surplus for trade to secure essential items and sufficient cash to meet their obligations. From the 1780s on, farmers exchanged "country produce" at stores in market towns for manufactured goods. As late as 1811, stores in Washington and Canonsburg continued to accept linen, beeswax, and other rural products as a substitute for cash.[13] Participation in the commercial network represented a source of cash to pay taxes and rent as well as to purchase property and goods. In 1810 farming in much of southwestern Pennsylvania by people of European descent was barely forty years old; the generation that had cleared much of the land—a generation whose members were often born in the north of Ireland—in many cases still worked it. Thus, older ideas of competency, independence, and moral economy remained prominent in the world view of the region's patriarchs, even as locally built boats carried ever-greater loads of flour down the Ohio.

The influx of Scots-Irish and other settlers reached the region by two main routes. One followed the Monongahela and Youghiogheny rivers north from Virginia (which claimed the area until 1781). The second and the primary route was from eastern and mid-Pennsylvania, New Jersey, or Maryland across the Allegheny Mountains via Indian trails and the colonial-era military roads named for British generals Braddock and Forbes. A large number of these migrants had Irish (and overwhelmingly Ulster) back-

Peter Gilmore and Kerby A. Miller

grounds, although it is likely that a majority of settlers were of English and German descent. But the Ulster proportion of the population was considerable. Scholars working in the first half of the twentieth century, who largely relied on surname analyses in estimates of population origins, tended to overestimate Scottish at the expense of Ulster immigration. By contrast, an examination of naturalization applications in Allegheny and Washington counties during this period indicates that most of the applicants who had distinctively "Scottish" surnames were in fact born in Ireland, almost certainly in Ulster. It is probable, therefore, that in 1780–1810 settlers of Ulster birth or descent—the great majority of them Scots-Irish Presbyterians—along with smaller numbers of Irish Catholics, Anglicans, Methodists, and others, also primarily from Ulster—constituted at least one-fourth to one-third of the inhabitants of southwestern Pennsylvania. The Scots-Irish alone may have been the largest single group in the region, and they likely constituted a majority of inhabitants in many townships—thus replicating their earlier settlement patterns in eastern and central Pennsylvania.[14]

In 1780–1810 the Ulster-born population of southwestern Pennsylvania was composed of representatives of several different waves of trans-Atlantic migrants. The first comprised those who had immigrated prior to the Revolutionary War of 1775–1783. The second included migrants who came to America after the Revolution, often impelled by economic crises in Ulster in the early and mid-1780s or by political turmoil and repression in the 1790s. The last contingent was composed of immigrants who fled the North in the immediate aftermath of the 1798 Rebellion or who left Ulster to escape famine (in 1801–1802) and economic travails (including soaring wartime inflation and taxation) in the decade following the Act of Union in 1800. Of course, accompanying all the waves of immigrant settlers to southwestern Pennsylvania were earlier Ulster immigrants' American-born descendants, for people from the north of Ireland had been settling in the American colonies since the 1680s, most heavily since the 1720s and 1730s.

For instance, Thomas Marquis, who came to Washington County in the 1770s, was among those settlers of Irish background who traveled north from Virginia. Born in the lower Shenandoah Valley in the largely Scots-Irish settlement at Opequon and the son of Ulster immigrants of Huguenot background, Marquis eventually abandoned weaving and farming to become a revivalist preacher.[15] Many more of the region's new residents, however, hailed from Ulster enclaves in Pennsylvania east of the mountains. "A great proportion of them were farmer's sons, or farmers themselves, with rising families, who emigrated from the old counties, and were generally acquainted with each other," wrote William Findley, whose own westward movement is emblematic. Findley left County Antrim in 1763 for the Scots-Irish communities of eastern and central Pennsylvania; his family made a final move west in the 1780s, relocating to Loyalhanna Creek in Westmoreland County.[16] After 1783, thousands more came to the region directly from Ulster, among them Joseph and Mary Donahey, Presbyterians from near Omagh in County Tyrone, who in 1790 emigrated and settled along Washington County's Buffalo Creek.[17]

Those settling in southwestern Pennsylvania during the final decades of the eighteenth century replicated a pattern long employed in the east: they named their new communities for places in the old country. From Blair County (Tyrone) and Bedford County (Dublin, Colerain, and Londonderry), west to Westmoreland (Derry, Donegal, and Rostraver), Fayette (Menallen and Tyrone), and Washington (Donegal and Strabane) counties, the surge of Scots-Irish migration planted Ulster place-names on the Pennsylvania frontier. Thus in 1792 the Seceding Presbyterians, James and Margaret Graham, led seven families to the wilderness of Indiana County and a community they christened Armagh. Similarly, in the early 1800s, several Catholic families from southwestern Ulster settled on the border of Butler and Armstrong counties, naming their township Donegal. Farms, too, not infrequently received Ulster toponyms. For example, in 1785, John Welch secured a tract in East Bethlehem Township, Washington County, that he called "Enniskillen." The prevalence of Ulster immigrants also meant that the new entrepôts would have market squares known as "diamonds"; such was the case in Washington, Pittsburgh, and Butler, as well as in smaller market towns like Mount Pleasant in Westmoreland County and Newport in Indiana County.[18]

The dramatic expansion of Presbyterian churches in the region paralleled the population explosion and provides still more evidence of the strong Scots-Irish presence in southwestern Pennsylvania. Indicative of the simultaneous development of Presbyterianism and secular society was an advertisement, in an 1810 Washington newspaper, for a three-hundred-acre tract in nearby Westmoreland County. Among its other attractions, the "plantation" was reputed to be located "[c]onvenient to two merchant mills, and a Presbyterian clergyman," as well as "within ten miles of a navigable stream of water."[19]

Prior to 1785, Presbyterian settlers in the area had organized eleven congregations, most of them in Washington County where, by 1798, nineteen churches were established. Presbyterians in Pittsburgh came together as a congregation in the 1780s; their first minister was a recent Irish immigrant.

Peter Gilmore and Kerby A. Miller

The year 1781 saw the organization of the first mainstream Presbyterian judicature west of the Allegheny Mountains, the Presbytery of Redstone, which took its name from a Monongahela River outpost and nearby creek in Fayette County. Rapid growth soon necessitated the erection of another new presbytery to bring together congregations west of the Monongahela and south of the Ohio. Thus, in 1793 the Ohio Presbytery was organized, with five ministers who had responsibility for more than twenty congregations.[20] By 1802, the Ohio Presbytery had twenty-one settled ministers as well as twenty-seven additional churches with vacant pulpits.[21] Nearly one out of every five of those ministers had been born in Ireland, while a little more than half had been born in Scots-Irish settlements in eastern or mid-Pennsylvania.[22]

Perhaps an even more telling denominational index of the region's strong Irish Presbyterian influence was the rapid proliferation of dissenting congregations, that is, of churches whose clergy and communicants were not affiliated with the dominant Synod of Ulster in northern Ireland or with the mainstream Presbyterian Church in the United States (its official title), formally organized in 1788. Indeed, Seceders and Covenanters came to enjoy roughly the same proportion of Presbyterian congregations in western Pennsylvania as they did in contemporary Ulster, about one out of every three. By 1802 the Associate, Associate Reformed, and Reformed Presbyterian churches had organized more than thirty congregations in Allegheny, Beaver, Fayette, Washington, and Westmoreland counties in Pennsylvania and in adjacent Ohio County, Virginia (now West Virginia).

The Associate Reformed Church had been formed in 1782 as a merger of the Associate Presbyteries of Pennsylvania and New York and the Covenanters' Reformed Presbytery. Covenanters unhappy with the union organized the Reformed Presbytery in North America, under the leadership of Ulster-born ministers exiled in the 1790s because of their association with radical politics. Meanwhile, a minority of Seceders likewise rejected the merger. Their Associate Synod convened in 1801 with four constituent presbyteries: Philadelphia, Kentucky, Cambridge (New York), and Chartiers, the last-named centered on Washington County.[23]

Numerous Seceders settled in Washington County following the American Revolution.[24] The Seceders in southwestern Pennsylvania, as in Ulster, may have established congregations in those areas of late Irish and Scots settlement that were perceived as underserved by the mainstream Ohio Presbytery. A map of Washington County in 1817 locates the majority of Associate and Associate Reform congregations in the western half of the county, within townships that generally had been settled later than those along the river valleys.[25] These rival organizations competed for communicants among Scots-Irish and Scottish settlers with the mainstream Presbyterian Church and with each other. Seceder churches provided an alternative to the innovations of the Great Awakening for those in southwestern Pennsylvania whose Calvinism owed more to Old World religion. The presence of Seceder and Covenanter congregations, therefore, is yet another sign of the numerical strength and vitality of Scots-Irish society in the region, and an indication as well of the continued salience of religious and other developments in Ulster to the immigrants in the New World.[26]

Even if Ulster Presbyterians did not comprise an absolute majority of the region's inhabitants, their great numbers and high visibility nonetheless gave an impression of Scots-Irish predominance. In 1784, Arthur Lee, brother of two signers of the Declaration of Independence, notoriously described Pittsburgh as "inhabited almost entirely by Scots and Irish, who live in paltry log houses, and are as dirty as in the north of Ireland, or even Scotland."[27] In the following decades, steady immigration from Ulster to southwestern Pennsylvania only strengthened that impression. Thus a Scottish missionary passing through Pittsburgh in 1798 wrote home that "A great many of the inhabitants have come from Ireland."[28] Thomas Ashe, an Irish tourist of roguish reputation, stayed in Pittsburgh for some months in 1806–1807, when he described the city's inhabitants as largely Irish or of Irish origin.[29] "[T]he 9/10 of the people of pittsburg is Irish and the[y] are flocking here Every day," wrote a Methodist immigrant from the north of Ireland in 1810.[30]

The numerical significance of Irish immigrants—as well as their prominent role in the region's economy, politics, and religion—is also reflected in the frequent attention given to Ireland by newspapers published in Washington and Pittsburgh. News from Ireland, sometimes printed alongside romantic Irish nationalist verse, featured prominently. Likewise, newspapers with radical (or at least not conservative) politics sharply criticized British policies toward Ireland, reprinted favorable reports of Irish revolutionary movements, and decried any perceived "British" or "royalist" influences in the United States. Thus, in 1800, Pittsburgh's *Tree of Liberty,* a Democratic-Republican organ, denounced "Anglo-Federalists" and warned of the dangers posed by a pro-British, monarchial clique in American politics.[31] Similarly, in 1810 one issue of the Washington, Pennsylvania, *Reporter* published a sentimental poem titled "The Grave of Russell" (commemorating Thomas Russell, the "advocate for Irish independence," who was executed in 1803) near an advertisement for the Presbyterian "shorter and larger Catechism," which was available for sale at the newspaper's office.[32]

Clearly, the editors of these papers both identified and appealed to a strong affinity between their Scots-Irish readers' communal memory of Ireland and their ethnic identity and political sympathies in the United States. Clearly also, an older sense of "Irish" freedom—of freedom from "monarchical," "aristocratic" British rule (and from the rents, tithes, and taxes associated with it)—found contemporary expression in the republicanism of Ulster Presbyterians. Political dissidence framed the world view of the many thousands forced to emigrate in the 1780s and 1790s due to repression or economic exigencies. Thus, both Irish memories and American sensibilities often became associated with defiant expressions of radical-republican or ultra-democratic political ideals on both sides of the Atlantic. In the backcountry, these ideals combined with and reinforced frustration with elite obstruction to the goal of "happiness and independence."

Hence, the widespread opposition of western Pennsylvanians of Irish origin—first to the ratification of the United States Constitution and then to the policies of the early Federalist administrations—may have reflected not only their uniquely American circumstances but also a coherent ethnic source for their political opinions and behavior. Certainly, their political adversaries both noted and scorned the frequently "Irish" character of Pennsylvania's Ulster American politics. For example, in a 1788 satire on Antifederalist objections to the Constitution, Hugh Henry Brackenridge (a Scottish immigrant) claimed that one of the document's obvious weaknesses was its failure to specify the requisite ancestry of senators—"whether they should be altogether Irish or only Scotch-Irish." In addition, he joked that, without a bill of rights, the Presbyterians' Confession of Faith and Shorter Catechism would be "swept away."[33] Later, in what Brackenridge and other "friends of order" would regard as even greater crises, their associations of "Irishness" with Ulster Presbyterian fomenters of "disorder" would become even more numerous and strident.

Of course, not all the Scots-Irish in southwestern Pennsylvania were Antifederalists in the 1780s, Jeffersonian Republicans in the 1790s and early 1800s, or even opponents of British rule in Ireland itself. However, the jibes of Brackenridge and of other conservatives testified to the prevalence in the region of both Irish immigrants and of sharp social and political antagonisms. Moreover, it appears that a very large number of those immigrants— perhaps the great majority, both early on and after the 1798 United Irish Rebellion—were staunchly democratic in their political sympathies. For example, the letters written by Ulster Presbyterians who came to America in the post-Revolution decades, and often well into the mid-nineteenth century, indicate that they understood and conflated their economic and political motives for emigrating in terms of the "freedom," denied in Ireland, which they hoped to enjoy in what one immigrant eulogized as a "promised land" with a "free republikan goverment." As the Ulsterman John Gamble observed, his Presbyterian countrymen carried "their industry, talents and energy, to a distant and happier land, and never think of the one they have quitted but with loathing, and of its government, with a feeling, for which hatred is but a feeble word."[34]

Yet although Ulster immigrant James Dinsmore hopefully named his new Washington County farm "Land of Canaan," he—like many of his countrymen who poured into the region—in fact found no promised land. As latecomers with meager resources discovered to their grief, farmland in southwestern Pennsylvania was not inexhaustible in either quantity or quality. Between 1783 and 1796 the region rapidly ceased to be a "frontier" in any meaningful sense, particularly after the cessation of Indian hostilities in 1794. At the close of the eighteenth century, settlement remained fluid, but it was marked by a growing concentration of wealth at one extreme and a growing mass of transient poor men at the other. Even within the first generation of settlers, writes historian R. Eugene Harper, "a very large and important landless class developed. It constituted at least a third of the population, and in some townships it was over half." In the 1790s the percentage of landowning individuals in the area's more-settled townships continued to trend downward, as population pressures also led to smaller-sized landholdings.[35]

As a result, Harper concluded, southwestern Pennsylvania increasingly resembled Ulster in at least two important respects: landlordism and tenancy, the latter of which became "a solution for the increasing number of landless people coming into the region as it matured." Between the 1780s and the 1790s, the proportion of the area's taxable population who were tenants rose from 12 to 20 percent, while tenant farmers represented half of the region's landless or dependent class. The remainder consisted mostly of mere laborers, often farmers' sons who had little hope of inheriting their fathers' farms unless the latter agreed to subdivide their holdings—a process which, over time, would condemn increasing numbers of small farmers to bare subsistence livings. As Harper concluded, "Large landowners, both local and absentee," employed the "labor of propertyless people for the tasks of clearing and working their farms."[36] Also, as in contemporary Ireland, many of southwestern Pennsylvania's largest landholders were absentees as well as speculators. Although in some areas speculation and absenteeism declined, as early owners parceled and sold their land grants to newcomers (thus signal-

Peter Gilmore and Kerby A. Miller

ing the end of frontier settlement), in other districts absenteeism continued to increase. For example, between the 1780s and 1790s, the number of absentee landlords in Westmoreland County rose from 280 to 366. Likewise, speculation remained rampant on the unsettled margins, but those lands were often poor in quality, and many of their settlers could only squat on farms they could not afford to purchase. In more mature districts, the size of the lower classes steadily increased, as indicated by Washington County's tax records on livestock: between the 1780s and the 1790s, an increasing number of families possessed a few cattle, but a declining number were able to own even a single horse, both trends signifying farmers' entrapment in a hardscrabble, subsistence economy.[37]

The declining fortunes of the family of Elizabeth Guthrie, a daughter of one of Westmoreland County's earliest and most prominent Ulster-born citizens, illustrate the downward social mobility that afflicted many in the postwar, postfrontier era. During the Revolution, Guthrie's first husband and son were slain in an Indian raid, while she and her youngest child were taken prisoner. After thirteen months' Canadian captivity, the Derry-born woman returned to Westmoreland County in 1783, marrying her second cousin, William Guthrie, the following year. Unfortunately, in the late 1780s and 1790s, Elizabeth's second husband failed in his attempts at land speculation in an increasingly stratified Westmoreland County, forcing the family to the region's geographic margins: northward to Armstrong County circa 1810 and later to the still more remote and backward Clarion County. There they settled as squatters, eking out a bare living by combining subsistence farming with the meager state and federal pensions Elizabeth received for her deceased and current husbands' Revolutionary War service.[38]

In southwestern Pennsylvania, as elsewhere, wealth translated into political dominance. At the apex of regional society was a "mushroom aristocracy" of substantial farmers, merchants, manufacturers, and lawyers. In addition to profiting from landownership and speculation, the members of this nascent elite also grew wealthy from gristmills, sawmills, ferries, distilleries, and iron manufacturing. In the late 1700s almost all those who assumed political leadership had begun to amass fortunes as young men, early in their careers. Usually, they had arrived in southwestern Pennsylvania in the region's early stages of settlement and development—before, during, or shortly after the Revolutionary War—and had succeeded in acquiring title to large amounts of land at relatively little cost.

Sharp disagreements over the state and federal constitutions provided the initial fault lines of Pennsylvania politics in the 1780s and 1790s. Those whose power derived from commerce, manufacturing, and the professions tended to favor stronger government and elite rule, while those associated with farming and home production joined the democratic opposition. The western counties generally elected candidates who defended the radical democratic Pennsylvania constitution of 1776; prominent among them were Ulster immigrants such as William Findley, John Smilie, David Redick, and John McDowell—the western allies of the Dublin-born Presbyterian George Bryan, leader of the democratic forces in Philadelphia. Like Bryan, the Scots-Irish in the backcountry usually opposed the federal Constitution as well. "The vote for western Pennsylvania stood seven to two against the Constitution and probably was representative of the sentiment of the region," according to historian Russell J. Ferguson. Attitudes toward the Constitution and the first presidential administrations created under it formed the basis of political allegiances. The farmers in the West distrusted the concentration of political and economic power exercised by the federal government and its elite backers in the East. Within southwestern Pennsylvania itself, these divisions increasingly pitted the countryside against the mercantile and professional classes of Pittsburgh and Washington.[39]

Recent immigrants no doubt noticed that, in a pattern alarmingly reminiscent of Ulster, Episcopalian landowners and office seekers figured prominently among these elites. General John Gibson, Episcopalian, merchant, and former commander of Fort Pitt, chaired a meeting of prominent Pittsburgh residents who resolved in support of the federal Constitution. General John Neville, an Episcopalian who was the region's largest landowner, cast one of the two votes from western Pennsylvania for the Constitution at the state's ratification convention. Indeed, the "Neville Connection" of extended family members stood at the center of the commercial elite that controlled Pittsburgh's Federalist politics. A Neville son-in-law, Major Isaac Craig, was a landowner, sawmill owner, and major distiller associated with Pittsburgh's Presbyterian congregation. Craig and business partner Lieutenant Colonel Stephen Bayard purchased the first land in Pittsburgh sold by the Penn family following the Revolutionary War. John O' Hara, the Army's quartermaster general and a prominent merchant-banker, joined with Craig in launching a glassmaking works in 1797. Born in Ireland, O'Hara was a nominal Presbyterian who housed a peregrinating priest and donated land for Pittsburgh's first Catholic church, St. Patrick's, dedicated in 1811. Whiskey merchant and distiller John Wilkins was an elder in the Presbyterian church. John Ormsby, an Irish-born Episcopalian, first came to the region with the British army during the French and Indian War; he became a major landowner and manufacturer.[40] This elite circle also encompassed Dr. Nathaniel Bedford, retired British army surgeon and landowner.[41]

As in Ulster, this Anglican aristocracy often treated local Presbyterians in an overbearing fashion. Thus, Rev. Samuel Barr, a recent immigrant from County Derry, who in 1785 had accepted an invitation to serve as Pittsburgh's first settled minister, was forced to leave town five years later because of his conflict with Episcopalian power brokers who expected to enjoy privileges in, if not control of, a nominally Presbyterian congregation. At a sensational ecclesiastical trial, Barr faced charges that he refused to officiate at the wedding of Dr. Bedford and an Ormsby daughter or baptize a daughter of John Gibson. Among those testifying against Barr was Major Abraham Kirkpatrick, brother-in-law of Neville and scion of a Scottish Jacobite family.[42]

To counter the dominance of the politically conservative and economically powerful elites, rural and village radicals organized Democratic-Republican societies in the early 1790s in three areas that would soon be associated with the 1794 Whiskey Rebellion: Washington Town, Mingo Creek, and the Forks of the Yough. Washington's Democratic-Republican Society appears to have been an offshoot of the more prominent club in Philadelphia. One of its leading figures was James Marshel, an Irish immigrant who had arrived early in the region and had prospered as a landowner and county official. Washington's society was the most conservative of the three, dominated as it was by aspiring "gentlemen" such as Marshel and David Redick. In February 1794, Washington County's farmers, most of them less successful or affluent than the county seat's Democratic-Republicans, organized the Society of United Freeman—a name that suggests conscious imitation of the contemporary and radical (indeed, soon revolutionary) Irish nationalist organization, the Society of United Irishmen. These rural "Jacobins" met in the Mingo Creek Presbyterian congregation's log meetinghouse; their territory (and apparently their membership) was coterminous with that of the local militia. Reminiscent of the mutual aid practiced in Ulster when United Irishmen were incarcerated, these embattled farmers demonstrated opposition to the whiskey tax by collecting funds to sustain those who had run afoul of the excisemen. And similar to the practice in other Pennsylvania frontier settlements where the Scots-Irish predominated, they instituted their own court system to settle disputes amongst themselves, thus avoiding the professional lawyers whom they despised as "parasites" on "honest farmers." Shortly afterward, the Republican Society of the Yough grew out of the Mingo Creek United Freemen. Its members also were relatively poor farmers, and, like its parent organization, it too would earn a radical reputation.[43]

In 1794, increasing social stratification, profound political conflicts, and the cultural distinctiveness of the backcountry Scots-Irish all coalesced explosively in a Whiskey Rebellion that both revealed and sharpened the uneven and painful effects of southwestern Pennsylvania's transition from a subsistence to a commercial economy. Judicial salaries and official fees perceived as excessive further fueled popular discontent, as farmers complained bitterly that in the absence of an adequately circulating currency, they could not pay exorbitant "land-office fees, surveyor fees, and prothonotors and lawyers fees, which are the worst of all." The farmers' anger only intensified when wealthy men used political connections to monopolize local offices and reap even greater emoluments at public expense. Thus, John Gibson had become an associate judge under the state constitution of 1790, and Neville brother-in-law Abraham Kirkpatrick was a judge of the Court of Common Pleas. Neville's son Presley, an occasional land speculator and surveyor, served in the state legislature. Major James Brison, a rising Federalist politician who had testified against Barr, served both as justice of the peace and Allegheny County prothonotary.[44]

Among many of the region's farmers, the imposition in 1791 of a federal excise on distilled spirits at the point of production seemed both reminiscent of Irish taxation and confirmation of the dangers posed even by an American government that was dominated by "aristocratic," eastern interests. The particular effect of the excise in the Monongahela Valley seemed manifestly unrepublican: large distillers gained unfair advantages. By increasing production, the largest distillers could gain an enormous competitive advantage by significantly reducing the effective tax rate. These distillers were linked to a commercial elite connected to military procurement, the U.S. army being the largest single purchaser of whiskey. Military procurers, through their large-volume purchases, were effecting consolidation in the industry and driving its transition from a customary to a strictly commercial enterprise. Western Pennsylvania distilling, however, was still dominated by a number of small, family distillers, many of whom combined part-time whiskey manufacture with subsistence farming. Most distillers, like millers, provided a public service to the farming population; their economic role was similarly defined by custom. The excise could be seen in part as enforced rationalization of distilling, with the "elimination of small, inefficient, seasonal distillers"; a central government mandate was accelerating the transition from a customary to a cash economy.[45] The pain of economic adjustment was severe in a cash-poor, postfrontier society. The tenant farmers, who distilled their grain to get cash to pay their rents, naturally viewed the excise as a tax they could ill afford;

Peter Gilmore and Kerby A. Miller

small operators faced ruin. Not surprisingly, the most determined opposition to the excise occurred where the majority of inhabitants were not commercial farmers but tenants and others engaged in a subsistence economy.

Community solidarity enforced by sporadic violence soon rendered the excise a dead letter, especially in Washington County, but in the summer of 1794 the government's insistence on compliance produced a brief but explosive confrontation. The often-ritualized violence that occurred in the Whiskey Insurrection seems at times reminiscent of the Oakboys' and Steelboys' agrarian protests in Ulster during the 1760s and 1770s, with nocturnal barn-burning and cattle-maiming accompanied by threatening letters, mock trials, and public humiliation. Likewise, in southwestern Pennsylvania the targets of violence included not only the hated excisemen but also many others who had enjoyed unusual degrees of economic success. For example, all the distillers who complied with the law and were subsequently terrorized were affluent men.[46]

The single greatest target of popular fury, the "Neville Connection," stood at the center of the political-commercial nexus, promoting and benefiting from economic change. John Neville became excise superintendent for the western region, making himself "obnoxious" to his neighbors, as William Findley put it. That office gave Neville and his family decisive control over the military supply business, a principal source of cash in the western economy. His son-in-law, Isaac Craig, became deputy quartermaster of the U.S. army; brother-in-law Abraham Kirkpatrick, another major landholder, supplied grain to distilleries and worked as an agent for army contractors.

Neville's mansion, Bower Hill, regarded as the finest home west of the Alleghenies, became in July 1794 the scene of the most violent and one of the most overtly insurrectionary acts of the rebellion. Aroused inhabitants of the Washington and Allegheny county borderlands, among them members of the Mingo Creek militia, twice marched on Bower Hill to demand that Neville repudiate his commission. Both forays were accompanied by loss of life. The two men slain—farmer Oliver Miller and Major James McFarlane of the Mingo Creek militia—appear to have been Irish immigrants long settled in Pennsylvania. On the second march to Bower Hill, the presence of federal troops inside the mansion raised the stakes of the regional protest but did not deter the rebels. Their hatred of Neville and of what he had come to represent translated into the systematic destruction of the mansion and its ostentatious expression of wealth.[47]

Bower Hill was not the only loss suffered by the Neville family connection. In August 1794 Kirkpatrick's barn and grain stacks, across the

Monongahela from Pittsburgh, were fired by rebels following their muster at Braddock's Field and march to Pittsburgh—which the rural rebels reportedly (and revealingly) called "Sodom." St. Luke's Episcopal Church, near to Bower Hill in the Chartiers Valley and established by the Nevilles in 1790 as that denomination's only church in the region, seems to have been another victim. "The Whiskey Rebellion destroyed even this solitary sanctuary of the Episcopalians," according to one account, although it appears more likely that the hostilities merely discouraged attendance and the abandoned building fell into disrepair. In any case, local legend holds that the Scots-Irish looked with disfavor at an Episcopalian church in their midst—perhaps because of their traditional animosity toward the Church of Ireland and the tithes it had imposed on their ancestors in Ulster; perhaps also because of their disapproval of Anglican ritual as well as their anxiety over the imagined threat of a Federalist-imposed American religious ascendancy.[48]

Naturally, contemporaries both perceived and usually condemned a strong "Irish" influence in the Whiskey Rebellion and in Jeffersonian Republicanism, generally. Judge Alexander Addison, a Scottish immigrant, wrote, "Many now in the country talk of their having seen the riots and resistance against the excise in Ireland. In Ireland, the ordinary power of government seems incompetent to suppress riots, which have perpetual existence, from successive and varying causes. This country [referring to western Pennsylvania] is in a great measure settled from Ireland." Hugh Henry Brackenridge, another jurist and Scottish immigrant, also believed that the ethnic composition of Pennsylvania's western counties inclined their inhabitants to oppose the excise. Rev. James Carnahan, during the rebellion a student at the Presbyterian academy in Canonsburg, Washington County, likewise emphasized the settlers' Irish origins. Judge Samuel Wilkeson, who, like Carnahan, was a youth at the time of the insurrection, reported that the region's large Irish immigrant population was the major component of the "insurgent party." And not only inveterate Federalists shared this belief. William Findley reported that his neighbors believed "opposition to excises was brought into the country with the settlers, many of whom inherited an aversion to them from their fathers."[49]

Moreover, there were specific traditional Ulster Presbyterian beliefs that may have reinforced the rebels' opposition to the excise and even to the oath-demanding amnesty the government offered to the unrepentant. With regard to the excise itself, for example, William Findley observed, "The great error among the people was an opinion, that an immoral law might be opposed and yet the government respected." Many believed the excise to be immoral, Findley wrote, and "[t]his theory became with many a religious principle" and as such "one of the greatest obstacles" to convincing dissenters to signal acceptance of the law. Likewise, some orthodox Presbyterians refused to countenance the amnesty oath itself, regarding it as a violation of scripture-based beliefs.[50]

Yet the local Presbyterian clergy did not encourage their congregants to apply such notions to either the excise or the amnesty. Indeed, an enduring image of the Whiskey Rebellion is that of an elderly Presbyterian minister resolutely confronting the Mingo Creek militia on their march to Bower Hill—an image drawn from the experience of John Clark, pastor of two congregations in southern Allegheny County, who failed in his attempt to dissuade the aroused farmers and laborers. His story is inevitably recounted as symbolic of ministerial efforts to keep the peace, but it may be suggestive of something quite different. Apart from Clark's dramatic (and unsuccessful) intervention, there is little documentary evidence to indicate the Presbyterian clergy's active opposition to illegality and violence until after the insurrection had failed. Nor is there evidence of clerical complicity in opposition to the excise; by all accounts, no ministers endorsed the movement. Rather, their apparent silence suggests resignation (or a tactical retreat) in the face of local Presbyterians' overwhelming hostility to the excise tax. According to a church historian, "Presbyterian pastors had consistently sought through preaching and counseling to check angry passions and deeds of violence." However, while that statement describes a plausible and even likely scenario, it is not an assertion easily confirmed by the record. [51]

To be sure, Presbyterian elders of social and political prominence were notably outspoken in counseling moderation. Judge James Edgar was born in York County, Pennsylvania, and moved to Washington County during the Revolutionary War. He was a delegate to the convention that approved the radical state constitution of 1776, a delegate to the federal constitutional convention who voted in opposition to that document, and an associate judge from 1788. Unsurprisingly, neighbors elected him as a delegate to the pivotal meetings of opposition to the excise. There he assumed a crucial role in steering the deliberations away from outright armed resistance to the United States government. Edgar also preached before large gatherings in Washington County, reminding his listeners of their scriptural obligation to obey the constituted authorities. His counsel was credited with mitigating violence. Not all listeners, however, were swayed. In Nottingham Township, Washington County—where the settlements along Mingo Creek and Peters Creek were particularly noted for their violent opposition to the whiskey tax—the erstwhile peacemaker received a barrage of stones and mud when he tried to speak. Other prominent Presbyterian elders counseled peaceful submission, among them the Irish-born John McDowell (brother-in-law of insurrectionary leader David Bradford) and Congressman William Findley.[52]

Opposition to illegal and violent actions by so many prominent local Presbyterians, and by men who were simultaneously church elders and public officials, indicates the depth of the social conflict within southwestern Pennsylvania's Ulster American community. Men of property and prestige opposed not only open confrontation with the United States government but also the generalized assault on those benefiting from economic change. By contrast, advocates of violent opposition to the law were concentrated among those who had little or no property. Historian Dorothy Fennell notes that the rebellion "occurred in the most economically developed neighborhoods, where landless men accounted for 30 to 60 percent of the taxable residents, and that commercially successful men were among its primary victims." This pattern indicates, she argues, a connection between the prevalence of rebellion and "the hardening of class lines and the decreasing opportunities to own land that characterized the western country at the turn of the century." For example, in her analysis of twenty-three rebels from southwestern Allegheny County's Moon Township (adjacent to Washington County), Fennell found that few were actual distillers and that a majority, who "evidently had little or no property to lose," abandoned their meager possessions and moved out of the area after the rebellion collapsed. This finding accords well with the contemporary observations of William Findley, who, along with fellow Ulsterman David Redick, was commissioned to parley with President Washington on his neighbors' behalf. Findley claimed that those promoting rebellion were "the most ignorant and obstinate class of people"; lacking in property, they had taken advantage of "this season of disorder" to abuse the region's prominent and successful citizens. Findley likewise attributed the disturbances that continued after the rebellion to the intransigence of the area's transient, nonpropertied, and hence least "respectable" inhabitants.[53]

As in Ulster following the 1798 rebellion, once the Whiskey Insurrection was over, most Presbyterian clergymen quickly evidenced what a critic in Ireland later called a "pious and loyal servility."[54] Findley noted that the clergy exerted significant influence only *after* the subsidence of a popular "agitation of mind" that "for a time" had "rendered men deaf" to their ministers' advice. Hence, the ministers' most energetic and best-documented efforts began only after the citizens present at a popular meeting, held in Brownsville on August 28–29, 1794, resolved to submit to the laws and accept an amnesty.

186   Peter Gilmore and Kerby A. Miller

From that point, led by the Reverend John McMillan, the reputed "founder" of western Pennsylvanian Presbyterianism (and an outspoken Federalist), the clergy labored to secure a large vote in favor of submission at the balloting scheduled for September 11, 1794. Under the terms of the arrangement agreed upon between commissioners from the federal and state governments and representatives from the disaffected townships, amnesty required a vote by a majority of all citizens over age eighteen in favor of submitting to federal laws and accepting amnesty. In addition, voters were obliged to sign a pledge that avowed their submission to the laws, their renunciation of further opposition to the excise, and their full support for civil authority.[55]

Just prior to the September 11 balloting (which was open and public), McMillan—like many other Presbyterian clergymen—posted himself at the polling place and personally exhorted the electors to vote for submission. Even more intimidating, he postponed the planned celebration of the Lord's Supper—an event which occurred only two or three times a year—until after the poll, clearly implying that those who failed to ratify the amnesty agreement would be turned away from the communion table. McMillan thus employed a stratagem that, for the Scots-Irish, was perhaps even more laden with traditional and symbolic power than any acts of ritualistic violence that the insurgents had committed![56]

Nonetheless, the Presbyterian clergy and other proponents of submission could take only partial satisfaction from the vote. A majority voted to submit—but the number of total votes was very low. The United States commissioners reported that, out of 11,000 taxable inhabitants in the Fourth Survey (the tax district encompassing southwestern Pennsylvania), merely 2,700 votes had been cast for submission. The voting process in some areas, such as the volatile Mingo Creek district, was marred by intimidation. In the Forks of the Yough, another bastion of rebellion, voters chose defiance. But in Derry Township, Westmoreland County, 139 voted for submission, and only 3 voted against it. Much confusion accompanied the voting, and some communities chose to frame the question in their own ways. East Bethlehem Township in Washington County declared for "Peace with no Excise." Findley believed that, in many areas unaffected by disturbances, the voters had reasoned that, since they had not committed any illegal actions, they need not affirm their lawfulness. Faced with objections—presumably from orthodox Presbyterians, i.e., Seceders and Covenanters—to the word "solemnly" in the submission paper, the United States commissioners announced, just five days prior to the poll, that voters could strike out the offensive word before signing. Perhaps unaware of this concession, some Presbyterians with strict religious scruples were averse to subscribing to what seemed suspiciously like an oath. It may not have been coincidental that, after an army of some thirteen thousand advanced into western Pennsylvania to quell the insurrection, at least one adherent of the Associate Reformed Church, from southern Allegheny County, was among the thirty or so "unrepentant rebels" marched to Philadelphia to face charges of treason.[57]

Perhaps partly in response to the poor turnout by voters on September 11, Presbyterian clergy and elders rushed to demonstrate their support for "law and order" on behalf of their community, in very public and collective ways. Thus, in September 1794 the mainstream Presbyterian Synod of Virginia (which included southwestern Pennsylvania) resolved that November 2 would be a "day of fasting and prayer" to atone for "the late very sinful and unconstitutional opposition which has taken place to some of the laws of the United States." Likewise, that autumn the Presbytery of Redstone (encompassing the territory east and north of the Monongahela River) decried the "present calamitous and threatening situation of our Country and . . . the great prevalency of Sabbath-breaking, swearing, lying, and other vices innumerable which abound in many parts of the land." Finally, in April 1795 both the Redstone and the Ohio presbyteries issued statements deploring the "late disturbances" and requiring those who had violated the law to make public repentance as a condition of receiving communion.[58]

The Whiskey Rebellion was over, but southwestern Pennsylvania remained disturbed. The processes of submitting and signing the amnesty continued for another five years. "The Rebellion and the government's response . . . exacerbated rather than cured the political conflict that rent America in the 1790s," concludes historian Thomas P. Slaughter. "It contributed as much as any single event to widening the breach between self-styled friends of liberty and friends of order, and to the birth of the Republican and Federalist parties in the years after 1794." That breach was exemplified by the actions of the Federalist-dominated state legislature immediately following the rebellion's collapse. To express their disdain for the western rebels, legislators invalidated the results of the October 1794 state elections (ostensibly because voting had occurred during the insurrection), a triumphalist gesture that did nothing to assuage transmontane Pennsylvania's sense of alienation and victimization.

Moreover, if the rebellion was, as Slaughter contends, a "frontier epilogue to the American Revolution," the Great Revival of the West that blazed in Washington County beginning in the 1790s may be regarded as an epilogue to the Whiskey Rebellion. Arguably, the revival broadly reflected the on-

Peter Gilmore and Kerby A. Miller

going social transformations that had given opposition to the federal excise its violent edge. Indeed (and ironically), the rebellion only accelerated the transition from a subsistence (and moral) economy to a cash-driven, commercial economy. The presence of thirteen thousand troops in southwestern Pennsylvania strengthened the hand of the "Neville connection" of military contractors as it rapidly multiplied the number of cash transactions for whiskey and other commodities.[59]

However, a direct relationship between the Whiskey Rebellion itself and the subsequent revival is at least implicit in "Macurdy's War Sermon," delivered at a sacramental occasion at the Upper Buffalo congregation in Washington County in November 1802. Like others, this celebration of the Lord's Supper drew Presbyterian communicants from a wide area; this event reportedly saw "the largest assembly" ever convened for services in western Pennsylvania, a crowd estimated at ten thousand. At the height of the solemn proceedings, as the elements were served, the Reverend Elisha Macurdy announced to the communicants that he would preach on politics, claiming he had received a request to do so from the government. He took as his text the Second Psalm, "Why do the heathen rage?" There had been an insurrection, he railed, a rebellion against the lawfully constituted authorities. Similarly, sinners were rebels against God and His government as well. But, said Macurdy, again citing the Second Psalm, just as the government had proffered amnesty to those who returned to their duty, so too had God offered clemency through the sacrifice of his Son: "Kiss ye the Son," Macurdy demanded, "lest He be angry." The alleged effect of Macurdy's sermon was electrifying: hundreds fell to the ground writhing and weeping. Another minister present recalled, "the scene appeared to me like the close of a battle, in which every tenth man had fallen fatally wounded."[60] A similar revival took place the year after the Whiskey Rebellion, in John McMillan's Washington County congregation, followed by another in 1799. Both revivals, McMillan reported, were accompanied by "silent weeping under the preaching of the word." Revivals likewise occurred within other Presbyterian congregations in Washington County.

It may be, as sociologists of religion might argue, that through these cathartic experiences, settlers found psychological and emotional release from the social and political tensions that the failure of the Whiskey Rebellion had left unresolved. It must also be acknowledged, however, that the Presbyterian clergy encouraged, organized, indeed manipulated the revivals for social and political, as well as for spiritual, purposes. Accompanying their desire to bring souls to Christ were at least two additional, interrelated motives. The emotional power of the revivals, centered on the traditional Scots-Presbyterian sacramental occasions, was intended to bring apostate Scots-Irish back into the fold, thus enhancing the institutional viability of a church with far more congregations than ministers. In 1799, for example, the Ohio Presbytery reported only nine settled ministers and fifteen vacant pulpits.[61] Furthermore, this quest for communicants took place at a time of stiff competition between mainstream Presbyterians and numerous varieties of Seceders and Covenanters—as well as with Baptists and Methodists. At least equally important, however, were the revivals' political connotations. The Federalist-aligned clergy regarded the expansion of church influence as urgently necessary to ensure order and deference—more specifically, to combat Jacobinism and deism, the pernicious spread of which threatened Presbyterian ministers' vision of America as a uniquely "Christian nation."

It appears, however, that these Federalist ministers were only partly and temporarily successful in their religious crusade against Jacobinism, Jeffersonianism, and "infidelity." Thus, Macurdy's biographer noted sadly that a period of "painful declension" followed the 1799 revival. Likewise, John McMillan also feared that post-revival religion was in steep decline, as sinners were emboldened while the pious had become weak "and much buried in the world."[62]

McMillan doubtless had in mind the steady expansion of Democratic-Republicanism in western Pennsylvania—and perhaps also the simultaneous growth of radical republicanism, embodied by the United Irishmen, in Ulster itself. Indeed, the two political phenomena were linked, practically as well as ideologically. New Irish immigrants—often influenced prior to their departures by Irish republicanism (and by its inspirations: the French Revolution and the writings of Tom Paine)—opposed Federalist policies overwhelmingly. In return, the Federalists regarded the immigration of "wild Irishmen," infected with Jacobin ideas, as a major source of Republican strength statewide, as well as a factor contributing to the "terrorism" in southwestern Pennsylvania during the Whiskey Rebellion. In 1798 these concerns led the Federalists to enact the Alien and Sedition and the Naturalization acts designed to throttle this "Irish" opposition. Irish-born Republican congressmen William Findley and John Smilie, among other western Pennsylvanians, relied upon their long experience in defending civil liberties to combat the legislation. By contrast, Federalist judge Alexander Addison, who had been mentored by McMillan, defended the Alien and Sedition Acts and excoriated the French Revolution and the pernicious influence of aliens on American life. In December 1800 in an address to the grand jury on the "Rise and

Progress of Revolution," Addison warned of the presence of revolutionary elements in the United States, among them the Society of United Irishmen. According to Russell Ferguson, Addison's "polemic, delivered under the guise of a charge to the jury, included also the observation that the recent election of [Thomas] McKean as governor of Pennsylvania was the result of the baneful influence of a revolutionary spirit."[63]

The 1799 Democratic-Republican candidate, Thomas McKean, had indeed gained Pennsylvania's governorship, amid rumors that this son of Ulster immigrants intended to import "Twenty Thousand United Irishmen" into the state to influence the outcome.[64] The state election that year assumed crucial importance because of its presumed impact on the following year's presidential contest. By gaining a majority in the lower house of the state legislature, Republicans hoped to deliver Pennsylvania's crucial eight electoral votes to Thomas Jefferson in 1800. With the stakes so high, Washington County's Presbyterian elders had entered the political arena; in 1799 they provided James Ross, McKean's Federalist opponent, with testimonials attesting his religious values. Revealingly, Ross was a protégé of the Reverend John McMillan, who no doubt encouraged, if not orchestrated, the elders' efforts to sway the voters.[65] Nevertheless, McKean's election meant that the tide had turned against the state's "friends of order," for whom the town of Washington was increasingly a Federalist island in a Republican sea. In 1800 Pennsylvania did play a deciding role in the outcome of the bitterly fought presidential election between Jefferson and Federalist John Adams. The contest for the state assembly, held on October 14, 1800, ensured the Republicans' national triumph. The state election "was a crushing defeat for the Federalists," and Washington and other southwestern counties gave hefty majorities to the Jeffersonians.[66]

One reason for the Republicans' victories in southwestern Pennsylvania was that the immediately preceding years had witnessed a large influx of Ulster immigrants who sympathized with the United Irishmen. More than a few had been active rebels who had barely escaped arrest, execution, forced enlistment in the British army's "condemned regiments," being stationed in the fever-ridden West Indies, or transportation as convicts to Britain's Australian penal colonies. Along with ordinary farmers, weavers, shopkeepers, and laborers came Presbyterian ministers with radical credentials. For instance, the Reverend Robert Steele, found guilty of treason to the Crown, sought refuge in America and settled in Pittsburgh. The Reverend John Black, minister to the Pittsburgh area's Reformed Presbyterians, had escaped prior to the 1798 Rebellion; his revolutionary sermons in Ulster had made him a target of military reprisal. According to a contemporary, the Reverend Joseph Kerr also had to flee because of his radical sympathies; he became a minister to Seceders in southern Allegheny County. Thomas Hoge was twenty-three years of age when he fled County Derry in 1798; following residence and business ventures in a succession of Scots-Irish enclaves in Pennsylvania, he turned to the ministry and in 1817 began serving congregations in Washington County. Most notorious was Rev. Thomas Ledlie Birch from Saintfield, County Down. Formerly minister to one of the largest Presbyterian congregations in Ireland, Birch escaped both a military execution and an Orange lynching to minister to Scots-Irish immigrants and Jeffersonian Democrats in Washington County. Like their lesser-known coreligionists and fellow emigrants, these clergymen benefited from an already-well-established chain migration linking western Pennsylvania and the north of Ireland. For example, Birch had former congregants in Washington, and Steele had a brother who was an established businessman in Pittsburgh and who for a time served as Allegheny County treasurer.

After his arrival in the United States, Birch experienced an increasingly bitter and ultimately unsuccessful effort to win admission to the Ohio Presbytery. His Federalist antagonists said pointedly, "Birch's politicks were not suited to Washington [County]."[67] But Birch's difficulties were as much theological and ecclesiastical as overtly political: a rigid, old-fashioned Calvinist who had welcomed the French Revolution as heralding Christ's Second Coming, Birch had little understanding and less sympathy for the revivals zealously nurtured by the Ohio Presbytery; he was conspicuously, in the Presbytery's view, "unconverted." Furthermore, Birch's willingness to ordain elders and carry out other ministerial functions without the presbyters' express approval seemed to the latter an outrageous and potentially schismatic breach of protocol. Failing to secure satisfaction in church judicatories, Birch turned to the civil courts when his religious and political archenemy, the Reverend John McMillan, defamed him as "a liar, a drunkard, and a preacher of the Devil." [68]

The trial in the libel case of *Birch v. McMillan* had strong echoes of the Whiskey Rebellion. The presiding judge, Jasper Yeates, had been a United States commissioner to the rebels, as had McMillan's defense attorney, James Ross, a former United States senator and Federalist gubernatorial candidate. Alexander Addison, recently impeached and removed from the bench, also served as a defense attorney. John Holcroft, rumored to have been rebel leader "Tom the Tinker" and an informer in the insurrection's collapse, served on the jury. Birch won his case, which was appealed to the Pennsylvania Supreme

Court. There, among the justices who reversed the lower court's decision, was Hugh Henry Brackenridge, another prominent figure in the rebellion, while Birch's attorney, James Mountain, was a fellow Irish immigrant and prominent Republican. With Mountain's aid, Birch reinstated his suit in 1808; this time McMillan agreed to settle out of court, paying the immigrant the not-inconsiderable sum of three hundred dollars. McMillan's willingness to settle seems linked to the renewed gubernatorial bid of his protégé, James Ross; the Birch controversy had emerged as an issue in the campaign.

More than a decade after Birch first applied for admittance to the Ohio Presbytery, Washington County residents read with surprise in the Washington, *Reporter* that Birch had been received by the Presbytery of Baltimore and finally admitted into the General Assembly of the Presbyterian Church. Apparently, Birch prevailed upon the sympathy of fellow United Irish émigrés in the Baltimore Presbytery to secure this rather surprising result.[69]

Robert Steele also experienced difficulty in gaining admittance to the American church, and he too endured considerable political controversy, but Steele's circumstances were quite different from Birch's, as were the results. Similar to the Ohio Presbytery's stance toward Birch, the Redstone Presbytery initially refused to accept Steele on the basis of his Irish ordination and credentials. Steele submitted to repeated examinations and a lengthy probation, and eventually he won acceptance nearly three years after his first application. As minister to Pittsburgh's mainstream Presbyterian congregation, Steele maintained his republican credentials but gravitated toward the business-oriented, moderate wing of the state's Jeffersonian party. Steele's political trajectory was likely a consequence of his social position: he mixed comfortably with fellow Masons in the upper echelons of Pittsburgh's Presbyterian society. Indeed, Steele served as chaplain to Masonic Lodge No. 45, which brought together such members of the local elite as Isaac Craig, Abraham Kirkpatrick, Hugh Henry Brackenridge, and Ebenezer Denny, the city's first mayor in 1816. Controversy soon brushed Steele's ministry, however, as Pennsylvania's Republicans, following their 1799–1800 electoral triumphs, began to wrangle with each other.[70]

The 1800–1810 decade saw the emergent Ulster American middle class rent by clashing political allegiances, with divisions shaped as much by pursuit of power as by contesting visions of republicanism. The Republican Party in southwestern Pennsylvania, formerly a unifying force for the region's Scots-Irish, now fragmented along factional, regional, and social fault lines. Irish Republican leaders in Pittsburgh and Washington battled with each other (as well as with recrudescent Federalists) for town, county, and state offices and their spoils. Their strategies were numerous; for example, the proliferation of Pennsylvania counties after 1800 had as much to do with the state Republican administration's interest in appointing sympathetic officials as it did with a need to accommodate the burgeoning western population. At least equally important, party chiefs redoubled their efforts to enlist recent Irish immigrants as supporters of one or the other of the state's warring Republican factions.

One consequence of this intra-party strife was that Pittsburgh's Reverend Robert Steele soon faced complaints from dissident congregants led by Irish immigrant William Gazzam. Church legend has it that Gazzam's faction was displeased that in the traditional psalm-singing, two lines were given out instead of one. However, the petition presented in 1803 to the newly created Synod of Pittsburgh failed to mention that or any other specific grievance. Gazzam and the petition's three other signatories stated only that they and their brethren had found "no kind of spiritual advantage" in Steele's preaching and had therefore withdrawn from the congregation. They also asked permission to create a second Presbyterian congregation in Pittsburgh, in order, as they told the Synod, "to receive the immediate benefits of what we deem to be a Gospel Ministry."[71]

Despite its seemingly narrow compass, this internal church controversy appears to have been inextricably associated with a political dispute that had embroiled Pittsburgh's Republicans for several years prior to the petition against Steele. In 1800 the *Tree of Liberty,* a Jeffersonian newspaper, had identified William Gazzam as the secretary of a Republican meeting and as an officer in the state militia. Gazzam and another signatory to the 1803 petition, William Barrett, owned adjacent stores on Market Street, amidst a series of buildings known as "Clapboard Row"—a name that Pittsburgh residents also applied to a Republican faction or "junto" composed of shopkeepers and professional men. In August 1801 a meeting of Republicans in Washington County had selected Scots-Irish Federalist William Hoge, one of David Redick's in-laws and a member of Washington town's "founding family," as their candidate for Congress. Barely a fortnight later, other Republicans in Pittsburgh met and nominated General Alexander Fowler for the same seat, but Fowler then encountered internecine opposition from Gazzam's "Clapboard Row junto." Fowler in turn bitterly denounced Gazzam in the *Pittsburgh Gazette,* charging him with seeking political office under "the cloak of Republicanism and religion." In other words, it appears that Fowler was ascribing the schismatic movement against Steele to Gazzam's secular and political ambitions rather than to the latter's alleged spiritual con-

Peter Gilmore and Kerby A. Miller

cerns. Adding to the melee, arch-Federalist Alexander Addison joined the battle against Republican Gazzam by pressing the case for maintaining a single, undivided Presbyterian congregation. At this point, the Democratic-Republican *Tree of Liberty* condemned William Steele, the Reverend Robert Steele's merchant brother, for supporting a Federalist candidate (the son of church elder John Wilkins) and for expressing sympathy for the despised Addison.[72]

Indicative of the strength of Irish-nationalist identification among many prospective voters, in 1801 Fowler's foes spread a rumor concerning the latter's alleged support for the Orange Order, the ultra-Loyalist (and then overwhelmingly Anglican) organization that had aided Ulster's landlords and the British government in crushing the United Irish Rebellion of 1798. As a former English army officer in the Royal Irish Regiment, in 1774 Fowler was alleged to have proposed a toast following an officers' dinner in Fort Pitt to "the immortal memory of King William the Third" and then to have ordered the band to strike up the "Boyne March," commemorating William of Orange's famous victory in 1690. Such Orange and royalist sympathies, declared an open letter in the *Pittsburgh Gazette,* were prominent "feature[s]" in the character of General Alexander Fowler."[73]

During Jefferson's first presidential term, these and other divisions among Pennsylvania's Democratic-Republicans became increasingly fratricidal, culminating in the 1805 gubernatorial election when rival party factions vied openly for control. Radicals backed the candidacy of Simon Snyder, called for the restoration of the ultra-democratic state constitution of 1776, and demanded that state judges be elected by the people, rather than appointed for life, to ensure their sensitivity to popular grievances. By contrast, conservative and moderate Republicans supported Governor Thomas McKean's re-election and the "balanced" state constitution that the Federalists had written and ratified in 1790; equally, they abhorred radical demands for democratic control over the state's legal and judicial systems. According to Sanford W. Higginbotham, "Though the election was to a great extent a struggle between conservatives and radicals—between those opposing and those seeking change—it reflected as well the old personal feuds over patronage and political power, and it foreshadowed the passing of political hegemony in the State from Philadelphia to the country regions." These divisions also fractured the Ulster American base of Democratic-Republicanism in southwestern Pennsylvania and may have pitted generational cohorts of Ulster immigrants, as well as different social classes among the Scots-Irish, against one another. Congressman William Findley associated himself with the moderate Republican faction defending McKean's reelection; in return, he received contemptuous rebukes from the Washington, *Reporter,* a newspaper aligned with former United Irishman William Duane and his radical paper, the Philadelphia, *Aurora.* It appears likely that many younger, more recent Scots-Irish immigrants supported the radical candidate, who captured both Washington and Greene counties. McKean owed his narrow victory in part to Pittsburgh's Federalists but also to moderate Republican voters in Fayette and Westmoreland counties, who remained loyal to the older Ulster-born congressmen, Findley and John Smilie.[74]

Revealingly, Snyder's forces seized on and publicized any indication of anti-Irish bias on the part of their opponents. Along with rumors that McKean had disparaged his critics as "clodhoppers," the radical Pittsburgh paper the *Commonwealth* circulated the report that the governor's local supporters had denigrated naturalized citizens, focusing particularly on an anti–United Irish outburst in a courthouse. By contrast, the newspaper devoted its front page to the address adopted by a pro-Snyder meeting of Irish immigrants, printing a verbose endorsement of the gubernatorial candidate replete with references to an ecumenical pantheon of martyrs to Irish freedom. Not coincidentally, perhaps, the political foes whom the *Commonwealth* most frequently condemned were newcomers from New England of English ethnic and non-Presbyterian backgrounds. Indeed, in 1806 one of these men, Allegheny County prothonotary Tarleton Bates, would be shot to death by an Irish immigrant in Pittsburgh's last recorded duel.[75]

Some recent Irish immigrants played significant roles in this intra-ethnic factional contest. At a Fourth of July celebration in 1802, Joseph McClurg offered the toast, "The Irish emigrants, may they all become citizens, and remain true republicans." McClurg, one of Pittsburgh's first ironmasters, did more than express a wish. As a member of William Gazzam's "Clapboard Junto," McClurg served on a committee to encourage and assist the naturalization of aliens. Such efforts appear to have enjoyed success. For example, in September 1808 a committee of "naturalized citizens, natives of Ireland," met at William McCullough's public house in Pittsburgh to express support for the Jefferson administration and the election of James Madison, and to deplore "friends of British connection" and "federal tories." The meeting, chaired by James Irwin, also expressed support for Simon Snyder in yet another gubernatorial contest that pitted him against the inveterate Federalist James Ross. The Ross candidacy provided ample opportunities for radical newspaper editors to make rhetorical flourishes designed to rally recent immigrants to Snyder's cause. The *Commonwealth* excoriated Ross as the can-

Peter Gilmore and Kerby A. Miller

didate of the "old tories, traitors and apostate whigs," as well as an "enemy of liberty," a foe to Irish immigrants, an "Enemy to Christianity," and—perhaps especially appealing to traditional-minded Ulster Calvinists—as "a man desirous of pomp and parade."

Thus the fissures in the state's Democratic-Republican Party, themselves in part a reflection of underlying socioeconomic tensions, introduced new and more threatening political divisions among southwestern Pennsylvania's Scots-Irish. One example of such intra-communal conflict is that, in 1807, Saint Patrick's Day was celebrated locally by two rival organizations: the Sons of Erin, more reflective of middle-class moderation, and the Sons of Hibernia, which exhibited more democratic and more stridently anti-British sentiments. As the names and purpose of the two organizations indicate, however, most Ulster immigrants and their polemicists still referred to themselves unambiguously as "Irish."[76]

For at least several decades, a broad "Irish" self-identification continued, reflected in these and other social organizations as well as in most of the few surviving letters written by ordinary Presbyterians who emigrated from Ulster in the late 1700s and early 1800s.[77] Likewise, Saint Patrick's Day celebrations long remained both ecumenical and Presbyterian-led affairs. Southwestern Pennsylvania's first recorded Saint Patrick's Day event appears to have occurred as early as 1795, when on March 14 the *Pittsburgh Gazette* reported, "There is to be a meeting on Tuesday the 17th inst. at the house of Norris Morrison to celebrate the memory of Saint Patrick." In 1802 the Pittsburgh Irish community organized the Hibernian Society and commemorated that year's Saint Patrick's Day at the home of William Irwin. On that occasion, reported the *Gazette,* "no discordant note, no jarring string in their harp [was heard]—the most perfect harmony prevailed"—as the immigrants lifted their glasses to the scarcely veiled Irish-nationalist proposition that "the sons of Hibernia and Columbia be a terror to the Oppressor, and a shield to the Oppressed."

In the same tradition, about 1815, Joseph McClurg and his son and business partner, Alexander, mobilized Irish newcomers through the organization of one of the region's earliest fraternal associations, the Erin Benevolent Society, which welcomed members of Irish birth regardless of whether they were Protestants or Catholics. Designed to promote charity and philanthropy among Irish immigrants, the society's constitution established a three-man committee to visit the city's wards and mandated an annual meeting every March 17 to elect officers. A report of its 1823 Saint Patrick's Day gathering cited memorial toasts to the heroes of the 1798 and 1803 Irish rebellions, as well as to leading figures in the federal and state governments and to tariff protection for western Pennsylvania's burgeoning industries. Like its predecessors, although inclusively "Irish," the Erin Benevolent Society appears to have been a predominantly Presbyterian organization.[78]

For many years, annual Saint Patrick's Day gatherings in southwestern Pennsylvania would usually mask—albeit sometimes explosively reflect—social, political, and intergenerational conflicts, as Ulster American radicals continued to confront Ulster American moderates and conservatives. Thus in 1828 an Independent Republican committee, consisting of two officers of the Erin Benevolent Society (Alexander McClurg and J. H. Hopkins) among other Irish Americans, battled with Democratic-Republicans, whose ranks included various Presbyterian notables.[79]

Already, however, an alternative mode of self-identification was coming into vogue, as radical notions of "Irish" freedom increasingly clashed with new accommodations to bourgeois authority and standards. Indeed, the origins of this revised ethnic identity lay earlier, in the tumultuous 1790s, when Federalist politicians nationally had denounced Ulster Presbyterian Antifederalists, whiskey rebels, and Democratic-Republicans as "wild Irish," and locally when Federalist polemicist David Bruce had posed "Scots-Irish"—or, more commonly, "Scotch-Irish"—as a conservative, respectable ethnic substitute for Ulster Americans who wished to dissociate themselves from the "dangerously" democratic connotations of "Irishness"—as well as from the latter term's traditionally negative associations with Ireland's "papists."

From the early 1790s, even before the Whiskey Insurrection, David Bruce, a Federalist poet and propagandist, had sought to sway southwestern Pennsylvania's voters from their allegiance to Jefferson, in part by adopting the nom de plume of "the Scots-Irishman" to appeal to those whom he claimed as his fellow countrymen.[80] David Bruce claimed he chose his pseudonym in part simply because of the large Ulster Presbyterian population in the frontier townships: "The Author thought . . . as the people, who are distinguished by the name of Scots-Irish, were the most numerous in the country . . . to assume the language and appellation of a Scots-Irishman, would add to his celebrity."[81] A clever writer and canny shopkeeper, Bruce also appealed to the Ulster immigrants with whom he lived, worked, drank, and worshipped through his use of the Scots language and his occasional references to Ireland. Bruce aimed not at personal celebrity, however, but rather to undermine Ulster immigrants' allegiance to "Irish" republican ideals and radical politics.

Bruce employed his verse to war against "the factious, jacobinic spirit" so widespread in the region, and he hoped to persuade his neighbors to support "the genuine principles of their balanced government." His poetry appeared in the *Western Telegraphe,* a Washington newspaper that ardently championed the Federalist Party's conservative policies. Bruce's first published poem, "Land of War," was a lengthy exercise in blank verse that vilified the French Revolution and stoked contemporary fears of a possible French attack on the United States. However, his claim to fame was assured by "To Whiskey," a Scots-language commentary on the Whiskey Rebellion. Bruce claimed he wrote this poem to show "there was still one faithful Scots Irishman who was as fond of whiskey as any of his countrymen, but was still willing to pay for the liberty of drinking it"; however, he also wrote it to counter the influence of William Findley's sympathetic history of the insurrection.[82]

The popularity of Bruce's label seems to have grown in tandem with Ulster America's increasing social stratification and political factionalism, and with the growing size and influence of an Ulster American bourgeoisie. Revealingly, in an 1812 autobiographical letter, William Findley, perhaps the region's most prominent figure, described himself as among the people "frequently called Scotch-Irish." Yet back in 1790, Findley, while in Philadelphia as an elected official, had joined that city's inclusively "Irish" Hibernian Society for the Relief of Emigrants from Ireland shortly after its organization. Likewise, in 1803 he had taken part in a Saint Patrick's Day celebration of "Irish and American gentlemen" in Lancaster. Indeed, early in his political career, the then-radical Republican had been subjected to taunts from political opponents who labeled him an "Irish Teague" and mocked his Hibernian origins and Ulster accent as well as his lowly former (and stereotypically "Irish") occupations of weaver and schoolmaster.[83]

But as Findley had aged his politics had become more conservative, and he now grumbled rancorously at the gibes of recent immigrants who were too "Irish": i.e., radical, disruptive, and plebeian. By 1812, he championed the Constitution he had once opposed, favored the national bank he had formerly campaigned against, and reversed previous votes in Congress on military preparedness—stands that earned him the censure of more militant Irish-born Republicans. In a letter written in 1805, Findley had complained of the new voters rallying to William Duane and radical factionalists in western Pennsylvania: "No other state is cursed with such a number of unprincipled emigrants." Unsurprisingly, then, he may have found the act of distancing, through the use of the "Scotch-Irish" label, a more attractive option than close identification with political rivals as unhyphenated "Irish."[84]

The region's ironmasters and merchants in the 1810s and 1820s often continued to identify themselves as "Irish" in association with recent immigrants. Very shortly, however, new or accelerated economic and political conflicts (particularly over protective tariffs) and nascent "culture wars" (sparked by new waves of evangelical revivals and their offshoots—the anti-Masonic, temperance, abolitionist, and Sabbatarian crusades)—as well as dramatic increases in the immigration from Ireland of both Catholics and "Orange" Protestants—would create new rifts and alignments within western Pennsylvanian society and American politics generally. These in turn would encourage further refinements of ethnic identification, nationally as well as locally, with the process culminating in the late nineteenth-century formation of the Scotch-Irish Congresses, notable alike for their hyper-patriotism, political conservatism, pride in their ancestors' "British-Protestant" origins, and strident opposition to Irish Catholic immigrants and to Irish nationalist movements.

Nevertheless, it is arguable that, in 1780–1810, Washington, Allegheny, and their adjacent counties provided a vital center for the evolution of Ulster American society, culture, and identity. Quite possibly, the new immigrants who would define their collective identity in terms of "Scotch-Irishness" would be relatively recent arrivals such as the fabulously wealthy financier and arch-reactionary Thomas Mellon, whose own Ulster background and American interests invoked no broader or all-inclusive "Irish" ethnic sensibility and, indeed, found expression only in contempt for the "Irish" (Catholics) who led and manned the labor unions that he vehemently opposed. It may be, as well, that such recent immigrants, like Mellon, would "naturally" assimilate to the "respectable" ethnic imagery that successful older settlers, like William Findley, and their descendants had already begun to embrace.

"Irish" had seemed appropriate enough while the nation still gloried in its revolutionary fervor. But success enjoyed by the upwardly mobile in politics, commerce, and industry would induce later nineteenth-century immigrants, and the offspring of previous immigrants, to shed the increasingly discredited "Irish" label for a more fashionable descriptor that invoked (in part, at least) the allure of Sir Walter Scott's tartan-wrapped romances, all the while assuring an image of sobriety and moral fitness. Yet for several decades to come, the Presbyterian farmers in the western Pennsylvania countryside would continue to be "Irish" in their support for the party of Jefferson and Jackson, even as Pittsburgh steadily became the "smoky citadel of Scotch-Irish enterprise" and a bastion of Presbyterian power, wealth, and respectability.

Notes

1. We employ the term *Scots-Irish* without quotation marks, as a neutral synonym for Ulster Presbyterians, usually for Ulster Presbyterian immigrants in America. By contrast, in our usage, the label "Scotch-Irish," in quotation marks, has problematic social, cultural, and political connotations, as has also our use of the term "Irish," also in quotation marks. For similar reasons, however, we do not employ the currently fashionable term, "Ulster Scots," either with or without quotation marks; indeed, given the determinedly "Irish" political consciousness of most of those we discuss here, it would be ahistorical to do so.

2. James G. Leyburn, *The Scotch-Irish: A Social History* (Chapel Hill: University of North Carolina Press, 1962), 327–34. The interpretations set forth in this and the six following paragraphs are elaborated in Peter Gilmore, "Rebels and Revivals: Ulster Immigrants, Western Pennsylvania Presbyterianism, and the Formation of Scotch-Irish Identity, 1780–1830," PhD diss., Carnegie Mellon University, 2009; Peter Gilmore, "'A Fiddler Was a Great Acquisition to Any Neighborhood': Traditional Music and Ulster Culture on the Pennsylvania Frontier," *Western Pennsylvania History* 83, no. 3 (Fall 2003): 148–65; Gilmore, "'Minister of the Devil': Thomas Ledlie Birch, Presbyterian Rebel in Exile," in David A. Wilson and Mark G. Spencer, eds., *Ulster Presbyterians in the Atlantic World: Religion, Politics and Identity* (Dublin: Four Courts Press, 2006); and also in Kerby A. Miller, Arnold Schrier, Bruce D. Boling, and David N. Doyle, *Irish Immigrants in the Land of Canaan: Letters and Memoirs from Colonial and Revolutionary America, 1675–1815* (New York: Oxford University Press, 2003); Kerby A. Miller, "The New England and Federalist Origins of 'Scotch-Irish' Identity," in William Kelly and John R. Young, eds., *Ulster and Scotland, 1600–2000: History, Language and Identity* (Dublin: Four Courts Press, 2004), 105–18; Kerby A. Miller, "Ulster Presbyterians and the 'Two Traditions' in Ireland and America," in Terry Brotherstone, Anna Clark, and Kevin Whelan, eds., *These Fissured Isles: Varieties of British and Irish Identities* (Edinburgh: John Donald Press, 2005), 260–77; Kerby A. Miller, "Forging the 'Protestant Way of Life': Class Conflict and the Origins of Unionist Hegemony in Early Nineteenth-Century Ulster," in Mark G. Spencer and David A. Wilson, eds., *Transatlantic Perspectives on Ulster Presbyterianism: Religion, Politics and Identity* (Dublin: Four Courts Press, 2005), 128–65.

3. Miller et al., *Irish Immigrants,* chapter 58.

4. John Gamble, *Views of Society and Manners in the North of Ireland* (London: Longman, Hurst, Rees, Orme, and Brown, 1819), 367.

5. John McBride, Watertown, N.Y., January 9, 1820 (T.2613/3, Public Record Office of Northern Ireland, hereafter cited as PRONI).

6. On the meanings of "independence," see Kerby A. Miller, *Emigrants and Exiles: Ireland and the Irish Exodus to North America* (New York: Oxford University Press, 1985), 156–67, 174–79, 190–92, 201–10.

7. John Caldwell, *William Findley from West of the Mountains,* vol. 1: *A Politician in Pennsylvania, 1783–1791* (Gig Harbor, Wash.: Red Apple Publishing, 2000), 96.

8. See the letters of the Kerr and McElderry brothers, in MIC 144/1 and in T. 2414 and MIC 26, respectively, in PRONI.

9. Miller, *Emigrants and Exiles,* 164.

10. Patrick Griffin, *American Leviathan: Empire, Nation, and Revolutionary Frontier* (New York: Hill and Wang, 2007), 22–23; Kevin Kenny, *Peaceable Kingdom Lost: The Paxton Boys and the Destruction of William Penn's Holy Experiment* (New York: Oxford University Press, 2009), 217; Peter Gilmore, "From Rostrevor to Raphoe: An Overview of Ulster Place-Names in Pennsylvania, 1700–1820," unpublished manuscript, 2009, 19. A few Scots-Irish illegally settled in what became Belfast Township, Fulton County, as early as the 1740s; others squatted in what later emerged as Colerain, Bedford County, in the 1750s.

11. Solon Buck and Elizabeth Hawthorn Buck, *The Planting of Civilization in Western Pennsylvania* (Pittsburgh: University of Pittsburgh Press, 1939; 1995 reprint), 144, 146, 214–15.

12. David Hoge, Esq., a native of Ulster, owned the land that became Washington Town; see Miller et al., *Irish Immigrants,* 574–75; Belfast reference cited in Victor Anthony Walsh, "'Across the Big Wather': Irish Community Life in Pittsburgh and Allegheny City, 1853–1855," PhD diss., University of Pittsburgh, 1983, 152; Buck and Buck, *Planting of Civilization,* 217, 153.

13. While less common in the 1820s, some merchants continued to accept country produce, although apparently with more stringent conditions. Isaac Harris, who operated a store on Market Street in Pittsburgh, in 1822 announced that domestic goods "will now be sold for Cash or approved Barter." The list of items sought for purchase included beeswax, deerskins, and "country Carpeting." *Pittsburgh Gazette,* January 11, 1822. Robert Steele (nephew of the 1798 exile) undertook business along the Ohio River and announced he was prepared to "receive, store and sell or forward all kinds of goods and country produce." He gave as references Pittsburgh merchants Cunningham & Wilson and Alexander Johnston, plus the Philadelphia firm of McCullough & Dixon, suggesting an ongoing Ulster American commercial network. *Pittsburgh Gazette,* March 30, 1820.

14. Buck and Buck, *Planting of Civilization,* 152–53; R. Eugene Harper, *The Transformation of Western Pennsylvania, 1770–1800* (Pittsburgh: University of Pittsburgh Press, 1991), 214–15; *A List of Immigrants Who Applied for Naturalization Papers in the District Courts of Allegheny County, Pennsylvania* (Pittsburgh: Western Pennsylvania Genealogical Society, 1978); Sanford W. Higginbotham, *The Keystone in the Democratic Arch: Pennsylvania Politics, 1800–1816* (Harrisburg: Pennsylvania Historical and Museum Commission, 1952), 4.

15. Joseph Stockton, *A Historical Discourse on the Fortieth Anniversary of the Author's Ministry in Cross Creek* (Pittsburgh: Errett, Anderson, 1867), 8–10; Presbytery of Washington, Presbyterian Church in the U.S.A., *History of the Presbytery of Washington* (Philadelphia: James B. Rodgers Printing, 1889), 121.

16. William Findley, *History of the Insurrection in the Four Western Counties of Pennsylvania* (Philadelphia: Samuel Harrison Smith, 1796), 20; John Caldwell, *The Family of William Findley of Westmoreland, Pa.* (Rock Island, Ill.: Five Rhinos Book Company, 2002), 3.

17. *History of the Presbytery of Washington,* 232, 212–13. Joseph Donahey became an elder in the East Buffalo congregation in Washington County; two of the sons of Joseph

and Mary also became elders. As was true of a significant minority of Ulster Presbyterians and other Irish Protestants, the family surname Donahey indicates native Irish and Catholic antecedents. In nineteenth- and early twentieth-century America, however, such families were often especially keen to claim "Scotch-Irish" ancestry and, hence, "British/Protestant" superiority.

18. Based on an unpublished survey of Pennsylvania place-names of Ulster origin by Peter Gilmore. Menallen may have been inspired by the similarly named township in York County, which in turn represents a corruption of Moyallon, a townland in County Down that was home to a Friends community. Perhaps coincidentally, the Fayette County township contained a Quaker settlement. Rostraver represents a somewhat phonetic spelling of Rostrevor in County Down. See also Karen J. Harvey, "Diamonds in the Rough: Scotch-Irish Town Planning in Northern Appalachia during the Early Republic," *Journal of Scotch-Irish Studies* 1, no. 2 (Summer 2001): 107–24.

19. Washington, Pa., *Reporter,* January 15, 1810.

20. *History of the Presbytery of Washington,* 10; Wayland F. Dunaway, *The Scotch-Irish of Colonial Pennsylvania* (Chapel Hill: University of North Carolina Press, 1944), 82. Pittsburgh's first settled minister was Samuel Barr. (See note 44 below.)

21. *Minutes of the General Assembly,* 186, 240–41. The churches with vacant pulpits in 1802 were found in what are now West Virginia and Ohio as well as in western Pennsylvania.

22. Conclusion based on a list of ministers found in *Minutes of the Presbytery of Ohio* and biographical sketches in *History of the Presbytery of Washington.*

23. William Melanchthon Glasgow, *Cyclopedic Manual of the United Presbyterian Church of North America* (Pittsburgh: United Presbyterian Board of Publications, 1903), 10; Rev. John T. Brownlee, *History of the Associate and United Presbyterian Presbytery of Chartiers* (1877, reprinted by Chartiers Presbytery, 1936), 4–5; Basil G. McBee and Reid W. Stewart, *History of the Associate Presbyterian Church in North America* (Apollo, Pa.: Closson Press, 1983), 22. Calculation based on information contained in the section titled "Congregations" in Glasgow, *Cyclopedic Manual,* 377–585.

24. William Lyons Fisk, *The Scottish High Church Tradition in America* (Lanham, Md.: University Press of America, 1995), 54.

25. Scrutiny of a map of Washington County made in 1817 locates the bulk of Associate and Associate Reform congregations in the western half of the county, within townships that tended to be settled later than those along river valleys.

26. An example of New World innovation was the movement to hymns and abandonment of traditional Scottish metrical psalms; on several occasions mainstream Presbyterian congregations protested the introduction of Watts' Psalms by defecting to an Associate or Associate Reformed body. See, for example, the defection of congregants of the Three Ridges Church in Donegal Township, Washington County, to the Seceders in *History of the Presbytery of Washington,* 279. The hymns of English poet Isaac Watts were in vogue in mainstream Presbyterian churches but rejected by Seceders as unscriptural. Presbyterian minister Adam Rankin, later a vitriolic critic of revivalism, unsuccessfully fought use of

Watts' Psalms all the way to the General Assembly before leading his congregation into the Associate Reformed Church; see John B. Boles, *The Great Revival, 1787–1805* (Lexington: University Press of Kentucky, 1972), 22, 98.

27. Neville B. Craig, *The History of Pittsburgh* (1851; rpt. J. R. Weldin, 1917), 173.

28. John M'Kerrow, *History of the Foreign Missions of the Secession and United Presbyterian Church* (Edinburgh: Andrew Elliot, 1867), 25.

29. Thomas Jefferson Chapman, *Old Pittsburgh Days* (Pittsburgh: J. R. Weldin, 1900), 176.

30. William Heazelton, Pittsburgh, October 22, 1810, reprinted in Miller et al., *Irish Immigrants,* 621.

31. Pittsburgh, *Tree of Liberty,* September 13, 1800.

32. Washington, *Reporter,* September 3, 1810.

33. Hugh Henry Brackenridge, "Cursory Remarks on the Federal Constitution," in Daniel Marder, ed., *A Hugh Henry Brackenridge Reader, 1770–1815* (Pittsburgh: University of Pittsburgh Press, 1970), 127. In speculating on the requirement that senators be "Irish" or "Scotch-Irish," Brackenridge continued, "If any of them have been in the war of the White Boys, Hearts of Oak, or the like, they may overturn all authority and make the shillelah the supreme law of the land"—a revealing comment in that it not only associated Pennsylvania's Scots-Irish Democratic-Republicans with Ireland's illegal and violent secret agrarian societies, but it also conflated the exclusively Protestant adherents of Ulster's Oakboys (1760s) with the exclusively Catholic Whiteboys of Munster (1760s–80s).

34. Gamble, *Views of Society,* 191. For numerous quotations from letters written by late eighteenth- and early nineteenth-century Ulster emigrants, see Miller, *Emigrants and Exiles,* chapters 5–6, as well as the pertinent documents in Miller et al., *Irish Immigrants.*

35. Noah Thompson, *Early History of the Peters Creek Valley and the Early Settlers* (self-published, 1973), 52; *History of Allegheny County, Pennsylvania* (Chicago: A. Warner, 1889), 618; Harper, *Transformation,* 39, 172, 30, 33. Dinsmore received his grant for land on Millers Run in 1785 (his tract was in that part of Washington County that later became southern Allegheny County). Dinsmore was an original elder of Bethel Presbyterian Church, among the oldest in western Pennsylvania. He later moved to Canton Township, Washington County. *History of Allegheny County,* 618; Joseph Smith, *Old Redstone, or Historical Sketches of Western Presbyterianism; Its Early Ministers and Perilous Times* (Philadelphia: Lippincott, Grambo, 1854), 353–54; Boyd Crumrine, ed., *History of Washington County, Pennsylvania, with Biographical Sketches of Many of Its Pioneers and Prominent Men* (Philadelphia: L. H. Everts, 1882), 689.

36. Harper, *Transformation,* 58, 63, 124–25, 128.

37. Ibid., 47, 56–57, 74; *Pittsburgh Gazette,* April 24, 1820.

38. Miller et al., *Irish Immigrants,* 179–84.

39. Harper, *Transformation,* 145; John Caldwell, *William Findley,* 54; Russell J. Ferguson, *Early Western Pennsylvania Politics* (Pittsburgh: University of Pittsburgh Press, 1938), 90.

40. Ferguson, *Early Western Pennsylvania Politics,* 114–16; Findley, *History of the Presbytery,* 319; Dorothy E. Fennell, "From Rebelliousness to Insurrection: A Social History of the Whiskey Rebellion," PhD diss., University of Pittsburgh, 1981, 125, 251–52; Leland D. Baldwin, *Whiskey Rebels, The Story of a Frontier Uprising* (Pittsburgh: University of Pitts-

burgh Press, 1939), 45–47; *The History of Lodge No. 45, F.&A.M., 1785–1910* (Pittsburgh, ca. 1912), 93; Anne Hemphill Herbert, *Personal Memories of the Darlington Family at Guyasuta* (Pittsburgh: University of Pittsburgh Press, 1949), 10; Kirk Q. Bingham, *Major Abraham Kirkpatrick and His Descendants* (Pittsburgh: J. P. Durbin, 1911), 44; Oliver Ormsby Page, *A Short Account of the Family of Ormsby of Pittsburgh* (Albany, N.Y.: J. Munsell's Sons, 1892), 13, 17; *History of Allegheny County,* 294, 396, 399.

41. Ferguson, *Early Western Pennsylvania Politics,* 114; Bingham, *Major Abraham Kirkpatrick,* 8; *History of Allegheny County,* 475, 491, 648, 651; Erasmus Wilson, ed., *Standard History of Pittsburg, Pennsylvania* (Chicago: H. R. Cornell, 1898), 197, 603, 664.

42. Peter Gilmore, "Rev. Samuel Barr and the Social Origins of the Whiskey Rebellion" (paper presented to the Carnegie Mellon University History Department Graduate Research Forum, January 17, 2007).

43. The Forks of the Yough comprised the territory between the Youghiogheny and Monongahela rivers, on the border of Westmoreland and Allegheny counties. Eugene Perry Link, *Democratic-Republican Societies, 1790–1800* (New York: Columbia University Press, 1942), 147–48; Dwight Raymond Guthrie, *John McMillan: The Apostle of Presbyterianism in the West, 1752–1833* (Pittsburgh: University of Pittsburgh Press, 1952), 163; Thomas P. Slaughter, *The Whiskey Rebellion, Frontier Epilogue to the American Revolution* (New York: Oxford University Press, 1986), 164–65; *Inventory of the Church Archives of Pennsylvania Churches: Presbyterian Churches,* prepared by the Pennsylvania Historical Records Survey, Works Progress Administration, arranged and indexed by Candace W. Belfield (Philadelphia: Presbyterian Historical Society, 1971), 05649–50.

44. James Patrick McClure, "The Ends of the American Earth: Pittsburgh and the Upper Ohio Valley to 1795," PhD diss., University of Michigan, 1983, 566, 538–9; the quote from the December 1786 *Gazette* appears in McClure, 538. "In addition to being a county judge and administrator of the public lands set aside for veterans of the Revolution, [George] Wallace engaged in lumbering, distilling and manufacturing. He also [in the 1790s] dealt exclusively with the quartermaster department." Wallace, a member of Pittsburgh's Presbyterian church, aligned himself with the Neville Connection and testified against Rev. Samuel Barr during a sensational ecclesiastical trial. Fennell, "From Rebelliousness to Insurrection," 138. In the early 1770s, similar grievances had driven the largely Scots-Irish "Regulators" of western North Carolina into outright rebellion against the colonial government, and from the mid-eighteenth into the early nineteenth century tenant farmers in Maine, among them also many Scots-Irish, were in a state of smothered (but sometimes violent) insurrection against Boston authorities and absentee landlords—the latter and their middlemen often of upper- or middle-class Irish Protestant birth or descent. Likewise, the reputed leader of New York's tenants in their Anti-Rent War of 1766 was an Irish immigrant, as were many of his alleged followers.

45. Fennell, "From Rebelliousness to Insurrection," 229.

46. Ibid., 99, 123–35; Miller, *Emigrants and Exiles,* 61, 66–67; Jim Smyth, *The Men of No Property: Irish Radicals and Popular Politics in the Late Eighteenth Century* (London: Macmillan Press, 1998), 35–36; George Thornton Fleming, *A History of Pittsburgh and Its Environs* (Chicago: American Historical Society, 1922), 33.

47. Smith, *Old Redstone,* 258. If the Oliver Miller who was slain was the father of farmer-distiller William Miller, as suggested by Baldwin (*Whiskey Rebels,* 116), then he was likely an Irishman who settled in Bedford County prior to the Revolution. James McFarlane (or McFarland), a Revolutionary War veteran, had a brother in County Tyrone and paid the passage of two men to America; see Jerry A. Clouse, *The Whiskey Rebellion: Southwestern Pennsylvania's Frontier People Test the American Constitution* (Harrisburg: Bureau for Historic Preservation, Pennsylvania Historical and Museum Commission, 1994), 16; Baldwin, *Whiskey Rebels,* 120; Fennell, "From Rebelliousness to Insurrection," 104.

48. Baldwin, *Whiskey Rebels,* 164; Slaughter, *Whiskey Rebellion,* 187 (the reference to "Sodom" is from Brackenridge); William Wilson McKinney, *Early Pittsburgh Presbyterianism* (Pittsburgh: Gibson Press, 1938), 65; *History of Allegheny County,* 333.

49. Letter of Alexander Addison to General Henry Lee, November 1794, qtd. in Roger H. Kohn, ed., "Judge Alexander Addison on the Origin and History of the Whiskey Rebellion" in Steven R. Boyd, ed., *The Whiskey Rebellion: Past and Present Perspectives* (Westport, Conn.: Greenwood Press, 1985), 52; Thomas P. Slaughter, "The Friends of Liberty, the Friends of Order, and the Whiskey Rebellion: A Historiographical Essay," in Boyd, *Whiskey Rebellion,* 12–13; Samuel Wilkeson, qtd. in Smith, *Old Redstone,* 256; Findley, *History of the Insurrection,* 241. Wilkeson grew up in Washington County's Chartiers Valley; his father, wrote Neville Craig, "was one of those Irish Presbyterians"; see Craig, *Exposure of a Few of the Many Misstatements in H. M. Brackenridge's History of the Whiskey Insurrection* (Pittsburgh: J. S. Davison, 1855), 61.

50. Findley, *History of the Insurrection,* 300–301; Baldwin, *Whiskey Rebels,* 72.

51. The anecdote about the Reverend John Clark recurs frequently in the literature, beginning with Findley's 1796 history (p. 86). It also informs a dramatic incident in Henry C. McCook's *The Latimers,* an 1898 novel about the rebellion. Smith, *Old Redstone,* 252; Daniel J. Yolton, "Upholding Moral Standards," in William W. McKinney, *The Presbyterian Valley* (Pittsburgh: Davis & Warde, 1958), 90. Ministers were placed in a difficult circumstance; their salaries were often in arrears as it was. Certain hefty arrearages may have represented indirect protests directed at ill-received ministerial exhortation. On the other hand, Findley and other writers credit the Irish-born Samuel Porter, a minister in Westmoreland County, with consistent and vigorous intervention throughout the tumult. Findley wrote: "Mr. Porter of Westmoreland . . . laboured publicly and privately with success from the beginning, to prevent the spirit of disorder from spreading in his congregation" (*History of the Insurrection,* 182).

Although no Pennsylvanian minister appears on the record as openly sympathetic to the movement against the excise, a Virginian clergyman faced physical threats from enraged militia for suggesting that the wrongs of the whiskey tax outweighed the rebellion in seriousness. The Reverend William Graham, speaking at a meeting of the Synod of Virginia in Harrisonburg, Virginia, in September 1794, helped to defeat a motion that would have appealed to those within the Synod's bounds to obey the law. Graham, "of Scotch-Irish parentage," was born near Harrisburg, Pennsylvania; see *Centenary Memorial of the Planting and Growth of Presbyterianism in Western Pennsylvania* (Pittsburgh: Benjamin Singerly, 1876), 408–9.

52. *History of the Presbytery of Washington*, 207–8; Harper, *Transformation*, 149, 163; Ferguson, *Early Western Pennsylvania Politics*, 52, 90; Ronald W. Long, "The Presbyterians and the Whiskey Rebellion" in the *Journal of Presbyterian History* 43 (March 1965); Baldwin, *Whiskey Rebels*, 210. For the strength of Edgar's intervention, see Findley, *History of the Insurrection*, 123, 125–26. Ferguson, *Early Western Pennsylvania Politics*, 47, 52, 65, 102, 269, 270; Harper, *Transformation*, 149; Long, "Presbyterians and the Whiskey Rebellion," 31–32. Findley asserted that he "attended every meeting that was held for the purpose of restoring order," including "different worshipping congregations . . . and at every place I could get an opportunity to converse with the people." Although Findley claimed that his immediate vicinity was unaffected by disturbances, Slaughter observes that malcontents disrupted the September 11, 1794, poll in Findley's Unity Township and absconded with the list of signatories. Findley, *History of the Insurrection*, 272; Slaughter, *Whiskey Rebellion*, 203.

53. Fennell, "From Rebelliousness to Insurrection," 139–40, 142, 145; Findley, *History of the Insurrection*, 173, 177.

54. Miller, "Forging the 'Protestant Way of Life,'" 156.

55. Yolton, "Upholding Moral Standards," 90; Findley, *History of the Presbytery*, 182.

56. Yolton, "Upholding Moral Standards," 91; Guthrie, *John McMillan*, 162–63.

57. Fleming, *History of Pittsburgh*, 38; Clouse, *Whiskey Rebellion*, 35–36; Slaughter, *Whiskey Rebellion*, 202–4; Baldwin, *Whiskey Rebels*, 72, 209–11; Findley, *History of the Insurrection*, 133–34. On Redick, see Miller et al, *Irish Immigrants*, 574–75. The reference is to Isaac Walker, who migrated from Lancaster to Allegheny County in 1772. A Covenanter, Walker was among the founders of the Robinson's Run Associate Reformed congregation organized by 1794; see Samuel S. Glass, *A History of the Associate Reformed Now United Presbyterian Congregation of Union, Robinson Township, Allegheny County, Pa.* . . . (Pittsburgh: Duncan & McElvany, 1994), 9; J. W. English, *A History of Robinson's Run Associate Reformed, Now United Presbyterian Congregation, Allegheny County, Pa.* . . . (Pittsburgh: Stevenson and Foster, 1890), 6, 8–9; Bicentennial Book Committee, Union Presbyterian Church, *Bicentennial History of Union Presbyterian Church, 1794–1994, Robinson Township, Allegheny County, Pennsylvania* (Franklin, Tenn.: Providence House Publishers, 1993), 11; William G. Johnston, *Life and Reminiscences from Birth to Manhood of Wm. G. Johnston* (Pittsburgh: Knickerbocker Press, 1901), 118.

58. Long, "Presbyterians and the Whiskey Rebellion," 34–35; *Minutes of the Ohio Presbytery*, April 28, 1795, 11.

59. Slaughter, *Whiskey Rebellion*, 221; Andrew Shankman, *Crucible of American Democracy: The Struggle to Fuse Egalitarianism and Capitalism in Jeffersonian Pennsylvania* (Lawrence: University Press of Kansas, 2004), 57–58. For the economic causes of the rebellion and the operations of the "whiskey junto," see Fennell, "From Rebelliousness to Insurrection," 249–58.

60. Clarence J. Macartney, *Not Far from Pittsburgh* (Pittsburgh: Gibson Press, 1936), 30; David Elliott, *The Life of the Rev. Elisha Macurdy* (Allegheny: Kennedy and Brother, 1848), 73–75. Macurdy, the grandson of an Irish immigrant, was born in Chester County, Pennsylvania.

61. *Minutes of the General Assembly of the Presbyterian Church in the United States of America, from Its Organization A.D. 1789 to A.D. 1820 Inclusive* (Philadelphia: Presbyterian Board of Education, 1847), 186, 240–41. The vacant churches in 1802 were located in what is now West Virginia and Ohio as well as in western Pennsylvania.

62. Elliott, *Rev. Elisha Macurdy,* 56; *Western Missionary Magazine* vol. II (1805), 354.

63. Edward C. Carter II, "A 'Wild Irishman' under Every Federalist's Bed: Naturalization in Philadelphia, 1789–1806," *Pennsylvania Magazine of History and Biography* 94 (July 1970), 334; Slaughter, *Whiskey Rebellion,* 194–95; Miller et al., *Irish Immigrants,* 587; Ferguson, *Early Western Pennsylvania Politics,* 48, 115, 149, 168–69; G. S. Rowe, "Alexander Addison: The Disillusionment of a 'Republican Schoolmaster,'" *Western Pennsylvania History Magazine* 62 (1975): 223–24, 238–42, 245–47; Guthrie, *John McMillan,* 135, 157 (n. 100); Harper, *Transformation,* 141–42.

64. Harry Marlin Tinkcom, *The Republicans and Federalists in Pennsylvania, 1790–1801* (Harrisburg: Pennsylvania Historical and Museum Commission, 1950), 231; Ferguson, *Early Western Pennsylvania Politics,* 149–50.

65. Tinkcom, *Republicans and Federalists,* 234–35; Ferguson, *Early Western Pennsylvania Politics,* 48, 115. Ross had been accused of deism. Both Ross and Addison, a particularly prominent political pair, served as McMillan's defense attorneys when Birch brought a suit of defamation against their mentor.

66. Tinkcom, *Republicans and Federalists,* 245–46; Ferguson, *Early Western Pennsylvania Politics,* 90, 163.

67. Thomas Ledlie Birch, *Seemingly Experimental Religion . . . or, War against the Gospel by Its Friends . . .* (Washington, Pa.: n.p., 1806), 138.

68. See Gilmore, "'Minister of the Devil,'" 62–86.

69. Washington, *Reporter,* August 5, 1811; David A. Wilson, *United Irishmen, United States: Immigrant Radicals in the Early Republic* (Ithaca: Cornell University Press, 1998), 129.

70. *Minutes of the Presbytery of Redstone, Sept. 19, 1781–December 1831,* 148–49, 161–64, 166, 167, 170–71, 179; McKinney, *Early Pittsburgh Presbyterians,* 101–6; *Centennial Volume of the First Presbyterian Church of Pittsburgh, Pa., 1784–1884* (Pittsburgh: Wm. G. Johnston, 1884), 152.; Scott C. Martin, "Fathers against Sons, Sons against Fathers: Antimasonry in Pittsburgh" (University of Pittsburgh seminar paper, n.d.), 17. Steele was licensed in Ulster by the Presbytery of Route in 1789 and ordained in Dungiven by the Presbytery of Londonderry in 1791. The Derry Presbytery reported in 1798 "[t]hat the Revd Robert Steel, having pleaded Guilty to a charge of Treason & Rebellion before a Court Martial, his name was erased from the List of the Presbytery," in *Records of the General Synod of Ulster from 1691 to 1820,* Vol. III [1778–1820] (Belfast: Archer and Sons, 1898), 109, 129, 205.

71. *Centennial Volume,* 33–34.

72. *Tree of Liberty,* October 11, 1800, November 8, 1800, October 30, 1802; Martin, "Fathers against Sons," 14–15; Higginbotham, *Keystone,* 38.

73. *Pittsburgh Gazette,* July 4, 1801; the letter was signed by William Semple.

74. Higginbotham, *Keystone,* 77; Ferguson, *Early Western Pennsylvania Politics,* 194–95; *Tree of Liberty,* various issues, 1805.

75. Pittsburgh, *Commonwealth,* July 24, 1805, July 31, 1805, August 14, 1805, August 31, 1805, September 28, 1805, September 14, 1805; Higginbotham, *Keystone,* 117. The address of the Irish gathering, which had taken place in Montgomery County, alluded to William Orr, a Presbyterian; Father James Quigley (or Coigley), Catholic; and Wolfe Tone and Thomas Russell, Anglicans, among others. In the "United Irishman" incident, the *Commonwealth* objected to the emphasis placed on the Irish origins of a young man convicted of larceny and how authorities allowed an obviously intoxicated man to interrupt court proceedings with impunity. The drunk allegedly roared out, "Had he (the criminal) been in his own country, and committed the crime, he would have danced the United Irishman's jig!" (meaning hanging). The duelist who killed Bates was William Stewart.

76. *Tree of Liberty,* July 10, 1802; Ferguson, *Early Western Pennsylvania Politics,* 167, 207, 216–17; Washington, *Reporter,* September 19, 1808; *Commonwealth,* March 25, 1807.

77. On the "Irish" self-identification in late eighteenth- and early nineteenth-century Ulster Presbyterian immigrants' letters, see Miller et al., *Irish Immigrants,* especially chapters 64–68.

78. Officers included Hugh Davis, who in 1801 had emigrated with his parents from County Tyrone and who later became one of the three founding trustees of the Presbyterians' Western Theological Seminary. Another, banker and society treasurer Michael Allen, was also the seminary's first treasurer and a prominent member of Pittsburgh's First Presbyterian Church. Finally, trustee Robert Steele was a nephew of First Presbyterian's minister and son of wealthy merchant William Steele. Wilson, *Standard History of Pittsburg,* 889, 219; Fleming, *History of Pittsburgh,* 3:603; *Tree of Liberty,* December 25, 1802; *Pittsburgh Gazette,* March 19, 1802, March 21, 1823. For Hugh Davis, see John E. Parke, *Recollections of Seventy Years and Historical Gleanings of Allegheny, Pennsylvania* (Boston: Rand, Avery, 1882), 302; *History of Allegheny County,* 256; and *Centenary Memorial.* Hugh Davis married Elizabeth Henderson, daughter of Robert Henderson, whose Pittsburgh tavern was the frequent site of Democratic-Republican meetings; Rev. Robert Steele, exiled for his alleged connection to the United Irishmen, performed the ceremony. *Commonwealth,* March 23, 1806.

79. Wilson, *Standard History of Pittsburg,* 753.

80. Scholars have assumed, on the basis of the pseudonym and a few references in his poetry to the north of Ireland that David Bruce lived for a time in Ulster's Scottish diaspora. (The allusions to Ireland in his verse were rather few and largely appeared earlier in his poetic career—in order, perhaps, to create his "Scots-Irish" persona.) Harry R. Warfel, in a 1925 article, expended some effort in speculation on the movements back and forth between Scotland and the north of Ireland; see Warfel, "David Bruce, Federalist Poet of Western Pennsylvania," *Western Pennsylvania Historical Magazine* 8 (1925): 176–77. Recently, Michael Montgomery assigned to Bruce "roots along the north coast of Ulster" and suggested that the poet "apparently spent his formative years in north County Londonderry." See Montgomery, "The Problem of Persistence: Ulster-American Missing Links," *Journal of Scotch-Irish Studies* 1 (Spring 2000): 108.

The full title of his 1801 collection of verse—*Poems Chiefly in the Scottish Dialect, Originally Written under the Signature of the Scots-Irishman, by A Native of Scotland; with*

Notes and Illustrations—suggests the essential facts of the pseudonym and Bruce's place of origin. The poet's publisher, John Colerick of Washington, Pennsylvania, wrote that Bruce was born in Caithness, the northernmost Scottish county, where his father, William Bruce, was a farmer. Father and son immigrated to Maryland in 1784. Apart from the nom de plume and occasional Irish references in his verse, there is no evidence linking Bruce to Ulster. Such evidence as does exist suggests the Bruce family did not relocate to Ulster prior to passage to the United States. The Washington County Orphans Court disposed of his property when Bruce, a bachelor, died without legal heirs. That record refers to a sister and the children of three sisters in Caithness, Glasgow, Edinburgh, and Burgettstown. No Irish reference appears. There is the further circumstantial evidence of financial and political ties between Bruce and Scottish immigrants.

81. David Bruce, *Poems Chiefly in the Scottish Dialect, Originally Written Under the Signature of the Scots-Irishman, by A Native of Scotland; with Notes and Illustrations* (Washington, Pa.: John Colerick, 1801).

82. Ibid. Findley outraged his conservative opponents by attempting to explain the rebellion—which he opposed—and by criticizing the federal excise on whiskey and the Washington administration's handling of the affair.

83. Caldwell, *William Findley* 2:239, 1:194: "It was right that Findly should be put in nomination, because he can 'Addrass the chair,' and say, 'Myster Spaker,' and avoid being 'parsenal.'" This satire was likely composed by Hugh Henry Brackenridge. In the writings of the elitist Brackenridge, Findley was portrayed either as contemptible, ignorant Irish weaver Traddle, or as the equally disreputable Irish (and stereotypically Catholic) servant, Teague O'Regan. David Bruce, Federalist poet and shopkeeper, lampooned Findley as "Willie Thrum," likewise calling attention to the legislator's weaving background.

84. "William Findley of Westmoreland, Pa." (letter written to Governor William Plumer of New Hampshire, February 27, 1812), *Pennsylvania Magazine of History and Biography* 5 (1881): 440.; The letter is quoted in Caldwell, *William Findley,* 2:269; also see Miller et al., *Irish Immigrants,* 625.

Searching for Independence: Revolutionary Kentucky, Irish American Experience, and Scotch-Irish Myth, 1770s–1790s

Patrick Griffin

When considering the early experience of migrants from Ireland to America, some places and dates quickly come to mind: Donegal, Pennsylvania, in the early 1720s; the Shenandoah in the 1740s; as well as Washington, Pennsylvania, in the 1790s. In each of these settings, men and women whom we could say were Irish, Scotch-Irish, or Scots-Irish lived.[1] In each of these times and places, men and women from Ireland also had visible and well-articulated roles in developments that defined the early experience of the Irish in America. The first site, of course, represents arguably the most significant setting for initial settlement for the group, the home of the charter generation of the Irish in British North America.[2] The second captures the dynamic of movement that defined the group's experience in the eighteenth century, as thousands moved to, through, and from southeast Pennsylvania and Atlantic ports into the "backcountry" and down what would be called the Great Wagon Road.[3] The third place in time highlights the "Scotch-Irish" participation in epic events of the frontier, in this case the Whiskey Rebellion. While each site portrays a distinctive feature of the group, together they suggest that men and women from "Ulster"—and of course other Irish provinces—seemed perfectly suited to the frontier. It does not surprise us, nor should it, that the Scotch-Irish put their distinctive stamp on America's frontier. In Ulster in particular, or so we have been led to believe, they were prepared for a life in the New World in which they would champion radical notions of democracy, defy authority, and relish whiskey.[4]

Or at least we would like to believe so. Part of the Scotch-Irish story, after all, is shrouded in mythic notions that still animate our understandings of the group to this day.[5] In this essay, I would like to discuss Scotch-Irish myths and Irish American realities by exploring a perhaps less visible but no less significant feature of the group's history and the history of the United States: revolutionary Kentucky. This place at this time represented an important site for the Irish immigrant experience because so many men and women from Ireland—and crucially as we shall see, their descendants—settled there and because Kentucky featured so prominently in the story of the American Revolution. But it also should demand our attention because this place in time lends itself to coming to terms with frontier myths. Exploring revolutionary Kentucky, in light of the scholarship of the past thirty years—much of which has not been done as "Scotch-Irish" or ethnic history—enables us to reconsider the mythic lenses through which we still view the group's past.

Kentucky at the time of the Revolution proved significant for both the group and the broader American experience. Kentucky grew in population from both trans-Atlantic and trans-Appalachian migration during the years of the Revolution. The American Revolution in experience and memory loomed large in the history of the place, and in the Kentucky revolutionary experience, many of the fundamental contradictions that emerged as part of the larger settlement of the Revolution in America come sharply into focus. Finally, in the crucible of Kentucky, a critical theme of the broader migrant experience in microcosm emerges. At this place, at this time, for these people, the theme of "independence"—personal and political—defined the cultural parameters of experience. Independence was not only the watchword of the Revolution; its changing meanings also epitomized what lured men and women from Ireland and the eastern reaches of America—what impelled movement—to places like Kentucky, as it would come to embody how groups like the Irish would define themselves as "American" and "Scotch-Irish."

At first glance, the Kentucky experience would seem to epitomize the mythic Scotch-Irish search for independence. Kentucky was home to the prototypical frontiersman, Daniel Boone. Although Boone was not of "Ulster stock," many of his neighbors were. Fighting Indians, staunchly independent, suspicious of authority, fiercely Protestant, unerringly patriotic, these and other migrants became in Kentucky storm troopers for civilization, the leading edge of a broader white society. In this way, they had a critical role to play in taming a continent. If the frontier defined America, or so the thinking went, then the Scotch-Irish more than any group defined the frontier.[6] And in revolutionary Kentucky, most of the characteristics and processes that we associate with the American frontier were present from the beginning and animated the history of the place.

While any consideration of the group's past must deal with these "traits," it must not do so in an uncritical, self-congratulatory fashion. Instead of rely-

Patrick Griffin

ing on dated—and frankly racist—understandings of the Scotch-Irish past, any study of Scotch-Irish Kentucky must grapple with the notion that the Irish story in this place hinged on paradox and contradiction. In the 1760s and 1770s, Kentucky represented both a newfound Eden for those in search of land and economic freedom and a dangerous frontier region where neither life nor liberty was secure. Moreover, by the early nineteenth century, Kentuckians had achieved security for their persons and property but at the cost of unfettered access to land and economic opportunity. Finally, in places like Kentucky, white men and women came to basing their rights as citizens and their claims to land on the exclusion of Indians from white society. The Kentucky narrative of the Irish must confront these tensions as well as how ordinary men and women tried to make sense of them. These tensions, I believe, go to the heart of the changing migration patterns of Irish men and women, their shifting notions of identity, and the meaning the American Revolution—in experience and memory—would have for them and their descendants. The tensions also challenge us to rethink some of the fundamental conceptions we have had of the Scotch-Irish since the late nineteenth century.

The Scotch-Irish story in Kentucky reveals more. In fact, it serves as a case study for identity formation and the creation of mythic memory, as well as the complex relationship between the two. For it was the tension inherent in making sense of the Revolution's contradictions on the frontier that animated the Irish experience in Kentucky. Squaring contradictions amid swirling notions of race, class, and status would sustain an "American" identity. Ironically, it would also feed Scotch-Irish myth. Scotch-Irishness heightened and valorized some markers made meaningful by the Revolution—such as race—while muting others, especially class. This process began after the Revolution and reached its height at the end of the nineteenth century. In short, the struggles to come to terms with revolutionary tensions, especially in frontier regions, became the stuff of American exceptionalist ideals. The same struggles also helped create the group that would epitomize that mythic exceptionalism. Becoming American and Scotch-Irish, therefore, entailed not only remembering but also forgetting.

* * *

Like others seeking freedom from the fetters of eastern elites and speculators, large numbers of Irish settlers began moving down the Ohio River or through the Cumberland Gap into the Kentucky Country during the 1760s. Some were the descendants of migrants who had settled in Pennsylvania,

Virginia, or North Carolina, the so-called "Cohees"; others came directly from Ireland. We know that about a third of all white men and women who settled in Kentucky early on are what we could call Irish or Scots-Irish, and about a fourth of all settlers, black and white. Indeed, if we examine American population statistics from the 1790 federal census, the Kentucky District ranked in the top three states, territories, or districts for the proportion of citizens of Scots-Irish, Irish, and Scottish origins, lagging behind only Pennsylvania and the "old" Southwest Territory, Tennessee.[7]

The prevailing eighteenth-century model of Atlantic migration, therefore, was evident in Kentucky. The people who settled there played a prominent role in the transition from an English to a British Atlantic. Before eighteenth-century migrants boarded ships, men and women leaving England during the seventeenth century dominated the movement of peoples. After Irish migrants began leaving in large numbers at the beginning of the eighteenth century, that model fundamentally changed. From that point through the American Revolution, migration would be dominated by those from the margins of Britain and Ireland and those in other regions on or near the littoral tied into a broader Atlantic world of commerce and culture. This was the century of the Irish and the Scots, as well as Germans and, of course, Africans.[8]

Three patterns, overlapping and complementary, defined Irish movement to Kentucky within the broad Atlantic model of migration for the eighteenth century. Some Irish migrants made the trans-Atlantic crossing before traveling to Kentucky. This first pattern was a defining movement of the group for the years up to the American Revolution. From 1770 until the beginning of the War of Independence, approximately forty thousand left Ireland for America, making these years and those just preceding it and immediately after it the period of heaviest Irish migration to America in the eighteenth century. Often, these first migrants and/or their children made their way to older frontier regions such as southeastern Pennsylvania. A second pattern also emerged. Some who had already settled in older, quickly developing frontier regions made the trek to less settled areas. A great many made their way down the eastern edges of the Appalachian Mountains, first to the Great Valley of Virginia and then to the backcountry of the Carolinas. This internal movement, of course, was to become another defining feature of pre-revolutionary migration.[9]

The cumulative decision of thousands to venture to Kentucky created the first significant spillover west of the mountains. This formed the third pattern of movement. Up to this point, the predominant patterns consisted

Patrick Griffin

of either arriving in Atlantic ports and, for many, then moving to frontier regions east of the Appalachian Mountains, or of the sons and daughters of migrants seeking out new opportunities in places east of the Appalachians. In the wake of the Seven Years' War, the sons, daughters, and grandchildren of these migrants, as well as new arrivals, began seeking opportunities west of the mountains as rising land values in the east precluded easy settlement. We will never know for certain the numbers who made such journeys; the sources do not allow it. But this much is clear: The Revolution represented a temporal cusp for the Irish migration experience, and Kentucky stood at its geographic crossroads.

* * *

These migrants, whether originating in Ireland or places like Pennsylvania and Virginia, entered a contested world. That Indians in the region knew Kentucky as "Dark and Bloody Ground" is telling. Since the 1730s, when Shawnees began returning to the Ohio River valley from eastern areas including southeastern Pennsylvania, they and Cherokees living to the south had clashed over the region. By and large, both regarded the region as a vast hunting ground. Iroquois from farther north who claimed sovereignty over the Shawnees and later the Cherokees also had rights to the region, largely fictive but recognized by Euro-American governments to the east.[10] After the British defeated the French in the Seven Years' War, officials in London declared the area off limits to white settlement and speculation. The Royal Proclamation of 1763 established the Appalachians as a barrier between the eastern colonies and lands set aside for Indians. The British, in other words, could claim sovereignty over the Kentucky Country but chose not to exercise it in a vigorous fashion over western lands and peoples. They had tried to do so in the immediate aftermath of hostilities in North America but relented as Indians from the Ohio Country to the Great lakes attacked British frontier outposts. Despite the Proclamation Line, white settlers moved over the mountains to settle, heightening levels of tension.[11]

As pressures on the land grew throughout the 1760s, British officials in North America attempted to cede the Kentucky Country to white settlement. In 1768 the Irish-born superintendent of Indian affairs for areas north of the Ohio River, Sir William Johnson, met with Iroquois representatives, ostensibly to defuse the growing tensions of the region and to ensure that traders who had lost their goods in previous years were compensated in some fashion for their losses. Johnson argued that because a number of whites had already ventured into the Kentucky Country, the Proclamation Line would have to be bent west in order to keep the peace between Indians, the British, and colonists, as well as to repay "suffering traders" with land. At Fort Stanwix, the Iroquois, who declared themselves the masters of the region, agreed to cede the Kentucky Country in consideration for goods and land concessions in the East. Although it is unclear whether Johnson engaged in this shady dealing for altruistic reasons or to enrich himself and others, including his Irish-born deputy George Croghan, this much is clear: At the end of the day, without the blessing of the Shawnees or the Cherokees, Johnson ensured that the trickle of whites would turn into a steady stream. Although officials in London did not sanction the massive transfer of land, they could do little to stop what had been an Indian country becoming a focus of Euro-American settlement.[12]

Despite Iroquois pretensions to the contrary, Cherokees and Shawnees continued to view the region as their sovereign hunting grounds. This dispute over the validity of the Treaty of Fort Stanwix, and by implication the Royal Proclamation of 1763, made much of the Ohio River valley a killing field, as Indians and white settlers terrorized each other in attempts to make good conflicting claims in the Kentucky Country. Yet settlers continued to stream in, often at the connivance of Virginia speculators and government officials. The most famous of these officials was the infamous John Murray, fourth earl of Dunmore and royal governor of Virginia, who with his deputy John Connolly whipped settlers living in the Ohio Valley into an Indian-hating frenzy. Engineering a war against Shawnees and intimidating Cherokees, Dunmore raised an army that defeated Indians from the Ohio Valley at Point Pleasant in 1774. In so doing, he tried to lay claim to all of Kentucky for Virginia and its speculating elite. In general, such men, including the Virginia planter George Washington, hoped that large numbers of squatters and purchasers would clear the way for more ambitious land schemes, most notably the failed Transylvania venture.[13]

Dunmore's bid ultimately failed. But as it did, the population of Kentucky continued to grow, and tensions continued to mount. By 1775 more than a thousand settlers held often-overlapping claims to areas of central Kentucky. Less than a year later, squatters and speculators claimed more than twenty million acres of land in Kentucky. Migrants from Ireland and their direct descendants comprised about a third of early settlers in the region. Kentucky's settlement accelerated in the years just before the Revolutionary War. Early regions settled included the areas around the Kentucky River, the Green River, the Bluegrass, and the Bear Grass. Settlement surges re-

Patrick Griffin

flected the numbers of people looking for land, exacerbated by rising tides of migration from places like Ireland, the availability and affordability of land east of the mountains, as well as the ebb and flow of violence. Even during the Revolutionary War, men and women, as well as speculators, claimed land. The earliest settlements lay on rivers and included the towns of Boonesborough, Harrodsburg, Saint Asaph, and Boiling Spring, and along the Falls of the Ohio (present-day Louisville). (See map 9.1.) While poorer settlers came with little, wealthier young men on the make such as George Rogers Clark came with slaves. By 1776 tensions were growing between poorer settlers and the land company officials, who were already in the process of warning squatters off plum sites. This was not a new dynamic; the same had happened a generation earlier in Pennsylvania. But by the late 1760s and early 1770s, the stakes were a great deal higher in the trans-Appalachian west.[14]

* * *

In this fluid world, identity formation was a complex affair. In these isolated settlements, migrants and their children rubbed shoulders with settlers of English descent, men and women from various eastern colonies, German-speakers, African Americans, and even Native Americans.[15] Of course, such diversity in America did not prove unprecedented; indeed, most migrants from Ireland would have encountered such a plural world in places like Pennsylvania and Virginia, whether they had lived there or passed through. Even in southeast Pennsylvania, for instance, some Irish settlers owned slaves and lived beside a great number of Indians and traders of various "ethnic" backgrounds. Moreover, the enclaves in Lancaster County where many had first established themselves were by 1750 almost surrounded by German-speakers. Kentucky unsurprisingly presented more of the same.[16]

But Kentucky also proved exceptional because the tensions of the Revolutionary Period would throw these people together or pit them against one another in new and profound ways. We have been led to believe that the people we would regard as Scotch-Irish came over with ready-made identities. Scotch-Irish identity, then, would merge into a broader American sense of self. There is some truth in this claim. If part of the larger "Scotch-Irish" story in America is the loss of a distinctive identity, then it would be in places like Kentucky where we see this process unfold most clearly.[17] But this simple story is much more complex. For the diminution of "Scotch-Irish" identity—if it even existed in the eighteenth century, which is doubtful—as well as

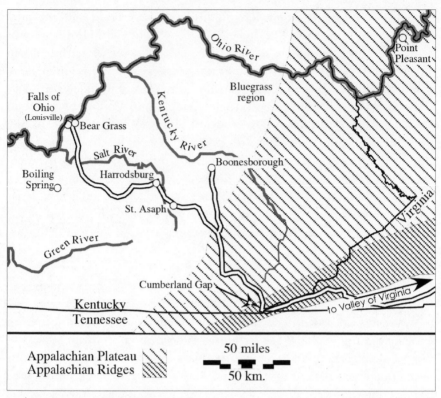

Map 9.1. *Kentucky from the 1770s to 1790s.*

its merger into a broader American identity did not take place only because of the plural conditions of the frontier or the "contagion" of liberty but also because of the exceptional circumstances migrants faced during the frontier revolution. Pluralism or toleration, the two great themes of the Pennsylvania experience, did not transform the reality of ethnic diversity into a virtue in Kentucky. Rather, brutal warfare and race hatred muted the significance of such categories. Yet here again, the vagaries of identity formation elude us. A sense of "American-ness" did not emerge at the expense of Scotch-Irish identity. Each emerged in tensions and in tandem with each other. Both, arguably, were products of the Revolution, and both were especially pronounced in frontier regions.[18]

One aspect of the process, however, is simple enough. Violence lay at the heart of revolutionary identity formation. Tensions between whites and Indians boiled over during the Revolutionary War. At first, settlers lived amid uncertainty, as no single group could prevail in the region. Virginians claimed

Patrick Griffin

Kentucky as theirs, as did Shawnees and Cherokees. So too, of course, did the British and the new American government. Small bands of Indians raided isolated frontier settlements from time to time, and whites repaid Indian communities in kind. From 1775 to 1777, as violence simmered, uncertainty defined the existence of most in Kentucky. Bloodshed rose to more appalling levels in 1778 when British commanders began coordinating Indian raids on the small settlements in Kentucky. Indeed, more people per capita died in Kentucky during the Revolution than in any other region, most after 1777. Numbers alone, however, obscure the nature of the bloodshed. Men, women, and children—white and Indian—died in shocking ways. Even when British Rangers led war parties, Indians were permitted and encouraged to kill and capture without constraint.[19]

Settlers holed up in small, stinking, and filthy forts or blockhouses for the better part of two years as Shawnees, Overhill Cherokees, Mingoes, and later Delawares launched daring raids. As much as anything else, these structures defined this place in time. Settlers constructed them at convenient sites throughout the countryside, usually close to rivers and located so that large numbers of men and women could use them for refuge. As forts, they were not impressive, usually consisting of a house or two, storage sheds, and a lot surrounded by pickets. Most had ditches for water and waste. Under the best of times, they proved difficult to defend from a concerted attack. At the worst of times, particularly during the winters of 1778 and 1779, they proved almost untenable. At that time, as men from settlements were called out to muster into militia units, women, the young, and the old were left to defend blockhouses that were either coming under attack consistently or were vulnerable to attack.

Although settlers had good reason to support the patriot cause, as they saw in the Revolution a chance to press for unfettered access to lands held by elites and Indians, disaffection with the Revolution grew as the new federal government and the state of Virginia showed little inclination to protect the suffering settlers. While the men and women in Kentucky dealt with Indian raids and provided for their own defense, the unremitting requests for manpower strained these communities to the breaking point. Federal officials deemed the area marginal to the broader War of Independence, understandably so. Barely able to hold the army together in the East, they proved reluctant to stage large-scale expeditions to stop Indian-British attacks. More gallingly for settlers, some officials were inclined to downplay the suffering of settlers or the type of violence they were confronting. Several officials in charge of Indian affairs for the revolutionary government, in fact, wanted to implement what settlers conceived of as a policy of appeasement in the West. Treaties and agreements, not costly military action, these officials argued, would ease the tensions in the West. In these circumstances, most settlers vacillated. Indeed, in places like Kentucky the "patriotic" cause came close to foundering.

Settlers had even more reason to distrust state authorities. Even George Rogers Clark's famous expedition out west failed to rally Kentuckians. In 1778, the young speculating transplant approached officials in Virginia, including that "Scotch-Irish" scion of revolutionary Virginia, Patrick Henry, with a daring idea to win the West. He promised to lead frontier militia units to destroy the British garrison at Detroit, the British nerve center of the West. As he gathered men in Kentucky for his expedition, weakening blockhouse defenses as he did so, he also promised to target the Shawnees who were striking frontier settlements. However, he bypassed Detroit and the Shawnee villages for the Illinois Country, a region he and other wealthy Virginians, such as the voracious Henry, hoped to lay claim to. In other words, elites, some of whom were of "Scotch-Irish" stock, were still trying to manipulate settlers, many of whom had ties to Ireland as well, to use them for land grabs at the very moment many men and women were struggling with appalling violence. Large numbers of settlers abandoned Clark, and ultimately his expedition proved a failure. The Indian raids continued, and Virginia could not lay claim to the Illinois Country.

No less than twenty thousand migrants moved into Kentucky in 1779 and 1780. Despite the continuing bloodshed, the uncertainty, the disorder, and the fear, poor settlers continued to stream in. Perhaps a better way of putting it is this: "Because" of these factors, men and women continued to arrive on foot and on boats to Kentucky. They came even though and because security and protection would fall to inhabitants themselves. The whole Ohio Valley, in fact, had become a Hobbesian world of all against all, a place in which society itself had come undone. Yet it also was a time when people were banding together. On the one hand, the state of affairs in Kentucky guaranteed that speculators could not claim whole tracts of land, allowing the daring and the desperate to settle. On the other hand, it's fair to say that as the warfare was impelling people to demonize Indians, speculators and common men and women were finding some common ground. They did not agree that the poor should inherit the earth; rather, they forged tacit arrangements suggesting that unfettered competition for land and elite manipulation in the face of Indian attacks made little sense.

Patrick Griffin

The violence on the frontier, therefore, acted as a cultural glue and as a cultural solvent. Class allegiances, for a time, melted before Indian violence. Bloodshed also created bonds between the men and women of various ethnic or national groups while attenuating distinctive ethnic identification. In Kentucky forts, what "ethnic," national, or linguistic group settlers belonged to—be it Irish, Scottish, Scots-Irish, or German—paled in comparison to the whiteness they shared. In fact, a better, less anachronistic question to ask about identity is not what these people were, but what they were not. Above all, they were not Indians. Viewed from this perspective, "Scotch-Irishness" as an idea or identifying marker was irrelevant. Whiteness mattered. Those who had settled in the Ohio Valley before the War of Independence may have had some affinity for Indian ways.[20] But by 1781, this was no longer the case. In the process, we could say that groups like the Irish were becoming American. But they were becoming something more as well. We could say that groups were also consciously becoming "white." As violence precluded the possibility of sustaining any sort of middle ground between Europeans and Euro-American settlers, on the one hand, and Indians, on the other, groups saw they had much more in common with other white settlers than they did with what settlers regarded as irredeemably bloodthirsty non-whites.

This process of racialization picked up momentum even after the War of Independence came to a close. At the end of the war, hostilities between Indians and whites continued in places like Kentucky. The arrival of yet more poor settlers and a growing coterie of wealthy Virginians strained the situation further. Federal authorities north of the Ohio River in the Northwest Territory seemed more interested in evicting squatters than in dealing with the Indian threat. To the south in Kentucky, a different dynamic took hold. Only as wealthier settlers began falling did local, state, and federal authorities draw up plans to protect the region. Smaller expeditions launched in the early 1790s failed to "chastise" Indians, as officials hoped, after which some settlers threatened the new nation with western secession. Authorities both local and federal decided they had to act to "conquer" Indians in the Ohio Valley or possibly lose the West. Finally, in 1794, as a combined federal and state force defeated a western confederacy of Indians at Fallen Timbers, a measure of peace and security came to Kentucky.

But more than race was at stake. Common settlers, of whom the Irish comprised a great number, won a great deal once peace came to the region. After the war ended, those who had settled during the bleeding years of the Revolution—the daring and the desperate—won on paper at least the right to hold onto the land they had claimed. Speculators, of course, retained the lion's share of land, arguing that their "sacrifice" during the war, not their wealth and status, gave them a right to hold what they could. As they did so, however, they could not ignore the pleas of those who held much smaller plots but who also had endured years of violence and fear. Later arrivals, those who had not had to survive the time of bloodshed and uncertainty, would not enjoy this privilege. Yet even if some had title to land, competing claims, speculators, and later courts would conspire to ensure that most land remained in the hands of the wealthy. Indeed, by the mid-nineteenth century Kentuckians were still dealing with land disputes that had first arisen at the time of the Revolution. In other words, many of the poorer sort never acquired the land they had sought, despite their sacrifice. Mobility would continue to provide the only reliable means for common men and women to acquire a measure of competency. And it is clear that, by 1800, many Irish settlers in Kentucky had moved elsewhere.[21]

At the end of the day, poorer settlers could not escape the margins of society. As Kentucky won statehood, the well-connected and well-heeled from out east began dominating the Bluegrass region of the newly admitted state. Poorer settlers—many of whom claimed land through "improvements," detested the slave-owning gentry emerging in their midst, and had few connections with or knowledge of the law—found themselves on the wrong side of the legal system, a burgeoning slave economy, and an elite-brokered political structure. Some would settle for marginal lives on marginal land in eastern Kentucky, others would struggle as tenants, and many would look to move north across the river to Ohio.[22] Despite sacrifice and suffering, Eden had once again eluded them.

Increasingly "American" and consciously white, the migrants from Ireland to Kentucky and their descendants had helped win the war by defining Indians as racial inferiors but had lost the Revolution at the hands of the wealthy. By the end of the war years, the only clear losers were Indians. The Treaty of Greenville, signed in the wake of the Battle of Fallen Timbers, mandated that Indians would never again live in what would be the states of Ohio and Kentucky. Drawing a line between white and Indian lands, the treaty was enacted to protect white settlement areas. It worked. Indians would never again raid Kentucky. And from this moment forward, whites and Indians as a rule could no longer live peacefully side by side east of the Mississippi. The period before the war when whites and Indians from time to time had forged some sort of middle ground now was a thing of the past, never possible in places like Kentucky again.[23]

Patrick Griffin

In many ways, the revolutionary frontier brought an end to the "Irish" story in Kentucky. Ethnicity as a meaningful marker had little purchase. But in other ways, identity had a great deal of meaning, particularly the Scotch-Irish variety. While only memories of violence remained after 1795, the realities of rich versus poor determined access to land and power. Over the course of the nineteenth century, the descendants of those whose ethnicity was melted down in the revolutionary crucible would discover their Scotch-Irishness. Why was this form of ethnic identity, if we could call it that, heightened, while "Irishness" was muted? The answer lies in myth. Mythically, Scotch-Irishness would be associated with the frontier. And as the frontier was associated with "American" traits, Scotch-Irishness could merge with American-ness. It became the anti-ethnic ethnic identity.

The process of frontier development, memories of violence, and tensions born at the time of the Revolution commingled to create Scotch-Irishness. This is a familiar story but one that reached its height in the late eighteenth century. As Kerby Miller has argued, Scotch-Irishness could be used to blunt the radical implications of revolutionary discourse, especially as "Irishness" became associated with radical republicanism. This was a nineteenth-century phenomenon, one that picked up momentum as Irish Catholic migration began surging in the 1820s. The frontier offers a variation of this theme. In 1892 federal officials declared that the frontier phase of American history had come to an end, as whites had officially conquered the continent. Also in that year—and not coincidentally—the historian Frederick Jackson Turner delivered a famous address before the American Historical Association at the World's Columbian Exposition in Chicago, exploring the formative meaning of the frontier for American development and the exceptional character of the nation. In many ways, the people who had struggled against superstitious and treacherous Catholics in Ulster, fled to America in the face of persecution, sought out the frontier, and conquered Indian savagery seemed to epitomize all that Turner deemed truly American. It was not a coincidence that at this time the Scotch-Irish Congress first assembled to extol the particular virtues of the "race," traits that dovetailed with the characteristics that made America exceptional and the frontier central to the birth of a nation. The "Scotch-Irish," therefore, invented themselves as the prototypical Americans at the moment Indians were deemed a conquered people.[24]

The merger of Scotch-Irish identity with frontier myth valorized common men, those with political rights but without unfettered access to land. In mythic memory, these people had become the storm troopers of civilization, the ideal Americans, perhaps even the first Americans. To be Scotch-Irish was not only to be non-Catholic. It also meant that one had a stake in a society, even if one lived on the geographic or socioeconomic margins. This was an identity that elites could buy into as well. To be white entitled one to rights. To be Scotch-Irish was to find some sort of peace with an American social contract that privileged Scotch-Irish participation in mythic events of the nation's past as well as its Americanizing crucible, the frontier. If radicalism lingered after the years of the Revolution, Scotch-Irishness served as an antiradical antidote, one that consigned meaningful tensions to the valorized past.[25]

Such sentiments defined Scotch-Irishness at the time that Turner delivered his famous lecture and as the frontier came to an end. One Scotch-Irish booster claimed that his forebears "first planted the flag of civilization and freedom, religion, law, order, and morality in the 'new world west of the Alleghanies.'" Not to be outdone, a Kentuckian at one of the Scotch-Irish Congresses asked how could he chronicle the story of Kentucky and not feature the Scotch-Irish "race": "Why Kentucky is Scotch Irish itself. I can't speak of Kentucky without speaking of the Scotch Irish, and I can't speak of the Scotch Irishmen that have lived in Kentucky without recalling the history of Kentucky." These men and women had "scaled" the mountains and, on reaching their destination, "commenced demanding their rights." They made America American. He mocked those who were claiming that the group amounted to a fiction. The Scotch-Irish had, in his estimation, "almost created the civilization of the modern world." They had adapted the religion and libertarian aspects of Calvin and Knox and sharpened them in Ulster before making their way to the American frontier. They then "laid the foundations of religious freedom [and] civil liberty."[26]

Scotch-Irishness worked for haves and have-nots. It claimed the mantle of what we could call bourgeois respectability but also made room for the "unrefined," the leading edges of civility. Common people could claim a share of its meaning. Kerby Miller and David Doyle in *Irish Immigrants in the Land of Canaan* are firm on this point. In this volume, we encounter John Dunlap, a migrant who left Strabane for Philadelphia and made a fine living as a printer. Dunlap also speculated in Kentucky lands, amassing ninety-eight thousand acres and becoming a gentleman in his own right. Like the mythical "Poor Richard," Dunlap studiously followed Benjamin Franklin's example; in this case, literally. Dunlap's experience, therefore, highlights the fact that some Irish migrants who settled in Kentucky were not faceless

Patrick Griffin

squatters. Nor did they all harbor stereotypical anti-authoritarian attitudes. Dunlap, for instance, styled himself a Federalist and lent a hand in suppressing the Whiskey Rebellion. The "rebellion," no doubt, revolved around an excise tax on distilled spirits. But it also serves as a barometer for social standing and social opinion in the West in the years after the Revolution. Dunlap was a "friend of order," a person who had a stake in Kentucky's transition to an orderly settled society where the wealthy monopolized political power, owned slaves, and had claims to the best land. The experience of those like him would become the stuff of Scotch-Irish myth.[27]

But although Kentucky contained some Dunlaps who had migrated from Ireland, it contained far more people like Thomas Hinds, landless men and women. Hinds set sail from Ireland to Philadelphia in 1770—a peak year in migration—before heading west to the promise and peril of Kentucky. Hinds extolled the glories of the New World, and Philadelphia in particular, to his father, encouraging him to sail the ocean to America. The father heeded his advice. But when the elder Hinds disembarked at the Delaware River port, his son was nowhere to be seen. The father searched in vain for him in the bustling city, finally learning that he had headed west to Kentucky. He never found his son. Hinds, much like most other trans-Atlantic migrants and Cohees, went missing from the historical record.[28] Another more typical migrant was Job Johnson, who left Derry for the New World just before the Revolution. Johnson served in the army during the War of Independence, fighting in some of its major campaigns. When the war ended, Johnson either purchased or received fifteen hundred acres in Kentucky as a bounty. He died, however, nearly penniless, as most of his deeds were in fact worthless.[29] Johnson's misfortune and Hinds's elusiveness speak volumes about the faceless and difficult experience of the vast majority of Irish immigrants who hoped to better their lot in Kentucky despite threats from Indians and the manipulation at the hands of the well-heeled, like Dunlap. But the experiences of Hinds and Johnson would also be incorporated into the Scotch-Irish myth. They had, after all, helped tame the nation's frontier. If they embraced the Revolution's radical promise, we will never know. This much is clear, however: Their elusiveness and our inability to label them plays into Scotch-Irish mythic conceptions that downplay class antagonism. They did, after all, play a valuable role in birthing a nation, even if they would not inherit the earth.

* * *

If there is any animating idea to the Irish Kentucky experience during the Revolution, encompassing the varied lots of both the Hinds and Dunlaps of Kentucky as well as the new meanings of whiteness that emerged in these years in this place, it would be the quest for independence. The search for independence, of course, in many ways sums up the impulse to cross the ocean and the mountains for a new life free from landlords and land jobbers. Moreover, the search for independence epitomizes much of what the American Revolution was about. But the Irish migrant experience in Kentucky gets to the heart of another notion of independence: the term's shifting ideological content and what it would mean for post-revolutionary American society. Independence was considered a classic virtue of the gentry. Freed from worries about money and blessed with time for leisure, only the few could become independent. Wealthy Virginia planters tried to impress on their sons the critical need to cultivate this virtue. Men like Franklin strived to become "independent"—as Franklin did when he grew wealthy enough to stop working in his print shop—so they could style themselves gentlemen.[30]

But the American Revolution, and especially republican ideology, challenged the relationship between gentility and independence. We know that in the years before the Revolution, Americans of all ranks and stripes were experiencing a breakdown of what we could call deferential attitudes, that notions of status meant less as Americans engaged in a larger Atlantic world defined by vital piety, consumer culture, and libertarian ideas. The participation of common men and women in the Revolution accelerated this process. With the democratizing influence of boycotts and fighting, when the lower sort could practice "virtue," there would be no going back to a status-driven society.[31]

Much of the mythic "Scotch-Irish" story, of course, hinges on the idea that "independence," a sentiment that had been the defining feature of a gentlemen, now became a cornerstone of the popular republicanism unleashed by the Revolution. As Americans democratized virtue—through boycotts, through sacrifice, through valor—so too did they reclaim independence from the gentry. All by birthright were entitled to strive for it. In late eighteenth-century terms, this normally meant that men and women could steer their own destinies, that they had it within their grasp to dictate the fortunes of their lives. Men like Jefferson extolled the independence of the yeoman farmer and his ability to stand unmanipulated by greater forces and more sinister interests. In the Jeffersonian scheme, to own and work land made one part of the political nation. Such ideas proved revolutionary in a place like America where the vast majority of men could own land.[32]

Patrick Griffin

But in Kentucky this notion changed subtly but profoundly in the years just after the Revolution. For Irish migrants in Kentucky during the heady years of revolution, independence entailed having access to land. But because landownership would be contested, they would disconnect independence from landownership and pin their status as independent citizens on universal white male suffrage. The years of revolutionary violence, defined by the creation, if you will, of white American identity—a process that the Irish were at the heart of—made this difficult and troubling trade-off possible. In places like Kentucky, to be white and to be male made one independent. The bloody crucible of violence in Kentucky in the 1790s—when Indians and whites slaughtered each other with gusto—paved the way for this notion of independence to gain broad acceptance. The growing friction between haves and have-nots made this notion of independence necessary. But such trade-offs came at a price. To comprise part of the political nation meant giving up a right for land. Individuals could be entitled to life and liberty, but property would be the purview of the few. Hence, the experience of Irish migrants in Kentucky sums up the limitations of the radicalism of the American Revolution.

Independence also had a darker aspect. Indeed, this liberating notion entailed fetters for others. In slaveholding Kentucky, white freedom—at least in the political sense—rested on unfreedom for blacks. By definition, a dependent slave could not be independent. African Americans could not provide for families, nor were they considered by law to be persons.[33] Indians were deemed by most settlers to be in a savage state lacking the virtue necessary to be truly independent. Throughout the eighteenth century, many social commentators wondered if Indians ever could practice virtue.[34] Could they, in other words, ever develop into civilized people? Did they possess such capacity? Frontier settlers, by and large, answered no. Easterners may have argued otherwise, but the logic of removal and displacement, separating the races by lines on a map, mooted the issue. Indians would not be part of a white, American society, one in which the eighteenth-century Irish had carved out a comfortable place, a society that their "Scotch-Irish" descendants would claim the group played a formative role in bringing into being.[35]

What does all this mean for the larger Irish or "Scotch-Irish" experience? Kentucky during the Revolution in many ways was both crossroads and crucible for the historical Irish in America as well as the mythical Scotch-Irish. At this place at this time, we see the group in transition with the shift from littoral migration to trans-Appalachian movement. We can also discern a shifting notion of identity, one definably American and definably white.

Finally, the quest of men and women for independence—or the search for freedom and security—reveals the contradictory legacy of the American Revolution, a contradictory legacy they would work to reconcile to their benefit and to their detriment. Scotch-Irishness, valorizing the sacrifice of the common men and women, allowed people to live with such contradictions. The search of the Irish for independence contributed to shifting notions of what independence would mean in America, a changing definition that would have critical implications for the future of the group and the future of America.

In Kentucky, Scotch-Irish myth and Irish American reality also collide in often uncomfortable ways. In the late nineteenth century, claiming that the group played a critical role in civilizing the West, taming it, and bringing civility to what had been savage regions won the Scotch-Irish a special place in the American story. Indeed, hagiographers—both real and imagined descendants of the "Scotch-Irish" migrants from "Ulster"—pointed with pride to these characteristics as the group's providential contribution to American society. Such ideas can no longer be sustained even if—and because—they share a popular following today. Any consideration of the group must encourage us to ask why we cling to such mythic formulations. For better and for worse, the Irish—as well as the Scotch-Irish in memory—had a prominent place in the revolutionary saga in Kentucky. This is not to say that we must now in almost puerile fashion chuck the proverbial baby out with the bathwater, arguing that those characteristics of the group we once hailed we must now condemn. Rather, we should strive to portray the group in a fair and mature light. After all, the group's experience, like that of nearly all Americans during this period, was marked by ambiguity and ambivalence. In this regard, what we call them matters less than the fact that—whatever their name—they did not prove exceptional.

Notes

1. Naming the migrants who left Ulster, or better Ireland, for America in the eighteenth century presents both tricky historical problems and, more to the point, thorny political issues. Indeed, even referring to them as "Ulster" migrants is a loaded and historically misleading statement, as some in the group's enclaves came from other provinces and none had the sense of an "Ulster" identity. This essay will not explore such issues, however interesting they may be, but it will instead use the term "Irish" for historical experience and "Scotch-Irish" when discussing identities. For my thinking on how we should conceive the eighteenth-century Irish migration to America, see "The Two Migrations Myth, the Scotch

Irish, and Irish-American Experience," in Andrew Higgins Wyndham, *Re-Imagining Ireland: How a Storied Island is Transforming Its Politics, Economics, Religious Life, and Culture for the Twenty-First Century* (Charlottesville: University of Virginia Press, 2006).

2. On this, see Patrick Griffin, *The People with No Name: Ireland's Ulster Scots, America's Scots Irish, and the Creation of a British Atlantic World, 1689–1764* (Princeton: Princeton University Press, 2001). T. H. Breen covers charter groups in "Creative Adaptations: Peoples and Cultures," in Jack Greene and J. R. Pole, eds., *Colonial British America: Essays in the New History of the Early Modern Era* (Baltimore: Johns Hopkins University Press, 1984), 195–232.

3. Another hallmark of the group was mobility and perpetual motion. See James Lemon, *The Best Poor Man's Country: A Geographical Study of Early Southeastern Pennsylvania* (Baltimore: Johns Hopkins University Press, 1972); Carl Bridenbaugh, *Myths and Realities: Societies of the Colonial South* (Baton Rouge: Louisiana State University Press, 1966).

4. The Scotch-Irish, of course, figure prominently in frontier myth. With a great deal of justification, nearly every book written on the group assumes the formative role the group played in frontier American life. Most also dwell on mythic conceptions of the group—how its members became so individualistic, for example. For a discussion of the group's traits and their contribution to frontier culture, see any textbook on early American history and arguably two of the most scholarly studies of the Scotch-Irish: James Leyburn, *The Scotch Irish: A Social History* (Chapel Hill: University of North Carolina Press, 1962), and David Hackett Fischer, *Albion's Seed: Four British Folkways in America* (New York: Oxford University Press, 1989).

5. See spate of popular books, including such telling titles as Rory Fitzpatrick's *God's Frontiersmen: The Scots Irish Epic* (London: Weidenfeld and Nicholson, 1989), and more recently, *Born Fighting: How the Scots-Irish Shaped America* by the amateur historian James Webb (New York: Broadway Books, 2004).

6. For a brief but solid analysis of the "Scotch-Irish" myth, see Maldwyn A. Jones, "The Scotch-Irish in British North America," in B. Bailyn and P. Morgan, eds., *Strangers within the Realm: Cultural Margins of the First British Empire* (Chapel Hill: University of North Carolina Press for the Institute of Early American History and Culture, 1991), 284–313.

7. Kerby A. Miller, Arnold Schrier, Bruce D. Boling, and David N. Doyle, *Irish Immigrants in the Land of Canaan: Letters and Memoirs from Colonial and Revolutionary America, 1675–1815* (New York: Oxford University Press, 2003), 106, 117. These statistics were compiled from Thomas L. Purvis, "The European Ancestry of the United States Population, 1790," *William and Mary Quarterly,* 3rd ser., vol. 41 (January 1984): 98, and Walter Rossiter, *A Century of Population Growth* (Washington, D.C.: Government Printing Office, 1909).

8. For a broad-brush interpretation of this changing movement, see the provocative, if underdeveloped, arguments in Fischer's *Albion's Seed*. For German-speakers, see Marianne S. Wokeck, *Trade in Strangers: The Beginnings of Mass Migration to North America* (University Park: Pennsylvania State University Press, 1999). On eighteenth-century slave migration, see Philip Morgan, *Slave Counterpoint: Black Culture in the Eighteenth-Century Chesapeake and Lowcountry* (Chapel Hill: University of North Carolina Press for

the Institute of Early American History and Culture, 1998); and Ira Berlin, *Many Thousands Gone: The First Two Centuries of Slavery in North America* (Cambridge, Mass.: Harvard University Press, 2000).

9. The best treatment of this type of movement is Warren Hofstra's *The Planting of New Virginia: Settlement and Landscape in the Shenandoah Valley* (Baltimore: Johns Hopkins University Press, 2004).

10. On these themes, see Michael McConnell, *A Country Between: The Upper Ohio Valley and Its Peoples, 1724–1774* (Lincoln: University of Nebraska Press, 1997), as well as Daniel Richter's *The Ordeal of the Longhouse: The Peoples of the Iroquois League in the Era of European Colonization* (Chapel Hill: University of North Carolina Press for the Institute of Early American History and Culture, 1993).

11. The best treatments of Pontiac's War are Gregory Dowd's *A Spirited Resistance: The North American Indian Struggle for Unity, 1745–1815* (Baltimore: Johns Hopkins University Press, 1992) and *War under Heaven: Pontiac, the Indian Nations, and the British Empire* (Baltimore: Johns Hopkins University Press, 2002). The best account of the Treaty of Paris ending the war, as well as the drafting and implementation of the royal proclamation, is Fred Anderson's *The Crucible of War: The Seven Years' War and the Fate of Empire in British North America* (New York: Vintage Books, 2001).

12. See Richard White, *The Middle Ground: Indians, Empires, and Republics in the Great Lakes Region, 1650–1815* (New York: Cambridge University Press, 1991). On Johnson, see Fintan O'Toole, *White Savage: William Johnson and the Invention of America* (New York: Farrar, Straus, Giroux, 2005).

13. On Lord Dunmore's War and the sordid land schemes that it sustained, see Woody Holton, *Forced Founders: Indians, Debtors, Slaves, and the Making of the American Revolution in Virginia* (Chapel Hill: University of North Carolina Press for the Institute of Early American History and Culture, 1999).

14. For the best accounts of this region during the period, see Stephen Aron, *How the West Was Lost: The Transformation of Kentucky from Daniel Boone to Henry Clay* (Baltimore: Johns Hopkins University Press, 1996); Craig Thomson Friend, ed., *The Buzzel about Kentuck: Settling the Promised Land* (Lexington: University Press of Kentucky, 1999); Kim Gruenwald, *River of Enterprise: The Commercial Origins of Regional Identity in the Ohio Valley, 1790–1850* (Bloomington: University of Indiana Press, 2002); Eric Hinderaker, *Elusive Empires: Constructing Colonialism in the Ohio Valley, 1673–1800* (New York: Cambridge University Press, 1997); Elizabeth Perkins, *Border Life: Experience and Memory in the Revolutionary Ohio Valley* (Chapel Hill: University of North Carolina Press, 1998).

15. Interestingly, the books on Kentucky noted above make few if any references to ethnicity. Being Scotch-Irish or Irish had little bearing on life in Kentucky, they would seem to suggest. More likely, ethnicity as a category is not something that interests historians exploring early Kentucky experience, with good reason. Arguably, it proved irrelevant in coming to terms with what was at stake in revolutionary Kentucky.

16. See Griffin, *People with No Name*.

17. On this standard story of the group, see Leyburn, *Scotch Irish*.

18. On the role of the contagion of liberty, see Bernard Bailyn, *The Ideological Origins of the American Revolution* (Cambridge, Mass.: Harvard University Press, 1992). On the pluralism/diversity thesis, which has been applied to Pennsylvania in particular, see Sally Schwartz, *"A Mixed Multitude": The Struggle for Toleration in Colonial Pennsylvania* (New York: New York University Press, 1987). For similar dynamics of race hatred and whiteness for the early American period, see Jane Merritt, *At the Crossroads: Indians and Empires on a Mid-Atlantic Frontier, 1700–1763* (Chapel Hill: University of North Carolina Press for the Institute of Early American History and Culture, 2003); and Nancy Shoemaker, *A Strange Likeness: Becoming Red and White in Eighteenth-Century North America* (New York: Oxford University Press, 2004). For the notion that the terms "ethnicity" and perhaps "identity" have been anachronistically applied to the eighteenth century, see Colin Kidd, *British Identities before Nationalism: Ethnicity and Nationhood in the Atlantic World, 1600–1800* (New York, 1999). That "Scotch-Irish" identity as we conventionally know it was an invention of the early nineteenth century and that for the eighteenth century the simple term Irish would seem to work better—denoting geographic realities, not mythic constructs—see the introduction to Miller et. al., *Irish Immigrants.*

19. This and what follows are covered in great detail in my book entitled *American Leviathan: Empire, Nation, and Revolutionary Frontier* (New York: Hill and Wang, 2006).

20. On this story, see Aron, *How the West Was Lost.*

21. Ibid.; Miller et al., *Irish Immigrants,* 106, 117.

22. On the movement north by some of these settlers, see Andrew Cayton, *Frontier Republic: Ideology and Politics in the Ohio Country, 1780–1825* (Kent, Ohio: Kent State University Press, 1986).

23. Scholars put distinct dates on this phenomenon—1763, 1795, or 1815—but this much is clear: In Kentucky at this time in the wake of Indian removal from the state, whites and Indians would no longer inhabit common worlds. On these other dates, see Daniel Richter, *Facing East from Indian Country: A Native History of Early America* (Cambridge: Harvard University Press, 2001); White, *Middle Ground;* and D. C. Skaggs and L. L. Nelson, *The Sixty Years' War for the Great Lakes, 1754–1815* (East Lansing: Michigan State University Press, 2001).

24. On this, see Jones, "Scotch-Irish," and Gregory Nobles, *American Frontiers: Cultural Encounters and Continental Conquest* (New York: Hill and Wang, 1997).

25. On this, see Kerby Miller, "Ulster Presbyterians and the 'Two Traditions' in Ireland and America," in Terry Brotherstone, Anna Clark, and Kevin Whelan, eds., *These Fissured Isles: Varieties of British and Irish Identities* (Edinburgh: John Donald, 2005), 260–77.

26. The Scotch-Irish in America: Proceedings of the Scotch-Irish Congress, vol. 9 (Nashville, 1900), 151; *The Scotch-Irish in America: Proceedings of the Scotch-Irish Congress,* vol. 3 (Nashville: Publishing House of the Methodist Episcopal Church South, 1891), 191–95.

27. Miller et al., *Irish Immigrants,* 107. On the "friends of order" and the Whiskey Rebellion, see Thomas Slaughter's, *The Whiskey Rebellion: Frontier Epilogue to the American Revolution* (New York: Oxford University Press, 1988).

28. Miller et al., *Irish Immigrants,* 105–6.

29. Ibid., 571.

30. On the meanings of independence, see T. H. Breen, *Tobacco Culture: The Mentality of the Great Tidewater Planters on the Eve of Revolution* (Princeton: Princeton University Press, 2001), and Gordon Wood, *The Americanization of Benjamin Franklin* (New York: Penguin Press, 2004).

31. See Gordon Wood, *The Radicalism of the American Revolution* (New York: Vintage Books, 1993), and T. H. Breen, *The Marketplace of Revolution: How Consumer Politics Shaped American Independence* (New York: Oxford University Press, 2004).

32. Drew McCoy, *The Elusive Republic: Political Economy in Jeffersonian America* (Chapel Hill: University of North Carolina Press for the Institute of Early American History and Culture, 1996).

33. For a provocative look at these themes, see Kathleen M. Brown, *Good Wives, Nasty Wenches, and Anxious Patriarchs: Gender, Race, and Power in Colonial Virginia* (Chapel Hill: University of North Carolina Press for the Omohundro Institute of Early American History and Culture, 1996).

34. See, for example, the debates raging at the time of racial and geographical difference that prompted Thomas Jefferson to write "Notes on the State of Virginia," in Dror Wahrman, *The Making of the Modern Self* (New Haven, Conn.: Yale University Press, 2004).

35. Anthony F. C. Wallace, *Jefferson and the Indians: The Tragic Fate of the First Americans* (Cambridge, Mass.: Harvard University Press, 2001).

Patrick Griffin

Afterword

Historic Political Moderation in the Ulster-to-America Diaspora

Robert M. Calhoon

The trek of Lowland Scots first to Elizabethan Ulster (beginning in the 1590s), of Ulster Scots to British colonial North America (peaking in the 1730s and 1740s), and the spread of the Scotch-Irish finally from Pennsylvania and the Virginia Piedmont into the Carolina backcountry (1750s–60s) roughly corresponded with the reemergence of political moderation in the political thought of the early modern Atlantic world from the French Wars of Religion to the era of the American Revolution (1572–1788). These contemporaneous demographic and ideological changes were closely related.

Moderation originated in Greece during and following the Peloponnesian War and during the final years of the Roman Republic. Absorbed into Christian humanism by Saint Augustine, it entered a twelve-century hibernation only to be revived by French humanists and their Huguenot allies during the sixteenth century, by Anglicans and Puritans in England during the late sixteenth and early seventeenth centuries, and by Pietists in northern Europe in the late seventeenth and eighteenth centuries. Each of these political and religious communities reinvented moderation in the form of philosophical insights, ethical teachings, and religious beliefs, empowering those on the margins of power and security to solve intractable political disagreements. There is, among historians, a generic, commonsense understanding of moderation as cautious and reasonable politics, wary of extremes. During the early modern era and well into the nineteenth century, *historic moderation* set a higher standard. *Historic moderation was not an absence of conflict nor the dawning of peace; it was instead a framework for survival and equanimity in the midst of intense social strife and political conflict.*

No one was a moderate all of the time—those who strived ceaselessly for conflict resolution (devout Quakers, for example) were radicals. Instead, moderates responded to circumstances, picked their fights carefully, and, after great struggles against the zealous extremism by others, retreated back into older, often more conservative, habits. Roughly two-thirds of all moderates began their movement toward the political center from conservative backgrounds, and the remaining third with liberal predilections were among the most inventive moderates. The theme of moderation runs through Scotch-Irish history because Scottish and Scots-Irish bookmen, clergymen, and laity took to moderation as a means of knitting institutions of modernity, communities of faith, and a rising middle class of merchants and men of letters into a coherent whole.[1]

This Afterword therefore announces two fairly recent historiographical moments in political history: first, that the discovery that moderation was not an American invention but a European and western Christian inheritance, with significant religious undertones; and secondly, that the southern backcountry—and, for that matter, its Connecticut Valley counterpart in New England and the keystone region of central, northeastern, and western Pennsylvania—was a seedbed of moderate politics and not at all remote from the Atlantic world. Rather, the crescent-shaped southern backcountry had Atlantic world entry points in Philadelphia and Savannah. The culture of what Carl Bridenbaugh called "the back settlements" in his groundbreaking 1952 study of southern colonial regionalism owed its vitality to the movements of peoples and their ideas, beliefs, material cultures, and their often-conflicting political aspirations from Europe and Africa to the Shenandoah Valley, the Carolina Piedmont, and the Georgia frontier (see map 10.1).[2]

To be sure, Scotch-Irish political moderation sounds like an oxymoron. Ulster Scots' reputation for displays of fierce anger, violent defense of personal and family honor, and aggressive pursuit of political power has fostered a one-dimensional historical image, and yet this distortion marks the path toward a more complete and paradoxical interpretation. By observantly examining historical evidence of anger, honor, and ambition as it scarred the Scotch-Irish soul, historians can locate the moderation intrinsic to their culture. How could seemingly immoderate people come to prize moderation? Did brushes with extremism in others and restless, unruly psyches in them-

Robert M. Calhoon

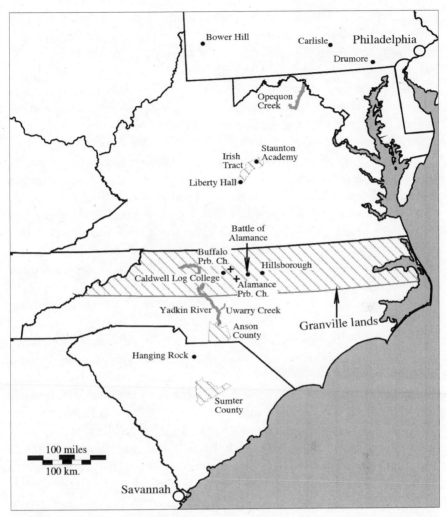

Map 10.1. *Places mentioned in Afterword.*

selves instill caution, prudence, forbearance, and civic-minded gregariousness into some of the communities constituting the American people during the formative years of American life?[3]

These questions, and the affirmative answers they elicited, had long resonated in Lowland Scottish history, and they continued to do so in Protestant Ulster. The seventeenth-century Scottish historian George Buchanan identified in the Scottish character two interlocking and irreconcilable ideal typologies: a *warrior* culture and a culture of *refinement,* alternately "barbaric" and "virtuous." In Ulster, Marilyn J. Westerkamp has discovered, this polarity structured theological controversies over "subscription" to the Westminster Confession between rationalists, reconciling Calvinism and the Enlightenment, and evangelicals, who made subscription to the Westminster Confession the touchstone of orthodoxy. Most Ulster Presbyterian clergy quietly positioned themselves somewhere in between orthodoxy and rationalism, and the zeal of the laity to enforce or relax orthodoxy waxed and waned. Noted for "the fierceness and the frequency with which battle informed all other topics of church debate . . . each clergyman was fighting for the integrity of his own religiosity and for control over the church and his congregation."[4] Thus it was vital for both minister and laity to believe and practice contradictory things and dwell uncomfortably between political extremes.

Primed by these early cultural experiences, moderation became embedded in the *structure* of Scotch-Irish historical consciousness as well as in *contingencies* that periodically and unexpectedly assaulted that structure and the *volitional* responses of allies and adversaries.

Structure

The history of moderation was, to be sure, a response to contentiousness, but it was also a chapter in the Atlantic world enlightenment. North Carolina governor Arthur Dobbs was a moderate because he climbed the ladder of preferment in the imperial bureaucracy while, at the same time, nursing a distinctively Irish Protestant moral contempt for English exploitation of, and insensitivity toward, colonial subjects. His long public career in North Carolina, first as a client and friend of land speculator Henry McCulloch and then as royal governor (1754–1765), tightened the duality of his *striving outsider/conscientious insider* identity. An arresting statement Dobbs made about Ulster Scots in America opens to view the fragility and also vitality of the imperial bureaucracy at the midpoint of the eighteenth century. In a report to the Board of Trade, Dobbs characterized seventy-five families of his Anson County tenants in 1755 as "a colony from Ireland, removed from Pennsylvania, of what we call Scotch Irish Presbyterians *who with others in neighboring tracts have settled together in order to have a teacher of their own opinion and choice*" (emphasis added).[5]

There is more to this cryptic observation than meets the eye. These people, Dobbs was telling the Board of Trade, would be productive, loyal subjects *if* no obstacle was placed in the way of their bringing Scottish or Ulster Scots Presbyterian ministers into their midst to educate their children and, in the course of doing so, bring Calvinist worship, theology, and moral teachings to a mixed population of Scotch-Irish and their Pennsylvanian neighbors (twenty-two German and Swiss Calvinist families then being absorbed into a Scotch-Irish/German enclave in Anson County). Dobbs's assessment of their potential value to the empire rested upon his detailed description of the geography, fertility, and hydrology of the territory between the Yadkin River and Uwarry Creek; his mapping of internal communication networks of roads, navigable streams, and rivers in the two Carolinas; his cataloguing of their crops, livestock, and the potential for mining minerals in the area; his estimates of their population growth; and his report of progress made in surveying boundaries between the North Carolina backcountry, South Carolina to the south, and the Granville lands to the northwest.[6]

The longest letter in Dobbs's official career as governor, the report emphasized geo-political realities: "as . . . the backcountry is much better settled than the sea coast," its political loyalty and social coherence was secured by the proximity of a large Catawba Indian population so that "no poor man dare take up lands upon an exposed frontier to the merciless Indians." Moreover, well-to-do Pennsylvania immigrants to the region would need "a large scope of land to divide among their children, so that 640 acre tracts will not be sufficient to these migrants." As a result "rich planters and German families from the northern colonies" would have to seek two or three separate land grants from the governor—mutually beneficial to Dobbs as a speculator and royal official and to the people he attracted to the province.[7] And like Virginia governor William Gooch in the Shenandoah Valley, he saw more possibilities than problems in a stabilizing mixture of Ulster Scots, Germans, and native peoples in the vanguard of settlement.

As an imperial middleman in this transaction between the Anson County Scotch-Irish and Whitehall (the building in the city of Westminster housing the Board of Trade), Dobbs was involved in what cultural anthropologist P. Nick Kardulias calls "negotiated peripherality"[8]—meaning that power relationships within empires are never completely one sided. Colonists may not be able to fight back, but they nonetheless retain room for maneuver. Center-Periphery Sociology in the 1950s to the 1980s prompted early American historians—notably Jack P. Greene in *Peripheries and Center* (1986)—to regard the London metropolis, and southern England generally, as a confident and purposeful location of power, while authority in Scotland, Ireland, and most dramatically colonial British North America appeared to be at the peripheries of the metropolitan center, where relative powerlessness engendered instability *and* creative spontaneity. The career of backcountry Indian trader and operative George Galphin, deftly extracted from fragmentary local records in Michael Montgomery's chapter in this book, illustrates the crucial economic role of the Carolina interior as a steady engine of economic activity beside the boom-or-bust economy of the mid-eighteenth-century lowcountry.[9]

The imperial interest in peopling North Carolina with Ulster Scots and German settlers from Pennsylvania, as well as Governor Dobbs's own bureaucratic and financial interest in Anson County settlement, made him the point man in negotiating concessions to non-Anglican religious communities.

As Warren Hofstra shows in his highly integrated analysis of geology, ethnicity, and economic theory, William Gooch played the same role in the Opequon Creek settlements of Jost Hite's German recruits and the Scotch-Irish settlers who joined them. The currency lubricating these negotiations was information. The fertility of limestone bottomland attracted Jost Hite and other settlers to the banks of Opequon Creek in the 1730s. Indian trails skirting the creek brought Indians ready to do business until the Seven Years' War curtailed this biracial collaboration. A more durable medium of exchange was indebtedness among backcountry settlers, which, among three-generation families, Hofstra in the Valley of Virginia and Marianne Wokeck in the Delaware Valley found to be the glue holding together families and whole communities in a currency-strapped barter economy. Rudimentary monetary and exchange practices moderated economic competition and, because they could be learned by anyone with a modicum of property and enterprise, were integral to the structure of backcountry society. As Wokeck observes, "Scotch-Irish customs and traditions in the New World—. . . language, material culture, and shared rituals, foremost among them those rooted in religious beliefs and practices—all point to the importance of families and the strengths of ties that bound them to neighboring communities." Those shared communications, material assets, and religious rituals moderated the exercise of power and tightened the gaps between social strata.

Contingency

A hallmark of political moderation, education was a pedagogical curriculum drawn from sixteenth-century study of classical history, oratory, political thought, and ethics known as Renaissance statecraft. Developed by classical scholars in the courts of rising monarchies as well as in countinghouses, in courts of law, and in churches and schools, statecraft became a staple in the training of merchants, lawyers, bureaucrats, and clergymen. Classical learning revealed how the ancients had leveraged limited power out of relative powerlessness, matched means against ends, imbued diplomacy with etiquette and personal presentation, and promoted a respect for law as a prerequisite for stability and constraint.

A prime example of a backcountry community coming together to learn statecraft occurred on Wednesday, March 3, 1768, in Guilford County, North Carolina, when the members of the Buffalo (New Side) and Alamance (Old Side) Presbyterian churches gathered for the ordination of their new pastor, David Caldwell. Hugh McAden, dean of North Carolina Presbyterian ministers, delivered the sermon, a model of statecraft in community affairs. McAden challenged Caldwell's Old School traditionalist and New Side revivalist parishioners to submerge theological differences in moderate reciprocity and charged their new pastor to clothe his clerical authority in diplomacy and love. Caldwell had worked as a carpenter in the Ulster Scots settlement of Drumore Township, Pennsylvania, for sixteen years before discerning his call to ministry and entering the College of New Jersey in the class of 1761. He remained a working farmer in North Carolina throughout his long ministry. Just as strong as his identification with working folk was his Scottish preference for order as an antidote to social conflict. [10]

Thus in 1771 he took two Guilford County Regulators, Robert Thompson and Robert Mateer, with him when he sought to intervene in the armed conflict between Governor William Tryon and backcountry rebels. The three men intercepted Tryon's force just three hundred feet from the Regulator encampment. Tryon put Thompson and Mateer in irons and sent Caldwell into the encampment carrying a thinly veiled surrender ultimatum in which Tryon promised not to attack the insurgents if they surrendered their ringleaders, laid down their weapons, and obeyed the law. With Thompson and Mateer held hostage, the Regulators agreed to a limited prisoner exchange, but before it would be arranged Tryon impulsively executed Thompson within sight of his compatriots. Over the next ten days, Tryon's troops dispersed the backcountry rebels.

Benumbed by Tryon's manipulation, Caldwell was in Hillsborough a month later to witness the hanging of six Regulators, standing only a few feet away from Herman Husband's brother-in-law, James Pugh, a religious mystic of unknown denominational affiliations but probably, like Husband, a Universalist. Mysticism was new to Caldwell but, considering the source, was an attitude he held in deep respect. In his speech from the gallows, Pugh spoke of the righteousness of the Regulator cause—the indignity of frontier farmers groveling before provincial officials in order to get land grants surveyed and deeds recorded, and all for extortionate fees. Warming to his theme, Pugh named the most notorious extorter, Edmund Fanning, only to have the box on which he was standing painfully on tiptoes kicked away by one of Fanning's cronies—his final words still wafting silently in the deadly air.

Four years later, in November 1775, North Carolina delegate Joseph Hewes explained to the Second Continental Congress the connection between seething Regulator tensions of 1771 and a political and military paralysis that gripped the Carolina Piedmont during the Revolutionary crisis of 1774–1775:

> In the present unhappy controversy between Great Britain and the Colonies it is the particular misfortune of North Carolina that in a very populous part of that province there is seated a body of men who not only refuse to become active . . . but from *a temper of mind which these people discover at present there is reason to apprehend that they might be . . . hostile to the friends of America . . . those who some years ago were concerned in the* [Regulator] *insurrection. . . . We know that the education of most of these men* [has] *been religious* [and] *that they look to their spiritual pastors with great respect* [emphasis added].

Congress voted to send two New Jersey Presbyterian clergymen, Elihu Spencer and Alexander McWhorter, to North Carolina "to go amongst the Highlanders and Regulators . . . for the purpose of informing them of the nature of the present dispute." Hewes had a more specific agenda for these emissaries: to confront the five North Carolina Presbyterian ministers—Caldwell and McAden most prominent among them—and determine whether traumatic memories of Tryon's invasion of the Piedmont now silenced the capacity of ministers as well as laity to speak and undermined their capacity to act politically.[11]

Though they spent nearly four months in North Carolina, McWhorter and Spencer must have confronted Caldwell immediately. After what must have been a dramatic and painful discussion, Caldwell, in early 1776, gathered available accounts of the proceedings of the First Continental Congress and in a cathartic burst of activity responded to the "temper of mind" argument about lingering Regulator trauma in a seven-thousand-word jeremiad against temporizing in the face of political oppression entitled, "The Character and Doom of the Sluggard" and based on Proverbs 12:24, "the slothful shall be under tribute." The heart of this sermon—which Caldwell preached at both the Buffalo and Alamance churches in February or March 1776, prior to news of Paine's *Common Sense* reaching the Piedmont—was

Robert M. Calhoon

not allegiance but rather obedience to the command of the Holy Spirit as the only force that could penetrate the encrustations of habit and inertia, which were the marks of submissiveness in the face of tyranny. "If I could portray to you, in something like their reality, the results of your conduct in this great crisis of your political destiny," he told the Buffalo and Alamance parishioners, "I should have no difficulty in persuading you to shake off your sloth and stand up manfully in a firm, united, and persevering defense of your liberties."[12] Manliness was the moderate key to throwing off slothful political indifference—not plunging recklessly from weakness to rash and heedless violence but taking the responsible middle path of firmness, unity, and perseverance.

Ulster Scots ministers and laity regarded each other warily, and yet, just as spontaneously, they respected each other's right to hold *somewhat* heterodox religious and political opinions, as Westerkamp observed of the Ulster subscription controversies and again during the Great Awakening in the middle colonies. As David Miller suggests in his wide-ranging examination of Ulster Scots identity, Presbyterian laymen asked rhetorically, "Why bother walking to the crossroads to hear a Methodist denounce your minister as unconverted when your own culture already gave you such latitude to take that minister to task?" That wariness—that willingness to listen to a controversial sermon but reserve one's own opinion and, in turn, Caldwell's counsel of courage in the face of tyranny while refraining from advocating independence or vilifying specific Crown officials—made backcountry Presbyterianism moderate.

Volition

Ulster Scots in America not only lived within a political, legal, and economic structure and responded to contingencies beyond their control; they also acted intentionally to create an identity consistent with structural realities like denominational emphasis on learning and contingent challenges like revolutionary warfare and settlement throughout a greater Pennsylvania of backcountry expansion. When in 1831 the Reverend Anthony Jefferson Pearson in the South Carolina upcountry entered a brief Pearson family memoir into his newly started diary, he lavished detail on two formative events: the grisly deaths in 1781 of two of his ancestors in partisan warfare and, immediately following, an account of his own formal schooling (at age thirteen to fourteen) in 1823–1824: "In the course of these two years, I read and reviewed the Latin Virgil, Horace, and Cicero and of the Greek, John, Acts of the Apostles, and Xenophon. . . . We met every third Saturday and either exhibited composition or debated some subject previously proposed. We also had a exhibition near the last of the school, which was acknowledged by the spectators to be the best performance ever seen in the backwoods."[13] The fact that people came from far and wide to witness students perform at graduation and that they had informed opinions about the quality of academic performance speaks to the social and cultural impact of frontier education.

Xenophon was the Greek political philosopher who declared that the moderate antidote to martial passions of vengeance, rage, and exhibitionism was the life of the polis—what classical historian Paul Rahe has called "the primacy of politics." In his great trilogy, *Republics Ancient and Modern,* Rahe discovered an important point of connection between ancient Greece and Revolutionary American political wisdom. The Pearson family's traumatic memory of backcountry revolutionary violence and Anthony's instruction in Cicero and Xenophon was a microcosm. After Aristotle, Cicero and Xenophon were the most well-known philosophers of moderation for backcountry readers.

Pearson was named for his grandfather Anthony Pearson and for Thomas Jefferson, the political hero of the southern backcountry. His grandfather's brother, whose given name he did not vouchsafe to his memoir, died at the battle of Hanging Rock, South Carolina, in 1780 when Mecklenberg County, North Carolina, troops commanded by William R. Davie and South Carolina militia recruited by Thomas Sumter attacked and "routed with great slaughter" Tory militia and well-trained members of Banestre Tarleton's British legion. Pearson's recitation of these Revolutionary War events merits our attention because Pearson's entire family internalized them and, in turn, allowed traumatic memory to shape their lives for decades.

Great-uncle Pearson's young son saw his father die and stumbled away in a daze mumbling something about walking back to his ancestral home in Pennsylvania, never to be seen again. Pearson's grandmother Stewart's first husband, Patrick Crawford, died in a bizarre "friendly fire" incident "near the close of the war," probably in 1781 or 1782 when two militia companies of "liberty scouts" ran headlong into each other, and mistaking the other with Tory partisans in the area, both opened fire on the other. Only when someone in Crawford's party recognized a dog (possibly a mascot) scurrying around amidst flashes of musket fire, did the shooting stop, and by that time Pearson's maternal grandfather lay dead, shot by a neighbor.

The Pearson family never got over the horror of those two deaths and the disappearance of Pearson's young son. Reminding the family members to whom he planned to bequeath his diary and family history of the horror of partisan warfare, Pearson commended to them the consolation of the classics and Christian scripture. The Xenophon text that Pearson studied in 1823–1824 was almost certainly *The Education of Cyrus,* a Renaissance and Protestant text on moderation. Cyrus was both an Old Testament hero and an exemplar of Greek humanism. In ruling Persia and directing Persian conquests throughout the Middle East, Cyrus learned that his pursuit of absolute power stood in creative tension with his need to rule leniently, that "both benevolence and despotism are needed to run a large state empire successfully." Eighteenth-century Enlightenment writers credited Xenophon, as an eminent teacher of religiously grounded moderation, with diagnosing why and how democratic political uprisings from the formation of the Greek polis to early modern America and Europe invariably turn despotic and violent—just as Cicero explained in his depiction of Julius Caesar's seizure of power.[14]

Recalling his rigorous backcountry training in Cicero and Xenophon was Anthony Jefferson Pearson's way of processing—and enabling his offspring to process—the trauma that three generations of Pearsons had not been able to shake off.

Historical Convergence

Five chapters in *Ulster to America* confirm the full range and backcountry convergence of structural, narrative, and traumatic dimensions of Ulster Scottish identity that surfaced in Scotch-Irish moderation as they chafed under structural constraints of empire, encountered contingent violence and other forms of immoderation, and sought to heal the wounds inflicted over a century and a half of diaspora.

Richard MacMaster associates colonial Donegal's "search for order" and Carlisle's search for "civic community" with historic moderation. At both locations, order and community were not imposed solutions. The case of Donegal Springs represented a colonial era "contest between at least two different visions of what an orderly community should be, . . . one . . . a more traditional society" in which community provincial institutions facilitated the creation of a productive rural society, and another in which enterprising individuals made rural Pennsylvania into "the best poor man's country" independent of communal institutions. The contest in Carlisle was a "more complex" effort, during the Revolutionary Era, to determine whether the town would realize its apparent potential to become a "dynamic. . . . distribution point for backcountry grain, flour, flaxseed, and British manufactured goods" or whether it would be merely a "frontier outpost, . . . a refugee camp for settlers fleeing more exposed frontier settlements, and the base for the British army's operations."

Both identities were classic moderate paradoxes. These polarities induced political moderation, and the politics that mattered most in these Scotch-Irish communities was the politics of Presbyterian-sponsored education. To a lesser extent, Old Lights and more frequently New Lights in Donegal Springs "included men of an entrepreneurial bent, interested in making the most of their opportunities in a market-oriented world, . . . enough to allow us to conclude that by 1745 the search for order in Donegal embraced an order that valued individual freedom and material gain more than community." And in 1782, Carlisle Presbyterian leader John Montgomery persuaded his friend in Philadelphia, Benjamin Rush, to lobby the legislature to charter Dickinson College—named for the state's most moderate Whig and patriot leader.

Kenneth Keller and Katharine Brown found even richer evidence of social and cultural cohesion in the Irish Tract, located strategically athwart the headwaters of the James and upper Shenandoah rivers and a desirable location for Scotch-Irish settlers already steeped in the Ulster etiquette of disagreement and softened by accommodation. Irish Tract families, in the Reverend John Craig's well-informed (if highly subjective) view, were "proud, Self interested, Contentious, & ungovernable"; and, sensitive to such allegations, they had every incentive to spread authority widely within their own ranks. The Irish Tract Presbyterian patriarchs modeled themselves on the Tidewater burgesses of whom the Huguenot descendant, Francis Fauquier, famously said, "any one who accuses them of acting upon a premeditated plan don't know them, for they mean honestly but are expedient mongers in the highest degree."[15] Spontaneous, unapologetic expediency was the form political moderation had taken in the colonial Tidewater during Fauquier's moderate governorship and which Ulster Scots, anxious to imitate their betters, brought with them to the backcountry.

What Jack P. Greene has called the politics of *mimesis* (self-serving imitation of actors in august institutions like the House of Burgesses, or among burgesses themselves, imitating the House of Commons) was not, as Craig's insult made clear, a pretty sight, but imitation did spread power widely within the new elite and acknowledged custom as the basis of the legitimate exercise of power within the region.[16] That Ulster Scots in the Irish Tract migrated to the already established (in the ecclesiastical as well as institutional sense) Anglican Church was less a sign of social climbing and more a case of putting to good use all of the institutional resources at hand. Stripped of Craig's gruff ministerial manner, Greene's concept anticipated Keller and Brown's finding that the Ulster Tract elite regarded "hard work, frugality, honesty,

Robert M. Calhoon

austere dissenting piety, avoidance of luxury, social harmony, and the opportunity to own land and slaves" as the proper "reward" for "white people like themselves." This mixture of virtues and privileges expressed well the moderate determination to live both virtuously and comfortably. And Augusta County Episcopalians, as local historian John Lewis Peyton observed, were "politically Episcopalians and doctrinally Presbyterians."

When the Revolution gave such believers the opportunity, they petitioned the General Assembly to apply glebe land income to the support of academies like William Graham's Liberty Hall and the Staunton Academy—the pride of the towns' leading families. "What is the difference between appetite and passion?" Graham rhetorically asked his Moral Philosophy students in the 1790s. The former is "general" derived from the *genus* of humanity, whereas the latter is "particular." Appetites could be satisfied, alleviated; passions could not.[17] It was to satisfy healthy appetites that Irish Tract landowners petitioned the General Assembly to convert to the cause of Presbyterian schooling "glebes which were purchased at common expense toward the lessening of our common debt." By the same token, Irish Tract leadership invested themselves in founding and maintaining Masonic lodges as institutions of "order, hierarchy, and reputation" as well as making the militia a compulsory school for up-and-coming community leaders. Keller and Brown rightly emphasize that "while the leaders of the Irish Tract worked to remove the last privileges of the old established church, build educational institutions designed to produce a new group of well-educated republican young men, and promote private virtue and [civic] order [a moderate polarity of the first order], they also sought to consolidate their power, incorporating the communities in which they lived so that resident elites like themselves might govern local affairs rather than depend upon the distant legislature in Richmond."

Moderation was often a response to local circumstances, and when moderates sought to govern the local communities in which they lived, they preferred to use nonbelligerent, prudential statecraft.

In their regional political and social study of southwestern Pennsylvania, Peter Gilmore and Kerby Miller call the socialization of Ulster Scots in America "a process of assimilation by which Ulster Presbyterians in the United States—once the quintessential 'Wild Irish' Jacobins of Federalist nightmares—eventually became socially respectable and politically conservative 'Scotch-Irish.'" That is a rough but reasonably accurate description of moderation within a religious and ethnic community. But it was not *only* the yearning for respectability that moderated Ulster Scots politics. More important than social conformity was the kind of Presbyterian piety and community building Westerkamp describes as *The Triumph of the Laity*. Presbyterian elders became pillars of an orderly community not because they lapsed into conservatism but rather because, as *moderate* conservatives, they had learned from their ministers to be humbled in the shadow of their long and turbulent history.[18] Gilmore and Miller rightly label that history as a quest for land and artisanal "independence." Those aspirations, they caution, "should not be confused with the capitalist acquisitiveness of later decades. . . . [When] Robert Morris accused his political opponent, the Ulster immigrant William Findley, of being just as avid in pursuing wealth as was Morris himself, . . . Findley's reply . . . made a clear distinction between the two men's ambitions and outlooks: 'Doubtless I do,' Findley rejoined; . . . but 'not as an end,' in itself, but rather only 'as a means enjoying happiness and independence.'"

Happiness and independence constituted a classically Aristotelian polarity between a manageable vice and a modest virtue eminently understandable to a man like Findley, a moderately energetic entrepreneur, a socially egalitarian political leader, and a conscientious Presbyterian elder.

The Whiskey Rebellion in western Pennsylvania brought down the wrath of the community on wealthy Ulster Scots distillers who flaunted their wealth. But it was *targeted* violence: notably, the "systematic destruction" of the lavish home of excise superintendent John Neville for its "ostentatious expression of wealth." The Whiskey Rebellion was thus nourished in large part by Calvinist tradition and Irish symbolism but also by class, ethnic, and religious hostility provoked by Neville's Federalist partisanship, Episcopal religious affiliation, and ostentatious landed wealth.[19] Responses to the excise were fired by communal passions, which both fueled violence and at the same time constrained and disciplined it. The Whiskey rebels were Regulators in the tradition of Charles Woodmason in South Carolina, Herman Husband in North Carolina, and Daniel Shays in Massachusetts.[20]

As Gilmore and Miller demonstrate, "The farmers' anger . . . intensified when wealthy men used political connections to monopolize local offices and reap even greater emoluments at public expense." Here was a communal threat justifying a rebellion in behalf of the public good. The destruction of John Neville's sumptuous home was not mindless anarchy but rather a necessary civic demonstration whereby the people could, in a ritualized, public way, deprive a greedy and oppressive public figure of the fruits of his avarice. As William Findley recognized, "the great error among the people was an opinion, that an immoral law might be opposed and yet the government [be] respected." By "opinion," he meant something very different from polling data. Opinion was the moral economy of the crowd learning liberty together.

Robert M. Calhoon

Rightly or wrongly, that opinion took on a life of its own as a "[quasi-]religious principle." The Presbyterian clergy, Gilmore and Miller brilliantly highlight, may not have condoned violence, but they did insist on moderation as the only way to heal deep wounds in the body politic. When "men of property and prestige opposed not only open confrontation with the United States government *but also the generalized assault on those benefitting from economic change*" (emphasis added), they implicitly distinguished between imprudent confrontationalism and sincere, if misguided, outrage at greed and dishonesty among their elite leaders.

The Presbyterian clergy, in a heavy-handed way in 1795–1798, persuaded parishioners to make peace with men of property and standing and considered themselves as trustees of a long Ulster and Scottish tradition of moderation within the kirk. The heart of the Scottish Reformation was the retention of "sacramental seasons" beloved by the Scottish populace. That communion services provided a Scotch-Irish community with "cathartic . . . psychological and emotional release" in the aftermath of the Whiskey Rebellion echoed an important Scottish and Ulster Calvinist tradition: the common people of the Scottish Reformation and their Scotch-Irish descendants alike revered the Eucharist as a defining moment of Presbyterian solidarity.[21] In this instance, as Gilmore and Miller astutely note, that release opened the door to a Presbyterian uprising at the polls in 1800 in support of Jefferson and the Republicans' moderate candidate for governor, Thomas McKean—a nonviolent expression of political opposition to the Whiskey excise.[22] A part of the moral economy of the crowd in the Bower Hill and other Ulster Scottish neighborhoods was Presbyterian moderation intermixed with Regulator zeal, righteous anger, and hierarchical hauteur. Without the presence and activity of pastoral peacemakers—admittedly, prudentially self-interested—the outcome of the rebellion would have been a different one, not better or worse, but almost certainly different—warier of confrontations with federal authority.

Patrick Griffin's Kentucky was the last Ulster American frontier to develop and also the most violent. The defining political experience of Ulster Scots settlers there was violent ethnic cleansing. For the many Scotch-Irish who arrived too late to become landowners, that violence substituted white savagery for Jeffersonian husbandry of the land. There was no moderation here, it would appear. Both for Griffin and the people he has so carefully studied, it could not be that simple. Considering all of the evidence of identity formation, especially its Hobbesian character, Griffin finds finally "a difficult and troubling trade-off." Ulster Kentuckians somehow knew that their experience "sum[med] up the limitations of the radicalism of the American Revolution." Forced to counterbalance bloody-mindedness against the loss of Edenic independence, the Kentucky Irish clung to their habitual recognition of moderating trade-offs between the world as it is and as it might have been.

Who speaks for the Scotch-Irish? Academic historians? Popular historical writers? The primary sources of the Ulster-to-America diaspora? The Ulster Scots' sometimes discerning adversaries? All of the above?

The question echoes the 1964 book title *Who Speaks for the South?* by James McBride Dabbs, Scotch-Irish descendant, Southern Presbyterian layman, college professor, and fifth-generation inhabitant of Sumter County, South Carolina, on the cusp of the backcountry. Beginning amid rumblings of opposition to school desegregation in the 1950s and maturing during the Civil Rights movement of the 1960s, Dabbs implored his fellow Scotch-Irish Presbyterians to honor their Christian and classical heritages by working to build a "world of justice, unity, and spiritual peace." "Against our will and in our own despite," he quoted Aeschylus, "wisdom comes to us by the awful grace of God." At the same time, he urged his readers to consider whether "southern history was God's way of leading two originally opposed peoples into a richer life than either could have found alone."[23]

Dabbs located the mid-twentieth-century closure of a trajectory dating from European settlement of the backcountry in the 1740s—and in a larger sense spanning Roman Stoicism and Niebuhrian Christianity. The tragic paradox framed by Aeschylus and Faulkner was one moderate liberal whites like Ralph McGill felt themselves drawn to irresistibly. As Staunton, Virginia, Presbyterian minister Joseph Ruggles Wilson had reminded southern whites in 1861, the only kind of slavery they could conscientiously fight to preserve was "slavery . . . embedded in the very heart of the moral law itself, a law which constitutes . . . the very *constitution* of that royal kingdom whose regulations begin and end in the infinite holiness of Jehovah." No one who knew Woodrow Wilson's father doubted that he was holding white southerners in 1861 to a moral standard they had yet to honor, and which, by virtue of their heritage, they had come deeply, *and ominously,* to appreciate.[24]

That was the meaning of moderation in the Ulster Scottish past—repeated reminders from religion and philosophy that irrepressible human beings are not quite as competent, wise, or entirely free as they imagine.

Robert M. Calhoon

Notes

1. Robert M. Calhoon, *Political Moderation in America's First Two Centuries* (New York: Cambridge University Press, 2009), 1–15. Although I employ "Scotch-Irish" most commonly in this afterword, all three terms including "Ulster Scots" and "Scots-Irish" refer herein to the *collective identities* of participants in the Ulster-to-America diaspora, what Jack P. Greene calls questions of "who we are, what kind of society we live in, and what sort of a place we inhabit," in *Imperatives, Behaviors, and Identities: Essays in Early American Cultural History* (Charlottesville: University Press of Virginia, 1992), 113.

2. Carl Bridenbaugh, *Myths and Realities: Societies of the Colonial South* (Baton Rouge: Louisiana State University Press, 1952), chap. 3.

3. Robert M. Calhoon, "The Scotch Irish and Political Moderation," *Journal of Scotch Irish Studies* 1 (2002): 122–41.

4. Marilyn J Westerkamp, *Triumph of the Laity: Scots-Irish Piety and the Great Awakening, 1625–1760* (New York: Oxford University Press, 1988), 106.

5. Calhoon, *Political Moderation,* 43–44.

6. William L. Saunders, ed., *Colonial Records of North Carolina,* 10 vols. (Raleigh: P. M. Hale, 1887), vol. 5: 355.

7. Ibid., 356.

8. P. Nick Kardulias, ed., *World-Systems Theory in Practice: Leadership, Production, and Exchange* (Lanham, Md.: Rowman & Littlefield, 1999), xviii, 63, 70, 78.

9. Jack P. Greene, *Peripheries and Centers: Constitutional Development in the Extended Polities of the British Empire and the United States* (Athens: University of Georgia Press, 1986), chap. 1–2; Greene, *Pursuits of Happiness: The Social Development of Early Modern British Colonies and the Formation of American Culture* (Chapel Hill: University of North Carolina Press, 1988), 193–204.

10. Calhoon, *Political Moderation,* 120–24.

11. Ibid., 122–23.

12. Ibid., 123–26.

13. Ibid., 175–77.

14. Ibid., 177–78.

15. Ibid., 38.

16. Jack P. Greene, *Negotiated Authorities: Essays in Colonial Political and Constitutional History* (Charlottesville: University Press of Virginia, 1994), 185–214; Richard R. Beeman, *The Varieties of Political Experience in Eighteenth-Century America* (Philadelphia: University of Pennsylvania Press, 2004), 180–82, 288–92.

17. Calhoon, *Political Moderation,* 171.

18. For a provocative account of this tradition, see J. G. A. Pocock, *Barbarism and Religion,* vol. 2, *Narratives of Civil Government* (Cambridge: Cambridge University Press, 1999), 261–68.

19. Peter Gilmore helped me fine-tune these characterizations of Findley and Neville.

20. Calhoon, *Political Moderation,* 35–36, 121–22, 205–6.

21. Leigh Eric Schmidt, *Holy Fairs: Scottish Communions and American Revivals in the Early Modern Period* (Princeton: Princeton University Press, 1989), 11–13, 63–64.

22. On McKean's moderation, see Calhoon, *Political Moderation,* 100–103.

23. David Hackett Fischer, "Two Minds of the South: Ideas of Southern History in W. J. Cash and James McBride Dabbs," in Paul D. Escott, ed., *W. J. Cash and the Minds of the South* (Baton Rouge: Louisiana State University Press, 1992), 161.

24. John M. Mulder, *Woodrow Wilson: The Years of Preparation* (Princeton, N.J.: Princeton University Press, 1978), 9.

Contributors

KATHARINE L. BROWN received her BA from Hollins University, Roanoke, Virginia, and PhD in history at the Johns Hopkins University, Baltimore. Much of her professional work has involved the interpretation of the Scotch-Irish in Virginia at the Stonewall Jackson House in Lexington; the Woodrow Wilson Presidential Library, Staunton; and the Frontier Culture Museum of Virginia. She has presented papers on aspects of the Scotch-Irish experience in America at conferences in the United States, Northern Ireland, and Canada and published in various journals. Essays appear in *Atlantic Crossroads: Historical Connections between Scotland, Ulster and North America* (Colourpoint, 2001) and *Ulster Presbyterians in the Atlantic World: Religion, Politics, and Identity* (Four Courts, 2006).

ROBERT M. CALHOON has been a member of the history department at the University of North Carolina at Greensboro since 1964, where he became professor emeritus in 2008. A graduate of the College of Wooster in 1958, he received MA and PhD degrees from Western Reserve University in 1959 and 1964. He has written books on the Loyalists, on American Revolutionary ideology, and on religion and politics in the American South. He recently published *Political Moderation in America's First Two Centuries* (Cambridge University Press, 2009) and, with Timothy M. Barnes and Robert Scott Davis, *Tory Insurgents: The Loyalist Perception and Other Essays* (University of South Carolina Press, revised edition, 2010). He is founding editor of the *Journal of Backcountry Studies*.

PETER GILMORE received a PhD in social history from Carnegie Mellon University in 2009 and is currently adjunct lecturer in history at Carlow University, Pittsburgh. His conference presentations and articles have examined the varieties of immigrant Irish Presbyterianism in the United States. Among his publications is "'Minister of the Devil': Thomas Ledlie Birch, Presbyterian Rebel in Exile," in *Transatlantic Perspectives on Ulster Presbyterianism: Religion, Politics and Identity* (Four Courts Press, 2006), edited by Mark G. Spencer and David A. Wilson.

PATRICK GRIFFIN teaches history at the University of Notre Dame. He is the author of *The People with No Name: Ireland's Ulster Scots, America's Scots Irish, and the Creation of a British Atlantic World* (Princeton University Press, 2001), as well as *American Leviathan: Empire, Nation, and Revolutionary Frontier* (Hill and Wang, 2008).

WARREN R. HOFSTRA is Stewart Bell Professor of History at Shenandoah University in Winchester, Virginia. In addition to teaching in the fields of American social and cultural history and directing the Community History Project of Shenandoah University, he has written or edited books on various aspects of American regional history including *The Planting of New Virginia: Settlement and Landscape in the Shenandoah Valley* (Johns Hopkins University Press, 2004); *A Separate Place: The Formation of Clarke County, Virginia* (Rowman & Littlefield, 1999); *George Washington and the Virginia Backcountry* (Madison House, 1998); *After the Backcountry: Rural Life in the Great Valley of Virginia, 1800–1900* (University of Tennessee Press, 2000); *Virginia Reconsidered: New Histories of the Old Dominion* (University of Virginia Press, 2003); *Cultures in Conflict: The Seven Years' War in North America* (Rowman & Littlefield, 2007); and *The Great Valley Road of Virginia: Shenandoah Landscapes from Prehistory to the Present* (University of Virginia Press, 2010).

KENNETH W. KELLER is professor emeritus of history at Mary Baldwin College in Staunton, Virginia. He is the author of *Rural Politics and the Collapse of Pennsylvania Federalism* (American Philosophical Society, 1982), numerous articles in professional journals, and book reviews on American history. He is a specialist in early American history. He received his PhD from Yale University.

RICHARD K. MACMASTER is co-editor of the *Journal of Scotch-Irish Studies* and co-director of the Center for Scotch-Irish Studies. He earned a BA and MA in history at Fordham University and a PhD in American history at Georgetown University. His research interests have been in eighteenth-century America: Virginia, Mennonites and other German settlers, and the Scotch-Irish. His books include *The Five George Masons: Planters and Patriots of Maryland and Virginia* (University Press of Virginia, 1975); *Conscience in Crisis: Mennonites and Other Peace Churches in America 1739–1789* (Herald Press, 1979); *Land, Piety, Peoplehood: The Establishment of Mennonite Communities in America, 1683–1790* (Herald Press, 1985); and most recently *Scotch-Irish Merchants in Eighteenth-Century America* (Ulster Historical Foundation, 2009.) He has taught at Western Carolina University, James Madison University, Bluffton University, and

Elizabethtown College and, in retirement, has been affiliated with the history department at the University of Florida since 2002.

DAVID W. MILLER is a professor of history at Carnegie Mellon University. He is author of *Church, State and Nation in Ireland, 1898–1921* (Gill and Macmillan and University of Pittsburgh Press, 1973); *Queen's Rebels: Ulster Loyalism in Historical Perspective* (Gill and Macmillan and Barnes and Noble, 1978, University College Dublin Press, 2007); editor of *Peep o'Day Boys and Defenders: Selected Documents on the Disturbances in County Armagh* (Public Record Office of Northern Ireland, 1990); and co-editor of *Piety and Power in Ireland, 1760–1960* (Institute of Irish Studies and University of Notre Dame Press, 2000). He has published a number of essays on Irish politics and religion and is currently working on a book on religion in the north of Ireland in the nineteenth century.

KERBY A. MILLER is Curators' Professor of History at the University of Missouri. His major publications include *Emigrants and Exiles: Ireland and the Irish Exodus to North America* (Oxford University Press, 1985), which won the Organization of American Historians Merle Curti Award; *Irish Popular Culture, 1650–1850* (Irish Academic Press, 1998), co-edited with J. S. Donnelly Jr.; *Irish Immigrants in the Land of Canaan: Letters and Memoirs from Colonial and Revolutionary America, 1675–1815* (Oxford University Press, 2003), with Arnold Schrier, Bruce D. Boling, and David N. Doyle, which won the American Conference for Irish Studies James S. Donnelly Prize; and *Ireland and Irish America: Culture, Class, and Transatlantic Migration* (Field Day, 2008); in addition to more than thirty major articles and essays. He is married to the former Patricia Mulholland of Magherafelt, County Derry.

MICHAEL MONTGOMERY is professor emeritus of English and linguistics at the University of South Carolina. He has written widely on Irish and Scottish links to American English as well as on the English of his native southern United States. His most recent books include the *Dictionary of Smoky Mountain English* (University of Tennessee Press, 2004); *From Ulster To America: The Scotch-Irish Heritage of American English* (Ulster Historical Foundation, 2006); the *Language* volume of the *New Encyclopedia of Southern Culture* (University of North Carolina Press, 2007); and *The Academic Study of Ulster-Scots: Essays for and by Robert J. Gregg* (Ulster Folk and Transport Museum, 2006). He is Honorary President of the Ulster-Scots Language Society and the Forum for Research on the Languages of Scotland and Ulster.

MARIANNE S. WOKECK is Chancellor's Professor of History at Indiana University–Purdue University, Indianapolis, where she teaches early American history. She is the author of *Trade in Strangers: The Beginnings of Mass Migration to North America*

(Penn State University Press, 1999), a reflection of her research interest in the history of the North Atlantic world in the seventeenth and eighteenth centuries. Other professional interests are focused on scholarly editing, to which her additional book publications speak: *The Papers of William Penn,* vols. 3 and 4 (University of Pennsylvania Press, 1986, 1987); *Lawmaking and Legislators in Pennsylvania: A Biographical Dictionary,* vol. 1 (University of Pennsylvania Press, 1991); *The Letters of George Santayana,* [1868]–1952, vol. 5 of *The Works of George Santayana* (MIT Press, 2001–8).

Index

Ulster to America was designed and typeset on a Macintosh OS X computer system using CS5 InDesign software. The body text is set in 11.5/13.5 Granjon LT Std and display type is set in Franklin Gothic Medium. This book was designed and typeset by Barbara Karwhite.